COGNITIVE THERAPY FOR CHRONIC AND PERSISTENT DEPRESSION

The Wiley Series in

CLINICAL PSYCHOLOGY

COGNITIVE THERAPY FOR CHRONIC AND PERSISTENT DEPRESSION

Richard G. Moore
Addenbrooke's Hospital, Cambridge

and

Anne Garland
Nottingham Psychotherapy Unit

WILEY

Other Wiley Editorial Offices

John Wiley & Sons Inc., 111 River Street, Hoboken, NJ 07030, USA

Jossey-Bass, 989 Market Street, San Francisco, CA 94103-1741, USA

Wiley-VCH Verlag GmbH, Boschstr. 12, D-69469 Weinheim, Germany

John Wiley & Sons Australia Ltd, 33 Park Road, Milton, Queensland 4064, Australia

John Wiley & Sons (Asia) Pte Ltd, 2 Clementi Loop #02-01, Jin Xing Distripark, Singapore
129809

John Wiley & Sons Canada Ltd, 22 Worcester Road, Etobicoke, Ontario, Canada M9W 1L1

Wiley also publishes its books in a variety of electronic formats. Some content that appears
in print may not be available in electronic books.

Library of Congress Cataloging-in-Publication Data
Moore, Richard, 1936–
    Cognitive therapy for chronic and persistent depression/Richard G. Moore and
Anne Garland.
       p.   cm.
    Includes bibliographical references and index.
    ISBN 0-471-89278-5 (Cloth)–ISBN 0-471-89279-3 (Paper : alk. paper)
    1. Depression,   Mental–Treatment.   2. Cognitive therapy.   I. Garland, Anne.   II. Title.
RC537 .M668   2003
616.85'2706–dc21   2003006736

British Library Cataloguing in Publication Data
A catalogue record for this book is available from the British Library

ISBN 0-471-89278-5 (hbk)
ISBN 0-471-89279-3 (pbk)

Typeset in 10/12pt Palatino by TechBooks, New Delhi, India
Printed and bound in Great Britain by TJ International, Padstow, Cornwall
This book is printed on acid-free paper responsibly manufactured from sustainable forestry
in which at least two trees are planted for each one used for paper production.

CONTENTS

ABOUT THE AUTHORS

Richard Moore works as a clinical psychologist in the Department of Cognitive and Behavioural Psychotherapies at Addenbrooke's Hospital in Cambridge. After obtaining an M.A. and a Ph.D. from the University of Cambridge and completing his clinical psychology training at the University of Edinburgh, he trained as a cognitive therapist at the Center for Cognitive Therapy in Philadelphia. He has been a therapist on major controlled trials of cognitive therapy for recurrent and residual depression in Edinburgh and in Cambridge. Through this and his subsequent experience working with depressed patients in the NHS, Richard has acquired expertise in providing cognitive therapy for both in- and out-patients with chronic and recurrent depressive disorders that have not responded fully to previous treatment. He is experienced at teaching practical clinical workshops to professional and postgraduate audiences and has presented research at a number of major international conferences. He is a Founding Fellow of the Academy of Cognitive Therapy.

Anne Garland is a nurse consultant in psychological therapies at the Nottingham Psychotherapy Unit. After training in cognitive therapy at Sheffield and Oxford, Anne worked as a therapist in two Medical Research Council funded trials investigating the efficacy of using cognitive therapy in the treatment of residual depression and bi-polar disorder. She has developed clinical expertise in the delivery of cognitive therapy across NHS service settings including primary care, community mental health teams, inpatient units and specialist psychotherapy services. Anne is also recognised nationally as a cognitive therapy trainer and clinical supervisor and has presented cognitive therapy skills based workshops and academic papers at both a national and international level. She was assistant course director to the Newcastle cognitive therapy course and also co-founder of the Salford cognitive therapy course. Anne is an active researcher investigating the impact of cognitive therapy training and clinical supervision initiatives on developing clinical competencies among health service staff. She is currently President-elect to the British Association of Behavioural and Cognitive Psychotherapies (BABCP) as a member of the psychotherapy accreditation sub-committee.

PREFACE

When we set out to write this book, we wanted to write a definitive work on the treatment of persistent depression with cognitive therapy. For some disorders, the development of cognitive therapy based on the cognitive model seems to have 'sewn up' treatment of the disorder in many cases. For example, for many patients with panic disorder, addressing the factors described in the cognitive model using the techniques recommended results in remediation of the problem with minimal risk of relapse. Such an approach to persistent depression would be welcome indeed. With this possibility in mind, we made heavy weather of describing cognitive therapy for persistent depression. It seemed that perhaps we were doing exactly what many patients with persistent depression do: having set our sights on an impossible ideal, we were thrown back by the disappointment of failing to live up to it. A different approach was needed. Therefore, the book does not present 'the answer to chronic depression'. Rather, it describes some of the ideas and experiences that were successful in endeavouring to develop and apply the therapy with many patients over the years ... and some of our interventions that did not result in the desired or anticipated outcome.

We believe our difficulty highlights something important about the nature of persistent depression. For more acute disorders, acquiring clinical experience enables the clinician to home in on the one or two factors that are most important in addressing the patient's problems. Working with persistent depression, increasing experience seems to have the reverse effect. As the clinician sees more patients or gets to know each individual better, they become more and more aware of an increasing number of factors, all of which seem to be contributing to the problems. These include not only intrapersonal, cognitive, behavioural and emotional factors, but also interpersonal, relational, environmental, biological, historical and cultural factors. If this impression is correct, we will have to accept that no single approach to the treatment of persistent depression is likely to be universally successful. In presenting a cognitive approach to treatment, we have tried to balance focusing on cognition with acknowledging the role of many other factors. Therefore, we aim to consider the role of cognition among the plethora of factors contributing to the persistence of depression, to describe how to minimise the ways that all these factors may undermine cognitive change and to suggest how cognitive changes may bring about changes in the wider sphere. We assume that patients might also benefit from biological, interpersonal and social approaches to which we do not give great attention here.

It would be remiss to present such an approach without considering the values on which it is based. In working with individuals with persistent depression, the clinician will repeatedly be faced with patients' conviction that the therapy will not 'work'. Given that previous treatments received by these patients may have met with little success, a concern to demonstrate the effectiveness of this treatment must be central. Demonstrations of the effectiveness of therapy have played a vital part in the development and success of cognitive therapy generally. The approach we describe arose within this framework of a commitment to implementing treatments of established efficacy. The approach was developed for use in a randomised-controlled trial of cognitive therapy for patients with persistent depressive symptoms following treatment with medication (The Cambridge–Newcastle Depression Study, see Paykel et al., 1999). As well as drawing on our clinical work in the NHS, many of the examples given in this book draw on our experiences in treating patients in that study. The beneficial outcomes in that study (see Chapter 12) give us some confidence in presenting the procedures we used in the therapy.

However, when working with persistent depression, the possibility that, for at least some patients, therapy may not result in the desired level of improvement remains all too real. To view the effectiveness of treatment as the only important value underlying it would put both patient and therapist in a very vulnerable position. If both parties are desperate for the therapy to work, the resulting pressure can even work against the chances of improvement. An exclusive obsession with outcome, as is often seen in the current interest in evidence-based medicine, can therefore be counterproductive. In his ground-breaking work on chronic depression, McCullough (2000) emphasises the importance of the opportunity in therapy for chronically depressed patients to engage with a decent, caring human being. We believe this valuing of human care and decency is as important when working with persistent depression as concern about outcome. Without the latter, professed care and decency can ring hollow. However, we assume that embracing values of respect and care for depressed individuals, whatever the outcome or effectiveness of treatment, is of paramount importance. We hope that our presentation of this approach will contribute to the care and decency afforded to depressed patients, rather than to the competitive fervour often present in health care systems.

This is particularly important given that the kind of problems we address in this book seem to be increasingly typical of those most commonly seen in psychological treatment settings. Many clinicians report that they are seeing more and more chronic and complex cases in their clinics. For many psychological therapists, it seems to be something of a rarity to see a case of acute depression, with a recent onset following long periods of good functioning. This may reflect the success of antidepressant medication in primary care in treating those acute cases, combined with increasing public awareness that depression can be treated. In attempting to grapple with this familiar problem of chronicity of depression, we have dodged some of the issues of definitional and diagnostic complexity. We use the terms chronic, persistent and resistant depression somewhat interchangeably. The essence of the problem we address is that patients have some symptoms of depression that persist despite treatments of known effectiveness and these continue to interfere with functioning and impair the individual's quality of life.

One result of this definitional imprecision is that patients considered to have persistent depression may have had varying degrees of exposure to psychological treatments. Some may have had exclusively biologically based treatments, others may have had various forms of psychological treatment. The majority will not have had an adequate trial of cognitive therapy. In view of the solid evidence of the effectiveness of standard cognitive therapy for depression, as described by Beck and colleagues (1979), we suggest that their approach should remain the basis for therapy with persistent cases. Much of the material we present therefore describes the application of standard cognitive therapy specifically with more persistent cases. Many of our suggestions—for example, relating to the rigidity of thinking in depression—can be traced back to the original work of Beck and colleagues. We believe there is merit in reiterating many aspects of the original approach and highlighting their importance in this patient group. In the years since the approach was first described, there has been important work in developing applications of cognitive therapy for more chronic disorders. Much of this has focused on intervening at the level of underlying beliefs. We attempt to illustrate how, in working with persistent depression, some of these more novel approaches can be integrated with standard cognitive therapy. In describing how the standard cognitive approach can be refined and broadened, we do not present that standard approach in detail. Readers who are not familiar with it should seek out Beck et al. (1979), Blackburn and Davidson (1990) or Judy Beck's *Cognitive Therapy: Basics and Beyond* (1995) before grappling with the approach described here.

Thus, our aim has not been to revolutionise the theory of persistence of depression or to present ground-breaking technical developments. Rather, it is to use material derived from working with many cases of persistent depression to show how existing clinical theory and techniques can be developed and applied in therapy. We have tried to convey as closely as possible the 'flavour' of working with people suffering from persistent depression and to be as practical as possible in suggesting how their problems may be addressed in cognitive therapy. To do this, we have used many clinical examples drawn from discussions with real patients. However, in order to protect their confidentiality and to ensure that the examples are generalisable, we have only used examples of situations described by multiple patients. The patients we describe are composites, each representing some features common to several patients that we have seen in our outcome study of NHS clinics. Of necessity, the more specific details are fictional. The dialogues are based on actual interventions, amended to protect confidentiality and edited in the interests of brevity. It should be remembered that work with patients often proceeds at an even slower pace and with more digressions than illustrated here. Despite these liberties with gospel truth, we believe that the dialogues, situations and 'factional' characters we describe are highly typical of patients with persistent depression seen in many clinics. We hope that therapists reading this book will recognise something of their patients in it and that any sufferers reading it will recognise something of themselves. To help readers to build up a picture of the patients that we refer to repeatedly throughout the book, we have provided brief biographies of each of the main patients described. The patients for whom such a biography is provided are indicated by their names being in italics when first mentioned within each section of text.

These clinical examples are used in the main body of the text in Chapters 1 to 10 to illustrate the model and clinical application of cognitive therapy with patients suffering from persistent depression. Chapters 1 and 2, covering the cognitive model and therapeutic relationship, style and structure, provide a framework that is essential throughout the course of therapy. Chapters 3 to 10 describe the nature of interventions implemented in each of the main phases across the course of therapy. In sequence, we describe assessment, socialising the patient into therapy, setting goals, using standard behavioural and cognitive techniques, working with underlying beliefs and helping the patients to maintain their gains beyond the end of therapy. Chapter 11 then discusses some of the practical and service-related issues that therapists encounter in working with these patients. Finally, Chapter 12 presents results of research into the outcomes and mechanisms of our own approach and those of other recently developed cognitive approaches to depression, before rounding up some of the main issues and themes presented throughout the book.

Before we present our clinical approach, our Introduction outlines the drastic significance of persistent depression in the lives of those who suffer from it, before setting out issues relating to definition, diagnosis, predictors of outcome and treatment of persistent depressive symptoms. Although this introduction does not contain any clinical material, we believe that this information is important in understanding the context for the application of therapy described in the following chapters. Because it does not contain any clinical material, we forgive any enthusiastic clinicians who cannot restrain themselves from skipping straight to Chapter 1. We then hope that our account of cognitive therapy with these patients will assist therapists in gaining some inspiration to work with chronic depression and in helping their patients to find a greater degree of satisfaction and fulfilment.

ACKNOWLEDGEMENTS

We wish to thank warmly the many people who have inspired and supported us, and otherwise contributed to the writing of this book. We would both particularly like to thank:

- The members of the Cambridge Newcastle Depression Study team, including the study psychiatrists, Alison Jenaway, Lenny Cornwall and Robert Bothwell; the research staff, Hazel Hayhurst, Marie Pope, Rosemary Abbott, Carolyn Crane and Maxwell Saxty; and the grantholders Gene Paykel, Jan Scott and John Teasdale. Special thanks to Jan Scott for her stimulating supervision and for her many contributions to the ideas presented in this book.
- The patients from the study and our NHS clinics, without whom we would not be in the position to present many of these ideas.
- We gratefully acknowledge the organisations who have supported us over the period of this work, including the Medical Research Council, the Psychological Treatment Service of Addenbrooke's Hospital and Nottinghamshire Healthcare NHS Trust.

RGM would like to thank:

- Lee Brosan, David Allison and Gillian Todd for their invaluable encouragement, supervision and helpful comments on drafts of parts of the manuscript.
- Jolanta Kruszewska and the staff and patients of Ward R4, Addenbrooke's Hospital for their kindness and sustenance.
- My past teachers, supervisors and colleagues, especially Ivy Blackburn, Cory Newman, Ruth Greenberg Fraser Watts and Mark Williams, whose helpful influence pervades every page.
- My family and friends for their unwavering support, and especially Stella and the boys for their love and forbearance.

AG would like to thank:

- John Jones, Steve Regel, Jan Scott, Melanie Fennell, David Clark and Ivy Blackburn, whose consummate clinical knowledge and skill have contributed significantly to my development as a cognitive therapist.

- Hazel Dunn, Pam Barnes and Julie Owen whose pragmatism, wisdom and wit have been an inspiration in times of self-doubt.
- Marian, John, Allyson, Craig, Vic, Bob, Rebecca, Rory and Katharina whose love and friendship I deeply treasure.
- Chris, for being himself and letting me be myself—this isn't getting the pigs in!

THE CHALLENGE OF PERSISTENT DEPRESSION

In this introduction, you will find information on:

- Symptoms and consequences of persistent depression
- Difficulties in defining and diagnosing persistent depression
- Rates of persistent depression
- Factors that predict the persistence of depression
- Pharmacological strategies for treating persistent depression
- The reasons for pursuing psychological treatments
- The existing evidence on the effectiveness of cognitive therapy in persistent depression
- Recent developments in cognitive therapy that may be useful in adapting the standard cognitive approach to depression

They say time flies when you're enjoying yourself. When you're depressed, the moments creep miserably by, and to those with chronic depression, this misery is endless. Looking back, misery predominates. To those who dare to look forward, it seems certain that they will never experience any lasting relief. Chronic depression casts a very long, black shadow over the person's life.

In this book, we will be illustrating the advances that a cognitive approach can provide in understanding and treating persistent depression by describing the stories of several patients. As will become clear, there are as many different precise presentations of persistent depression as there are patients. For example, *Kate* described being tossed about by extremes of every different kind of unpleasant emotion, whereas *Stan* was mired in an unvarying bleak flatness of mood. *Elizabeth* was struggling to keep up standards of performance that others would have been proud to attain, whereas *Peter* struggled to keep going at all. Amid all the variety, the common factor is the ongoing suffering of anyone afflicted by persistent depression. As we describe below, persistent depression has drastic effects, not only on the mood of individuals, but also on their overall mental and physical well-being, their daily functioning, their relationships, their working life and on society around them.

The scale of the problem of persistent depression has only recently begun to emerge. The latter half of the twentieth century saw great optimism surrounding the treatment of depression, as pharmacological and psychological treatments were found to be effective (Hollon et al., 1993). The substantial minority of patients who did not benefit from treatment seemed at first to receive little notice. Gradually, the continued suffering of individual patients and its effect on society has been reflected in consideration given to the diagnosis and treatment of persistent depression. It was not until 1987 that the diagnosis of chronic depression was included in the influential Diagnostic and Statistical Manual of the American Psychiatric Association with publication of the revised third edition (DSM-III-R). The lack of consensus over issues of definition and diagnosis has hindered the gathering of consistent information about predictors and possible causes of persistent depressive symptoms. As a result, although the potential treatment options are many, evidence that might inform decisions about the most beneficial treatments remains limited.

The majority of patients feel overwhelmed by helplessness in the face of the persistence of their depression. In view of the sketchiness of the available information on causes and treatments, clinicians too can feel helpless when faced with the prospect of treating persistent depression. In setting the scene for describing the treatment of persistent depression with cognitive therapy, we aim to present some of the information that is available. In this introduction, we first outline the nature of the problem by describing the symptoms of persistent depression and outlining some of its psychological and social consequences. We then discuss some of the main issues in defining and diagnosing chronic and persistent depression. We draw attention to the role of the inadequacy of treatment received by many patients, and highlight the distinction between chronicity and treatment resistance. We then review some of the main research findings on predictors of persistence of depression and put forward some of the reasons for pursuing psychotherapeutic treatments in chronic depression. Existing evidence on the use of cognitive therapy with patients with persistent depression is then reviewed, and more recent developments in cognitive therapy are described.

SYMPTOMS OF PERSISTENT DEPRESSION

There is considerable agreement across different diagnostic systems as to the symptoms required for diagnosing depressive disorders, whether

Table 1 Symptoms required to meet DSM-IV criteria for a Major Depressive Episode

To meet DSM-IV criteria, five or more of the following symptoms must have been present during the same 2-week period and must represent a change from previous functioning. At least one of the symptoms must be either (1) depressed mood or (2) loss of interest or pleasure.

1. Depressed mood most of the day, nearly every day, as indicated by subjective report (e.g. feels sad or empty) or observation by others (e.g. appears tearful).
2. Markedly diminished interest or pleasure in all, or almost all, activities most of the day, nearly every day.
3. Significant weight loss when not dieting or weight gain, or decrease or increase in appetite nearly every day.
4. Insomnia or hypersomnia nearly every day.
5. Psychomotor agitation or retardation nearly every day (observable by others, not merely subjective feelings of restlessness or being slowed down).
6. Fatigue or loss of energy nearly every day.
7. Feelings of worthlessness or excessive or inappropriate guilt nearly every day (not merely self-reproach or guilt about being sick).
8. Diminished ability to think or concentrate, or indecisiveness, nearly every day (either by subjective account or as observed by others).
9. Recurrent thoughts of death (not just fear of dying), recurrent suicidal ideation without a specific plan, or a suicide attempt or specific plan for committing suicide.

chronic or not. The symptoms required for diagnosing a major depressive episode in DSM-IV (Diagnostic and Statistical Manual of Mental Disorders (4th edition), American Psychiatric Association, 1994) are presented in Table 1. The same set of symptoms is used as the basis for diagnosing chronic depressive disorders.

There are differences between acute and chronic depression in the precise symptoms presented. Psychologically, patients with persistent depression are invariably demoralised and hopeless (Thase, 1994). For many patients, lack of motivation and lack of pleasure can present more of a problem than acute negative mood states. Patients usually experience their symptoms as being completely out of their control: they may feel powerless to change an unremitting background level of low mood or may experience upsurges of various unpleasant emotions 'for no reason'. This lack of control often results in helplessness and passivity. Thus, many patients have withdrawn from or compromised important roles or functions. Despite this perceived lack of control, patients often blame themselves and feel guilty, for both the depression and any external problems. There is some evidence that vegetative symptoms, such as appetite and sleep disturbance, occur less frequently than in acute depression (Keller et al., 1995). Biologically, complaints of lack of energy and fatigue seem to be more common and more disabling than other symptoms. This combination of hopelessness, uncontrollable low mood, fatigue and lack of response to previous treatment is often enough to make the most enthusiastic therapist's heart sink. The symptoms of persistent depression and their assessment are described in more detail in Chapter 3.

CONSEQUENCES OF PERSISTENCE OF DEPRESSION

The toll exacted by depression extends not only to the devastation of the well-being of individual patients, but also to their families, their wider social and occupational contacts and to the health care system. The high levels of disability due to depression were documented by Wells et al. (1989). Even without specifically selecting for chronic depression, levels of disability in depression were greater than in other chronic medical conditions with the exception of heart disease. Persistent depression has even more drastic effects on the individual and their ability to carry out their role in society. In research on the consequences of depression, it has proved difficult to disentangle the antecedents of depression from its consequences. Many individual (e.g. low self-esteem) and social (e.g. lack of supportive relationships) factors may be both antecedents and consequences of persistent depression. In the next chapter, we will describe how a cognitive model must incorporate the reciprocal effects of these factors on depression and the effects of depression on these factors.

Psychological Consequences

On an individual level, demoralisation and the entrenchment of hopelessness are almost inevitable consequences of persistent depression. Although hopelessness is itself a common symptom in acute depression, effective treatments can alleviate it as patients perceive improvement in their other symptoms. However, when treatments that a patient has been told are effective prove not to be, then the belief that things cannot get any better is confirmed, leading to an entrenched sense of hopelessness. Although self-esteem is commonly viewed as an antecedent or vulnerability factor for depression, the persistence of depression can have crushing consequences for an individual's self-esteem. Similarly, it has been argued that the experience of persistent depression can result in changes in personality, including increases in dependency and neuroticism (Akiskal et al., 1983).

Social Consequences

The social withdrawal characteristic of most depression tends to become more disruptive as depression persists. For patients with chronic depression, this can entail severe disruption of their ability to keep up various social roles. Frequently, this is seen in an inability to establish or maintain intimate relationships, leading to a deficit in the degree of social support available. Impairments due to the poor marital and family relationships that often accompany persistent depression may be particularly marked for women (Kornstein et al., 2000). Where a patient has been living in a well-established family unit before the onset of the depression, other members of the family often compensate for the difficulties experienced by the patient. It is not uncommon to find spouses who are themselves overburdened having taken over tasks or responsibilities from the patient, or who have given up their social life rather than trying to carry on socialising alone. Children of patients may also have taken on responsibilities for household tasks or childcare for their younger siblings.

Occupational performance is often drastically compromised in chronic depression. In contrast to impairments in marital adjustment, impairments in work functioning may be relatively greater in men (Kornstein et al., 2000). Where depression persists, this frequently results in patients having to take long-term sick leave or medical retirement. Where unemployment triggered the initial onset of the depression, persistence of symptoms can rule out the prospect of getting back into work. This then has financial consequences, not only for the patient and their family, but also for the social system more widely.

These psychological and social consequences of persistent depression all have further implications for the depression: they make it more likely that the depression will persist. In the next chapter, the cognitive model describes a long-term vicious cycle whereby chronic depression results in negative psychological and social consequences that then serve to maintain the depression. Somewhat similar processes have been described biologically, whereby the persistence of depression disrupts important homoeostatic processes, particularly in the hypothalamic–pituitary–adrenocortical axis (Gold et al., 1988). This can result in the kindling of depression, such that with each new episode a chronic course becomes increasingly likely (see page 9). The consequences for the health care system can be serious. If efforts are made to save resources by treating milder, acute cases of depression less intensively, at least some of these cases are then more likely to experience chronic depression and thus require more intensive, longer-term and more costly treatments.

DIFFICULTIES IN DEFINING PERSISTENT DEPRESSION

There have been two main approaches to the definition of disorders characterised by the persistence of depressive symptoms. One is to consider simply the duration over which depressive symptoms have persisted. In this approach, someone is viewed as chronically depressed if they have suffered from depressive symptoms for a number of months or years with little evidence of relief. The alternative approach is to consider the degree to which attempts at treatment have been unsuccessful. In this approach, someone is viewed as persistently depressed if their symptoms have not been adequately alleviated by a course of treatment that might have been expected to be effective.

Chronicity over Time

In DSM-IV, various forms of persistent depression are defined according to the course of the disorder. In these criteria, a chronic episode of Major Depressive Disorder is diagnosed when symptoms have persisted for two years or more at a level that merits a diagnosis of major depression. Other diagnoses involving persistent depressive symptoms are also distinguished by the particular time course of the disorder. These include:

• Major Depressive Episode, in partial remission
• Major Depressive Disorder, recurrent, without interepisode recovery
• Dysthymic Disorder
• Dysthymic Disorder and Major Depressive Disorder ('double depression').

A major depressive episode, partially remitted, is diagnosed when significant depressive symptoms persist, but at a level where they no longer meet the full criteria for major depression. Such a partially remitted episode can be a first episode of major depression, or can be the latest in a series of episodes. If previous episodes also did not remit completely before the onset of the next episode, this would entail a diagnosis of 'Major Depressive Disorder, recurrent, without full interepisode recovery'. There are many cases where low-level depressive symptoms have persisted for many years, with at best only brief periods of relief. Where such symptoms have persisted on more days than not for two years before the occurrence of any episode meeting full criteria for Major Depression, the ongoing symptoms are classed as Dysthymic Disorder. For some patients, these constant low-grade symptoms provide a backdrop to occasional more intense episodes that do meet the criteria for a full Major Depressive Episode. The term *double depression* has been coined for this pattern of disorder, where one or more depressive episodes are superimposed on pre-existing Dysthymic Disorder (Keller & Shapiro, 1982). In patients with persistent depressive symptoms, movement between higher and lower levels of symptoms is common: the presence of residual symptoms following partial remission or of dysthymia confers a high risk of recurrence of a major depressive episode (Judd et al., 1998).

This approach to definition and diagnosis takes no account of any treatments that a patient may have received. In these modern times when few patients with depression have not been treated with pharmacological and possibly psychological treatments, this presents a problem. For most patients, the time course of symptoms cannot be considered independently of treatments received over time. For example, two patients might receive a diagnosis of chronic depression by DSM-IV criteria. One may have received an inadequate dose of medication many months ago with little further follow-up. The other may have had trials of several classes of antidepressants at maximal doses along with augmentation with lithium. Clearly, the aetiology and prognosis for these two patients would be very different, as the latter patient is likely to present a far greater challenge in subsequent treatment. Chronicity of symptoms in itself is less of a problem, as the symptoms may respond to a suitable standard treatment. Persistence of significant symptoms even once standard treatments have been adequately implemented presents a greater challenge.

Treatment Resistance

An alternative to defining persistence of depressive symptoms simply according to time course or chronicity has therefore been to focus on treatment resistance (for comprehensive reviews, see Amsterdam et al., 2001). Little consensus has emerged as to standard criteria for defining treatment resistance in depression. However, it has become clear that definitions must address two issues: adequacy of treatment and degree of response to treatment. Attempts to define adequacy of treatment have focused exclusively on antidepressant medication. The term *treatment resistance* could include a lack of acceptable response to minimal standard doses of medication (e.g. 150 mg/day of imipramine or equivalent). Alternatively, the term could be reserved only for disorders that persist in spite of attempts to treat initial non-response more aggressively with higher doses of medication (e.g. above 300 mg/day of imipramine or equivalent). There has been a similar lack of agreement over what constitutes a lack of acceptable response to treatment. Treatment resistance could include those who respond only partially to treatment or could be reserved for those who do not respond at all. Failure to respond to treatment has variously been defined according to degree of improvement in symptom levels (e.g. less than 50% reduction in score on a standard measure of depressive symptoms) or through remaining above some criterion on a measure of symptoms (commonly 7 on the Hamilton Rating Scale for Depression; Hamilton, 1960).

One way of dealing with this lack of consensus has been to propose that different levels or stages of treatment resistance should be defined. The different stages reflect the number and intensity of treatments that have been tried without success. Thus, in Thase and Rush's (1995) system, Stage I resistance reflects failure of one adequate trial of an antidepressant medication and subsequent stages reflect failure to respond to a broadening range of subsequent treatments. Stage V resistance reflects failure to respond to numerous classes of antidepressant (including tricyclic medications and monoamine oxidase inhibitors) and a course of ECT. The stages in this system are thus based mainly on the number of different medications tried. For many patients, a lack of satisfactory response to strategies such as taking supra-maximal doses of a particular medication or combining such medication with mood stabilisers are further indicators of degree of resistance. If some consensus can be reached on the weighting of non-response to these various treatment strategies, this kind of approach seems to offer the most promise for some degree of standardisation to be forged.

Persistent Depression

Whether they are defined according to temporal chronicity or treatment resistance, persistent depressive symptoms are a problem in themselves, with a drastic impact on the well-being of the individual and their functioning in their social network. Comparing different diagnostic subtypes of persistent depression, McCullough et al. (2000) found few differences between them in demographic and clinical variables, family history and response to treatment. Even in patients who show some degree of response to treatment, the presence of residual symptoms following treatment is a strong predictor of subsequent relapse and recurrence (Paykel et al., 1995). Thus, patients do not need to meet full criteria for chronic major depression for their depression to follow a chronic and relapsing course, with a huge detrimental impact on their own lives and on the lives of those around them.

In this book, we have taken a broad view of persistent depressive disorders. We have mainly used the term *persistent depression* to encompass presentations involving either temporal chronicity or treatment resistance. Where we have used the terms *chronic* or *resistant* depression, this has generally been in the service of enlivening the text, and not to specify one kind of presentation rather than another. We assume that the therapeutic approach we describe will have some relevance to patients with any of the above disorders. It has been tested with patients suffering from residual depressive symptoms following adequate treatment of a major depressive episode in the Cambridge–Newcastle Depression Study (see Chapter 12 for details of the study design and outcomes). This study included patients with varying numbers of previous depressive episodes and patients with underlying dysthymia.

HOW COMMON IS PERSISTENCE OF DEPRESSION?

Although depression is often considered to be a treatable condition, it is now clear that a sizeable minority of patients suffer chronic or persistent depressive symptoms. The lack of consensus over definitions of persistent depression has led to variations in estimates of how commonly it occurs. The most widely used methodology has been to follow up samples of patients diagnosed with depression over a number of years. Such studies have rarely attempted any control over the treatment received, so can give little information on the relative numbers of patients with different degrees of treatment resistance. In a review by Scott (1988), rates of symptomatic non-recovery after two years of follow-up ranged from 1% to 23% across a number of studies. Some of these studies pre-dated the era of modern treatments, however. More recent studies still consistently show that rates of persistence of depression remain around 20% over two years of follow-up, despite the increased availability of effective treatments (Keller et al., 1984; see Paykel, 1994, for a review). Longer-term follow-up studies have also found evidence of significant persistence of depression. Winokur et al. (1993) found a poor outcome in over 10% of their depressed sample at a five-year follow-up. Two studies which examined outcomes over periods in excess of 15 years following hospitalisation found rates of chronic symptoms of 25% (Lee & Murray, 1988) and 11% (Kiloh et al., 1988).

Even when patients do make a satisfactory recovery from an initial episode of depression, rates of relapse are high. Rates of relapse within a year of recovery from an episode of depression are typically 30% (Lavori et al., 1984). The probability of relapse is strongly linked to the presence of residual depressive symptoms following response to treatment (Paykel et al., 1995). There is some evidence that each successive episode of depression carries an increasing risk of chronicity (Kupfer et al., 1989), which has been termed the kindling hypothesis of resistant depression (Post, 1992). Some individual patients show a pattern of less satisfactory response to treatment with each successive episode (for example, see the case of Marion described on page 113). The factors within the cognitive model that might contribute to this increasing risk of chronicity are discussed in the following chapter.

THE ROLE OF MISDIAGNOSIS AND INADEQUATE TREATMENT

A number of other psychiatric (e.g. early onset psychotic disorders) and physical conditions (e.g. thyroid dysfunction) can present with symptoms similar to depression. Where such conditions are diagnosed as depression, alleviation of the symptoms with antidepressant treatments is hardly to be expected. In such cases of non-response, chronic or treatment-resistant depression may be diagnosed. Such diagnosis is likely to be misleading, as treatment of the alternative condition may lead to alleviation of the depression-like symptoms. It is therefore important that such other conditions have been considered and are unlikely before a diagnosis of a persistent depressive disorder is reached.

In addition to such misdiagnosis, chronic depressive symptoms may result from inadequate treatment. It is self-evident that delay in starting an effective treatment will result in a longer duration of illness before treatment is introduced. Even once treatment is commenced, inadequacy of treatment with medication may account for some persistence of symptoms in some patients. Studies of depressed patients designated as treatment resistant have consistently found that a sizeable proportion of such patients have in fact received inadequate treatment (e.g. Quitkin, 1985). Many such patients have been prescribed subtherapeutic doses. Even when prescribing has been adequate, some patients are found not to have reached adequate plasma levels, possibly reflecting non-compliance. It is hardly surprising to find depressive symptoms persisting in patients who have received inadequate treatment. These findings suggest that in at least some cases, although the depression may be chronic in duration, it may not be resistant to treatment. In some cases where treatment has hitherto been inadequate, achieving satisfactory prescription and monitoring of medication may result in alleviation of the depressive symptoms.

More worryingly, there is also evidence that delay in starting treatment and inadequate initial treatment can increase the likelihood of subsequent non-response even when adequate treatment is commenced (Scott, 1988; Guscott & Grof, 1991). Thus, although failure to respond to inadequate treatment should not itself be considered as a sign of treatment resistance, true treatment resistance can result from a lack of prompt or adequate treatment. Such problems are likely to be less common with more recently introduced medications, due to lower side-effect profiles and easier prescribing. It is clear that, to lower the likelihood of depressive symptoms becoming persistent, pharmacotherapy should be prompt, adequate and properly monitored.

PREDICTORS OF PERSISTENCE OF DEPRESSION

In follow-up studies of depression, the associations of a wide range of factors with recovery from and, conversely, persistence of depression have been examined. In addition to the consistent relationship found between treatment factors and persistent depression described above, a number of sociodemographic and patient-related factors have been found to be important.

Social and Demographic Factors

A number of studies have found depression to be more likely to persist in older patients (e.g. Keller et al., 1986) and in women (e.g. Berti Ceroni et al., 1984). Negative life events occurring after the onset of an episode of depression have been found to be associated with chronicity (Scott et al., 1988). Of these life events, marital and interpersonal difficulties were found to be particularly common in patients with chronic compared to acute depression, and redundancy was particularly common in males with chronic depression. There has been some debate as to whether such events are causes or consequences of persistence of depression (Gotlib & Hammen, 1992). We shall discuss in the next chapter how undesirable events and situations are likely consequences of depression that serve to prolong and entrench depressive symptoms.

Patient Factors

A number of factors concerning the patient's history, premorbid personality and presentation of depression have been found to be important predictors of chronicity. A greater number of previous episodes and a family history of depression have both been found to predict persistence of depression (Scott et al., 1988). Neuroticism has consistently been found to predict chronicity and poorer treatment response in depression (Scott et al., 1988). Cognitive factors, in particular high levels of dysfunctional attitudes, are associated with poor response to medication or psychotherapy (Sotsky et al., 1991). Although biological or endogenous symptoms in themselves are not consistently associated with persistence, Scott (1994) found that a combination of neurotic premorbid personality with an endogenous symptom profile was particularly likely to be associated with chronic rather than episodic depression. This suggests that chronicity may result from an interaction between psychological and biological factors. Psychotic symptoms have been related to a more chronic course in several studies (including Scott, 1994).

Comorbidity

Comorbidity of depression with a number of disorders must be considered. Around a third of patients with major depression are found to have pre-existing dysthymia, which significantly influences the course of the depressive episode (Keller et al., 1995). In double depression, where a major depressive episode is superimposed on pre-existing dysthymia, patients are less likely to recover fully, but tend to return to their previous dysthymic level (Keller et al., 1983). Such patients remain at higher risk of relapse into a further depressive episode than patients without comorbid dysthymia. Other comorbid psychiatric disorders are common in depression, including anxiety states, substance misuse and personality disorders. Comorbid personality disorders have been found in around a half of patients with chronic depression (McCullough, 1996). They are associated with greater likelihood of persistent depressive symptoms following treatment (e.g. Shea et al., 1990).

PHARMACOLOGICAL TREATMENT OPTIONS

Not surprisingly, the rate of spontaneous remission in patients with chronic depressive symptoms is low (McCullough et al., 1988). This reinforces the importance of identifying effective options for active treatment. Given the possibility that lack of improvement may have been due to lack of adequate treatment, there is a need to ensure that patients presenting with persistent depressive symptoms have had an adequate trial of some standard treatment of established efficacy, whether biological or psychosocial. Even where the chronic course of symptoms to date may be in part attributable to not having received adequate treatment, response to standard treatments in patients with depressive symptoms of long duration is compromised (Scott, 1988). Thus, response to standard medication regimens in patients with persistent depressive symptoms is not high. In one large study of patients with chronic or double depression, less than one-fifth of patients responded fully to adequately administered medications (imipramine or sertraline), and nearly a half of the patients failed to show even a partial response (Keller et al., 1998). However, a number of studies have indicated benefits of persisting with standard medications beyond the usual 12-week trial. Response rates have been found to increase up to six months from the inception of treatment (e.g. Greenhouse et al., 1987). Again, this underlines the importance of ensuring that patients have had an adequate and sustained trial of standard treatments before they are classed as nonresponders and other options are considered.

Once it has been established that an adequate trial of standard medication was not effective, the options for pharmacotherapy include switching to a different medication or adding further medications to the existing regimen. Where patients have failed to respond to one adequate trial of a particular medication, rates of response to switching to a different medication appear to be around 50% (e.g. Thase et al., 2002). From a number of studies, response seems somewhat more likely when switching classes of antidepressant (for example, from a tricyclic to a serotonin-specific reuptake inhibitor, SSRI) as compared to switching to a different medication of the same class (for a review, see O'Reardon & Amsterdam, 2001). An alternative to switching medications, particularly where partial response has been achieved, is to seek to augment the response to the existing medication using one of a number of additional agents. The most common augmentation strategy is to supplement an existing antidepressant with the use of lithium. Rates of response when lithium is added to an existing adequate dose of medication are again around 50% (O'Reardon & Amsterdam, 2001).

THE POTENTIAL OF PSYCHOLOGICAL TREATMENT IN PERSISTENT DEPRESSION

From the above, it is clear that persisting with, switching or combining medications will be of benefit to a significant number of patients with persistent depressive symptoms. However, it is equally clear that a large proportion of patients will continue to experience persistent depressive symptoms even if these pharmacological strategies are tried. There are a number of reasons why psychotherapeutic approaches might be considered beneficial in persistent depression.

- Firstly, as described above, some of the most prominent symptoms in cases of chronic or resistant depression are psychological in nature, including hopelessness, low self-esteem and lack of pleasure. Where such symptoms have not proved amenable to pharmacological interventions, it makes some sense to consider addressing them more directly with psychological interventions.

• Secondly, whatever the original cause of the depression, persistence of depression entails considerable psychological and social consequences. These factors, such as learned helplessness and impoverished social networks, are likely to maintain or exacerbate the depressive symptoms. Being one step further down the causal chain from the original depressive syndrome, these factors may be less likely to benefit from medication than acute depressive symptoms. Again, these psychological and social consequences of persistent depression seem likely to benefit from psychosocial interventions.

• Thirdly, there is now convincing evidence that some specific psychological treatments are of similar efficacy in acute depression to medication (e.g. Elkin et al., 1989). Although evidence is surprisingly sparse (e.g. Imber et al., 1990), it is highly likely that medication and psychotherapy achieve their antidepressant effects through different mechanisms. In cases where the depressive symptoms have not responded to medication, it could be argued that trying a treatment whose effectiveness may be achieved through a different mechanism is more likely to be successful than persisting with a purely pharmacological approach.

• Finally, a significant proportion of patients with persistent depression have comorbid diagnoses of dysthymia or personality disorder. Whereas medication is generally viewed as appropriate in treating acute or Axis I disorders, psychotherapeutic approaches have long been conceived as more appropriate in addressing these problems of personality. In one large study of the treatment of acute depression, results suggested more favourable response to medication in more severely depressed patients, but more favourable response to cognitive therapy in patients with personality disorders (Shea et al., 1990).

Why Cognitive Therapy?

A number of psychological therapies have now been shown to be effective in the treatment of acute major depression, including cognitive therapy (Beck et al., 1979; see Hollon et al., 1993, for a review), problem-solving therapy (Mynors Wallis et al., 1995) and interpersonal psychotherapy (Klerman et al., 1984). These effective interventions share some common features: they are all structured, provide a clear rationale, and foster the development of the patient's ability to implement changes outside of the therapy setting. Although there is little evidence on the general characteristics of therapies likely to be of benefit with persistent depression, provision of therapy without a clear structure or rationale would appear unlikely to combat the demoralisation and helplessness that are cardinal features of chronic depression. Cognitive therapy is one of the range of psychological therapies that holds most promise in the treatment of persistent depression.

One of the main benefits of cognitive therapy in treating depression has been in the reduction of the risk of relapse. Compared to alternatives such as medication and interpersonal psychotherapy, there is evidence that patients treated with cognitive therapy are more likely to maintain any improvement after the end of treatment (Evans et al., 1992; Shea et al., 1992). Cognitive therapy provided as a maintenance treatment in patients who have responded to acute treatment but are at high risk of relapse has also been found to reduce rates of recurrence (Blackburn & Moore, 1997; Fava et al., 1994; Jarrett et al., 2001). The benefits of cognitive therapy thus extend beyond the alleviation of acute depressive symptoms. The potential of cognitive therapy for producing enduring changes may be of benefit in persistent depression, where enduring problems are the focus.

EVIDENCE FOR STANDARD COGNITIVE THERAPY IN PERSISTENT DEPRESSION

Outpatient Studies

Much of the evidence that addresses the effectiveness of cognitive therapy on persistent depressive symptoms comes from small-scale studies that have not been rigorously controlled. Data from a number of studies that examined response to cognitive therapy in outpatients who had failed to respond to adequate courses of medication or those with dysthymia are shown in Table 2. The earliest studies (e.g. Fennell & Teasdale, 1982)

Table 2 Studies of response to cognitive therapy in outpatients with persistent depression

Reference	Patients included	Sample size	Recovery rate (%)
Fennell & Teasdale (1982)	Drug refractory	5	20
Harpin et al. (1982)	Non-responders to medication	6	33
Gonzales et al. (1985)	Dysthymia	54	34
Stravynski et al. (1991)	Dysthymia	6	67
Mercier et al. (1992)	Atypical depression	15	40
Fava et al. (1997)	Non-responders to medication	16	75
Moore & Blackburn (1997)	Non-responders to medication	6	60

sounded a cautious note due to the low response rate. The rate of response in subsequent studies has varied very widely, resulting in a range of rates of recovery from 20% to 75%. The small sample sizes render these studies highly susceptible to biases due to the selection of patients for inclusion, in that the inclusion of any single patient particularly suitable or unsuitable for cognitive therapy can exert a large effect on the results. It must also be noted that only two of these studies (Harpin et al., 1982; Moore & Blackburn, 1997) included any kind of control condition. Despite the limitations of these studies, the overall pattern of findings suggests that cognitive therapy is likely to be of benefit in at least some cases of persistent depression in outpatients.

Inpatient Studies

A number of studies have examined the effectiveness of cognitive therapy in inpatient samples. Most of these (e.g. Bowers, 1990) did not specifically select patients on the basis of chronicity of depressive symptoms and reported rates of response of 60–80%. As such, these studies probably testify more to the effectiveness of combining cognitive therapy and medication in treating severe cases, than to the effects of therapy on persistent symptoms. Three studies have specifically selected inpatient samples on the basis of persistent depression. Miller et al. (1985) reported that four out of six drug-refractory inpatients achieved remission when treated with a combination of cognitive therapy and medication. De Jong et al. (1986) compared the response of inpatients with dysthymia to full cognitive therapy, cognitive restructuring alone or a waiting list control. Of the ten patients who received full cognitive therapy, six met criteria for recovery, which was higher than the recovery rate in the other groups. Scott (1992) describes two studies of inpatients with depressive symptoms of over two years' duration who had failed to respond to medication. The first study compared continued aggressive, pharmacological treatment alone with that treatment plus cognitive therapy. There was no difference in response rates between these groups. In the second study, 16 patients were treated with a combined treatment incorporating a 'cognitive therapy milieu' on the ward. Although standard recovery rates are not reported, a greater percentage change in symptoms was achieved using this upgraded version of cognitive therapy. Again, the results of studies of cognitive therapy in inpatients with persistent depressive symptoms suggest that worthwhile improvements can be achieved.

This review of the effectiveness of existing attempts to apply cognitive therapy to persistent depression leaves much open to interpretation. There is evidence of recovery in many patients and of good overall response rates in some studies. There is also evidence that many patients with chronic and resistant depression do not respond adequately to cognitive therapy, resulting in poor rates of response in other studies. The wide range of response rates found in these studies probably reflects differences in the degree of treatment resistance in the patients included. There may also be differences between studies in the nature of the cognitive therapy administered. The majority appear to have used standard cognitive therapy for depression as described by Beck et al. (1979). However, one study used a group format for some patients (Gonzales et al., 1985) and others broadened the administration of the therapy from the individual therapist to other members of the treating team (Miller et al., 1985; Scott, 1992). Overall, it seems safe to conclude that cognitive therapy is a plausible treatment option in persistent depression, as some patients may respond significantly. However, the degree of response is clearly considerably less than that expected in treating acute depression. This is consistent with evidence from studies of the efficacy of cognitive therapy in acute depression, which have found that chronicity of symptoms predicts poorer response to therapy (Hamilton & Dobson, 2002).

RECENT DEVELOPMENTS IN COGNITIVE THERAPY

The time period over which these studies have been conducted is at least 15 years. During this time, the field of cognitive therapy has evolved considerably. Since cognitive therapy was first shown to be effective in the treatment of acute depression, it has been applied to a number of different disorders, ranging from the anxiety disorders to psychosis. The novel application of most relevance to the treatment of persistent depression is cognitive therapy for personality disorders. Applying cognitive therapy to personality disorders has required the development of an account of long-standing patterns of thinking and behaviour (Beck et al., 1990; Young, 1990). This has entailed expansion of the model on which cognitive therapy was originally based to include a greater role for dysfunctional schemas. The emphasis of the model has shifted from the negative thoughts immediately apparent in the patient's experience when emotionally upset to the deeper level, enduring cognitive structures underpinning the way patients process their experience. These developments in the cognitive model have clear relevance to the treatment of persistent depression, which in its enduring nature has many parallels with personality disorder. A cognitive model of persistent depression that incorporates many of these recent developments is described in the next chapter.

This shift of theoretical emphasis has been accompanied by developments in the practice of therapy. A range of techniques has been proposed for addressing the structures underlying dysfunctional thinking or schemas (e.g. Padesky, 1994). Additionally, there has been a greater focus on the interpersonal difficulties evident in many patients with longstanding problems. Addressing these difficulties has required attention to adapting both the style of therapy and its content, with a relatively greater focus on the therapeutic relationship itself than when working with acute disorders (e.g. Safran & Segal, 1990). Much of this book concerns the attempt to incorporate these practical developments into therapy with patients with persistent depression.

One further relevant trend in the field of cognitive therapy has been an interest in how patients experience their negative thoughts, rather than simply the content of their thinking. Theoretically, this has been evident in an increase in interest in metacognition (e.g. Wells, 2000) and models of different levels of cognitive processing (e.g. Teasdale & Barnard, 1993). Practically, this has been reflected in the incorporation of techniques such as mindfulness into cognitive therapy programmes, particularly those aimed at relapse prevention. Such techniques may help patients to realise enduring benefits in areas of longstanding vulnerability (e.g. Segal et al., 2002). Although the approach described in this book does not directly include such practices, there is common ground with some of the principles underlying treatment strategies advocated here. In Chapter 12, we present evidence that patients' progress towards the development of mindful awareness of negative thoughts may be an important mediator of the benefits of therapy.

The Old and the New

Our starting point in approaching the treatment of persistent depression has been to retain the essential features of cognitive therapy that appear to have contributed to its established efficacy in treating depression. We maintain that many features of standard cognitive therapy are essential in treating persistent depression. These include the structuring of therapy both within sessions and over the course of therapy; the collaborative nature of the therapeutic relationship and an emphasis on helping patients to identify and question patterns of negative thinking. However, relying purely on standard cognitive therapy runs the risk of therapy foundering in the face of three significant obstacles presented by patients with persistent depression:

(a) their lack of motivation to engage in treatment that they are convinced is doomed to failure;
(b) their passivity and avoidance of behavioural change;
(c) the refractoriness of their negative thoughts to disconfirmatory evidence.

We have therefore attempted to balance retaining the core features of cognitive therapy with incorporating some developments that offer the greatest promise in addressing these obstacles presented by persistent depression. Most important in these adaptations are: the need to consider the patient's existing view of depression when socialising them into treatment (Chapter 4); the need to adapt the style of therapy (Chapter 2) and its delivery system (Chapter 11); the use of occasions when standard techniques are unsuccessful to enhance the therapist's formulation and the patient's awareness of the nature of the problems (Chapters 5 and 6); and the use of techniques specifically developed to address prejudicial systems of negative thinking (Chapters 7 and 8). This approach represents a 'snapshot' of our best endeavours at the time we started this work. The field of cognitive therapy continues to develop rapidly and there will remain a great need for effective developments in the treatment of persistent depression in the foreseeable future. In the final chapter, we describe some of the latest developments in research and practice in the area of persistent depression, including the results of the outcome study of the therapy described here, and outline some areas where further developments are needed.

SUMMARY POINTS

- Despite the existence of effective treatments for depression, depressive symptoms persist in large numbers of patients.
- Hopelessness, passivity and low self-esteem are prominent characteristics of persistent depression.
- Persistent depression has drastic consequences for the well-being of patients, their performance of social roles and hence for their families and society more generally.
- Adverse social consequences of depressive symptoms become increasingly likely as symptoms persist. The effects of these social changes make it more likely that symptoms will persist further.
- Research and the development of treatments have been hindered by the slow development of any consensus regarding definitions and diagnostic criteria.
- Chronicity per se is less of a problem than persistence of symptoms despite adequate treatment.
- Delay in starting treatment and provision of inadequate treatment are major contributors to chronicity, and are associated with a reduced likelihood of full response to subsequent adequate treatment.
- A number of biological, psychological and social factors predict persistence of depressive symptoms. Chronicity is most likely when biological and psychosocial vulnerabilities occur in combination.

- A range of options exists for treatment with medication, which are of modest benefit and require longer duration of treatment than in acute depression.
- Psychological therapies may help to address the psychosocial symptoms and consequences of persistent depression.
- Cognitive therapy holds particular promise because of its structured approach and its enduring benefits following treatment of acute depression.
- Existing evidence for the efficacy of standard cognitive therapy in persistent depression is highly variable, but suggests that a significant proportion of patients may benefit.
- The recent extension of cognitive therapy to long-term problems and personality disorders suggests ways in which standard cognitive therapy might be adapted to address the particular problems of patients with persistent depression.

Chapter 1

THE COGNITIVE MODEL OF PERSISTENT DEPRESSION

In this chapter, you will find information on:

- The standard cognitive model of acute depression
- Problems encountered in applying this model in persistent depression
- Three kinds of avoidance that obscure the relationship between negative automatic thoughts and negative emotions
- The nature of overt negative thinking and important underlying beliefs in persistent depression
- Social factors that can trigger or maintain persistent depression
- Early experiences that can contribute to the formation of maladaptive belief systems
- How beliefs, overt negative thoughts, avoidance processes and social adversity combine to manifest in low self-esteem, helplessness and hopelessness
- The implications of the model for the overall conduct of cognitive therapy

---

Cognitive therapy for depression is based on the theoretical and clinical model described by Beck, Rush, Shaw and Emery in their influential book *Cognitive Therapy of Depression* (1979). This model describes the negative thinking characteristic of depression and how this relates to the symptoms and to other emotional, behavioural and situational aspects of the illness. Factors contributing to the manifestation of negative thinking are also considered. These factors include early experiences that influence the development of beliefs and attitudes, and subsequent situations or events that trigger the disorder in vulnerable individuals. The model is used as a guide for the therapist in formulating how depression is maintained in a particular case.

The application of the standard cognitive model in cases of persistent depression can result in confusion and frustration for both patient and therapist. In this chapter, we discuss how the cognitive model for acute depression needs to be adapted in order to apply it to persistent depression. In outline, we propose that the crucial cognitive characteristics in persistent depression are low self-esteem, helplessness and hopelessness. Vulnerability to these thinking patterns arises from the enduring and rigid nature of patients' negative beliefs about themselves and their social world. The persistent threat of distress results in the adoption of maladaptive coping styles, which exacerbate the problems that patients face. Once depressed, patients' experiences, shaped by their beliefs and coping style, confirm and entrench low self-esteem, helplessness and hopelessness. As we have described in the introduction, persistent depression is not a homogeneous problem. Patients' histories, course of current episode and presentation can vary widely. The model describes factors that potentially contribute to the maintenance of depression and help to account for some of the variation in presentations of persistent depression. These factors then need to be considered in constructing a cognitive formulation and treatment plan for each individual case.

THE COGNITIVE MODEL OF ACUTE DEPRESSION

Automatic Thoughts

The standard cognitive model of Beck and colleagues (1979) describes negative thinking in depression at three levels: negative automatic thoughts, thinking errors or biases and underlying beliefs or assumptions. Firstly, many of the spontaneous or automatic thoughts of people with depression are manifestly negative. Such negativity focuses on the self, the world and the future: the negative cognitive triad. People suffering from acute depression tend to see themselves as defective or inadequate, and see the world as presenting them only with insuperable obstacles and difficulties. They see such problems persisting indefinitely into the future and are pessimistic to the point of hopelessness and perhaps suicidal wishes. When these negative automatic thoughts come to mind, they trigger feelings of misery and despair or exacerbate an existing low mood state. Negative emotions or low mood can prime these negative thoughts, making them more likely to come to mind and more believable when they do. As low mood primes the negative thoughts, which then further exacerbate low mood, a vicious circle is set up whereby the person's mood can spiral downwards. This can also lead to procrastination and inactivity, which further feed into the vicious circle, as illustrated in Figure 1.1.

Cognitive Biases

The negative content of thinking manifest in these negative automatic thoughts results in part from certain biases or distortions in the processing

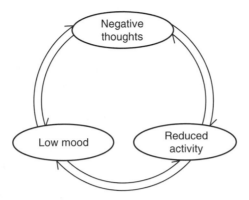

Figure 1.1   The vicious circle in depression

of information. These biases include all-or-nothing or 'black and white' thinking, personalisation and jumping to conclusions. Dichotomous or 'black and white' thinking is central, whereby the person sets unrealistically high standards for their own performance. If these standards are not met, negative judgements ensue. For example, this processing bias could readily be identified with one patient, *Elizabeth*, from the early stages of therapy and was a target for intervention. If something did not meet Elizabeth's exacting high standards it was dismissed as substandard and of no value. Elizabeth saw no shades of grey, so that even an adequate outcome was seen as not making the grade. Black and white thinking can lead to a mental filter, such that positive or neutral aspects of a situation are ignored, whereas negative aspects are selectively focused on and dwelt on at length. Having such high standards served to focus Elizabeth continually on her shortcomings. Her expectation of failing to meet her standards accounted in large part for the avoidance and procrastination that had pervaded her life since the onset of her depression. Elizabeth's thinking biases are evident in the following discussion that took place while reviewing one of her homework assignments.

T: How did you get on with keeping your diary of automatic thoughts?
E: Not very well.
T: Have you got it with you?
E: Yes. It's a mess.
T: Could we take a look at it together?
E: Okay (*shows completed diary to therapist*).
T: Right. Mmm . . . You've written down three examples. What makes you say you have not done it very well?
E: My handwriting is very untidy.
T: I can read it though, isn't that the most important thing?
E: It looks awful.

T: Anything else you are unhappy with?

E: I don't think I've done it properly.

T: Mmmm.... We've spoken about your sense of not doing things properly before. How are you defining properly in this instance?

E: I haven't written down all the thoughts I intended to. I'm bound to have missed some important thoughts, I'm so forgetful these days. Also, I didn't always write them down immediately as you suggested. I waited half an hour or so.

T: Okay let's summarise. You have very ably identified what you see as your shortcomings in completing the diary. You see your handwriting as untidy and as far as you are concerned it has not been done properly. Can I ask—even if it has not met your exacting standard, is it of no use to us today in our session?

E: Mmmm... I see what you're saying.

T: So if this is the black and white position are there any shades of grey here?

E: (sighs) I suppose. I guess I did write down three thoughts and like you said you can read it, which is the point really.

In addition, depressed people frequently personalise any negative outcomes, by assuming the blame for things that go wrong or seeing personal rejection in any uncomfortable social situation. Thoughts that exemplify this kind of bias include 'It's all my fault' or 'I should have stopped this happening'. Personalisation pervaded *Jean's* thinking in most interactions with other people. For example, if she argued with her partner she invariably concluded it was her fault. This was sometimes taken to the extreme that if someone refused a request, Jean took this as evidence that she had offended them in some way or that they were exacting revenge for some past misdemeanour on her part.

Negative biases may also be in the form of arbitrary inferences, where the depressed person jumps to the most negative conclusion about a situation in the absence of any evidence. Patients often predict quite catastrophic outcomes for future events, while perfectly plausible benign or beneficial outcomes are never conceived or are dismissed as highly unlikely. This way of thinking is particularly characteristic of depressed patients who present with significant anxiety symptoms. *Marion* tended to predict that any event from making a request of her daughter to attending a social gathering or therapy session was likely to end in absolute disaster. In the early stages of treatment, Marion asked to end the therapy. After some discussion, it transpired that before each treatment session Marion's mind was bombarded by negative thoughts regarding the fact she had not completed her homework. This typically began with thoughts such as 'I'm too tired' and 'It won't help' and then turned to predicting that the therapist would think that she was lazy. This thinking quickly got out of proportion to such an extent that she would picture the therapist shouting at her and telling her she was a waste of space. She imagined the therapist writing to her psychiatrist to tell him the same, resulting in the psychiatrist washing his hands of her. Her request to be discharged helped her to exert some control over what she perceived with absolute certainty would be the inevitable outcome of the non-completion of homework assignments. Marion had no evidence to support these predictions, but when depressed and anxious her thinking was dominated by this kind of negative processing.

Dysfunctional Assumptions

The third level of negative thinking is that of longstanding cognitive structures that predate the onset of the episode of depression and whose activation results in cognitive biases and automatic thoughts. In cases of acute depression, conditional beliefs or assumptions are thought to confer the cognitive aspect of vulnerability. These conditional beliefs typically set out the conditions that must be satisfied for the person to adopt a sense of worth, fulfilment or happiness. *Elizabeth's* rule 'If you can't do something properly then there is no point in doing it at all' was manifest in the above example. If rigidly applied, such a belief increases the likelihood of depression when those high standards are not met, whether this is due to internal or external factors. The limitations imposed by the symptoms of depression prevented Elizabeth living up to her standards and so caused her much distress. Other common conditional beliefs in depression are 'If anyone criticises or rejects me, it shows I am an unlikeable person' and 'I cannot be happy unless I am loved by others'. These conditional beliefs are similar to quite functional beliefs held by many people, in that most people would prefer to be loved and not to be criticised or rejected. However, they are unhelpful in their extremity or the rigidity with which they are applied to situations where the conditions are perceived as not being met.

In the cognitive model of depression, these conditional beliefs are thought to develop in many cases through early life experiences. Where parents have been excessively critical, the child may internalise the implicit rule that being valued only comes from perfect performance, as was the case for Elizabeth. This assumption may become latent or silent during parts of adult life where any endeavours are met with a reasonable degree of success. Thus, prior to becoming depressed, Elizabeth had, by unrelenting hard work, managed to live up to the excesses of her conditional belief. However, any notable failures activate the latent assumption and the person becomes sensitised to any signs of falling short of their perfectionistic standard. The onset of Elizabeth's depression was triggered by public criticism from her coworkers for dutifully following company procedures that were commonly flouted. The demand she placed on herself always to do things 'properly' (in this instance, stick to the rulebook) led to her being criticised. This criticism was perceived by her as a failure to live up to others' expectations of her. However, had Elizabeth decided to flout the rules along with everyone else, she would in her eyes have failed in the expectations she set for herself. This illustrates the impact of stringent adherence to inflexible rules, which in this instance put Elizabeth in a no-win position.

PROBLEMS APPLYING THE COGNITIVE MODEL IN PERSISTENT DEPRESSION

In using this model of depression with acute cases, pertinent negative thoughts are often self-evident. Once the patient is socialised to the cognitive model, automatic thoughts can readily be identified and are often amenable to cognitive interventions. It would seem reasonable to expect that persistent depression would be characterised by a thinking style in which these negative automatic thoughts, processing biases and structures would be chronically manifest. Indeed this is often the case, and the therapist is assailed by a barrage of self-criticism and overwhelming negativity from the patient. A chronic cognitive triad (see pages 55–59) of low self-esteem, helplessness and hopelessness is often manifest in overt negative thoughts about the self, the world and the future. The extremity and rigidity of this negative thinking can be difficult to contain and manage, as was the case with Elizabeth. However, this barrage of negativity is not the only notable thing in the experience of therapists working with resistant depression. A number of common features of presentation in these patients can make it hard to see immediately how the cognitive model applies. These include a reluctance of some patients to discuss their problems or thoughts; globality of thinking that is hard to relate to particular problems; and an apparent lack of relationship between the patients' negative thoughts and low moods.

Firstly, with some chronically depressed patients, it can be hard to gain from them any idea of what their problems are or even that they have any problems. In the early stages of contact, some patients are reluctant to talk about any problems they are having. Although some reluctant patients will assent to direct questions about their problems, others may explicitly refuse to discuss certain issues. Even where an initial assessment has seemed fairly innocuous to the therapist, the patient may express reluctance to continue with the therapy during or after the initial contact.

The therapist's difficulty applying the cognitive model does not always stem from this reluctance of patients to discuss their problems. Plenty of patients with persistent depression have many problems that they wish to discuss and on occasion the therapist can be faced with an apparent tidal wave of different problems affecting every area of a patient's life. Patients may indicate various relationships in which they have been slighted, rejected or let down and various endeavours that have failed or been incomplete. As they flit from one to another of an apparently vast array of problems, the patient's moods may be quite turbulent. However, the negative cognitions described in the standard cognitive model may still be hard to identify. It can be difficult to focus a patient on one particular problem for long enough to identify the related meanings and interpretations. Having been hit by this wave of various problems, the therapist can still be left with a lack of clarity as to the nature of the patient's difficulties. Importantly, the cognitions crucial to applying the model may not be immediately apparent.

Other patients respond to the therapist's questions about their problems quite readily, but show or describe little sign of upset or distress. Where patients do not readily provide information about their problems or feelings, the therapist is often left with a description of symptoms but little information about other aspects of the cognitive model with which to build a formulation. For example, at his first session *Stan* complained of a number of symptoms of depression, particularly memory loss, which he worried was due to dementia or a brain tumour. However, he did not think he had any other problems, although he acknowledged in response to the therapist's questioning that being unemployed and various family situations might be problems. Although he said he did not like talking about these things, Stan did not appear to be upset. Similarly, when any overt negative thinking was apparent, such as when he described himself as pathetic, this was accompanied by an air of resignation rather than any sign of acute distress.

AVOIDANCE IN PERSISTENT DEPRESSION

A common factor that interferes with the application of the cognitive model in these apparently disparate presentations of persistent depression is avoidance. In persistent depression, avoidance can serve to mask negative thinking patterns or inhibit the effects of negative thoughts on mood. On occasions, negative thinking may not be overt or apparent due to such avoidance. Pinpointing such avoidance in persistent depression is often a prerequisite to identifying negative thoughts. To understand the ways that negative thinking manifests in and contributes to persistent depression, it is important first to consider different forms of avoidance and their effects.

In acute depression, avoidance is often plain to see and is frequently acknowledged by the patient. It is manifest in gross behaviours, such as staying in bed all day or steering clear of particular work or social situations. The patient is usually willing and able to describe the negative feelings and thoughts that result when their attempts to avoid these situations are not successful. In chronic depression, the avoidance is often more subtle in nature. It can take three interrelated forms: behavioural avoidance of certain external circumstances, cognitive avoidance of certain mental ideas or images and emotional avoidance through the direct suppression of emotional experiences. Each of these forms of avoidance can obscure the distressing feelings and thoughts that are crucial in constructing a cognitive formulation of the patient's problems.

Behavioural Avoidance

Patterns of behavioural avoidance associated with depression have to be sustainable within the patient's lifestyle. Because in chronic cases the depression is of some duration, the gross withdrawal seen in acute depression is usually not sustainable and is encountered relatively rarely. Although some patients avoid whole classes of situation, such as work or social situations, in many cases the avoidance is of more subtle aspects of the situation. Thus, patients with persistent depression may not acknowledge or may not be aware that they are avoiding certain situations. Some patients may appear to be keeping up a good level of social contact. However, it may emerge that all their relationships are concerned with providing practical help to other people, and that in fact they become highly anxious about unstructured situations. For example, at assessment it appeared that *Rosemary* was maintaining a busy social life with friends and family. However, it emerged that most of her contacts involved helping others in some way, by cleaning or childminding for neighbours and by ferrying people in her car to shops or hospital appointments. At family gatherings and social activities, she would avoid mixing with people by engaging in activity, such as cooking or tidying up. Through managing the precise nature of social interactions in this way, patients like Rosemary can minimise the levels of distress they experience. Importantly for the cognitive therapist, overt negative thoughts may rarely be triggered and tend to emerge only when the patient is unable to manage in their usual way. For example, when Rosemary did have to engage in social interactions without recourse to helping people, she thought that people would see her as a miserable person and want nothing more to do with her.

Subtle avoidance is also commonly encountered in the form of routines that patients develop for carrying out activities of daily living. Some patients appear to be carrying out many activities, such as shopping or looking after themselves and their home, with little difficulty. This may be accomplished through a strict routine in which particular activities are carried out at a particular time on specific days of the week in a particular place. Any deviation, such as going to a different shop than usual, or doing something at a different time, represents an insuperable break from routine. As with overt withdrawal, this adherence to routine is often an attempt to manage the depression, and any variation is seen as risking a worsening of symptoms. For example, *Graham's* lifestyle included aspects of overt avoidance and routinised activity. Having experienced two very disabling episodes of depression, he had made a conscious decision 'not to rock the boat' by overstretching himself. His routine involved getting up at 9.30 a.m., then slowly having breakfast, watching television and getting washed and dressed, which took him until lunchtime. After lunch, his afternoon activities included a five-minute walk to the local shop for a paper and the evening would involve preparing a meal and watching more television. He made expeditions to the local supermarket (10 minutes' walk away) and visits to his neighbours on a weekly basis. Based on his fear of overstretching himself, Graham actively avoided exercise, working on his computer and making trips to the pub, cinema or town (to which he received frequent invitations from friends). The development of rigid routines can help patients to adapt their lifestyle to the depression and can successfully limit the acute distress experienced on a day-to-day basis.

Cognitive Avoidance

Many chronically depressed patients not only try to avoid being in certain situations but may also try to avoid thinking about them. Cognitive avoidance can manifest itself in a number of ways. It can be seen in the general reluctance to discuss or acknowledge problems described above. Some patients will discuss their problems in general terms but try to avoid thinking certain specific thoughts. This can influence not only their internal mental life, but also their reaction to the therapist's attempts to engage them in describing their problems. Some of the difficulties relating a patient's presentation to the cognitive model can be accounted for by this coping strategy and are manifest from the first meeting with the patient.

A general reluctance to discuss problem areas is sometimes evident from the very outset of any assessment. In some patients this is reflected in attempts to engage the therapist in discussions about issues of tangential relevance, such as the weather or a news item. Some chronically depressed patients will not spontaneously raise problems they wish to discuss, but will answer direct questions about their symptoms or problems that the therapist has gleaned from the referral, such as unemployment or social isolation. They may play down the impact of these problems or respond in an unrealistically positive way. Other patients may be more explicit about their desire not to discuss certain topics. In *Peter's* case, this desire was reinforced by his wife, who asked to attend his first session to ensure that the therapist did not ask Peter anything about the circumstances that had led to his depression. She explained that whenever Peter attempted to talk about this subject he cried, which was humiliating for him. She wished to protect him from this humiliation by preventing him having to talk about issues that might upset him.

Some patients readily describe their symptoms or problem situations, but the therapist may find it hard to elicit any negative thoughts associated with their current distress. This was the case for *Marion* who complained of being constantly tired and of her lack of motivation to engage in even the basic activities of daily living. Attempting to focus Marion on how her inactivity impacted on her view of self met with statements such as 'I don't know' or 'It doesn't'. In cognitive therapy, part of the therapist's brief is to help the patient to identify the negative thoughts that may be contributing to their distress. Patients' reluctance to focus on negative thoughts can lead them to react to therapy in an irritable or prickly fashion. When the therapist attempts to enquire about particular thoughts, the patient can become extremely upset. This can be manifest as anger at and disparagement of the therapist ('You don't understand' or 'You must be incompetent to be making me feel like this') or therapy ('I can tell right now this is not going to work for me'). When *Julie's* therapist asked what was upsetting her most about the fact that her 14-year-old son was currently in a remand centre, Julie initially responded, 'Isn't it obvious? Anyone would be upset.' Although on one level this seems a valid response, it did not clarify exactly what the situation meant to Julie. The therapist asked whose fault it was that her son was in such trouble. Julie then became quite irritable with the therapist and replied, 'I suppose you're blaming me.' Although tempted to apologise and back off, the therapist persisted, 'There may be a range of possible answers to the question and I was interested in how you see the situation.' Julie replied that her husband said it was her fault. The therapist then asked her how much she believed that. At this point, Julie began to cry and said, 'It is my fault—I'm his mother.' This suggests that her initial irritation at the therapist was a result of her attempt to avoid her own thought that she was to blame for this unfortunate situation. She remained unable to see that some of her distress was caused by her attributions of self-blame, and instead attributed her difficulties entirely to the events that occurred in her life.

Even when patients complain of a tidal wave of problems in a turbulent fashion, as described on page 27, this can be a reflection of cognitive avoidance. The patient may be trying to describe a problem situation, but as they start to think about aspects of the situation that make them feel particularly uncomfortable, they 'jump ship' only to hit on another area of their life that is not going well. Again, they may describe the situational aspects of the problem but shy away from focusing on the painful thoughts and feelings that accompany those situations. At assessment, Julie described a plethora of problems accompanied by a moderate degree of distress, but moved from one problem to the next in a somewhat chaotic fashion. This left the therapist initially overwhelmed and somewhat at a loss about where to start treatment.

Cognitive avoidance in persistent depression can also take the form of deliberate suppression of specific thoughts, memories and images. The role of cognitive avoidance of specific thoughts and images in persistent depression may be similar to its role in cognitive models of other disorders (e.g. Borkovec & Inz, 1990; Wegner et al., 1987). Many chronically depressed patients report experiencing intrusive thoughts and memories. When they notice a distressing intrusion, they try to eliminate the intrusion from their mind or to control the rumination by attempting to distract themselves. The consequence of this can be a rebound effect, which results in a recurrence of the intrusion or a reinstitution of the ruminative process, often with a worsening of the accompanying affective state. The individual may then intensify their efforts to rid themselves of the distressing thought, resulting in a processing loop accompanied by increasing distress and a decreasing sense of control over mental processing. Such unsuccessful attempts to suppress distressing memories were manifest in Julie's strategy of cognitive avoidance. She reported intrusive memories of episodes of physical violence and sexual assault that had occurred over ten years previously during her first marriage. Julie took the occurrence of these intrusions as evidence that she should really still be with her first husband and that she was being punished for divorcing him. She also saw the intrusions as evidence that she was losing control of her mind and feared a complete mental breakdown. She invested a great deal of mental energy in attempting to keep control by pushing her intrusive memories out of her mind.

Emotional Avoidance

It is striking when working with patients with persistent depression that many describe having 'no feelings'. Indeed therapy sessions can proceed for long periods with little sign of the mood shifts so common in acute depression. Many patients appear to be able to talk about apparently distressing situations and describe apparently disturbing or disparaging thoughts with little outward sign of emotional disturbance. Apparently positive events can be described in the same flat monotone in which negative events, such as redundancy or the threat of losing invalidity benefit, are greeted. Indeed, many of these patients show very little sign of acute emotional arousal about anything, presenting instead with a dull flatness of mood. For example, at assessment *Stan* described, in an even tone with no sign of distress, his redundancy two years previously from a job he had held for many years. He elaborated equally cheerlessly that it might have been quite a good thing, as it saved him the hassle of getting to work every morning. In a subsequent session he relayed news of the birth of a grandchild in a similarly flat tone. As well as responding to events in an emotionally flat way, patients can describe cognitive themes that would be expected to be associated with great distress in a matter of fact fashion. Stan described how he was unable to tell his wife that he did not wish to accompany her on various outings with her friends. He said that he knew that this was a sign of being pathetic and weak, but his tone of voice was mild, there was no sign of distress and he denied being upset.

This damping down of expected affective responses can reflect a form of direct emotional avoidance. Some patients report that suppressing or distancing themselves from their feelings is an intentional strategy. This is most often the case for men who are socialised to value emotional control and to see expressions of emotion (either positive or negative) as indicative of weakness or irrationality. The degree of effort involved in such emotional suppression seems to vary considerably. If questioned, some patients acknowledge directing a great deal of effort towards vetting and controlling their emotional experience. Although *Graham* would discuss potentially upsetting issues with no overt sign of distress or discomfort, it transpired that internally he experienced a range of emotional reactions. He believed these responses to be abnormal and unacceptable, and took them as evidence of his inadequacy. As a result, from his childhood onwards he had developed strategies for ensuring that these emotions were never publicly displayed. These included tensing his body, in particular 'pushing down' in his stomach, in order physically to suppress his feelings. Interestingly, Graham was not averse to letting his feelings out in private and had on occasions cried at upsetting events in the privacy of his bedroom or when alone reading a moving book or watching a film. Thus it was the public display of emotions that was most unacceptable to him rather than experiencing them per se.

For many other patients, the control of emotions seems to have become so automatic that it requires little effort. Such patients often have great difficulty identifying any acute emotional experiences at all. The lack of acute negative experience may explain patients' failure to consider manifest difficulties as problems in the way described above. Even the most grievous external circumstances, including redundancy or personal losses, may not be viewed as problems. The lack of emotional experience can impact on a patient's view of depression itself, such that some persistently depressed patients do not see themselves as depressed. For example, at the beginning of therapy Stan kept asking the therapist over and again whether he was depressed, and seemed unable to take on board the therapist's assurance that he did indeed have many of the common symptoms of depression. This made it difficult at the beginning of therapy to gain an accurate picture of the history of depression and its relation to his other life experiences. Stan thought that he had been like this for the two years since his initial referral by his general practitioner, which was shortly after he had lost his job. He also thought it possible that he may have been like this for some 20 years, as he had not seemed to be the same as other people over that time.

CONSEQUENCES OF AVOIDANCE

Adaptive Consequences

With many patients, the adoption of a range of avoidant coping strategies for dealing with unpleasant events, thoughts and feelings can be traced back to an early age. These avoidance strategies were often adaptive, given the context in which they emerged, and enabled the individual to deal with highly aversive experiences. This was the case for *Marion*, who as a child was treated as a pawn in the ongoing conflict between her alcohol-dependent father and depressed mother. She quickly learned that she could exert little control over the behaviour of either parent and frequently became highly anxious. Her own emotional needs were neglected and she learned to ignore these to such a degree that as an adult she had no real sense of what these needs were and how to meet them. Avoidance as a coping strategy may also be learned from the models presented in certain cultures. For example, male patients' concerns that the expression of emotions will lead to ridicule and humiliation are not entirely unfounded in many parts of the UK. In this environment, men are socialised to view open expression of any emotion (positive or negative) as a lack of inner strength and control. Cultural attitudes about the experience and expression of emotion may lead to the reinforcement of emotional suppression both within and outside the home.

These forms of behavioural, cognitive and emotional avoidance can all be seen as strategies the patient has evolved for dealing with the distress provoked by difficult events and thoughts. Successful use of such strategies in the avoidance or relief of anxiety and distress over many years will have been highly reinforcing. With the onset of depression, these same avoidant strategies can then be applied to dealing with depression itself. Patients who have experienced depression over a number of years learn that if they can avoid stressful situations or painful thoughts and feelings, then their depression will just grumble along in the background in a way that can be endured. Clearly, developing skills to regulate affect is a crucial aspect of psychological development, which facilitates adaptation to change or challenging situations. However, the avoidance strategies described here seem maladaptive in that they do not simply serve to make unpleasant affect more manageable to enable those problem situations to be addressed effectively. Rather, they seem to be intended to eliminate unpleasant emotions from conscious awareness. This has a number of self-defeating consequences.

Maladaptive Consequences

With increasing avoidance, patients' tolerance of upsetting emotions can become severely limited and the development of alternative ways of managing affect compromised. Problem situations frequently remain unaddressed and problem-solving skills may not be developed or practised. Through avoiding articulating or working towards personal goals, patients may be chronically deprived of the satisfaction this can bring. Where avoidance is intended to conceal perceived inadequacies from others, it may in fact serve to prevent erroneously negative self-evaluations from being re-evaluated.

Different styles of avoidance can have different consequences for patients' current behaviour and mood. Behavioural and cognitive avoidance of upsetting situations and thoughts entails engaging in particular physical and mental activities to manage mood. Where this active avoidance is the predominant way of coping, patients' moods can be highly labile. When not confronted by any particular problems, the person's mood can be good and they may present themselves as happy and coping well. However, when avoiding or ignoring problems becomes impossible to sustain, their mood may quickly crash and extreme negative thinking may become evident. This style of coping is often exhibited from assessment onwards. For example, *Kate* began her first therapy session saying that she felt quite well and could not think of any problems that she wished to discuss. When the therapist suggested reviewing different areas of her life in order to get to know her better, it soon emerged that she was jobless and facing considerable financial problems. In addition, she had suffered in a string of apparently abusive relationships and had recently fallen out with one of her neighbours. As the elucidation of all these problems progressed, Kate became extremely distressed, berated herself as a horrible person and left the room saying she did not want to carry on the therapy. It took considerable persuasion in a quiet corridor outside before she agreed to return to the therapist's office and discuss how therapy might be able to help her. In many patients, when their avoidance breaks down, the negative cognitions expected within a cognitive model are all too evident and the associated mood shifts quite overwhelming.

In contrast, where emotional avoidance is predominant, the patient's mood will tend to be flat and the outward appearance is of passivity. Whereas behavioural avoidance leads to an outward focus on controlling events, emotional avoidance focuses the patient's effort inwards on the control of emotional experience. Patients for whom this strategy predominates seem to show little initiative, instead going along with what seems to be expected of them. In this way, *Stan* had few friends of his own and never arranged any social contact. When confronted with gatherings of his wife's friends, which he found quite awful, he would go along with an air of resignation. For some patients, the elimination of emotions has become so pervasive that they have great difficulty identifying or expressing any desires or preferences at all. Although this coping style tends to prevent overwhelming mood shifts, this lack of emotional immediacy can be problematic in itself. Where patients have become very able to limit or distance themselves from their feelings, they often remain in situations that they find aversive or fail to take any action to bring about satisfying results. The constancy of undesired outcomes then feeds an increasing sense of gloom and hopelessness, which even further emotional suppression cannot alleviate.

Consequences for Therapy

Importantly, the processes of avoidance have major implications for the conduct of cognitive therapy, which are discussed in detail in the remainder of this book. The subtle and often successful implementation of behavioural avoidance can mean that important negative thoughts are not triggered. Cognitive avoidance can make it difficult for the therapist to focus on specific problems or to identify specific negative thoughts in therapy. The lack of emotional arousal which results from emotional suppression impedes the psychotherapeutic process generally and means that any negative thoughts that are identified are not 'hot' and are thus harder to work with. Even when patients have grasped the idea of recognising and identifying negative thoughts, avoidance may then affect subsequent attempts to develop new ways of dealing with them. Having successfully identified a negative thought, patients may then apply their usual coping strategy of pushing thoughts out of their mind rather than going through the process of examining the content of the thought itself and looking for a more balanced view.

A further effect of patients' avoidance on therapy is that initial cognitive therapy interventions frequently result in patients feeling worse in the short term. If this reaction is not expected and discussed as part of the initial treatment rationale, the patient can experience the emotional arousal provoked in therapy as aversive and unhelpful. This in turn can feed into beliefs about the perceived uncontrollability of depression as an illness. It can also lead the patient to perceive that the therapist is 'out to get them' in some way. This can explain the sometimes hostile or angry responses when it is suggested to patients with chronic depression that they should start therapy. It is important that the threat this presents to the establishment of a therapeutic alliance is anticipated and the potential for premature termination of treatment reduced. Ways of adapting the style of therapy (Chapter 2), the socialisation of the patient into therapy (Chapter 4) and the use of behavioural (Chapter 5) and cognitive (Chapter 6) techniques to lessen the adverse impact of these avoidance processes on therapy are discussed in detail in subsequent chapters.

LEVELS OF COGNITION IN PERSISTENT DEPRESSION

Addressing the thinking of patients with persistent depression can often seem like the unenviable task of stripping wallpaper in an old house. With considerable effort one layer of wallpaper is removed small strip by small strip, only to reveal another layer of paper of an even more unsuitable design bonded to the wall by an even stronger layer of adhesive. The thoughts that are easiest to identify often turn out to be manifestations of more deeply entrenched and more widely generalised beliefs. For example, some patients appear to attribute their perceived inadequacy to being depressed but, when questioned, attribute their inadequacy to having been repeatedly depressed, and when this is questioned they attribute their inadequacy to their make-up, viz. 'It's just me—the way I am'. In providing an account of cognition in persistent depression, the cognitive model must first describe the characteristics of overt negative thinking that are most immediately apparent. The belief systems underlying overt negative thinking must then be examined.

Overt Negative Thoughts

In the cognitive model of acute depression, Beck and colleagues (1979) described how negative thoughts impinge on conscious awareness in a spontaneous or automatic fashion. Such negative automatic thoughts are commonly associated with depressive affect shifts. As with the cognitive triad in acute depression, negative thinking in persistent depression manifests in low self-esteem, helplessness and hopelessness. However, the processes of cognitive and emotional avoidance in persistent depression influence the nature of the thoughts that are apparent to the therapist. In many cases of persistent depression, the evasion or suppression of shifts in affect limits the occurrence of spontaneous, 'hot' automatic thoughts.

The negative thoughts that are reported in chronic cases seem less affectively charged and are often quite stereotyped or habitual. Patients may say the same things over and over again, using the same negative descriptions of themselves and the situation each time. Thus, *Marion* repeated the phrase 'It's hopeless' like an incantation; *Catherine* would respond to any therapeutic intervention with 'It won't make any difference'; and *Stan's* comment on most situations was 'I'm just pathetic'. These repetitive negative thoughts are often global in nature and may be divorced from reference to any specific situation. They often contain the same thinking biases as in acute depression, with black and white thinking patterns and personalisation particularly common. Although accompanied by a general mood of gloom, such thoughts are often not associated with changes in emotional state. Perhaps because of the lack of accompanying emotional arousal, such thoughts can not only be repetitive and held quite rigidly, but also seem somewhat immune to tried and trusted modes of questioning, as will be discussed in Chapter 6. Attempts to question these negative thoughts often lead to rationalisation at a superficial level with little improvement in the patient's affective or motivational state. This global negative thinking may reflect an avoidance of thoughts about specific negative situations that may be inherently more emotional or 'hot'.

However, when avoidance processes break down, the negative thoughts driving that avoidance tend to become apparent. Such thoughts are accompanied by overwhelming levels of affect. This was true for *Jean*, who in the face of actual or perceived criticism from others would become simultaneously anxious, angry and guilty. At such times, she spontaneously proffered a stream of automatic thoughts in which she assumed others were viewing her in a negative light, which she believed would lead them to withdraw all attention and affection forever. She would become enraged at the injustice of this but would also blame herself and assume the burden of responsibility for making peace.

Not only was the situation itself blown out of proportion in this way, but her high levels of affect were then catastrophised as a total loss of control, thus further exacerbating her distress. Such outbursts of emotion were difficult to contain and manage for both therapist and patient, so in some respects it was understandable that Jean used avoidance as a means of managing her negative affect. In these circumstances, the high levels of affect coupled with the rigidity of her thinking made conventional efforts to question Jean's negative thoughts extremely difficult.

Thinking Style

In many cases of persistent depression, the style of the patient's way of thinking may be as important as its negative content. The global style of thinking is reflected in the kinds of cognitive biases or thinking errors seen in persistent depression. The negative thinking of patients with persistent depression is often categorical and extreme. This extremity of black and white thinking can make the thinking biases of acutely depressed patients seem moderate. For example, *Rosemary* could concede that other depressed people would benefit from making some allowance for the depression, but drew the line at the possibility that she might give herself more time to do things. To her, even to consider this possibility would be categorically 'selfish', as it would limit the time she had available to do things for others. Thinking biases such as overgeneralisation, jumping to conclusions and personalisation are also common in persistent depression. In acute depression, these thinking biases often reflect excessively negative inferences drawn from particular situations. Patients with persistent depression often seem to arrive at similar negative conclusions without any reference to any particular negative situation or trigger.

An overgeneral style of processing has been described as an important feature of cognition in depression that is associated with chronicity (Williams et al., 1997). Patients with persistent depression often seem to have great difficulty recounting particular incidents, whether from the recent or more distant past. They may be certain about some state of affairs at an abstract level, but be unable to back up their general view with specific instances. This applies to both positive and negative events, although the difficulty may be more marked when attempting to recall positive memories. For example, at one session when discussing the previous week, *Julie* reported that she had failed at just about everything she had attempted, but was unable to give any examples. She also said that the only thing that had gone well in the week was that her niece had made some kind remarks to her, but she could not think of the day on which this had occurred or the content of what had been said. It is likely that such overgeneral memories have less affective impact than more specific memories. As this overgeneral recall does not seem to be under conscious control, it may be different in nature to the forms of cognitive avoidance described above. It may result from a detrimental influence of an avoidant style of processing on the ability to access and elaborate specific memories at the time of recall (Kuyken & Brewin, 1996). Alternatively, it may reflect cognitive disengagement from situations at the time they are encoded into memory, which interferes with the registration of specific information about those situations.

This abstract style of processing may interfere with the accomplishment of particular tasks. For example, at one stage *Elizabeth* described having considerable difficulty completing a particularly complicated report at work. When the therapist asked for more details, Elizabeth could describe in general terms what the report was about but was unable to elaborate on its format or the more specific issues involved. This resulted in her difficulty in breaking the overall task down in order to tackle specific aspects of the report in a step-by-step fashion. Interestingly, this kind of clinical observation is supported by research suggesting that the difficulty depressed patients have in recalling specific memories contributes to their poor problem solving (Williams et al., 1997; Garland et al., 2000).

The overt negative thinking observed in patients with persistent depression is often ruminative in nature. Such rumination involves patients repeatedly focusing on the fact that they are depressed; on the symptoms of depression; on its causes and its persistence. Recent research has suggested that rumination may influence both the duration and severity of low mood (Nolen-Hoeksema, 1991). Importantly, this ruminative response style may reflect different cognitive processes to the negative automatic thoughts in depression. This processing style can reflect a deliberate or habitual strategy, rather than reflecting automatic differences in accessibility of emotionally toned material. It is frequently encountered in patients for whom the theme of control is a central concern, and it may represent part of a strategy for managing affect. Its presence can be detected when the patient's attention shifts in the session from the issue at hand to questions of the symptoms of depression or the likely duration and course of the illness.

Underlying Beliefs

The overwhelming affect occasionally triggered by some thoughts in persistent depression results from the profound personal significance of the thoughts. The thoughts that are accessible in awareness at times of acute distress may directly reflect the activation of deeper level assumptions and beliefs. The repetitive and flat nature of much of the thinking observed can be seen as a consequence of protecting against such activation of deeper beliefs. Whereas in acute depression it is often possible to treat cases by addressing behaviours and automatic thoughts with relatively minimal understanding of or attention to beliefs, this is less so in persistent depression. Beliefs relevant to persistent depression concern negative representations that patients have of themselves, their relationship to others and the world in which they live. Rather than being transient ideas that are to a large extent coloured by the mood state in which they arise—as in the automatic thoughts seen in acute depression—beliefs are of an enduring nature. The person gives them credence at different times, in different situations and in different mood states. In applying the cognitive model to persistent depression, it is helpful to consider three types of underlying beliefs: beliefs about depression, conditional beliefs or assumptions and unconditional or core beliefs.

BELIEFS ABOUT DEPRESSION

The beliefs that are often most immediately evident when working with cases of persistent depression are those concerning the depression itself. Beliefs about depression, its causes and its controllability may be fashioned by the patient's repeated or prolonged experience of being depressed and undergoing treatment. These beliefs about depression can have important implications for the persistence of depression.

Depression as a Sign of Inadequacy

The symptoms of depression, including lack of energy and motivation, entail reductions in what the person is able to accomplish compared to usual. As a result of such limitations, patients often view being depressed as a sign of weakness or inadequacy. For many patients, the specific belief that depression is a sign of weakness is guided by a pre-existing general belief that emotions are a sign of weakness (see below). When the symptoms persist, such weakness is viewed as characterological, rather than as a temporary or partial state. This view is then often reinforced by changes in role that may accompany the persistence of depression, such as being retired on medical grounds. Prior to his illness, Peter saw himself as strong, capable and in control of himself and his life. In his eyes, not having eradicated the depression at an early stage constituted a definitive failure.

He believed quite rigidly that 'my depression shows what an inadequate person I am' and he discounted as applying only to other people the view that depression is an illness.

An unsuccessful treatment process can reinforce the belief that depression shows a weakness of character. When first presenting with depression, patients are often told that their depression is treatable and are informed of the range of effective treatments that are available for depression. When such 'effective' treatments are tried and found to be ineffective, perhaps several times over, an attribution that the illness reflects a defect in character rather than being a treatable illness is reinforced. The explanation is often lent further weight by other aspects of the treatment process. For example, the clinician whose initial attempt at treatment has been unsuccessful may refer the patient on. Although to those who understand the health care system this is eminently sensible, patients who are forming a view that their depression proves that they are inadequate may see this as a sign that the clinician has given up on them. Similarly, if, as is often the case for psychiatrists in training positions, the treating doctor is moved to another position after an unsuccessful course of treatment, then this may again reinforce a patient's view that they are untreatable as a result of some fundamental inadequacy. Things are made even worse if the clinicians themselves, having initially approached their new patient with optimism and enthusiasm, become transparently discouraged and even disinterested when the patient fails to make a good response despite the clinician's best efforts. For example, *Catherine* had had several experiences of being referred on by different mental health professionals after their efforts to treat her depression had met with little success. She interpreted this lack of success of treatments that she had been told were effective as evidence of her own fragility and weakness. However, she continued to believe that there were effective treatments available, and so also believed that the various treating clinicians must be withholding these from her. Bitterness and resentment at the failure of the treatment system were thus mixed in with her own poor self-esteem.

Depression as a Biological Problem

As well as confirming a view of depression as a sign of personal inadequacy, past unsuccessful treatments can reinforce other beliefs about depression that affect the person's engagement in cognitive therapy. The majority of patients have initially been prescribed antidepressant medication as a first-line treatment for their illness. The treatment rationale provided for this usually involves presenting depression as a biological problem. Depression may be described as a chemical imbalance or as a hereditary complaint for which medication is the treatment of choice. Subsequent lack of treatment response may also have been explained in terms of biological disturbances in the brain. The view that depression is biological is reinforced by evident physical symptoms, especially lethargy and muscular aches or weakness. The apparent lack of relation between low mood and obvious stressors can also feed the idea that the problem is entirely biological. This idea can be integrated with the characterological view described above in a belief that depression is 'stamped in my genes'.

The strength of patients' attributions of their problems to character or to biology limits their expectations of cognitive therapy. The idea that a few hours of talking will alleviate flaws in a person's character is seen as implausible. It can seem similarly illogical to expect a psychological app-roach to change the nature of the brain or affect levels of neurotransmitters. Cognitive therapy is firmly expected to be the latest in the long line of failed treatments. This can result in therapy being commenced with an attitude of scepticism or overt antipathy towards the therapist, but an air of pas-sive resignation seems at least as common. As we discuss in Chapter 4, in presenting the rationale for cognitive therapy, it is helpful to discuss the interrelationships between biological changes and psychological changes. To encompass patients' beliefs about depression, explaining the mainte-nance of their problems using a psychobiosocial model is preferable to using exclusively psychological explanations.

CONDITIONAL BELIEFS

Beliefs about depression can be quite firmly held and have significant impact on engagement in therapy, but nevertheless represent only the outer layer of cognitive content (or 'wallpaper') in persistent depression. At the next layer, conditional beliefs are rules and assumptions that gov-ern behaviour. Such rules stipulate that if certain conditions are satisfied, self-esteem is preserved. These rules can often be articulated as 'if ... then' statements ('If I do everything perfectly, then I am a worthwhile person') or should statements ('I should always put the needs of others before my own'). Some examples of beliefs typical in persistent depression are: 'If I can't do something properly, there is no point in doing it at all' (*Elizabeth*); 'If I don't do what other people want, I will be criticised and rejected' (*Jean*); and 'If I can't control my emotions, it is a sign of weakness' (*Peter*). These beliefs can be viewed as values that confer some benefits, but also entail disadvantages. The rigidity with which such beliefs are adhered to by patients with chronic depression prevents them, to a greater or lesser extent, from functioning effectively.

Beliefs about Emotions

As discussed above, the belief that depression is a sign of personal inadequacy is often a specific application of a more general belief that emotions are a sign of weakness. The different forms of avoidance discussed above often result from negative beliefs about the experience and expression of emotion. The idea that open expression of any emotion reflects a lack of self-control prevails in many parts of British and other cultures. Control of emotions may be reinforced and viewed as strong or brave, whereas emotional display may be punished or derided as weak. Many patients with persistent depression firmly and wholeheartedly endorse the view that emotions are a sign of weakness and should be overcome or kept under control. As a result of such beliefs, many patients adopt a rule that their feelings should be hidden from others at all times. Any display of emotions is predicted to lead to ridicule and humiliation. This idea often leads to overt behavioural avoidance of upsetting situations. For example, since his business had gone into receivership, *Dave* had seen little of his extended family. He knew that he would feel embarrassed, predicted that he would be unable to hide his upset and believed that for others to see this would result in complete humiliation. He thus tried to avoid all situations where he thought that people might ask personal questions. Many patients believe that emotions should not only be kept hidden, but should be stamped out internally too. Where patients' rules entail overcoming their emotions completely, attempts at emotional suppression become mandatory. For example, *Stan* shared Dave's belief that any outward sign of emotion would lead to ridicule and humiliation, but also believed that any feeling inside rendered him weak and vulnerable. His view was so absolute that he did not allow any feelings even about major positive events, such as the birth of his grandchild.

Beliefs about Work

Negative beliefs about emotions are often accompanied by beliefs about the importance of being productive. Many patients derive their sense of worth from being productive and see emotions as irrelevant to or interfering with this goal. The importance of productivity is often reflected in beliefs about work, which are endorsed by many men (and, increasingly, women) in Western society. Individually, work can provide a sense of purpose and meaning in life. Socially, work is important in defining roles, particularly masculinity, and can be the means through which status and respect (in the eyes of self and others) are conferred. Work is also the means through which someone becomes able to provide materially for others, which can be important in maintaining self-worth. In persistent depression, such attitudes are frequently encountered in the form of beliefs such as, 'In order to have respect and worth I must work'. For some individuals, simply working in itself confers acceptability and respectability, and being hard working is seen as a virtue. For others, it is vital to achieve particular status and respect through being outstanding in the work role. For example, prior to becoming depressed, *Dave* worked long hours striving to make his business the most successful in its field. When the conditions of these beliefs are satisfied, and the person has gainful employment, then there are no grounds for depression. Many patients, whose persistent depression followed their being made redundant, claim that they had never had a moment's depression before in their life. Examination of the person's history bears out that when they have worked there has indeed been no problem with self-confidence or esteem.

However, for patients with these beliefs, being unable to work is a devastating blow. Its effect on perceived self-worth is crippling, even when not working is a result of redundancy that is obviously not the patient's fault. For example, *Peter* was retired on grounds of ill-health due to depression at age 50. As a man in his fifties still battling with his illness in an area of high unemployment, it was unlikely that Peter would work again. As he was no longer working or providing materially for his family Peter saw himself as worthless and avoided most social activities because he felt so ashamed. He saw himself as a 'scrounger from the state' and worried that this was how others also perceived him. Although Peter did not hold any belief that was radically different to any other man of his generation and social class, his belief that his worth depended on working and nothing else was categorical. Peter believed with an extreme degree of conviction that work was his only measure of worth and applied this belief rigidly. Although he now devoted time to his family, house and garden, he saw this contribution to family life as of absolutely no significance to his self-worth. Attempts at encouraging Peter to consider voluntary work as a means of deriving a sense of purpose were defeated by the fact that part of his definition of worth was how much an individual earned. Far from improving his self-esteem, for Peter to consider his worth as depending on family or voluntary work represented in his eyes a loss of respect and dignity. As a result of its extremity and rigidity, the effects of his conditional belief on his self-esteem were as pernicious as those of an unconditional belief.

Other Common Conditional Beliefs

As in acute depression, conditional beliefs in persistent depression often focus on the standards the patients should maintain in their personal and social behaviour. Patients commonly apply rules about perfectionism and meeting high standards to performance of any tasks. For example, *Elizabeth* maintained that it was essential to her always to do everything to the highest possible standard and to ensure that this standard was met by 'always doing things properly'. This meant that she was continually vigilant for any shortcomings in any of her efforts and viewed any such shortcomings in a highly self-critical fashion. As with many patients, she saw such a self-critical attitude as essential to maintaining an adequate standard of performance. She endorsed a belief that 'Unless I push myself constantly, things I do will not be of an acceptable standard'. For other patients, concerns about pleasing others and gaining approval in their relationships are more important in maintaining self-esteem. For example, *Rosemary* adopted a rule that she should always please others. She believed that 'If I do not do what other people want, they will criticise or reject me'.

As well as determining a person's view of their self-worth, conditional beliefs can also describe that person's view of the world. Beliefs about fairness, such as 'if you are fair to others they will be fair to you in return' are commonly encountered in working with patients with persistent depression. For example, *Peter's* way of life had been greatly influenced by the principle that 'if you work hard you will be rewarded'. When he was made redundant, not only was his sense of worth as an individual eroded, but his sense of justice in the world was severely compromised. This destruction of the contract he had always assumed existed between him and the outside world left him believing that life was pointless in an unfair world. Other changes in working practices, such as a shift from a perceived emphasis on quality of work to an emphasis on profit, can also infringe beliefs about fairness and result in the elimination of job satisfaction. Beliefs about fairness can also influence people's expectations in relationships and importantly affect their reaction to events such as perceived let-downs or injustices.

The Rigidity of Conditional Beliefs

Beliefs that are similar in content to these may be apparent in acutely depressed patients or in the population at large. As with beliefs about work, it is the extremity and rigidity with which conditional beliefs are applied in chronic depression that makes their effect particularly disabling. The extremity of black and white thinking can be striking. For *Elizabeth*, the slightest blemish in anything she undertook could render it completely useless in her eyes. For *Rosemary*, even to consider not doing something that someone else wanted would cast her as a 'horrible person'. The particular rigidity of these beliefs can be highlighted when the patient has been exposed to conflicting demands. Rosemary frequently found herself in the position of trying to satisfy conflicting demands from different members of her family. Her rule that she should please all other people all of the time was sometimes impossible to satisfy. When having to turn down a request from members of her family because of some prior commitment, she was unable to see this as an inevitable consequence of the situation. Instead, she would blame herself for being unable to meet all the demands, and would greatly fear the anger of whomever she had been unable to please.

The rigidity with which beliefs are applied can also lead to particular difficulties in situations where more than one belief is activated simultaneously. For example, Elizabeth's belief that 'if you don't do something properly there is no point in doing it at all' would often make her anxious about the tasks that confronted her. To attempt these tasks would then activate another belief that 'if I am emotional, it shows I am not in control of my faculties'. Her inability to suspend or tone down one rule in order to satisfy the conflicting demands of another resulted in her being in a state of almost constant dissatisfaction with herself. Where conditional beliefs are applied in an absolute and rigid fashion, their detrimental effects can be as inevitable as those of unconditional or core beliefs that often form the most fundamental layer of negative cognition in persistent depression.

UNCONDITIONAL BELIEFS

The cognitive model proposes that the chronic cognitive triad (low self-esteem, helplessness and hopelessness) in persistent depression is underpinned by unconditional beliefs about the self, other people and the world. These generalised negative beliefs are tacitly held as unquestionable truths and so guide the processing of information in a distorted or prejudicial fashion (Padesky, 1990). Unconditional beliefs about the self most commonly cluster around two main themes: that of weakness and that of unacceptability. Beliefs about weakness include 'I am inadequate or weak', where the person considers that they fundamentally lack the resources to meet external or internal challenges, and 'I am vulnerable', where the person has an enduring expectation of harm either from ridicule by others or from being overwhelmed by emotions. Beliefs about unacceptability include 'I am bad', where the focus is on selfish impulses and feelings seen as morally unacceptable, 'I am horrible or unlovable', where the person believes that they can only ever be criticised or rejected by others, and 'I am no good', where the person believes that they can never meet the standards required to gain the approval of others. Other common beliefs are 'I am a failure', 'I am worthless', 'I am inferior', 'I don't count' (insignificance) and 'I am neglected or deprived'. To the patient, the experience of these unconditional beliefs being activated is of the awful truth about them being cruelly exposed, so such activation can trigger overwhelming affect. Behavioural, cognitive and emotional avoidance can be understood as strategies to prevent such activation or limit its consequences. In some patients with persistent depression, these unconditional beliefs are evident from the earliest stages of therapy. For others they become clear only after considerable effort at cutting through the 'smokescreen' of avoidance.

Prejudicial Processing

Unconditional beliefs are maintained by cognitive and behavioural processes, which have been well described in previous texts (Beck et al., 1990; Padesky, 1994; Young, 1990). At a cognitive level, such beliefs serve as prejudices, such that only experiences consistent with the negative view get noticed and remembered. When positive information that could disconfirm the belief is encountered, it is ignored, dismissed or discounted in some way. This cognitive bias in the way that information is processed reinforces the unconditional beliefs. For example, *Marion* saw herself as 'unlovable' and so always expected that other people would reject or abandon her. An incident early in therapy suggested how biases in her processing of information might have served to maintain this belief. Marion was 15 minutes late for an appointment on a cold, snowy December day. The bus had been late and she had walked a mile to the session, where she arrived flustered, shivering and soaking wet. She apologised profusely and repeatedly for being late. The therapist hung Marion's coat on the radiator to dry off, offered her some paper towels to dry her hair and face, and then offered to make her a hot drink. Marion started to cry and when asked what was upsetting her, she replied 'You are being kind to me. It doesn't seem right—I was late. I don't deserve it'. This interaction was subsequently used to illustrate how experiences inconsistent with her view of herself as unlovable could not be processed. The therapist's reaction to her being late made no sense to her. She elaborated that it would be dangerous to trust the therapist's kindness because ultimately she would be discharged from therapy and the potential for future kindness would be lost. Similar processes operated outside the therapy setting: when anyone seemed to like Marion, she believed that this was only because she complied with their wishes rather than because they liked her as a person. In contrast, she considered any negative reactions to be truly reflective of her real, unlovable self. The idea of unconditional beliefs as self-prejudices is discussed in more detail in Chapter 7.

Schema Maintenance Processes

As well as being reinforced by these cognitive biases, unconditional beliefs are further reinforced by their reciprocal relationship with conditional beliefs and the behavioural strategies associated with them. Young (1990) has described these processes as schema compensation, schema avoidance and schema maintenance. Conditional beliefs can specify compensatory strategies, whereby the individual tries to make up for the deficiency defined by their unconditional belief. For example, *Kate* believed that she was a bad or 'horrible' person. To prevent people discovering this, Kate took great pains to try to please others. She believed that 'Unless I please other people, I will be rejected' and so had great difficulty asserting her own needs in relationships. Whenever Kate did receive positive feedback, she attributed it to having done everything she could to please. She saw this simply as maintaining a façade, and thus continued to believe she was horrible in essence. If she ever perceived someone reacting negatively to her, she would become distraught as she believed that they had seen through her façade to her real character. The compensatory strategy specified by her conditional beliefs thus left her unconditional negative view of herself untouched. This strategy had a number of other effects, which only served to reinforce her view of herself as horrible. Always doing what others wanted often resulted in her becoming silently resentful, which she interpreted as further evidence of being horrible. When on occasion her bottled up resentment exploded into poorly controlled displays of anger, commonly at innocent parties, this confirmed her horribleness. Further, her acquiescence to others' wishes meant that she had landed in a succession of relationships with men who had treated her in an abusive fashion. She believed that these relationships were indicative of what someone like herself could expect and that for the abuse to keep repeating itself must mean that in some way she deserved it. Thus, far from mitigating or weakening unconditional beliefs, conditional beliefs or compensatory strategies often serve to reinforce them.

Where unconditional beliefs concern unacceptability, conditional beliefs often specify compensatory actions that aim to achieve some external goal. Thus, someone who believes that they are unlovable will try to prevent this being noticed by pleasing other people. An individual who believes that they are no good will try to succeed in everything they undertake. The person's emotional state depends on the extent to which their compensatory strategies succeed in masking the unconditional belief. Thus, when beliefs about unacceptability are most dominant, patients will generally be vulnerable to experiencing high levels of affect. In contrast, unconditional beliefs about weakness are often associated with conditional beliefs about maintaining control over emotions. *Stan's* view of himself was summed up in therapy as an unconditional belief 'I am weak'. This resulted in his endorsing a rule 'I must never allow myself to get emotional'. As described above, this led to his suppressing all feelings, negative and positive. Thus, where beliefs about weakness predominate, emotional flattening tends to result. This prevents the acute emotional arousal that the patient is most likely to interpret immediately as weakness. However, it can still lead to the beliefs about weakness being reinforced. For Stan, as his gloomy state was so unvarying, it came to seem that he was unable to control it. The resulting sense of helplessness fed into his view of himself as weak. In addition, his suppression of his wishes and desires resulted in inertia and passivity. In comparison to this, when he saw other people satisfying their personal goals or desires, he interpreted it as further evidence of his weakness.

Conditional beliefs and the ensuing compensatory strategies are thus used to prevent activation of unconditional beliefs, but may also have the effect of maintaining or reinforcing those very beliefs. In a similar fashion, avoidance may also be used directly to prevent such activation and may also serve to maintain the beliefs. Where patients have core beliefs about unacceptability, a common strategy is to prevent other people from realising this by avoiding certain types of people, relationships or interactions. To return to *Marion*, her view of herself as 'unlovable' led her to avoid social contact as much as possible in order to avoid the possibility of rejection. Where she could not avoid social contact altogether, she would try to keep any contact on as superficial a level as possible. As a result, Marion's network of social relationships was indeed impoverished: she had few friends and those relationships she had were not close. She interpreted this state of affairs as a sign that she was not loved as much as others, which reinforced her belief that she was unlovable. Avoidance can also reinforce beliefs about weakness. For example, Stan's view of himself as weak meant that he believed himself to be incapable of making decisions and unable to cope with the consequences of making the wrong one. He thus tried to avoid making any. The result of this was that others tended to make any decisions for him and he would go along with things that would patently not have been his choice. He then interpreted being subjected to these undesired situations as evidence of powerlessness, which again reinforced his view of himself as weak.

A process of schema maintenance can also occur, where the person behaves in ways that are directly consistent with the schema. Believing that they are inherently unlovable can induce some people to behave in ways that are unpleasant or uncaring. By behaving in a hostile or rejecting fashion, the person can avoid appearing to have been rejected. This can give the sense of having decided to act this way and hence of having some control over the perceived inadequacies. However, this course of action reinforces a negative self-view. The patient is likely to interpret their own negative behaviour as confirmation of their unacceptability as well as in fact alienating other people and inviting hostile responses. This was sometimes true of Kate (described above). Although she usually attempted to compensate for her view of herself as 'horrible' by pleasing others, on occasion she would instead adopt a cynical and dismissive tone towards others. This tended to occur in relatively impersonal situations where she perceived that she had little chance of eliciting a good reaction however she acted. At her doctor's surgery, for example, she had acquired a reputation for being rude and aggressive over the way she handled requests for appointments or prescriptions. Although in these situations she appeared haughty and overconfident, she saw the ensuing reluctance of the staff to help her as further evidence of just how horrible she was.

Beliefs about Others and the World

Rigid, unconditional beliefs shape not only patients' views of themselves, but also of other people and the world around. Patients with a view of themselves as weak often have an exaggerated and fixed view of the infallibility or 'normality' of others. They believe that others always deal smoothly with any real problems that they encounter and are never subject to any unexplained mood swings or irrational reactions. For example, when asked to describe how he saw other people, *Stan* replied that they were 'normal'. As well as believing that other people's feelings always made sense and were in proportion to events, Stan believed that others had no difficulty expressing themselves and getting what they wanted in life. Patients who view themselves as unacceptable often have a complementary view of others as critical and judgemental. For example, *Marion* expected other people to demean or reject her at every turn. It was described above how she tended to interpret others' kindness or sympathy as patronising or, in the case of her therapist, as a purely professional reaction. Patients who see themselves as worthless or not good enough frequently express a view of self-in-relation-to-others that is hierarchical in nature. Underlying interactions with others, there is a comparison drawn in which patients usually see themselves as less than others in some way. Within this hierarchy, some patients at times attempt to bolster their fragile self-esteem by viewing themselves as superior to some others. In such instances the patient may be overtly critical of another or seem to bask in the misfortunes that have befallen someone else.

In considering patients' view of the world or life in general, the most common theme in persistent depression is that of harshness. Patients do not expect life to treat them well, either in terms of good fortune or from the results of their own efforts. One patient summed it up as 'Life has got it in for me'. The particular slant put on this view of the world as harsh depends on its interaction with beliefs about self and others. Patients with the hierarchical view of self and others described above talk about a competitive 'dog eat dog' world. Those with high levels of anxiety view the world as particularly dangerous and unpredictable, whereas a view of the world as unfair is common in those with anger as a dominant feature. These negative views of the world can be particularly associated with the helplessness of persistently depressed patients. Patients' beliefs that the world is harsh can be self-referent in that they may believe that the world is particularly cruel to them. However, this is not always the case. Some patients are sensitive in general to any signs of suffering or injustice in the world, whether on a small scale or a global level. In some patients, poring over news reports of every tragedy or attending to every sign of misfortune that they encounter, from the weather to bad driving, reinforces this sensitivity. In others, the view that the world is too awful to be faced is fed by avoiding or minimising contact with the world as far as possible.

SOCIAL FACTORS IN PERSISTENT DEPRESSION

Maintaining Factors

From the above descriptions, it is clear that persistent depression is maintained not just by beliefs held inside the person's head. These beliefs manifest themselves behaviourally, often with detrimental consequences for the nature of the social environment in which patients find themselves. Whatever the precise nature of their beliefs, most patients with persistent depression drastically restrict the kinds of situations or experiences in which they participate. Whether their beliefs are of weakness, badness or worthlessness, patients tend to hang back from social contact and to behave in self-effacing and placatory ways when in social situations. They may have few social relationships and those they have, whether with partners, friends or acquaintances, often seem to be with people they do not particularly like. Similarly, this reluctance to express or assert themselves limits the chances of fresh social and occupational opportunities. The result is that patients are often underemployed or stuck in jobs they do not like or to which they are not suited. The consequent lack of positive feedback or reinforcement from the environment clearly serves to maintain the depression and the negative beliefs. The interaction between negative beliefs and negative life situations thus forms a vicious circle that is crucial in the current, ongoing maintenance of persistent depression.

Triggering Factors

Negative events or situations also have an important role in the initial development of persistent depression, sometimes through triggering the onset of depression. The role of events in triggering onset is evident in cases where rigid conditional beliefs are apparent. Loss of or disruption in relationships has long been recognised as a common trigger for depression, particularly in those whose self-esteem depends greatly on being liked or approved of. In comparison, patients who believe that their work determines their personal worth are more susceptible to events that disrupt their working life. Redundancy is the most obviously depressogenic type of event, but more subtle changes in working practices can also be devastating to those with rigid beliefs. In business, recent examples of changes in the working culture include change from an emphasis on mutual support to an emphasis on profit and change from an emphasis on quality of product to an emphasis on presentation. In the public services, changes in the working culture have included changes in emphasis from caring to efficiency and from clinical judgement to standardised protocols. Particularly where such changes are imposed suddenly, such as when a company that has provided employment for many years is taken over, this can lead to unaccustomed pressure and conflict, which are not well tolerated (as was the case for Peter and Graham described in this book). The resulting stress results in the person taking time off for physical or mental ailments and consequently feeling more guilty and ashamed. When low mood and loss of motivation then set in, the patient is diagnosed as depressed, the sense of weakness or worthlessness deepens and the cycle of persistent depression is underway.

Predisposing Factors

In the cognitive model, as well as contributing to the triggering and maintenance of current depression, situational factors also have a longer-term influence on vulnerability to depression. In particular, events or circumstances play a crucial role in the development of maladaptive beliefs. Important beliefs about the self and others are often formed through learning from experiences during childhood and adolescence. The impact of early loss, trauma or abuse on the development of negative beliefs has been extensively considered in cognitive therapy (e.g. Beck et al., 1990). In patients with persistent depression, overt trauma is often absent and other factors, such as neglect or being subject to rigid standards or rules across a variety of situations, may be most important in the development of beliefs.

Some patients with persistent depression report histories of harsh or abusive upbringings, as would be expected. Repeated experiences of being harshly criticised, punished, beaten or, more rarely, sexually abused, result in a view that abuse is all that can be expected. As no alternative view is apparent, the child forms a view that such treatment is deserved and so develops a view of self as being inherently unacceptable or bad. The violence does not necessarily have to be directed at the future patient. Many patients with persistent depression report an aggressive atmosphere between their parents, where either they were given or they assumed responsibility for trying to maintain a fragile peace. For example, *Marion's* mother would use Marion as a barrier to prevent her being hit by her alcoholic husband. Even when there was no imminent threat of violence, Marion was petrified of provoking any trouble. She quickly learned to be quiet and not to ask for anything, but despite this was not successful in preventing the violent outbursts. Her thinking that her own needs were unacceptable and that she was in some way to blame for not preventing the violence contributed to her developing a view of herself as unlovable.

Neglect does not always occur in such obviously violent or abusive circumstances. It can occur through parents modelling an overemphasis on the value of achievement, productivity and work over caring, kindness or family values. Through observing such role models, the future patient comes to adopt beliefs that they only have any worth as long as they achieve things. For example, *Elizabeth* described her mother as a strict woman with very high standards. She expected Elizabeth also to meet the standards that she set and restricted Elizabeth's opportunities to do things in any other fashion by continually monitoring her activities. It was not surprising that Elizabeth saw herself as worthless unless she continually met these very high standards.

Although abuse or neglect are common in the backgrounds of patients with persistent depression, it is not uncommon for negative beliefs to develop in a context that is more ambiguous and less readily identified as negative. Indeed in many cases, the strength of the person's negative view of themselves seems inconsistent with their reports of a trouble-free childhood. On closer examination, it sometimes seems to be the extreme 'normality' and lack of any observable ructions that has been pathogenic. Certain families seem to emphasise a view that life proceeds smoothly at all times and that even when things go wrong, no one gets upset. Disagreements and anger are never expressed. When children who grow up in this family 'culture' experience upset, they perceive themselves as something of an oddity and start to form the view that they are weak compared to others. This was the case for *Stan*, who described both his parents in terms of being kindly and calm, but perhaps somewhat distant. He remembered repeatedly being teased as a little boy at school, for example about his ears sticking out, and becoming very upset. At home, he found himself unable to express his upset to his family and instead pretended he was fine. Because he knew he was not fine, he felt ashamed of his reaction and started to see himself as weak. Although thoughts about the particular taunts about his ears did not now bother him, the sense of weakness for being upset by it had persisted. Such a view of self as weak may be wittingly or unwittingly reinforced by the reactions of other members of the family to the child's upset. Whether told forcefully or gently not to be upset, the implicit message is that, if you are upset, there is something wrong with you. This can then form the template or schema that is fertile ground for later pathology.

Particular circumstances at home or at school can thus have a strong influence on the formation of negative beliefs. For some patients, the uniformity in the attitudes encountered across different situations may reinforce negative beliefs or foster their being rigidly applied. For many people, being subjected to some pernicious influence in one situation, for example at home, may be balanced by a supportive influence in another sphere, for example at school. Even traumatic or repeated negative experiences frequently do not seem to lead to the global or rigid negative beliefs often seen in persistent depression. Conversely, the imposition of relatively innocuous conditions across different situations is sometimes central to understanding the development of maladaptive beliefs. For example, *Graham* described being vigorously encouraged by his parents to strive for excellence. There was nothing exceptional about this, but Graham was sent to a church school that propounded similar attitudes. Graham's social life as a child revolved around home, school and church and so he experienced limited exposure to different attitudes and encounters with people outside of and disapproved of by his milieu. In the face of the constancy of this striving for perfection, the strength of his view of himself as inadequate became understandable. Similarly, if a child sees any display of emotions being scorned both within their family and in wider social circles, their view of emotions as a sign of weakness may be particularly firm. For example, *Peter's* upbringing in a working-class family in Scotland helped to explain his belief that showing emotions was a sign of weakness. In this wider culture, control over emotions generally is an important part of being seen as strong or masculine, but displays of joy or grief are often deemed acceptable 'behind closed doors'. That Peter's family did not display emotions even in private made his view of emotions as weak particularly categorical.

THE CHRONIC COGNITIVE TRIAD

In acute depression, the concept of the negative cognitive triad is helpful in conceptualising patients' problems. Negative thinking about the self, the world and the future can usually be identified with suitable prompting. In persistent depression, the negative thinking in each domain is not necessarily linked to specific triggers or to changes in emotional state. In some patients, negative thinking may be immediately apparent, whereas in others overt negative thoughts may be evaded or denied. The model proposes that the negative thoughts central to persistent depression are enduring in nature and have become more closely interwoven with associated behavioural strategies and their social and environmental consequences. The chronic cognitive triad encompasses the domains of low self-esteem (self), helplessness (world) and hopelessness (future). The chronicity of negative thinking in each domain is a result of three factors. Firstly, negative beliefs confer enduring vulnerability to negative thinking in each domain. Secondly, avoidance and compensatory processes are used to handle the distress that would otherwise be constantly present when the beliefs were activated. Thirdly, the recurrence of negative situations and events, which are made more likely by those avoidance and compensatory strategies, confirms and entrenches the beliefs.

Low Self-esteem

Although low self-esteem is virtually ubiquitous in chronic depression, it is manifest in different ways in different patients. In many patients with persistent depression, negative thinking about the self is overt and is evident in their persistent self-criticism or self-blame. For some patients, such as *Elizabeth*, each attack on the self is experienced as depressing, so chronic low self-esteem is a painful experience. For her, engaging in any task once she was depressed entailed almost certain failure to live up to her high standards, and resulted in a barrage of self-criticism and consequent upset. Some patients take responsibility for any actual or perceived problem they encounter, and are constantly racked by guilt. In many other cases, negative thinking about the self may not always be evident, but any apparent self-esteem is fragile. For example, *Kate* kept negative thoughts from her mind and denied thinking negatively whenever possible. However, even when she seemed well, she was highly vulnerable to any event that triggered any negative self-evaluation. As the negativity was often extreme, her self-esteem was very fragile. Whenever her self-esteem crashed down, it had devastating consequences for her mood. For other patients, self-criticism has a more ritualistic quality and, although set in a background of low mood, does not itself evoke distress. *Stan* tended to keep negative thoughts from his mind by avoiding any challenging situations. However, when challenged or presented with negative possibilities, he would endorse them in a resigned fashion. His passivity and emotional suppression protected him from any acute sense of devastation.

Whether chronically low or fragile in nature, low self-esteem needs to be formulated at a number of levels. For patients with persistent depression, underlying beliefs define the fundamental experience or truth about themselves as inherently negative. These negative beliefs provide the grounds for low self-esteem that is then cemented by the effects of avoidance, compensatory strategies, overt negative thinking and life changes once depressed. For example, beliefs about weakness and inability in patients like Stan often result in self-protective strategies. Thus, Stan rarely even set himself any goals or articulated any wishes for fear of not satisfying them. This led to a blanket lack of initiative and the suppression of any distressing feelings. However, the lack of pleasure, satisfaction or achievement and the dominance of others in his life provided constant proof of his negative self-image. In this way, beliefs about weakness and emotional control are often associated with chronic low self-esteem, which is characterised by a lack of self-confidence. Negative self-evaluative beliefs about badness and unacceptability are associated with more acutely painful low self-esteem, as is experienced by patients like Kate. When her belief that she was horrible was activated, she was subject to self-critical and self-punitive thinking and intentions, leading to intense self-hatred. When these beliefs had successfully been deactivated through avoidance or compensation, her low self-esteem was less evident. The fragility of self-esteem in such cases may be seen in lability over time or in the patient's self-protective prickliness or hostility when in a less depressed state.

Most patients attribute their difficulties—whether with persistent depressive symptoms, with never getting any satisfaction, or with flare-ups of extremely painful feelings—to their make-up or character. These characterological attributions for their difficulties provide further confirmation for their negative beliefs about themselves and their lives. Thus, patients who have difficulty initiating any satisfying activity may interpret this in terms of weakness; patients who have mood swings see them as unacceptable; patients who are subject to many unfortunate events see themselves as responsible or even as cursed. Importantly, patients do not see that they have any role in making these interpretations or attributions, but experience their view as 'the way I am'. This certainty that any ongoing difficulty reflects some inherent flaw or defect means that low self-esteem is continuously confirmed, reconfirmed and then entrenched.

Helplessness

Most depressed patients see the world as an unrewarding or hostile environment affording only unpleasant outcomes that cannot be prevented. In acute depression, perceptions of helplessness can result from the biasing effect of low mood on judgements of control or from overgeneralised conclusions drawn from particular events. In persistent depression, helplessness results from a more complex interplay of beliefs and coping strategies. It can be manifest in different ways in different patients. For patients with beliefs about weakness and incapability, helplessness arises mainly through seeing positive outcomes as unattainable and manifests itself in passivity. Other patients are helpless in the face of the consistent failure of their often frantic efforts to prevent negative outcomes, such as the surges of overwhelming distress that occur when attempts to conceal presumed inadequacies break down. Either way, the result is that patients see good reasons to believe that they cannot get what they want from life.

Passivity is one of the most striking features in the presentation of many patients. It is a particularly common manifestation of helplessness in patients for whom emotional suppression is strongly evident. Such passivity is often based on the perception that no activity could have any desirable effect. Taking *Stan* as an example, his passivity and reluctance to initiate action resulted in his life being lacking in sources of reward or reinforcement. Rather than setting goals or working towards the satisfaction of any desires, he simply tended to suppress any wishes. Even when apparently desirable outcomes arose in his life—for example, when his family were pleased with anything he had done for them—he did not allow himself any pleasure in case it did not last. This reinforced his view that there was nothing he could do to feel any better. Helplessness in such cases arises from the unremitting flatness of the emotional landscape. Helpless passivity can also result from life events that shatter the person's view that their life has some value. For *Peter*, redundancy was a severe blow to his self-esteem. Moreover, it wiped out the value of any of his remaining social and leisure activities. While he was working, activities such as socialising and playing sports served to confirm that his life had value and were thus reinforcing. His redundancy undermined any reinforcement from these activities. To him, there seemed to be nothing he could do to restore the overall value to his life, which was previously conferred by working. His helpless outlook was therefore a result of the combination of his rigid belief about the value of work combined with the event of redundancy.

In other patients, helplessness focuses on inability to control negative outcomes, rather than from the impossibility of attaining any positive outcomes. For some patients, the chronicity of material and social adversity in the external environment is the key factor in triggering helplessness. For *Julie*, the initial onset of her depression was related to her divorce from her first husband, and since then she had experienced several bereavements, had entered into an unhappy second marriage and her teenage children were having serious problems. This series of major life events, some of which may have been made more likely by her depression, undoubtedly contributed to her view that there was nothing she could do to stop bad things happening. Moreover, her inability to avert these events confirmed her longstanding belief that she was responsible for bad things. For other patients, it is the uncontrollability of negative emotions that forms the focus of their helplessness. For *Kate*, lapses in her behavioural or cognitive avoidance of difficulties led to surges of overwhelming emotion. Whenever these struck, she saw them as entirely beyond her control and felt extremely helpless and frantic. Even in her better moments, she had a sense that emotional disaster could strike at any time. Her constant efforts to prevent or relieve distress through keeping painful thoughts and feelings out of her mind could not prevent these crises. She did not see the possibility that her avoidance was contributing to her problems and concluded that she was helpless to avert this overwhelming distress. In such patients, each crisis feeds back into their underlying view of themselves as unacceptable, confirming the view that they will not be able to prevent further disasters.

Hopelessness

Most patients with persistent depression believe that things cannot get better for them. They tend to see their depression stretching ahead indefinitely into the future and believe that any treatment is doomed to fail. In part, such hopelessness may be based on the person's current experience of low mood, as in acute depression. However, as with low self-esteem and helplessness, there are usually additional factors contributing to hopelessness in persistent depression. Again, patients' ongoing experiences, the influence of their avoidance and compensatory strategies on those experiences and their long-held underlying beliefs can all contribute to their hopeless perspective. The failure of previous treatments to produce the desired alleviation of the depression is usually the most obvious factor supporting the patient's hopelessness. Especially where such treatments have initially been presented as 'effective', the persistence of symptoms despite treatment results in a view that nothing will work. Patients often view such lack of response to treatment as showing that the depression has become part of their make-up. This feeds into both their low self-esteem and into their hopelessness about the chances of things ever improving.

In many cases, while these recent experiences of treatment are important contributors to hopelessness, they often serve to confirm and solidify a previous tendency to view life from a hopeless standpoint. Some patients endorse a long-held belief that always assuming the worst will protect them from disappointment. Such a pessimistic outlook is often part of an over-all strategy of emotional suppression and control. For example, *Stan* had always believed that by not allowing himself any expectation of any posi-tive outcome he could keep the potential for failure or disappointment to a minimum. He described going into most endeavours in his life, including his marriage and his job, with this attitude. Since he had become depressed, he viewed his symptoms and their lack of response to treatment in simi-lar terms and thought it best not to let anything raise his hopes. Thus, his long-term tendency to adopt a pessimistic outlook had become entrenched in his hopelessness about his depression ever improving. In such patients, pessimism can be seen as a strategy that has been adopted pre-emptively in order to avoid or control negative emotions.

For other patients, pessimism is a consequence of repeated experiences of external setbacks or recurrences of depressive experiences. Some pa-tients are desperate to avoid experiences of failure, rejection or depression that will reconfirm their negative view of themselves. However, they have learned 'the hard way' that no matter how much they try to succeed, be liked or stay in control, things will always go wrong. Patients such as *Kate*, who are highly avoidant of the possibility of failure or rejection, become extremely sensitive to any signs of the outcomes they fear. Whenever they encounter any sign of failure or rejection, it seems like another disaster and confirms to them that things in their life will never improve. Attributing any ongoing difficulties to inherent defects of character not only maintains low self-esteem, but also means that patients can see no possibility of things improving. As with low self-esteem and helplessness, the hopelessness of persistently depressed patients becomes more and more entrenched as on-going difficulties are interpreted in terms of long-held negative beliefs.

A SUMMARY OF THE COGNITIVE MODEL OF PERSISTENT DEPRESSION

The cognitive model of depression is represented in Figure 1.2. The main pathways contributing to the model of acute depression are shown as bold lines. In acute depression, the centre of the action is at the level of the nega-tive automatic thoughts that trigger or maintain negative emotions. These thoughts are specific to certain situations or times of low mood and are fuelled in the main by conditional beliefs. As the beliefs are conditional,

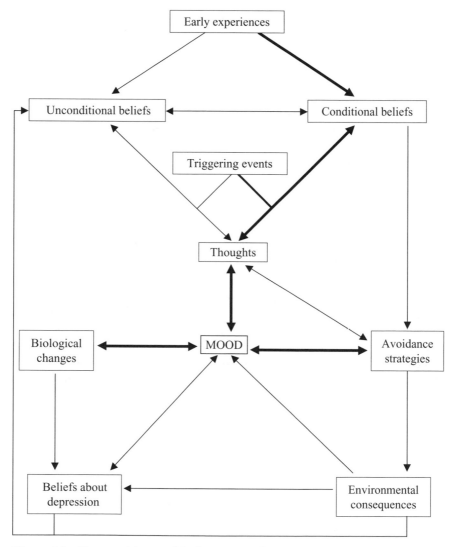

Figure 1.2   The cognitive model of persistent depression
➤   Main pathways in cognitive model of acute depression
➤   Additional main pathways in persistent depression

thinking errors and specific negative thoughts arise under certain conditions and are then sustained by the low mood they provoke. Low mood can also result in avoidance, which also feeds into the vicious cycle.

A number of additional factors contribute to the persistence of depression, as shown in the pathways indicated by fine arrows. The cognitive triad cannot be described simply in terms of automatic negative thoughts. Rather, low self-esteem, helplessness and hopelessness reflect more enduring and deeply held beliefs. These beliefs are closely interwoven with patterns of behaviour and their social consequences. In many cases, unconditional beliefs about the self, others and the world are evident. Furthermore, rigid conditional beliefs are often applied inflexibly across many different situations. The unconditional nature and rigid application of these beliefs renders the person pervasively vulnerable to low mood. However, the actual experience of low mood is mitigated by the employment of various avoidance strategies driven by these beliefs. Whereas in acute depression, avoidance tends to be gross in nature and triggered by low mood, the avoidance in persistent depression is subtle and ubiquitous. Subtle forms of behavioural, cognitive and emotional avoidance can all be identified, and can be related to the precise nature of underlying beliefs. Aggressively negative views of the self as unacceptable tend to be associated with behavioural and cognitive avoidance of situations and thoughts associated with those beliefs. Views of the self as weak and vulnerable are more likely to result in a blanket restriction of emotional experience. These attempts to limit acute emotional distress lead to dysfunction in the regulation of affect, resulting in either overwhelming, unregulated distress or in the suppression of much vital experience.

Beliefs and avoidance strategies are thus seen as important in rendering patients vulnerable to the persistence of low mood. The environmental and psychological consequences of long-term use of avoidance are then important in reinforcing and maintaining low mood. One result of avoidance is that patients restrict the range of activities in which they engage. Failure to express their own wishes or to work towards desired goals results in their becoming trapped in unfulfilling situations at best. At worst, a patient's passivity or acquiescence to undesirable situations culminates in extremely aversive outcomes, such as exploitation or abuse. Life becomes devoid of any positive rewards that could lift the person's low mood. Environmental changes arising as a result of the depression, such as medical retirement or divorce, further deprive the patient of sources of pleasure or satisfaction. The constant influx of negative information reinforces the negative beliefs. Persistent low mood states may then be reinforced by the constant activation of negative beliefs through these negative experiences, and this can lead to an intensification of avoidance strategies and further deterioration of the environmental conditions.

Whether the depression has persisted lifelong or has been triggered by a life event such as redundancy, its persistence results in the emergence of beliefs about the depression itself. When attempts to control depressive feelings and symptoms are unsuccessful, this supports the view that the depression is entirely beyond the patient's control. This belief that the depression is uncontrollable increases the sense of helplessness and exacerbates the patient's passivity. Further, the lack of response of the depression to assuredly effective treatments confirms beliefs of inadequacy and intrinsic defectiveness. The beliefs about the depression itself thus feed back into the central negative beliefs, which in turn serve to maintain the depression. As can be seen in Figure 1.2, a long-term vicious circle arises, whereby the environmental consequences of the avoidance and depression reinforce the negative beliefs which feed back into the depression.

An important factor that differentiates persistent depression from acute depression, as may seem obvious, is the timescale over which these vicious circles operate. In acute depression, the vicious circles of automatic thoughts and negative feelings are instantaneous. Changes in the extent to which activities are engaged in or avoided also occur across timescales of days or weeks and have concomitant effects on emotions within this timescale. By comparison, the vicious circles in persistent depression reflect patterns occurring across months and years. Central beliefs, dysfunctional affect regulation, behavioural passivity, and unsustaining or aversive environments may also have gradually and cumulatively fed into each other for many years.

VARIATIONS IN CLINICAL PRESENTATION

The Introduction outlined the heterogeneous nature of persistent depression, and a number of subgroups of patients with persistent depression were identified. These include:

(1) patients who have suffered from at least low-grade depressive symptoms for most of their adult life;
(2) patients who have experienced multiple, recurrent depressive episodes, with incomplete recovery from the most recent;
(3) patients whose symptoms persist following treatment of a first acute major depressive episode, often following a major life event.

Genetic, neurochemical or even changes in the structure of the brain may play a role in the persistence of symptoms in any of these groups. However, the nature of the central beliefs and the predominance of different processes of avoidance can make important contributions to understanding differences in the presentation of cases. In grouping different kinds of chronically depressed patients, two factors are particularly important: history of depression and the variability of emotional experience. In terms of the history of depression, some patients report always having had problems with depression, whereas others can identify a clear onset. In terms of the variability of depression, the emotional experience of some patients is intense and highly labile, whereas for others, emotional experience is depleted and flat.

Patients who report always having had problems with depression have often been described as having a depressive personality (group 1 above). In these patients, the model supposes that unconditional beliefs will be important. Some patients, such as *Stan*, describe continuous, usually low-grade depressive symptoms throughout their adult life. Because of the lack of variation in the patient's mood state, it is often hard to date the onset of any particular depressive episodes and the course of disorder tends to be one of gradual deterioration. In these cases, the self-concept is usually of being lacking in some essential qualities that others are perceived to possess. Stan thus perceived himself to be weak compared to others, who he saw as normal, and he saw the world as a daunting place. In common with many other patients, he saw unpleasant feelings as inevitable, and so coped with them by suppression and control. In his attempt to clamp down on all negative feelings, his positive motivation and initiative were also eliminated. Such patients' lives become socially impoverished or dominated by external demands and the wishes and desires of others. Stan's low mood resulted in part from a lack of much vital experience and in part from his surrender of external control to others. In this group of patients, it is often hard to identify specific problems. Patients often do not complain of depression itself, but focus on symptoms such as tiredness or memory problems. They have often been persuaded to seek treatment by others. Figure 1.3 illustrates some of the main features in the presentation of patients where beliefs of weakness and coping through suppression and control are predominant.

For other patients, such as *Kate*, the lifelong pattern is of intense mood swings rather than flatness of mood (group 2 above). During spells of depression, they experience intense combinations of self-hatred, anxiety and rage. With Kate, the difficulty in establishing the precise history of the depression arose from the sheer number of episodes, which lasted for periods of days, weeks or months. As with many patients, Kate described days or weeks of being well, sometimes exaggeratedly so, in between these episodes. Such chronic instability of mood is often associated with central beliefs about the self as unacceptable or bad. Kate saw herself as horrible, expected other people to be critical and rejecting, and saw the world as hostile. For such patients, their mood state depends on the success of strategies to mask these beliefs or avoid their activation. Behavioural and cognitive avoidance and compensatory strategies, such as subjugation to others or striving for achievement, are marked. The active nature of compensation and avoidance strategies tends to result in many projects and relationships initiated and abandoned, rather than a

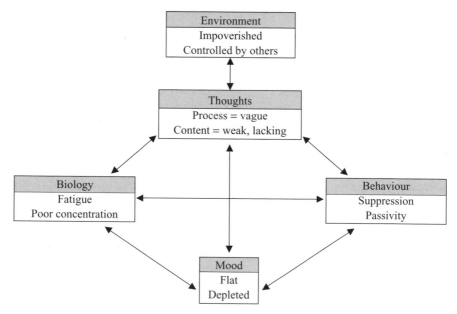

Figure 1.3   Relationships between factors in the cognitive model for patients with predominant beliefs about the importance of emotional control

blanket lack of initiative. Kate's intense low moods resulted whenever she could not avoid the latest in a long line of setbacks and problems, which confirmed her extreme negative views. Figure 1.4 illustrates relationships between key features in patients where compensation for beliefs about unacceptability and badness is central.

In many cases there is a specific onset of the persistent episode of depression after extended periods of apparently good functioning (group 3 above). The cognitive model here supposes that the conditional beliefs have previously been satisfied or unconditional beliefs successfully compensated for. Some event or change of circumstance then violates an important assumption or exposes an unconditional belief. The crucial change can be an external event, such as a major loss, redundancy or divorce, or the experience of illness or depression itself. The precipitating event or change explodes the basis for the person's self-worth because the rigidity of the belief system renders the impact of the event catastrophic. Subsequently, even when mood or symptoms are temporarily boosted by medication, there are no convincing alternative sources of self-worth to which the patient can resort.

For many of these onset cases, it appears to be the violation of beliefs about the importance of control that shatters self-esteem. Many patients with longstanding low-grade depression, such as Stan, see themselves as

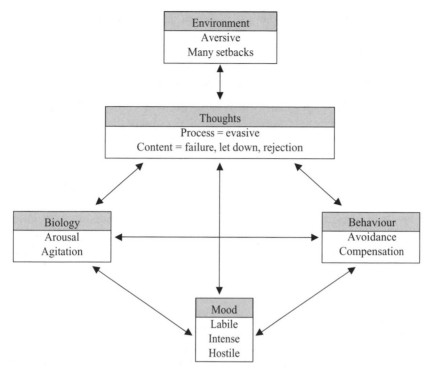

Figure 1.4   Relationships between factors in the cognitive model for patients with predominant beliefs about unacceptability and badness

striving to maintain control of their emotions. In comparison, many cases with more recent onset of depression, such as *Peter*, perceive themselves to have lost control. This may be due to an external event, most commonly the stresses in the field of work described previously. Importantly, the experience of illness, including depression itself, can also do this. Thus, in some patients, an initial experience of depression, which may result from a combination of biological or psychological factors, is so devastating to the person's self-image that recovery is not possible. For Peter, both external and internal factors were important: his redundancy was devastating and resulted in the onset of his depression. The depression itself was experienced as a total loss of control, which then compounded all his other concerns. His attempts to cope focused on controlling his unpleasant moods and emotions, for example by attempting to keep upsetting thoughts out of his mind. As these attempts rarely result in the elimination of low mood, patients like Peter tend to experience the depression as unpredictable and out of control. For other onset cases, the crucial events are those that trigger devastating negative self-evaluations, most commonly experiences of failure or rejection. Subsequent experiences that have previously been associated with self-worth, such as being liked or achieving things, may lead to lifts in mood. However, these tend to be short-lived as the patient is likely to have become highly sensitive to signs of failure or rejection, which cause mood to crash back down.

In presenting these groupings, it is not intended to imply that there are distinct and easily discernible subtypes of persistent depression. Some patients do exemplify quite clearly one of the different types presented here. In many, particular constellations of features described here predominate, but other features are mixed in. For example, it would be rare indeed to encounter a depressed patient who coped exclusively by emotional suppression with no behavioural avoidance or whose beliefs exclusively related to weakness and self-control with no sign of negative self-evaluation. Weighing the relative predominance of direct suppression of feelings versus compensation for perceived shortcomings or the relative influence of beliefs about control versus acceptability can prove helpful. Although most patients present in such a way that some particular features can be seen to predominate, some patients seem to have a cocktail of the different types of presentation described here. This can render formulation and treatment particularly complicated. Beyond this, these groupings of patients by different factors in the model do not seem readily to lead to the identification of differences in overall 'difficulty' or response to the therapy. Clinical impressions abound of people who seem deeply damaged but who respond surprisingly well, and of those who seem to be suffering relatively minor impairment but do not seem to change in the slightest degree. These are backed up by research data supporting the difficulty of predicting response from a variety of measures (see Chapter 12).

IMPACT OF THE MODEL ON THE NATURE OF COGNITIVE THERAPY

The model described has implications for each aspect of cognitive therapy as conventionally practised. The style of therapeutic relationship, the formulation, the strategies and techniques employed, and the structuring of the therapy all need to be amended in the light of this model. These changes are to be described in detail in the rest of this book. Two of the most crucial differences in the conduct of therapy relate to the attention paid to the regulation and management of affect and to the relative emphasis on automatic thoughts versus central beliefs.

In therapy with acute cases, the regulation of affect tends to take care of itself as long as the other tasks of therapy are being addressed. Focusing on problem areas and identifying the associated negative thoughts can usually be expected to provoke the appropriate negative affect. Questioning and reality testing those thoughts then usually results in modulation of excess negative affect. As we have described, these processes of activation and modulation of emotion cannot be assumed to occur naturally during therapy with chronic cases. In some instances, a combination of behavioural avoidance and emotional suppression result in a paucity of acute affect in the sessions. Although negative thoughts can be identified, the absence of affect renders attempts to question them ineffective. At other times, the breakdown of the patient's attempts to avoid painful affect results in overwhelming levels of emotion. Even when the patient does not blame the therapist or therapy for this, the high levels of affect and extremity of thinking are not conducive to re-evaluation or new learning. Thus when working with persistent depression, the therapist has to pay more deliberate attention to the regulation of affect, either by encouraging or provoking emotional experience when it is absent or by taking steps to stem its flow when it is overwhelming. This emphasis pervades all stages of the therapy. Particular effects on the style and structure of the therapy are described in Chapter 2 and effects on the implementation of standard behavioural and cognitive techniques are described in Chapters 5 and 6.

For many patients with persistent depression, automatic thoughts are few and far between, and for the rest automatic thoughts seem to reflect long-held beliefs. Therefore, working at the level of automatic thoughts presents considerable difficulty. In acute depression, working at this level is often sufficient to achieve considerable relief of symptoms and may even provide strategies to lessen the likelihood of relapse. In persistent depression, working at the level of automatic thoughts rarely accomplishes sufficient change in thinking or symptoms in itself. However, this level of work remains a vital precursor to the endeavour of modifying key underlying beliefs directly. Work on automatic thoughts is important in increasing patients' awareness that their thoughts are just thoughts, not reality (so-called meta-awareness, Moore, 1996, see Chapter 12). In addition, it introduces patients to skills in regulating affect. Any cognitive changes achieved at the level of automatic thoughts may also have effects at deeper levels of cognition. Thus, in working with persistent depression, the aim of intervening with automatic thoughts is not only to modify those thoughts themselves, but also to facilitate modification of underlying beliefs. At all stages of therapy, therapists working with chronic cases need to be constantly aware of the potential impact of core beliefs and, once therapy is underway, to be able to employ techniques for their modification. Working with automatic thoughts is the focus of Chapter 6 and, with more central beliefs, of Chapters 7 and 8.

SUMMARY POINTS

- In the cognitive model of acute depression, negative automatic thoughts, cognitive biases and dysfunctional assumptions contribute to the onset and maintenance of depression.
- In persistent depression, patients use subtle behavioural, cognitive and emotional forms of avoidance to limit negative affect.
- Avoidance can make specific negative automatic thoughts hard to identify and can obscure the link between negative automatic thoughts and negative feelings.
- When avoidance breaks down, patients can experience extreme negative thinking and intense negative emotions.
- Overt negative thinking in persistent depression is often global and repetitive, and is not always accompanied by acute affect shifts.
- Thinking style and conditional beliefs in persistent depression are often characterised by rigidity and extremity.
- Unconditional negative beliefs can be self-perpetuating through a prejudiced style of information processing.
- Common themes in the beliefs of patients with persistent depression are those of weakness/control and unacceptability/compensation.
- In addition to early trauma and abuse, less evidently malign factors, such as rigidity or lack of emotional expression by caregivers, may contribute to the formation of underlying beliefs in persistent depression.
- Patients' attempts to avoid or compensate for their underlying beliefs often have negative consequences, such as getting overwhelmed by trying to please others or gaining little pleasure, which maintain depressed mood.
- Beliefs about depression itself, such as the belief that depression is a sign of inadequacy, can feed the persistence of depression.
- The combination of negative beliefs, overt negative thinking, avoidance and their negative consequences results in enduring low self-esteem, helplessness and hopelessness, which are the cognitive hallmarks of chronic depression.
- In conducting cognitive therapy for patients with persistent depression, the prominence of avoidance and beliefs mean that processes for regulating affect and modifying beliefs are important developments from standard cognitive therapy.

Chapter 2

THE FOUNDATIONS OF THERAPY: THERAPEUTIC RELATIONSHIP, STYLE AND STRUCTURE

In this chapter, you will find descriptions of:

- The difficulties establishing a solid therapeutic relationship with persistently depressed patients
- Therapist qualities and techniques that assist in developing empathy
- The use of a questioning style in therapy with persistent depression
- How to adapt the style of therapy to regulate the intensity of affect
- Structuring the use of time within therapy sessions
- Procedures that help in transferring in-session gains to the patient's everyday life
- Different stages of therapy and the sequence in which different therapeutic tasks are addressed

Few would disagree that a sound therapeutic alliance is essential to good therapy. However, the success of cognitive therapy does not rest only on the warmth and care of the therapist. Cognitive therapy aims to help patients to address their symptoms and problems through identifying and modifying maladaptive behaviours, thoughts and beliefs. The intention is to promote changes during the time-limited course of therapy that will be of some enduring benefit once therapy has ended. The nature of the relationship is therefore shaped by the need to integrate developing a sound alliance with implementing interventions to effect cognitive change. Such interventions are more likely to be meaningful, effective and enduring if patients learn to recognise and question their own thoughts. Therefore, the style in which interventions are delivered is geared to maximise the involvement of the patient in self-discovery and change. Questioning is an important aspect of this style which facilitates collaboration between therapist and patient. The precise nature of the therapeutic relationship and the style in which therapy is conducted can be viewed as foundations of cognitive therapy. The therapeutic relationship and style of cognitive therapy distinguish it from other psychotherapies and are essential to the competent conduct of therapy.

It is important that therapy is structured to ensure that the various goals of therapy are addressed in the limited time. Cognitive therapy is structured within each session, in that different tasks are addressed at different stages of the session. It is also structured across the course of therapy, in that different goals are pursued using different strategies at different stages of therapy. The general style and structure of cognitive therapy have been described in detail in previous texts (Beck et al., 1979; Beck, J., 1995). In this chapter, we describe how aspects of the therapeutic relationship, style and structure of therapy can be adapted to address particular difficulties that emerge when applying the treatment to persistent depression. We also highlight additional aspects of therapy that can maximise the consolidation and generalisation of changes achieved.

THE THERAPEUTIC RELATIONSHIP

The practice of cognitive therapy is not possible unless the therapist is able to facilitate the establishment of a sound therapeutic relationship. Therapist characteristics of genuineness, warmth and empathy are as essential in cognitive therapy as in other psychotherapies (e.g. Rogers, 1951). Recently, McCullough (2000) has highlighted the importance for chronically depressed patients of the experience of interacting with a 'decent, caring human being' in therapy. Patients with persistent depression can present considerable obstacles to the conveying of warmth or care and to the development of empathy. For example, in her first few sessions, it was evident that *Catherine* was feeling very hopeless, did not readily accept that the cognitive model could apply to her and did not think that cognitive therapy would help. Her reluctance led the therapist to be gentle, kind and solicitous in attempting to engage her in therapy and to keep probing or confrontation to a minimum. At the end of the second session when the therapist asked how she had found the session, Catherine said irritably that she found it very upsetting and that she thought the therapist was trying to 'pin her to the ground' emotionally. Even when the therapist believes that they have displayed ample warmth and care, the patient may experience it differently.

Challenges to Developing a Therapeutic Relationship

Avoidance of emotionally charged thoughts and feelings has a central role in the cognitive model of persistent depression. Given that focusing on such thoughts and feelings is an integral part of therapy, many patients react to therapy in an aloof or even hostile fashion. Patients often begin therapy with a conviction that the therapist cannot help and that it is therefore pointless and potentially disappointing to engage with any attempt to try. They may therefore find it hard to accept any expressions of warmth or caring from the therapist. The particular nature of the patients' underlying beliefs and personal styles may also affect how they perceive warmth or care from the therapist. Highly autonomous patients or patients who see emotions as a sign of weakness may interpret the therapist's care as a sign that they have become incapable of 'standing on their own two feet'. Expressions of warmth or caring may be taken as confirmations of inadequacy and can result in a worsening of hopeless passivity or in hostility to the therapist. Even patients who view themselves as unlovable, and might be thought to crave warmth, may be deeply suspicious of the therapist's apparently positive intentions. Such patients doubt that the therapist will stay positive when they discover what the patient is really like, and may try to maintain a stance of detachment in therapy.

Patients' detachment from, or hostility towards, the therapist's care can present a challenge to the motivation of the therapist to help. Not only do many patients not readily warm to the therapist, they also do not provide any sort of stage for exhibiting technical excellence. Indeed, interventions that brilliantly illustrate the distorted nature of the patient's thinking often backfire with persistently depressed patients, who may see these as designed to make them look stupid. The satisfaction of performing manifestly successful interventions can therefore be a long time coming. The absence of sources of 'job satisfaction', such as gratitude or therapeutic success, can provoke frustration in the therapist. Patients are often vigilant for such signs in their therapist, and may interpret them in terms of hopelessness (viz. 'I always knew I could not be helped') or rejection. In addition to any sensitivity to rejection that the patient may have had before becoming depressed, they may since have had several experiences of an initially enthusiastic professional becoming frustrated and referring them on. Professional assurances designed to convince the patient of the therapist's genuineness are thus likely to prove inadequate.

Therapists' Personal Qualities

The therapist's confidence in their own motivation for trying to help the patient is therefore essential. Reliance on the patient's immediate response will undermine this, so therapists need to rely on their own resources of beneficence and patience. The latter is particularly vital, as many of the sessions are far from exciting. Maintaining motivation and concern in the face of a lack of positive response can demand considerable tenacity.

Supervision and support within the service context in which therapy is delivered (see Chapter 11) can help to build these personal resources in the therapist. Developing an affection for the foibles of this patient group can also be an asset. Therapists can be on the lookout for characteristics of these patients that touch or move them despite the frustration. For example, in filling out the question on indecision on the Beck Depression Inventory (Beck et al., 1961), one patient circled all the response options, some of them several times! Remembering this helped the therapist to maintain a certain sympathy for the internal torture of this and other patients in the face of the frustration caused by that very indecisiveness. Developing a kindly attitude to such frustrations is one of the advantages of experience that may be as important as the development of more technical aspects of competence (Persons et al., 1985).

Developing Empathy

Assuming that the therapist manages to maintain their internal sense of motivation to help, appropriately adapting the expression of warmth or care for the patient depends on the development of empathy. In acutely distressed patients, empathy is often achieved through acknowledging and reflecting the patient's feelings. However, cognitive and emotional avoidance in persistent depression confound the conveying of empathy in this way. For patients who are emotionally flat, it is often unclear what to empathise with. Simply mirroring the emotional flatness of the patient would result in the session grinding to a halt. With an emotionally turbulent patient, reflecting the patient's emotional state could result in a counterproductive escalation of feelings. In cognitive therapy, conveying empathy depends not just on the mirroring of patients' feelings, but also on conveying an understanding of how the world looks through their eyes. Empathy consists of accurately sensing how patients construe events in their lives, how they view themselves, and how this shapes how they feel. Conveying this understanding when working with chronically depressed patients helps to build their trust in the therapist and in fostering their engagement. Thus, in working with a patient who eschews any emotional display, the therapist can usefully follow up any expressions of concern for the patient by acknowledging the discomfort provoked by being in therapy. For example, over the course of her first two sessions, *Rosemary* had described an array of problems and stresses with little outward sign of distress. At the third session, she volunteered with some agitation that her cat had just died. When the therapist tried to express sympathy, Rosemary responded rather curtly, 'I'm fine'. The therapist ventured a 'guess' that perhaps Rosemary didn't really want to go into how she felt. Rosemary agreed with this with something of a sigh of relief and the therapist could then empathise with her worries about such feelings 'coming out'.

Helping patients to become more aware of and better able to identify what they are feeling can contribute to developing empathy with chronically depressed patients. Some patients try not to give the therapist any verbal or gross non-verbal cues (e.g. crying) that they feel upset. The therapist needs to be particularly sensitive to signs of any potential affect shift, including subtle changes in tone of voice, direction of gaze or body posture. Rosemary tended to describe herself as fine when discussing problem situations and would do so in a curt, clipped tone of voice followed by an attempt to return the conversation to more superficial aspects of daily living. The therapist learned to pick up on this and gently to draw her attention to it. Over time Rosemary became more able to recognise and acknowledge when all was not well with her. Other patients react catastrophically to any sign of emotional arousal, perceiving their state simply as 'awful' or 'terrible'. Helping them to discriminate between different negative emotions or different degrees of emotion can help to establish a sense that the therapist understands their feelings without criticising or rejecting them. This process of using feedback to train patients in recognising and labelling affective changes is prerequisite to more conventional expressions of empathy in many cases of chronic depression.

THERAPY STYLE AND THE REGULATION OF AFFECT

The style of therapy refers to the role the therapist takes in shaping the nature of the interaction with the patient. In any cognitive therapy, the therapist is active, collaborative and uses primarily a questioning format to facilitate guided discovery. The activity of the therapist is important in pacing the session appropriately. The therapist is also active in drawing relevant information to the patient's attention, so that neither important problems nor important assets are overlooked. Where the therapist endorses a certain viewpoint or promotes a particular activity, this is done collaboratively through helping the patient to ascertain whether that view or action would be acceptable or helpful. Collaboration and discovery on the part of the patient are facilitated by the use of questioning to help patients come to their own understanding or draw their own conclusions. There are several ways in which different facets of chronic depression impact on the style of therapy. These include passivity in behaviour and social interaction, rigidity of thinking and avoidance of emotion. The style of therapy therefore needs to be adapted in order to balance the activity levels of patient and therapist, to maximise the chance of cognitive change and to manage the levels of emotion evoked in the sessions.

The Use of Questions

The passivity of many patients with persistent depression often leaves the therapist with little option other than to be even more active than usual, at least initially. This may take the form of making active suggestions as to suitable goals for the therapy or items for the session agenda or of explaining how the cognitive model applies to particular situations discussed. There is a danger that this greater activity on the part of the therapist could reinforce patients' lack of engagement in the process and thus undermine the goal of helping patients to develop ways of helping themselves. When a patient is very passive, the use of questions helps to balance increased therapist activity with fostering involvement from the patient.

Patients often find questions about their thoughts and feelings hard to answer and often take some time to do so. However, it is essential to leave the patients to answer the questions posed. Answering the question for the patient, even when the answer seems obvious to the therapist, precludes helping the patient to make cognitive and behavioural changes. Thus the therapist may need to wait very patiently for an answer or assist the patient to be able to answer. It is impossible to convey in text or transcript the style of this kind of therapy, which is slow, sometimes painfully so, and characterised by long pauses and silences. An intervention with one patient does illustrate that waiting for an answer can sometimes pay off. Over the course of the first six sessions with Simon, a number of depressive thoughts had been identified and questioned, including being 'unable' to perform work tasks, letting down his children and being 'useless' in the face of criticism from his wife. The therapist and patient reviewed the issues covered in therapy so far and the therapist asked:

T: Do you see any themes in what we've talked about so far? ... (*long pause*) Do these discussions seem to have any common thread?
S: Errm ... er ... hmmm, I don't know ... yes, er ... thought I had something there but it's gone ... no ... sorry, it's erm ... blank ... can't concentrate ... I guess, erm ... er ... I seem to ... er ... I get an emotional perception that things are really bad before I see what's actually happening ... then even when it's clear what's going on I still follow the emotional side.

On saying this, the patient described a sense of seeing things more clearly ('The penny's dropped') accompanied by a feeling of relief. He then took an active interest in subsequent discussion of how he expected everything in his life to go wrong and saw himself as incapable of preventing this.

The therapist can help by making questions as easy to answer as possible. It often maximises the chances of getting answers if questions are concrete and specific rather than abstract and general. Thus, questions about specific sensations in the body are easier for some patients to answer than those about feelings. Similarly, questions about particular behaviours may be more productive than those about thoughts. The answers can then be followed up gradually to get information on feelings or thoughts. Another approach is to use questions that are less open-ended than usual. Patients can be provided with a choice of answers, which can take an 'either–or' format or be presented as a multiple choice question. For example, at his second session *Stan* could not generate any goals for therapy. When asked how he would like his life to be different, he spent some time pondering the question without being able to answer. Therefore, the therapist tried some more specific questions.

T: Would you prefer to be happier with your lot as it is or would you like your life to be different in some way?
S: (*pause*) The latter.
T: What would have to happen for your life to change?
S: (*long pause*)... I guess I'd have to fight my corner more.
T: Oh, you'd fight your corner more. How would that show itself?
S: I don't know.
T: Do you know who you would fight your corner with?
S: Hmm... not really.
T: Would it be most important to do that with people close to you or people in general? Your wife, your mother-in-law, your family, people at church, at the shops?
S: (*pause*) I suppose it would be most important with my wife. She's the one I spend most time with.
T: Okay, so you'd like to be a bit different with your wife. What would you do differently?
S: (*long pause*) Well, we always do what she wants. It would be nice to do what I want for a change.
T: Yes, and how would that happen?
S: I suppose I could ask.
T: What sort of things would you like to ask her to do?
S: I would like to go on some days out. You know, to places of interest just locally.
T: So would it be good for you to suggest to your wife ideas for days out together sometimes?
S: Yes, it would be good if I could carry them through.

Pacing of Interventions

In view of the rigidity of thinking in many patients with persistent depression, gains in awareness or changes in thinking processes can be difficult to achieve. Slow pacing and persistence are often required to implement any intervention. It is important that plausible strategies are not abandoned prematurely should they not immediately reap the intended rewards. Interventions may need to be repeated across several sessions for any gains made to be robust. Where the aim is for patients to practise particular techniques for helping themselves between sessions, the pace at which techniques are introduced needs to be adapted to the patient. For example, the methods of identifying and modifying automatic thoughts were grasped quickly over the course of two sessions by one patient, *Graham*, whereas with *Julie* three sessions and three homework assignments were spent just on identifying thoughts. When working at this slower pace, it can be difficult for both therapist and patient to see any progress. It is particularly important for the therapist to maintain vigilance for the smallest signs of changes in the patient's behaviours or thoughts, whether in terms of successful completion of some task or just of attempting something different. The therapist should greet any change, however small, with energy and enthusiasm. Not only does this provide vital reinforcement for the change, it can also enliven sessions that are otherwise very dull.

Regulating the Intensity of Emotions

In view of the different kinds of avoidance described in the model, the therapist has to adapt the style of therapy in order to regulate the intensity of affect within the session. In therapy with acute disorders, regulation of the intensity of emotion occurs through engaging in the different tasks of therapy. Thus, focusing on problems or painful thoughts tends to evoke distress, which can then be ameliorated by identifying coping strategies. In persistent depression, inappropriate levels of affect can interfere with many of the tasks of therapy. This interference can result from the suppression of affect or from the overwhelmingly high levels of emotion when cognitive avoidance breaks down.

In cases where emotional arousal is insufficient, it can be hard even to identify problem areas, and automatic thoughts about any problems may not be 'hot'. When these 'cold' automatic thoughts are questioned, it can lead to rationalisation or rumination, rather than real restructuring or re-evaluation (see Chapter 6). The therapist needs to gear the style of therapy to increase the chance of fostering or provoking some degree of affect. The therapist must guard against coming across as overly warm or 'touchy-feely', as this may be perceived as aversive by the patient. It often helps for the therapist to 'play dim' and adopt an inquisitive style. The therapist creates an impression that no assumptions are being made about what is going on or about what the patient is doing, thinking or feeling. This puts more onus on the patient to go into these details in order to be able to tell the therapist. It may also give the patient more of a sense of being in control. As in the example of Stan above, predominant use of questions, rather than statements or explanations, and waiting for answers can help to maintain any small emotional charge. Fostering emotions in this way rarely leads to an overt or intense emotional display. The goal is gradually to increase the emotional relevance of the discussion, which is often accompanied by small, subtle signs of arousal, such as fidgeting or speeding up of speech.

In contrast, where the patient has little control over overwhelming emotional reactions, it increases the chances that the therapy is perceived as unhelpful, inhibits the learning of new skills, and increases the likelihood of disengagement from therapy. Where the patient is emotionally labile, the therapist may have a sense of 'walking on eggshells'. At these times, it is helpful for the therapist to be a step ahead of the patient in order to guide them down a steep and uneven path. In working to contain excessive emotions, the style of therapy needs to be directive rather than probing. Where a patient is already struggling to control intense emotions, simply asking more questions may increase the emotional intensity, further reduce the patient's perceived control and result in a view that the therapist does not know what is going on either. To maintain collaboration, the therapist needs to convey to the patient that, although their feelings seem out of control, there is some control remaining in the therapeutic situation. The therapist can exhibit this greater degree of control over the emotional intensity of the session by providing some explanation for the patient's emotional state and suggesting ways of managing it.

From the beginning of therapy with patients who show emotional instability, it can be helpful to prepare or forewarn them of the likelihood that they will experience some of the discussions in therapy as intensely upsetting. While sympathising with the distress, the therapist needs actively to provide explanations of this as potentially helpful. The therapist can point out that these emotions can be experienced more safely in the therapy sessions than in the outside world, as there is less likelihood of any ramifications from the patient's reaction. In addition to predicting possible emotional reactions, the therapist can actively provide an explanation for reactions as they occur. Reminding the patient that these reactions are common signs that a fundamental negative belief has been tapped, and using the nature of the emotional eruption to suggest the nature of these beliefs, can be helpful. Actively suggesting coping strategies is also indicated at these points, even if these strategies contain elements of distraction or avoidance; it is also beneficial to help the patient to arrange social contact when they are in need of comfort.

Summarising can also be a helpful tool for modulating affect and regulating the pace of the session when working with patients with persistent depression. Providing mini-summaries during the course of each intervention is particularly useful. Where patients are highly upset, ventilation of their feelings can dominate the session. Here, a summary from the therapist can help to slow the pace, restore some balance in the interaction and contain the emotion. When patients are vague and not forthcoming, it can be helpful for the therapist to check whether they have understood correctly by summarising back what the patient has said. Providing a summary as far as possible in a patient's own words can help to reinforce what they have contributed and provides a platform for the therapist to direct subsequent questions. In rounding off discussion of any issue, there should be some attempt to summarise what has been discussed in order to consolidate any progress that has been made.

STRUCTURE WITHIN COGNITIVE THERAPY SESSIONS

Cognitive therapy sessions are structured to follow a general outline or plan. Having a plan enables the best use to be made of the limited time, typically 50 minutes to one hour. Having a structure can also assist with helping patients to adopt new perspectives or skills in two ways. The structure makes the procedures of therapy more predictable and so assists patients in learning aspects of those procedures. It also ensures that attention is given in each session to the patient's progress with self-help or homework assignments that aim to help them to apply what has been discussed in therapy.

Sessions usually begin with some brief discussion of how the patient has been since the last meeting. It is helpful for the therapist to get an idea of how things have been overall, as well as identifying any particular episodes of low mood. It is also important to enquire about any times the patient has not felt so low, as these may not be spontaneously reported. Trying to identify such times can help to counter the processing biases encountered in depression. A questionnaire, such as the Beck Depression Inventory (Beck et al., 1961), can be used to cover information about symptoms in a standardised way. This assists the therapist and patient in monitoring progress from session to session. Consistent use of such questionnaires can help the patient to become more aware of changes in their mood state that might benefit from further investigation.

Setting an Agenda

Following this brief enquiry into how the patient has been, the therapist and patient set an agenda for the session. Some aspects of this are fixed 'standing items', which are included in every session. At the beginning of the session, the agenda includes feedback from the previous session and discussion of the self-help tasks or homework that the patient attempted between times. At the end of each session, the session is summarised, feedback on the session is exchanged and a plan of further self-help tasks to be attempted before next session is agreed. Items for discussion during the main body of the session are agreed between the patient and therapist at the beginning of each session and put on the agenda. The overall structure of the session is as follows:

- Brief review of time preceding session
- Set agenda for session
- Feedback on previous session
- Review of homework
- Agreed issues for discussion
- Summary of discussion
- Setting new homework tasks
- Feedback on session

Setting the agenda gives both parties an opportunity to indicate matters they consider important to discuss. This can include problems arising in the time since the previous appointment; particular spells of low mood; reactions to forthcoming events or situations; discussion of self-help skills, such as breaking down overwhelming tasks or questioning negative thoughts; discussion of aspects of the cognitive model, such as core beliefs and their effects; and salient events from the patient's past. Once relevant issues for discussion have been identified, the therapist and patient mutually agree the priorities for that session. Because both therapist and patient are involved in putting forward ideas on what to cover and agreeing which are the priorities for that particular session, setting the agenda is important in establishing the collaboration that is essential to cognitive therapy.

In acute depression, although patients may initially be unused to structuring their time in this fashion and may be unsure of which issues it is appropriate to raise, they are, after a few sessions, usually willing and able to put forward relevant issues for discussion. Patients with persistent depression more often have difficulty doing this. Cognitive avoidance may mean that problems or low points from the week are not readily recalled. Emotional suppression may mean that there simply were no particular lows that stood out from the general gloom. A patient's low self-esteem and helplessness can entail a view that depression is a part of that individual's make-up and that nothing can be done about it. This means that patients with persistent depression are unlikely to wish to try to understand how various factors contribute to depression or to discuss techniques for addressing these factors. Not wanting to run the risk of looking foolish may also inhibit patients from raising relevant issues. Patients who have categorical beliefs about their worthlessness often assume that they have no right to express their opinions, which precludes their contributing to setting the agenda. Patients' responses to the therapist's invitation to set the agenda are thus usually passive.

In the face of this, it may be tempting for the therapist to dispense with the apparently fruitless endeavour of trying to obtain the patient's input. This would reinforce the patient's passivity and avoidant tendencies. Therefore, setting the agenda should still be done with the aim of modelling collaboration and gradually eliciting more participation from the patient. The therapist usually has no option but to take more responsibility than usual for raising appropriate issues for the agenda. Participation from the patient is more likely to be obtained by asking them what might be helpful about discussing a particular issue, or in asking them to set the priorities or suggest how much time to give to each issue. It is then important for the therapist to respond attentively to any output elicited from the patient, no matter how small and insubstantial this may be at first. Even mid-way into therapy with *Catherine*, it was proving difficult for the therapist to elicit any participation in setting an agenda. In the following extract, the therapist draws her into helping to decide what to discuss through the use of questions and empathy.

T: So overall it sounds like you have been rather flat and low this week, like before. What things would it be helpful to talk about today?

C: I don't know.

T: From what we've talked about so far, we could discuss these rather upsetting letters you've had or talk more about day to day things, like the difficulty remembering any 'lifts' you had or trying to do things at your own pace. Which would be most helpful today?

C: I don't know.

T: Is it that you know what you'd prefer but don't want to say or is it that you just don't know?

C: I just don't know.

T: What do you think makes it hard to have a preference about what we talk about?

C: When you feel so drowsy, you just don't care. Everything seems the same.

T: Well, I could decide instead what we talk about. What would be the effect of that?

C: I don't know.

T: If we just talk about what I want to talk about, would that relate to how much you care?

C: I guess I'd care less about it, but it just makes it so much easier.

T: And do you see any link between not caring and the depression?

C: It's all part of it.

T: (*sitting forward*) Right—not caring or not taking any interest is one of the main symptoms. It's number two on the list after low mood.

C: Yes, I've got a list somewhere and I think that's on it. But it's just so hard to care about anything when you don't have any energy.

T: That sounds like quite a hard struggle to take any interest when you don't have the energy.

C: It's like being asked to fight a war without any ammunition.

T: . . . Or without any petrol to put in your tank.

C: That's right.

T: So trying to take an interest or make a decision when you don't have any ammunition is really hard. But then if you don't take an interest, you stay in your shell, things get decided for you and the depression and symptoms stay the same. Coming back to this decision about what to talk about today, do you have any further thoughts?

C: Well, I don't want to talk about those letters, so we could talk about the other things like pacing myself.

T: Good—that's a decision! How do you feel about having made it?

C: Doesn't make any difference.

T: So even if you do make a decision it doesn't make any difference. Does that make it even harder to decide?

C: Whatever I decide, I'll just end up shattered.

T: That's really important—when you do make the effort to decide you end up shattered. What do you think then?

C: That nothing I do will help. It's pointless to try.

Through working to engage Catherine in setting the agenda, thoughts inherent to her low self-esteem and helplessness were made more explicit. These thoughts about having made the decision were then related to the cognitive model. Catherine took an increasing part in further discussion about how she perceived punishment as an inevitable result of any effort. Ways that she might modify this perceived punishment through tailoring her activity levels to her level of energy and through monitoring any satisfaction (see Chapter 5) were then discussed.

In contrast, if the patient raises a number of highly upsetting issues, the therapist should try to acknowledge them all and then help the patient to identify which is the priority. If the patient raises a large or longstanding problem, the therapist can model breaking this down into parts of the overall problem that can feasibly be addressed in the therapy hour. For example, if the patient wishes to put their lack of self-confidence on the agenda, different aspects of this may be appropriate according to the stage of therapy. Early in therapy the focus for discussion might appropriately be 'finding out any ways your thinking might be playing a part in situations in which you lack confidence', whereas later in therapy the topic might be 'discussing how your experiences when you were small might affect your confidence'.

Session Feedback

Allotting time for summarising the session and obtaining feedback is vital. The issues discussed are frequently complicated and concentration and memory are frequently impaired in chronic depression. If patients are to stand any chance of maintaining any potential gains from the session, the important points covered must be recapped and emphasised. As vagueness and overgenerality are characteristic of the thinking of patients with persistent depression, it is important to train or retrain patients in recalling specific points from the session initially by modelling and then prompting them to engage in such recall. It is most helpful if summary points from the session are written down (see below).

To get feedback on the session, the therapist enquires actively about both negative and positive reactions the patient may have had to aspects of the session. Many patients with chronic depression are particularly sensitive to criticism and can construe things the therapist has said as critical or rejecting. However, such patients are often loath to say anything that could be critical of others or could lead to unpleasantness. They may thus not spontaneously volunteer concerns raised by the session. It can be helpful for the therapist to predict things that might have been difficult and check them out with the patient. For example, at her fifth session, *Rosemary* had been talking about how difficult she found it trying to fulfil the many demands made upon her. When the therapist asked for feedback at the end of the session, she denied any negative reactions to the session. The therapist then expressed a concern that Rosemary might worry about how talking more freely about her difficulties had been perceived. Rosemary then 'confessed' to thinking that the therapist would think she was a 'pain' for 'whingeing on'. The therapist asked if there had been any actual sign of that sort of reaction. When Rosemary acknowledged that there had not, the therapist confirmed that it had been very welcome that Rosemary had been able to talk more freely. Both parties then agreed that Rosemary's 'mindreading' was a problem that would merit further discussion in the next session. This potentially damaging incident provided a valuable opportunity to build empathy, demonstrate the operation of cognitive biases and correct her misperceptions. Seizing on any positive reaction to aspects of therapy at the time and ensuring the maximum attention and processing of it can also be important in counteracting the cognitive biases predominant in these patients.

FACILITATING SELF-HELP AND THE CONSOLIDATION OF LEARNING

When patients have made advances in understanding problems or developing new skills during sessions, their ability to apply these advances in real life situations is key to the success of cognitive therapy. The style and structure of therapy are geared to engaging the patient during the session in the process of changing patterns of thinking and behaviour. A number of aspects of therapy assist in consolidating these changes made during sessions and maximising the generalisation of learning to the patient's life outside of therapy. Homework or self-help tasks provide the patient with an opportunity to practise the skills acquired in therapy repeatedly and independently in the life situations where the problems are most evident. Consolidation of learning in therapy with persistent depression can also be supported by writing down summaries of learning, the use of handouts, developing a personal therapy folder and listening to audiotapes of sessions.

Homework Assignments

Homework is a central mechanism of change in cognitive therapy (Burns & Spangler, 2000; Garland & Scott, 2000), and there is some evidence that the extent of engagement in homework exercises predicts outcome in cognitive therapy (Kazantzis et al., 2000). Acutely depressed patients can usually suspend any initial reluctance to attempt self-help in order to gain some benefit. In patients with chronic depression, a number of factors are particularly likely to interfere with the completion of homework assignments. Behavioural and cognitive avoidance work directly against engagement with any task involving the possibility of effort, distress or negative thoughts. Emotional suppression often results in passivity and a deficit in generating motivation to execute new tasks. Patients' beliefs that whatever they do will not improve the outcome can also render them passively helpless. Even if patients can find the motivation to attempt self-help, poor concentration and overgenerality of thinking can make even apparently simple tasks hard to execute. These factors all undermine the likelihood of the patient engaging in self-help tasks that are likely to be of some benefit. These difficulties can be addressed in a number of ways.

The clinician needs to establish assigning and reviewing homework as a routine part of the structure of each session. The most useful homework tasks often emerge from work done during the session, so planning tasks as the session progresses is more productive than allocating them at the end. Tasks agreed during the session should be summarised at the end of the session. As far as possible the task should be negotiated collaboratively between therapist and patient, not prescribed by the clinician. This is often difficult to achieve with the chronically depressed patient, and the therapist is frequently in the position of doing much of the work in devising homework tasks. This can reduce the patient's ownership of the task and can result in a reduced sense of responsibility for carrying it out. Encouraging the patient to summarise the purpose of the task can increase their sense of involvement. Potential obstacles to homework completion should be identified immediately after the assignment is agreed so that solutions can be found to any problem.

The therapist should adjust assignments according to the difficulties these patients have in attempting and completing tasks. Care should be taken not to overload the patient and it is usually advisable to agree on tasks that are smaller and more specific than in acute depression. Patients often find small behavioural tasks less daunting than written monitoring. Where the latter is necessary, specific limits should be agreed on what is to be written. For example, where an acutely depressed patient may agree to keep a diary of negative automatic thoughts, a patient with persistent depression may agree to note down one situation in the coming week where they notice a change in their mood. As treatment progresses and a degree of symptom relief is achieved then more complex tasks may be negotiated or the patient may choose to complete more than one task.

A common reason given by patients with chronic depression for not attempting homework is that they weren't sure what they had to do. Because of the lack of tolerance of the possibility of not doing things right, it is helpful to be as simple, explicit and concrete as possible about what the task actually involves. For example, presenting a patient with a thought record and instructions such as 'I would like you to record your automatic thoughts over the next week' may not only be unclear to the patient but also be completely overwhelming. Patients may be only too aware of how much their mind is plagued with negative and unpleasant thoughts and they may think they have to record every automatic thought they experience.

This would be a daunting task for anyone, let alone someone who is suffering from depression. When *Graham* was introduced to the concept of monitoring his automatic thoughts, key automatic thoughts about social activities were first identified in session. The therapist asked Graham to record these for himself in the session on a Dysfunctional Thought Record (Beck et al., 1979) to provide him with a concrete experience of the exercise. It was then agreed that before the next session Graham would try to record two examples of these putting-off thoughts, using the supporting handout as a guide. The therapist then asked Graham to summarise the assignment and the rationale for the task. This was routinely recorded on an audiotape that Graham could use at home to remind him of the assignment, the rationale for it and the steps involved in completing the thought record.

Reviewing homework should be prioritised as the first agenda item at each session. A chronically depressed patient may interpret a therapist's failure to review homework as dismissive, neglectful or as a sign that it has not been completed correctly. It will certainly reduce motivation for completion of future assignments if any efforts made are not acknowledged. Given the sensitivity of most chronically depressed patients to any signs of failure, the smallest signs of any effort to complete assignments should be reinforced enthusiastically. To counteract the patient's helplessness, some positive outcome needs to be highlighted from their efforts. Thus, whether the intended goal of the assignment is achieved or not, the objective is to reflect on what has been learned during the process of attempting the task and to elicit what new information is now available to the patient. Ideally this discussion results in a written summary of what has been learned from the assignment and how this new learning can be applied in future situations.

Written Summaries

Written summaries of sessions or of homework can be extremely helpful when working with chronic depression. Writing a summary of what has been learned in a session can help to combat the influence of memory deficits. A summary of what has been learned from homework assignments can help to reinforce and consolidate any new understanding or skills that have been gained. In the early and middle stages of therapy, the therapist will have to model this process to the patient. Later in therapy the patient will become more able to reflect and summarise for themselves on what they have learned from a session or task. A written summary drawn up in the course of a session with *Julie* is illustrated below. She had been involved in a fracas with some neighbours, in connection with her son's antisocial behaviour. Julie was taken to court and was bound over to keep the peace. One particular neighbour then began systematically trying to goad her into further fighting, which could have resulted in her imprisonment. At one particular session, Julie was angry and distressed about this and was very concerned that she would eventually rise to the bait. The session was spent devising an action plan of how to deal with the situation. Julie realised it would be helpful to involve the police, but was wary of the police and extremely sceptical that they would help 'someone like her' (i.e. with a son in a remand centre and with her own recent record). Her negative thoughts about going to the police were identified and she agreed to test them out in practice. The summary jointly constructed by Julie and her therapist at the next session outlined her thoughts before going to the police, the outcome and what she learned from the experiment.

- *Behavioural test*   To visit the local police station, explain my situation and ask for their advice.

- *My automatic thoughts/predictions regarding this course of action*   'It's pointless—they won't believe me.' 'I'm a criminal, I have a record now, the police won't want to help me.' 'The police won't do anything.'

- *What happened when you carried out the behavioural test?*   The policeman listened and told me that next time Angela bothered me I was to ring them. He promised that someone would visit me and her. Angela turned up on my doorstep drunk at two in the morning shouting and swearing, so I rang the police. It took half an hour for them to come, so she had gone. The policeman was fine with me and took the details. They must have gone round because I've seen her three times since and she hasn't said a word.

- *What have you learned from this?*   The police can be helpful and not all of them judge you negatively—even if you have a record. I was wrong in my assumptions—don't judge how things are going to work out before they have happened.

- *How can you apply what you've learned to other situations?*   When I get threats and hassle from people the most sensible thing to do is go to the police and not try to sort it out myself.

Handouts

Giving patients handouts can be a useful supplement to individually tailored homework and summary sheets. Handouts can provide general information and education on aspects of depression and the treatment, as well as providing practical instruction in developing new skills. Standard handouts for patients on cognitive therapy for depression; identifying and questioning automatic thoughts; and relapse prevention can be found in Appendix 2. Useful handouts on these and other topics relevant to depression, such as activity scheduling and graded task assignment, can be found in many other texts (e.g. Fennell, 1989).

While tailoring information given to the particular concerns of each patient is vital in therapy, patients with persistent depression often benefit from the provision of more general information. Patients typically observe that the most helpful thing about reading a handout describing various aspects of depression is that they realise that they are not alone in the problems they face. This can help to counter characterological attributions for symptoms and can have an important role in engendering a small degree of optimism early in treatment. In view of the likelihood of verbal information being forgotten or distorted, providing written information is particularly important in this patient group. Handouts should therefore be short and easy to read.

Written materials can also provide instructions to reinforce new skills introduced in sessions. Making clear what patients have to do will increase the likelihood of their practising the new skill. Using the same diary sheet and guidelines for homework as are used in the session can also increase this likelihood. For example, the clinician can model in the session how to complete a diary sheet using accompanying guidelines on identifying or questioning negative automatic thoughts. This is preferable to using one method in the session (verbal identification with no written summaries) and negotiating a different method (keeping a thought diary) as part of the homework assignment.

Personal Therapy Folders

The records from homework assignments, written summaries generated in sessions and handouts mean that therapy can generate a significant volume of paperwork. In chronic depression, it is important to minimise the extent to which patients feel daunted by or detached from these products of therapy. One method for maximising the sense of ownership and use of these materials is the development of an individualised therapy folder for each patient. At the first assessment session, the patient is given a wallet file or asked to bring one to the following session. It is explained that during the course of treatment there will be written information and diary sheets which the wallet can be used to keep together. The patient is encouraged to view this as a personalised guide to which they can refer whenever they are working on problems under their own steam. The patient is asked to bring the folder to each session so that the folder can be used to refer back to information learned in previous sessions. Of the patients described in this book, many (e.g. *Elizabeth* and *Dave*) reported finding their folder helpful, particularly during the follow-up phase of treatment when they were practising the independent use of CT skills (see Chapter 10). Others (e.g. *Jean* and *Julie*) seemed to store handouts and diary sheets in various handbags, drawers and jacket pockets. Several (e.g. *Kate* and *Marion*) did not manage to keep a wallet, rarely completed a diary sheet and rarely consulted written materials, despite their therapists' best efforts.

Taping Sessions

Given generally poor levels of recall following treatment consultations, patients with chronic depression are unlikely to recall much about a treatment session without prompting. The recording of treatment sessions on audiotape that the patient can take away to listen to is recommended to counteract the memory deficits symptomatic of depression. However, therapists and patients are often reluctant to use this method. It can be useful to both parties to approach the exercise as a behavioural experiment. Eliciting the patient's predictions about listening to the tape can be a useful starting point for socialising the patient to the cognitive model. Frequently cited thoughts include 'I hate the sound of my voice', 'It will make me feel miserable' and 'Someone else in my family might hear it'. Many are surprised to learn that their predictions are not realised and that they can gain from listening to the tape. Some patients find that the tape gives them a different 'third person' perspective, which helps them to stand back from their problems. For example, a few sessions into therapy, Joe said that when he was listening to the tape of the previous session, he observed that he often did not seem to be listening to what the therapist said. When asked what he thought was going on, he reflected that he was probably trying to sort his own thoughts out in his head. He concluded that this was probably counterproductive and resolved to keep a check on 'retreating into his thoughts' and its effects. A tape also functions as a useful reminder regarding homework assignments and what has been learned from sessions.

It is important to establish that the patient has the necessary equipment to listen to the tape and the opportunity to listen to the tape in privacy. Patients sometimes find it helpful to listen to the tape with their spouse or partner. However, this can lead to difficulties. For example, after listening to three tapes and finding them useful, *Julie* asked to stop taping the sessions. Her reason for this was that her husband insisted on listening to the tapes. In the previous session, Julie had confided how she perceived her husband as controlling her and that she wanted this to change. On hearing this, her husband had become angry and tried to insist that she terminate treatment. Julie asked if the taping could cease as she recognised she would avoid talking about important topics. However, situations like this are an exception rather than the rule. Such obstacles can be negotiated in the course of treatment by discussing how the patient might be able to listen to the tape in private or agreeing not to tape some sessions or parts of sessions.

THE COURSE OF COGNITIVE THERAPY

A course of cognitive therapy for acute depression typically consists of approximately 16 sessions. In many cases with persistent depression, significant benefit can be obtained from a course of therapy of 18 sessions (see Chapter 12 for research data). Even with these improvements, the majority of these patients are not restored to non-depressed status within this duration of therapy, and it is likely that many of these patients may benefit from longer courses (see Chapter 11). Engaging in cognitive therapy with no indication of time limits is not recommended even for the most recalcitrant of depressions, as it undermines efforts to focus therapy on specific goals and may serve only to obscure small steps taken towards their accomplishment. Where longer courses of therapy seem desirable, structure can be maintained by 'blocking' the sessions into groups of, say, ten. Goals can then be set for each block of sessions and progress reviewed at the end of each period.

Within the typical duration of therapy, the order of addressing different aspects of the therapy and a rough guide to the sessions in which these tasks occur would be:

- Assessment, including developing a problem list   1–2
- Setting and prioritising goals for therapy   1–3
- Socialisation into the cognitive model   1–4
- Behavioural re-activation   2–6
- Identification and questioning of automatic thoughts   2–10
- Identification and modification of assumptions and beliefs   8–16
- Preparation for termination and relapse prevention   14–18

The sequence of these tasks is determined by the idea that each task is easier to address if the preceding tasks have been accomplished. Thus, setting goals would be impossible without some idea of the problems to be addressed. Similarly, socialising the patient to the cognitive model depends on relating the model to the problems described by the patient. Behavioural re-activation can be important, not only for improving mood directly but also to foster re-engagement in situations where relevant negative thoughts occur. Identification and questioning of negative automatic thoughts and training the patient in skills to do this independently occupies much of the central period of therapy. Information gained on themes occurring in automatic thoughts is important in identifying underlying assumptions and beliefs. Only when the patient has acquired some ability to question their own thoughts does therapy generally attempt to modify more deeply held assumptions. Preparation for finishing therapy and coping with possible setbacks in the future involves recapping and consolidating skills learned throughout therapy and planning how to put them into practice in the future. Even when a longer course of therapy has been agreed, addressing the tasks in broadly the order outlined above is likely to be helpful.

When working with persistent depression it can be difficult to maintain this structure across the course of therapy. For example, cognitive and emotional avoidance can make it hard for the therapist initially to identify specific problem areas, as problems may be denied or alluded to only in the most vague terms. Significant problems that the patient did not spontaneously report during the assessment phase may subsequently emerge when trying to implement standard cognitive and behavioural techniques. Similarly, setting appropriate goals for therapy often depends on the patient having some recognition of how their behaviours, thoughts and feelings may be contributing to some problem. In many cases this recognition emerges over the course of therapy. The tasks of problem identification and setting goals may therefore have to be revisited over the course of therapy. This means that even when an initial problem list or set of goals has been agreed in the second or third session, it is helpful to raise the possibility that additional problems may be encountered or goals discussed as therapy proceeds. Although it is recommended that the different tasks of therapy are raised in the same order for chronic depression as for more acute presentations, there is often less of a sense of closure or completion of each task before moving on to the next one.

The Timing of Belief Modification

An important issue in working with chronic depression is when to attempt to tackle underlying assumptions or core beliefs. The model of persistent depression proposes that avoidance behaviours are likely to be driven by core beliefs and the avoidance of their activation, whereas in acute depression they may simply reflect attempts to manage acute negative affect. Similarly, the automatic thoughts in persistent depression may reflect central beliefs. These beliefs can thus be manifest or their influences felt from the earliest stages of therapy. As will be discussed in detail in Chapters 4, 5 and 6, these rigid beliefs can inhibit engagement in therapy and interfere with the implementation of standard techniques for addressing behaviours and automatic thoughts. Therapists with even the briefest of acquaintances with chronic depression will probably have encountered examples of this. Patients are often crushingly sceptical of the cognitive model or apparently refuse to shift on some negative view despite an impressive array of evidence contradicting it. Faced with these unfortunate manifestations of underlying beliefs early in therapy, it can be tempting to conclude that an attempt to modify them should precede more standard or superficial cognitive and behavioural approaches. However, early attempts at modifying underlying beliefs are perilous and can be detrimental to the course of therapy.

A number of considerations weigh against trying directly to pinpoint and modify underlying beliefs prior to intervening at a more superficial level. Firstly, although patients may already be dimly aware of their negative beliefs as they go about their lives, to focus directly on identifying and confronting these beliefs is often extremely uncomfortable. For the therapist to attempt this before having established any kind of trusting relationship often works against engaging the patient in therapy. Secondly, the beliefs are usually strongly held, so the chances of directly obtaining significant change early in therapy are slim. Thirdly, although underlying beliefs influence peripheral behaviours and thoughts in persistent depression, targeting these less fundamental thoughts and behaviours will maximise the likelihood of change in the short term. Even if only a small degree of success is achieved in making behavioural changes or questioning peripheral thoughts, these interventions can model a process of standing back from and questioning depressive experiences that is valuable in working with more central beliefs. The development of this ability to see thoughts as thoughts rather than as reality, or meta-awareness (Moore, 1996), may ultimately contribute to successful outcomes (see Chapter 12). For these reasons, some work on behaviours and automatic thoughts is still to be recommended before focusing on beliefs. The prospects for belief modification are improved once a working alliance has been established and once the patient has achieved some flexibility in more peripheral, less fundamental ideas through using more standard cognitive techniques.

Nevertheless, important beliefs stand to interfere with the tasks of engagement, behavioural activation and questioning negative thoughts in persistent depression. Therefore, it is often important to acknowledge and discuss the existence of longstanding patterns of thinking early in therapy with these patients. This can help to limit the potential for underlying beliefs to undermine the early stages of therapy. Suggestions on how to discuss the existence and possible effects of beliefs without directly confronting them are discussed in Chapter 4. Given that work on engaging in activities and questioning thoughts may initially be only partially successful, it can be useful to return to building these skills later in therapy once some flexibility in core beliefs has been obtained. Again the structure of the procession from behavioural engagement to automatic thoughts to underlying beliefs is more blurred in working with persistent depression than with acute depression. The approach described in this book attempts to balance maintaining structure and focus despite the difficulties patients may present in doing this with responding flexibly to the particular difficulties presented by chronic depression.

Maintaining a therapeutic relationship, structuring the therapy appropriately and adapting the style of therapy in the ways described in this chapter provide essential foundations for working with particular problem behaviours, thoughts and beliefs throughout the course of therapy. These aspects of therapy are particularly important in maintaining the engagement in the therapeutic process of patients who have become helpless and passive. More specific issues of establishing engagement at the beginning of therapy are discussed in Chapter 4. Through adopting the structure and style described, therapy sessions can provide a model for the experience, expression, containment and control of emotions in which the therapist at first takes the active role. Through their experience of the structure and collaborative style of cognitive therapy, the patient may gradually develop a greater sense of agency and begin to attempt for themselves techniques for managing emotions, thoughts and behaviours that have been modelled in the sessions. Later in therapy, the focus shifts to identifying the beliefs underlying passivity, avoidance and lack of emotional control. The patient is then explicitly given more responsibility for modifying these beliefs and developing their own skills for the regulation of their experience. These issues are discussed in Chapters 7 and 8.

SUMMARY POINTS

- The detachment or hostility of many patients with persistent depression can make it hard to develop a collaborative therapeutic bond.
- Patience and good humour are essential characteristics for therapists working with persistent depression.

- Developing empathy depends on helping patients to identify and discriminate their own emotional reactions.
- Questions are essential in fostering patients' involvement and often need to be simple and concrete.
- The therapist's style can be adapted to be more inquisitive when the intensity of emotional expression is low and more directive at times of intense emotion.
- Setting an agenda is particularly important in facilitating the engagement of chronically depressed patients in therapy.
- Self-help assignments often need to be simpler and more specific than those in standard cognitive therapy.
- Written summaries, tapes of sessions, handouts and therapy folders are essential to 'hammer home' any gains made during sessions.
- Particular therapeutic tasks may need to be revisited at several stages over the course of therapy, making the stages of therapy less distinct than when working with acute disorders.
- Although underlying beliefs and their effects need to be acknowledged early in therapy, attempts to modify underlying beliefs are best left until a solid relationship and some cognitive flexibility have been established.

Chapter 3

INITIAL ASSESSMENT AND FORMULATION

In this chapter, you will find suggestions on:

- Gathering information on the patient's current symptoms, problems, emotions, behaviours and cognition
- Developing a problem list
- Assessing the history of depression and factors that have contributed to it, including relevant early experiences
- Identifying attitudes to depression and its treatment that can influence the patient's response to cognitive therapy
- Integrating information about the current problems and the patient's history into a comprehensive cognitive formulation

Cognitive therapy with each individual patient is based on a formulation of how the cognitive model applies in that particular case (Butler, 1999; Persons, 1989). Arriving at a helpful formulation involves eliciting an accurate description of the problems affecting the patient, understanding the relationships between different aspects of the problems, and constructing an account of the factors involved in the development of the problems. The patient's difficulties are formulated at two levels: a formulation of how problems are currently being maintained and a longitudinal formulation regarding factors that may have made the patient vulnerable to the onset of the disorder. Understanding how the problems developed and are maintained guides the therapist in devising a treatment plan for tackling them. The formulation also helps to predict difficulties that might arise in the course of therapy and to plan how these might be addressed (Persons, 1989).

Conducting an initial assessment is an important step in developing a formulation of the case. A good initial assessment can help therapist and patient to begin to develop new ways of making sense of the difficulties. This provides an essential foundation for beginning to tackle the problems and planning subsequent interventions. Furthermore, when the therapist is able to convey that he or she understands the problems described by the patient, it can lay the foundations of a solid therapeutic alliance. Using this understanding to gear the treatment rationale to the patient's particular difficulties can help greatly in engaging them in therapy. A productive assessment session can be a first step towards reducing the patient's hopelessness regarding any current difficulties. In this chapter, we describe the main factors in the patient's current presentation and past history that need to be covered in a thorough assessment. We consider the relevance of each factor within the formulation and then suggest how these factors can be integrated into an overall cognitive formulation.

GATHERING INFORMATION

When working with chronically depressed patients, two common problems make it difficult to conduct an assessment that is comprehensive enough to support an accurate formulation. Firstly, there is frequently a large volume of information to be gathered due to the complicated nature and the often extensive history of the problems. As described previously, patients can be vague or evasive in their style and are often interpersonally sensitive. This means that the pacing of the interview often needs to be slower and more careful than with patients with more acute presentations. Thus, it usually takes the best part of two or more sessions to cover the areas recommended for assessment. This is often accomplished in tandem with presenting the cognitive rationale for treatment and collaboratively generating treatment goals (see Chapter 4). Secondly, because of the vague or evasive style of some patients, it is frequently difficult to obtain complete and accurate information about all the areas required for a comprehensive formulation. In many cases, the information from the assessment interview can be supplemented by information about the patient's difficulties and history in records of past correspondence from contacts with other professionals. For some areas of assessment, such as the history and course of past depressive episodes, this can provide reliable information. However, in general the information gathered at assessment and the formulation resulting from it has to be regarded as incomplete. As will be discussed, it is usually essential to continue to gather further information about the patient's problems and to develop more precise ideas about the factors contributing to them throughout the course of therapy.

In cognitive therapy, the assessment is structured around the areas that need to be considered in developing a cognitive formulation. Three broad areas need to be covered in the assessment:

1. The patient's symptoms and problems involved in the current vicious circle of depression.

2. The development of the problems and the patient's personal history, including social and environmental factors potentially contributing to depression.
3. The patient's view of depression as an illness, and its treatment.

These areas will be considered in detail, but every aspect considered here will not necessarily be relevant in the assessment of every patient. At the end of each section is a list of questions that may be useful in eliciting the information relevant to the assessment of that domain.

ASSESSING THE PATIENT'S CURRENT SITUATION

The patient's current symptoms and problems are assessed in order to arrive at a problem list that can form the basis for the cognitive formulation and for setting the goals of therapy. In assessing symptoms and problems, basic information is obtained about the problem, including its nature, timing and intensity. To develop the formulation, it is essential to elicit how these symptoms and problems contribute to negative thinking, particularly in the key areas of low self-esteem, helplessness and hopelessness. Therefore, the patient's thoughts about any problem are consistently sought in order to understand how the cognitive model applies to that patient's particular difficulties. The therapist should also establish how the patient's current problems impact on their life in concrete and specific terms.

Examples of each of the main areas that need to be covered are given below, and are then described in detail. The nature of the current vicious circle maintaining the depression is formulated by clarifying the relationships between these different domains.

- *Symptoms* Tiredness; tearfulness; sleep disturbance; loss of libido; agitation; indecisiveness; poor concentration; memory deficits; butterflies; tremor; restlessness; breathlessness; dizziness; pins and needles

- *Current problems* Relationships; work; home; life events (redundancy; unemployment; bereavement; divorce; jail sentence); illness (self or close friends/relations)

- *Emotions* Sadness; anger; anxiety; shame; guilt

- *Thoughts*
  —*Content:* negative automatic thoughts; perceived loss; negative view of self, world and future; helplessness; hopelessness and suicidality
  —*Process:* interpretational, memory and attentional biases; worry; rumination; intrusions; overgenerality

- *Behaviour* Inactivity; overactivity; avoidance; procrastination; crying; temper outbursts

Symptoms of Depression (including Physiological Symptoms of Anxiety)

Assessment generally begins by getting information on how the patient is currently affected by the symptoms of depression. The symptoms required for diagnosis of depression are discussed in the Introduction. Although formal diagnosis is not usually part of assessment for cognitive therapy, diagnostic interview schedules such as the SCID (Spitzer et al., 1992) can provide a useful template for covering the main symptoms of depression. It is helpful to ask the patient to focus on a specific time period, usually the week preceding the assessment interview. The therapist should establish whether this period would give an impression typical of the patient's usual depressive symptoms. As most patients with chronic depression are prescribed a therapeutic regime of pharmacotherapy, they do not generally describe the full spectrum of depressive symptoms seen in more acute depressive presentations. Most patients describe two or three persistent symptoms that cause them particular difficulty or distress.

It is helpful to try to gain an assessment of the overall severity of the patient's depressive symptoms. The patient's cognitive and emotional avoidance can render this difficult. Some patients with persistent depression are reluctant to acknowledge, think about or discuss their symptoms, and this can lead to a tendency for patients to underreport their symptoms. Scores on standard self-report measures of severity, such as the Beck Depression Inventory (Beck et al., 1961), while useful, thus need to be viewed with some caution. They should be supplemented by more detailed questioning about each symptom, how often it is experienced and to what degree, as described below. In gauging overall severity, the patient's degree of impairment in functioning in their everyday life should also be considered. In this way, both subjective and objective aspects of the severity of the symptoms can be taken into account.

Commonly reported persistent symptoms in patients with chronic depression are fatigue, sleep disturbance, poor concentration, loss of interest, tension, and agitation. A profile of the patient's troublesome biological and physiological symptoms should be ascertained. To be clinically useful, some detail of the extent to which each symptom interferes with activities of daily living is required. For example, if concentration is impaired, it is useful to know the activities that are impaired by poor concentration and the time of day when concentration is at its best/worst. *Elizabeth's* concentration difficulties meant that she could no longer do a crossword, follow the plot of a book or film or follow instructions in a recipe. She found it hard to follow conversations in groups of three or more, although she could take in individual conversations up to about 20 minutes. As a result of impaired concentration, she had stopped socialising, reading books and visiting the cinema. She saw these difficulties as a sign that she was 'stupid not to be able to do simple tasks', 'losing my mind' or that she had senile dementia.

As patients are likely to be on high doses of antidepressant medication often augmented with lithium or mood stabilisers, it is important to give consideration to the side-effects of any prescribed medication. It can be helpful to try to distinguish between the biological symptoms of depression and such side-effects. The patient's attributions about the causes and consequences of a particular symptom or side-effect should be assessed as these can have a significant impact on the persistence of low mood. For example, *Peter* confided that he had what he described as 'a terrible shake'. As he was sitting upright in the chair with his hands clenched, the therapist encouraged him to unfurl one hand and rest it on the arm of the chair. The therapist observed a fine but indeed noticeable tremor. Peter believed the cause of his tremor to be his weakness, which he was having difficulty controlling. He ruminated daily regarding the tremor, focusing much of his attention on trying to control it, and would not mix socially in case it was noticed by others, which would be humiliating. Further questioning revealed that the occurrence of the tremor—which is a common side-effect of lithium—coincided with an increase in his lithium dosage eight months previously. The identification of a biological symptom helped with beginning to identify important cognitive factors in the formulation, including interpretative biases (seeing the tremor as a terrible shake), the content of cognition ('I'm weak'), cognitive processes (rumination) and possible beliefs about the acceptability of emotions.

An important area for assessment in this domain is loss of libido. While loss of sexual interest is common for both men and women, difficulty reaching orgasm or maintaining an erection is also found. Patients rarely raise this topic for discussion but are usually willing to discuss any problems if the therapist asks the relevant questions. Many patients are unaware that sexual difficulties are a common problem in depression either as a symptom of the illness itself or as a side-effect of prescribed medication. It is best if the therapist discusses this in an open and matter of fact way, indicating that this is a common problem described by many patients who suffer with depression. As is to be expected, loss of libido can have a detrimental effect not only on an individual's self-esteem but also on that person's relationship with their spouse or partner. Both *Peter* and *Dave* described a loss of sexual interest. For Peter this served to reinforce his perceptions that he was 'weak' and 'had no control over himself'. Prior to becoming depressed Peter and his wife shared an active and enjoyable sexual relationship. While his wife was extremely understanding, Peter felt humiliated by his loss of interest and despite her reassurances he felt he was letting his wife down. In contrast, Dave's loss of sexual interest led to frequent arguments with his wife, who perceived his loss of interest as rejection. She questioned him regarding his fidelity and frequently suggested that he leave their home. Although Dave accepted his loss of sexual interest as a symptom of his depression and did not berate himself as inadequate, the conflict it caused in his relationship did exert a detrimental effect on his mood.

Finally, the issue of self-harm and suicidal intention needs to be addressed. Although hopelessness is a strong feature of persistent depression and most patients report wishing their life to end, active suicidal intent tends to be surprisingly low. A number of factors may inhibit active suicidal impulses: a strong sense of duty and responsibility towards others; generalised passivity and helplessness; or simply having lived with the depression for a long time. The extent of any suicidal plans should be ascertained. Some patients have barely considered any means for ending their lives, and others admit to keeping such means in reserve, such as a stash of tablets, a rope or a hosepipe to use in their car. Such items have often been acquired months or years before and are not necessarily associated with immediate suicidal intent. Where the patient does express such intent or has a well-prepared suicidal plan, obviously this needs to be taken extremely seriously. In this case, an emergency plan involving regular contact with the therapist or other professionals, consistent social contact in the patient's life, planning of activities until the next appointment and back-up emergency contacts is essential. If it is at all unlikely that suicidal intent cannot be managed by such a plan, inpatient admission needs to be considered.

Questions for Eliciting Patient's Perceptions re: Biological/Physiological Symptoms

- Can you describe any particularly troublesome symptoms that cause you problems on a day-to-day basis?
- How frequently is symptom x a problem?
- Are there any times of day when symptom x is more/less problematic?
- What activities does symptom x interfere with?
- What does symptom x stop you doing?
- Are there any strategies you use to deal with symptom x?
- How effective are these strategies?
- What is your understanding of the cause of symptom x? What do you put it down to?

Current Problems

In the literature on the aetiology of depression, much attention is paid
to the role environmental factors play in the onset and course of depression. Recent stressful life events and more enduring adverse circumstances
can both contribute to the adversity encountered by the patient (Brown &
Harris, 1978). Considering *situational, interpersonal* and *intrapersonal* problems can provide a useful template for the assessment of current difficulties.
Obviously, these categories overlap enormously and any single problem
may span each of these domains. Some patients report that they should
not be depressed, as they do not have any significant problems. This view
can lead them to dismiss problems that may in fact be contributing to their
depression. It can be helpful to use these domains as prompts for actively
eliciting potential problems that might otherwise be overlooked. Within
a cognitive formulation, the psychological distress of patients living in
adverse social circumstances cannot be accounted for exclusively in
environmental terms. The formulation must also include the patient's
attributions regarding any given adverse situation or environmental stres-
sor, so these should be elicited in the assessment.

Situational problems include factors clearly located in the environment,
such as unemployment, financial difficulties or problems with housing.
Serious illnesses that the patient has suffered should be considered, as
should illness in those with whom the patient has a close relationship. The
demands of caring for an elderly or sick relative can impose both psychological distress and practical burdens. Specific life events in the patient's
relationships may include bereavement and divorce. The therapist should
also enquire about any potentially positive aspects of the patient's situation, as opportunities to secure a clean break from an adverse situation
and make a fresh start are associated with remission of depression (Brown
et al., 1992). Recent work has suggested that some patients, particularly
women, take responsibility not only for life events that occur to themselves but also to their spouse, siblings and members of their extended
family (Nazroo et al., 1997). Thus it is important to consider life events that
occur not only to the patient but also to significant others in the patient's
life.

Interpersonal problems are often not acknowledged by patients, who often
report that there are no problems in their relationships. Whether or not
the patient complains of or acknowledges interpersonal difficulties, it is
essential for the therapist actively to gain an idea of the quality of the
patient's close relationships. In particular, marital discord and criticism
from the patient's spouse have been found to predict poor prognosis in
depression (Hooley & Teasdale, 1989; for a review, see Gotlib & Hammen,

1992). Some patients complain of difficulties in managing their children, and longstanding difficulties in relationships with parents are also common in persistently depressed patients (Crook et al., 1981). Social support has consistently been shown to be protective against depression (Brown & Harris, 1978; Brown et al., 1986), so an absence of supportive or confiding relationships is likely to contribute to chronicity. Social isolation or restricted range of opportunities for social contact is common, although again this may not be a spontaneous complaint. The patient's access to a circle of friends or family should therefore be considered. Many patients who report that there are no problems in their relationships describe a pattern of attempting to meet continuous demands in various relationships. The effort involved may contribute to their symptoms, so information on 'who does the running' in the patient's relationships is useful. This information can provide important insights into how the patient views any relationships, which is essential to the formulation. Fears of letting others down, ideas of responsibility for the well-being of others and fears of criticism or rejection can often be elicited even when the patient does not spontaneously raise any problems in ongoing relationships.

Intrapersonal problems may include the longer-term aspects of patients' negative perceptions of themselves, such as chronically low self-confidence or low self-esteem. Patients with chronic depression frequently locate the source of some of their difficulties within themselves and define various of their own attributes as a problem. They may describe personal shortcomings which result in difficulties they have in areas such as establishing relationships, sticking at things which go wrong or trying things they would really like to do. They may report difficulties of a psychological nature, such as never having been bright enough to do what they want in life or feeling unable to take any kind of risk, particularly in situations where they might fail. Other patients report personal problems of a more physical nature, particularly lack of attractiveness in women or lack of physical prowess in men.

It can be helpful to formulate the patient's current problems around themes of loss, as described in Beck's (1976) model of depression. External losses, such as bereavement, redundancy or divorce, often involve attendant internal losses, including loss of role, status or security. In chronic depression it is important to assess not only losses experienced by the patient through life events at the onset of the illness but also actual and perceived losses that are a direct result of depression itself. For example, *Peter* became depressed as a result of radical changes in working practices in the company where he had worked for 25 years. He had been receiving treatment for depression for seven years prior to commencing cognitive therapy. After some years of absence from work due to his depression, Peter was retired against his wishes on the grounds of ill health. He had lost his job, entailing considerable financial loss in terms of his current income and also his future pension (external losses). Moreover, he also felt he had lost his role and purpose in life, his status in the eyes of his family, friends and the wider community, and lost his 'sense of security' (internal losses). The use of this model to formulate Peter's difficulties helped both therapist and patient to identify how Peter's external problems fed into important cognitive themes pertinent to his experience of depression.

Particularly for problems that are described in situational or interpersonal terms, the formulation must include the patient's attributions for the problem. Such attributions are key to understanding the impact of the events and are essential in integrating social and environmental aspects of the patient's problems into a cognitive formulation. For example, *Julie* was divorced from the father of her four children and was now in her second marriage. She was very distressed throughout her first assessment session and described a number of problems. Her young son was currently in a remand centre for persistent petty crime. Her teenage daughter was pregnant to a married man from a family notorious for their criminal activities. In addition, for the past two years she had been experiencing difficulties with her husband, whom she described as critical and controlling. It would be easy to conclude that experiencing these life events would make anyone depressed. However, although the first two life events described had occurred in the previous two months, she had a five-year history of depression. As assessment progressed, a catalogue of further life events emerged which included her divorce and the repossession of her house. In assessing Julie's attributions regarding these events, it became clear that she not only held herself entirely responsible for their occurrence but saw it as up to her to sort them out as well. Julie viewed her problems as existing entirely in her environment and blamed herself for them, but did not recognise the part her overinflated sense of responsibility played in maintaining her depression.

In developing a formulation, it can be extremely difficult to disentangle circumstances that may have contributed to the onset of depression from social difficulties that have resulted from experiencing depression on a long-term basis. The causes and effects of depression can become entwined in various different life areas. For example, redundancy or changes in working practices are frequently implicated as possible triggers for the onset of depression. Such changes are also common consequences of suffering from persistent depression, where patients find it hard to keep up with the demands of their employment. Similarly in the social arena, social isolation or conflict in close relationships can be a trigger for or a consequence of the prolonged experience of depressive symptoms. The therapist can try to gain some indication of the relative degree to which environmental problems reflect cause or consequence of the depression by paying careful attention to the timing of events in relation to onset or worsening of symptoms. In many cases, however, it is impossible to separate out causal from consequential aspects. Environmental problems form one aspect of the vicious circle that can maintain depression, and must be incorporated not only into the therapist's formulation of the case but also into the model that is presented to the patient (as discussed in the next chapter).

Questions to Elicit Attributions about Situational/Environmental Factors

- What is it about this situation/event that you find most upsetting?
- How do you explain that this situation/event has occurred?
- Where do you lay the blame for the occurrence of this event?
- Whose responsibility is it to sort out this particular problem?
- What action can you take to deal with this event?
- If you don't sort out the problem what do you predict will happen?
- What is the worst thing you can imagine happening?
- Who generally sorts out problems in the family?
- If you were to say no to sorting out this particular problem, what do you predict the consequences would be?

Emotions

An important idea in the cognitive model of persistent depression is that patients often control or avoid the experience of emotions. The formulation therefore needs to cover not only the emotions experienced by the patient, but also their thoughts and attitudes about emotional experience. Emotions commonly described by patients with acute depression, such as sadness, guilt and anxiety, should be assessed. In chronic depression, irritability and shame are also particularly common. As shame may drive the concealment of perceived undesirable qualities, including emotions, from the gaze of others, it and other emotions may not be readily reported. As described previously (page 30), *Peter* was accompanied to his first assessment session by his wife, who requested that she join Peter and the therapist in the session. On enquiring as to her reasons for this, the therapist was politely told that she wanted to ensure that Peter was not asked about the circumstances leading to his taking sick leave from work, which would cause him undue distress. When Peter attended the second session alone, it transpired that whenever he attempted to talk about this subject he became overwhelmed with emotion and started to cry. Peter viewed this as a sign of inherent weakness about which he felt deeply ashamed. The therapist was careful to label Peter's thoughts about showing emotions, which proved central to the formulation of his illness. When Peter and the therapist developed a problem and target list, Peter identified his most pressing problem as his feelings of shame regarding the fact he had become depressed, which led to avoidance of all social situations.

Patients who have beliefs that showing emotion is shameful or unaccept- able often do not display the usual non-verbal cues that would indicate that someone was feeling distressed. In some chronically depressed patients, the anxiety often inherent in attending a first assessment can result in the patient presenting as hostile, mildly paranoid and even aggressive. In other cases, the emotional arousal can seem minimal and such patients typically describe feeling numb or having no feelings at all. It is tempting for the clinician to assume that the patient is experiencing little emotional arousal and vigorously pursue the elicitation of some degree of affect. To the patient struggling to retain control over their feelings, this may seem controlling or even persecutory. It is preferable to use current difficulties to gain some estimation of the degree of the patient's cognitive and emotional avoidance. The best way to facilitate this is to engage the patient in discus- sion of a recent upsetting event. For the patient who is reluctant to discuss feelings, it is sometimes helpful to begin by discussing positive emotions such as happiness, excitement or pleasure in the context of a recent event. It is important to allow the patient to exert some control over the topics that

---

Questions for Eliciting Information about Affect

- How did you feel when *x* occurred?
- What is the most common feeling you experience at present?
- Do you ever feel sad/angry/anxious/guilty/ashamed?
- Can you think of a recent situation where you have felt sad/anxious/ angry/guilty/ashamed?
- How easy/difficult do you find it to talk about your feelings?
- How easy/difficult do you find it to show your feelings?
- If you showed people how you really feel, what is the worst thing you can imagine happening?
- When you show you feel sad/angry how do other people react?
- How do you think other people see you when you show your feelings?

are discussed and the pace and depth to which these discussions progress. The patient's ability to tolerate, label and describe a range of emotions and engage with these emotions at an experiential level can then be gauged. It is useful to encourage the patient to compare how they feel now with prior to becoming depressed to assess differences in their ability to experience and describe emotional states between these two points in time. This will provide information as to whether the absence of affect is a symptom of the depression itself or more characteristic of a coping strategy for dealing with affect in general.

Thoughts: Content and Process

As has been described, in assessing the patient's affect, symptoms and current problems, important cognitions about each domain are noted or elicited. The meanings or attributions that patients attach to life events and difficulties and their perceptions of symptoms constitute important aspects of the *content* of cognition in persistent depression. The therapist thus uses assessment of these domains to begin to build a picture of the patient's potential for negative thinking about the self, the world and the future. As described in Chapter 1, the concept of a chronic cognitive triad, including low self-esteem, helplessness and hopelessness, can be useful. The therapist can probe further for thoughts relating to each aspect of the triad. In relation to self, self-criticism ('I am stupid'; 'I shouldn't have made such a silly mistake') and self-blame ('It's my fault'; 'It is up to me to sort the problem out') are common. In developing a formulation of chronic depression, it is particularly important to assess helplessness and hopelessness. Helplessness is assessed through the extent to which the individual believes that there is nothing that they can do to change the circumstances or that the world is full of negative outcomes that cannot be averted ('Things always go against me'). Assessing hopelessness involves gauging the degree of belief that the current difficulties will not improve in the future ('My life will never get any better').

For example, when *Elizabeth* described her current difficulties during assessment, it was immediately apparent that she was highly self-critical. When discussing her symptoms of tiredness and inactivity, she explained them in terms of seeing herself as 'lazy' and 'not trying hard enough'. Her exacting standards led her continually to focus on her perceived deficits, totally ignoring or discounting any assets highlighted by the therapist. In describing a recent endeavour to complete a complex piece of embroidery, Elizabeth's assessment was 'I was careless', 'I made a mess of it' and 'The workmanship is shoddy—it's just not up to scratch'. Elizabeth's self-criticism, which was associated with irritation and low mood, would persist for perhaps two to three hours following any perceived setback.

When particular negative thoughts are identified, it can be helpful to assess whether this is a common perception held by the patient across a range of situations, or specific to a given situation. It is not generally possible to identify with any precision or certainty the underlying beliefs held by chronically depressed patients at initial assessment; however, it can be helpful to begin to identify any particularly strong themes in the patient's perception of issues and problems raised. As discussed in Chapter 1, a number of common themes typify chronic depression. With regard to self, these include themes clustering around ideas of unloveability and badness; incompetence and failure; and inadequacy, weakness and vulnerability. With regard to beliefs concerning the world, common themes include unfairness, harshness and uncontrollability. Themes concerning other people include untrustworthiness, unreliability, superiority, criticism and hostility. In terms of strategies patients use to bolster self-worth, the themes of attaining respect and approval, performing one's duty and achieving perfection or control are central.

As well as assessing the content of cognition, various aspects of the process of cognition can be important in the formulation of chronic depression. The thinking errors identified in Beck's (1976) cognitive model of emotional disorders can be seen as biases in cognitive processing and these should be noted during assessment. It is also important to consider biases in memory and to assess the impact these may exert over the patient's everyday functioning. The relative ease with which some patients can recall negative compared to positive incidents can play a big part in the rumination over past setbacks and failures that can fill a large proportion of their day.

In addition to these cognitive biases, there is often a more general impairment of cognitive functioning in depression (Williams et al., 1997). Difficulties in accessing specific memories seem especially pronounced in some chronically depressed patients. Vagueness and overgenerality in cognitive processing can make it very difficult to obtain specific information about affect, symptoms, problems and cognitive content. The therapist needs to gauge the extent of such difficulties and needs to give the patient time to answer questions. *Julie* described a particular difficulty of not being able to complete her sentences and would often take up to thirty seconds to answer a question posed by the therapist. She took this as evidence of her inherent stupidity and viewed it as an indication of the depths to which she had plummeted. At the end of assessment, Julie indicated to the therapist that it had been useful to discover that this phenomenon could be

---

Questions to Assess Negative Views of Self and World

- How would you describe yourself as a person?
- How would you compare yourself to other people?
- How do you think other people see you?
- What aspects of yourself do you like? What do you see as your strengths?
- What aspects of yourself do you dislike? What do you see as your shortcomings?
- What does that experience/event/occurrence say about you as a person?
- What type of place would you describe the world as?
- How does this experience influence your view of the world?
- How do you deal with anger or arguments?
- What is it about anger or arguments that you like/don't like?
- How do you deal with someone paying you a compliment or giving you praise?
- What is it about someone paying you a compliment or giving you praise that you like/don't like?
- How do you deal with someone showing you affection or being kind to you?
- What is it about people showing you affection or being kind that you like/don't like?
- How do you deal with criticism?
- What is it about criticism that you find difficult to handle?

---

explained as a common symptom of depression. She also appreciated that the therapist did not complete sentences on her behalf but gave her time to answer questions for herself.

Rumination is another important factor to assess, as it is likely to be particularly pertinent to chronic presentations (e.g. Nolen Hoeksema, 1991). It is seen, for example, when the patient repeatedly focuses on the fact that they are depressed and on their depressive symptoms, or when they ponder extensively the possible causes. The therapist should ask about the extent to which the patient engages in this type of rumination in their everyday life. Any tendency of the patient to shift the focus of the session back to questions of why they are depressed and how long it will last should also be noted.

This apparently excessive focus on the symptoms and persistence of depression can be contrasted with the cognitive avoidance exhibited by other patients. Such avoidance can be manifested in patients' explicit refusal to discuss some upsetting issues. More commonly, the subject under discussion may be changed with varying degrees of subtlety. A further sign of possible cognitive avoidance is where a patient's responses seem at odds with the subject under discussion, as when someone greets discussion of the ending of a close relationship by reciting the benefits of being alone. Where the therapist suspects cognitive avoidance is underlying the patient's responses, it can be informative to introduce gently into the conversation content that is likely to be avoided and note the patient's response to its introduction. Persistent probing by the therapist of seemingly avoided issues during the assessment is not recommended as it will be experienced as threatening by the patient.

Formulating cognitive processes as well as content was particularly important in the case of *Peter*. He was highly self-critical of the way he had handled situations at work prior to the onset of his depression and he blamed himself for his current illness and for not being able to control his depression. Typically, Peter's bouts of depression would start with intrusive memories of events that occurred the day before he commenced sick leave from work. He would think 'I should have seen it coming' and 'It's all my fault' (self-blame). This was associated with high levels of anxiety, triggering thoughts such as 'I'm a wreck' and 'This is so pathetic'. In turn, this gave rise to a profound and persistent dysphoric mood state that could last several days in which Peter described his mind as 'racing out

---

Questions to Elicit Information about Cognitive Processes

- What differences do you notice in your thinking patterns when you are having a bad day in comparison to when you are having one of your better days?
- Do you ever ruminate/become preoccupied/seem to get things stuck in your mind and you can't get rid of them? What sort of things trigger this?
- What type of things do you become preoccupied with? Can you give me an example?
- When something gets stuck in your mind what do you do to try to get rid of it?
- What helps to stop you ruminating/get the stuck thing out of your mind?
- Are there any strategies you use to try to avoid ruminating/becoming preoccupied?

of control'. This would typically involve his mind being bombarded with other upsetting events that had occurred in his life both from recent years (i.e. the death of his mother) and his earlier life. This further reinforced his perception that he was 'losing control' and 'going mad' and resulted in further self-criticism ('I should be able to control this'). Understandably Peter tried to institute strategies to 'control his mind', which included distraction and cognitive avoidance. Understanding what Peter experienced once this cognitive process was instituted made sense of the reluctance of both Peter and his wife to initiate a conversation regarding the onset of his illness.

Behaviour

The formulation requires gathering information concerning behavioural deficits and excesses that have arisen since the onset of depression. In terms of overall levels of activity, chronic depression can be associated with inactivity, as is common in acute depression, and many patients assert that they do nothing. However, many patients with persistent depression can seem to be overactive. The therapist thus tries to get some account of the patient's activity levels during the assessment. If the relevant information has not emerged in the course of discussing other problems, the therapist can ask the patient to describe a typical day, perhaps starting with the day before the assessment. This information generally needs to be supplemented by asking the patient to complete an activity schedule with mastery and pleasure ratings as a homework assignment after the first or second assessment session. It is important that a thorough explanation of the task and its purpose is given during the session. The patient is asked how their current activity levels compare to activity levels prior to the onset of illness.

It is not unusual for patients to be reasonably active, with some structure and focus to their day, even when they assert that they have done nothing. When patients deny that they have been doing anything, mastery and pleasure ratings can help to make sense of the discrepancy between levels of specific activities and patients' protestations that they have done little. Mastery and pleasure ratings are usually low, reflecting the appraisal of the task at hand. For example, *Peter* was reasonably active on a daily basis helping his wife around the house. This activity was discounted as he saw housework as 'women's work' presenting no intellectual or physical challenge. Far from registering this activity as constructive, Peter found it humiliating that he had been reduced to such a level.

Some patients with a chronic presentation deliberately fill every minute of the day with a task or a social engagement. For *Jean*, this was a typical pattern. She would fill her day with household chores or have friends to her house or visit them at home. She also worked part time two nights per week in a local shop. She actively avoided time alone, particularly if it involved sitting down. Jean was able to make her own very accurate assessment of the purpose of this strategy—it stopped her 'dwelling on her problems'. As long as Jean was able to use excessive activity to distract herself from her low mood and attendant negative thoughts, her depression remained low grade and relatively stable. In such cases, it is important to ask what happens if the patient is prevented from engaging in activity. Jean reported that on an occasion when she sprained her ankle and had to rest, her mood had plummeted.

Even when patients appear to be active, it is important to ascertain what activities they have stopped engaging in since becoming depressed. As in acute depression, patients may have stopped engaging in previously pleasurable activities simply because they do not believe these activities will give any satisfaction. However, more deliberate procrastination and avoidance are extremely common. The patient may have been postponing specific tasks (e.g. filling in a form) or more general classes of activity (e.g. social situations). Discussing procrastination can be a rich source of negative thoughts, both at the time the activity is postponed ('I can't be bothered', 'I'll only mess it up', 'I'll wait until I feel more like doing it') and on later reflection ('It's pathetic', 'I can't even do the simplest thing', 'I'm useless'). Asking the patient about their reasons for putting things off can reveal important negative attitudes, for example not being able to bear doing something to a lower standard or not wishing to run the risk of failure or disapproval. When they became depressed, *Elizabeth* and *Peter* both stopped mixing socially, but their reasons for doing so were very different. For Peter, it was fear of negative evaluation from others and what people would think about the fact he had become depressed. In comparison, Elizabeth experienced concentration deficits as a result of her depression, which meant that she did not enjoy mixing in groups because she found it extremely difficult to keep track of a conversation.

It is vital for the clinician to enquire into more positive aspects of behaviour as well. Identification of any activities from which the patient still obtains some sense of satisfaction can contribute to behavioural strategies early in therapy. Coping strategies and problem-solving tactics that the patient is using to deal with ongoing stressors should be identified and their effectiveness assessed. As well as constructive coping strategies, the use of food, alcohol, tobacco and recreational drugs to cope with low mood should be assessed.

Questions for Assessing Patients' Behaviour

- In what ways has your behaviour changed since you became depressed?
- Are there activities you have stopped doing since you became depressed/anxious?
- What are your reasons for not doing *x*?
- What enjoyable activities do you do at the moment?
- What activities did you enjoy before becoming depressed?
- Are there any activities you actively avoid since becoming depressed?
- Are there any activities you have been putting off?
- If you were to try to do *x* now, what do you predict would happen?
- What is the worst thing you could imagine happening?
- Are there any times of day when activities/tasks are harder/easier?
- Are there activities/behaviours you do more since becoming depressed/anxious?

The Problem List

Once the different domains related to the patient's current problems have been assessed, it is helpful to sum up the problems in a problem list. The problem list can be written during the first assessment, as homework for the patient or therapist between the first and second session, or at the start of the second session as a summary of the first meeting. As well as stating the problem as reported by the patient, it can be helpful if each problem statement includes the main domains (biology, situations, thoughts, etc.) affected. Problem statements should be defined in order to help to identify any signs of change. In particular, describing the impact of the problem on functioning and behaviour leads to problem statements that are more open to the measurement of change. For example, *Elizabeth's* problem list was as follows:

- Periods of low mood three to six times per week lasting 2–4 hours, which lead me either to take to my bed or to start brooding over things.
- Poor concentration on a daily basis which interferes with my ability to mix socially.
- Excessive tiredness which makes me put off activities because everything is too much effort.
- A tendency to like to 'do things properly' and difficulty achieving this at present, leading to avoidance of certain activities (e.g. embroidery).

- Worry about what other people think of me, which means I have difficulty saying no to others and always put other people first.
- A difficult relationship with my mother, who is very critical of me and always gets her own way, leaving me feeling guilty and depressed.

For some patients, the problem list established at the outset of therapy is not comprehensive. Some patients may initially deny problems of which they are aware, such as marital conflict. Some patients do not see that some aspects of their lives could be problematic (e.g. helping everybody all the time) and may not be aware of intrapersonal problems (e.g. taking responsibility for things). For example, it was described above that *Julie* perceived her problems entirely in terms of the life events that occurred frequently in her life. She was initially unable to see the role of her own tendency to take excessive responsibility in contributing to her low mood. In these circumstances, problem areas can be added to the list as they are identified later in therapy. It can be helpful to mention at assessment that it is not uncommon for further problems to be identified as therapy progresses, as this can avert the interpretation that therapy is causing an increase rather than a decrease in the number of problems. For Julie, the issue of responsibility was not added to her problem list until Session 5, after a series of further life events provided the therapist with the opportunity to formulate links between a variety of life events and her low mood. Julie responded well to this and productive work ensued on trying to modify this intrapersonal problem area.

ASSESSING THE DEVELOPMENT OF THE DISORDER AND CONTRIBUTORY FACTORS

In formulating the development and onset of depression and factors contributing to it, three areas should be considered:

1. History of the disorder
2. Social and environmental factors in childhood and adolescence
3. Personal and family beliefs and rules.

Again, some information about these areas can be gathered at initial assessment, but will usually need to be supplemented as therapy progresses.

History of the Disorder

The aim here is to try to develop a picture of the course of the disorder across the patient's lifetime. The therapist establishes when the patient first experienced an episode of depression and then gets an indication of the severity and duration of subsequent episodes. The clinician gathers details of the onset, severity and duration of each episode and assesses the extent of the recovery the patient has made in between episodes of depression. Where a patient has experienced numerous episodes of varying severity, it can be helpful to establish some markers of significant episodes, such as seeking help, taking medication or taking time off work. The extent of recovery following each episode is gauged from the patient's subjective reports of their symptoms and functioning and indicators such as coming off medication or resuming activities and responsibilities. As well as providing information on the details of the patient's history, the nature of responses can also shed further light on their current processing of emotional material. Some patients become anxious or irritable in response to questions about their past experiences of depression. Others respond in vague or general terms, and find it difficult to give the details the therapist is requesting. It is usually inadvisable to push the patient for precise details, and any areas of confusion can be returned to in future sessions if necessary.

In chronic depression, two extremes are defined with some patients having never experienced significant depression prior to the current episode and others who have experienced countless previous episodes. Some patients' claims never to have experienced a moment's depression before can seem almost unbelievable, but perhaps help to explain how depression for them is such a catastrophic and bewildering experience. For others, a history of many episodes is consistent with research data (Thornicroft & Sartorius, 1993) that each recurrence tends to be of greater severity and duration than the previous episode. This is exactly what *Marion* described at assessment. She recounted a 25-year history of depression and was very clear that, although she made a full recovery from the first two episodes, following her third episode she never made a complete recovery. Indeed, she had been taking prescribed medication for the past 16 years and at assessment reported a number of persistent symptoms. Specific episodes of depression can be superimposed over different levels of recovery between episodes. Some patients report being symptom free, off medication and returning to their normal functioning following previous episodes. Others experience only a partial remission of symptoms following an episode and yet others report never having been free of depressive symptoms. For patients with likely dysthymic disorder in between episodes, it is helpful to try to establish what constitutes their best level of functioning and for which periods this has been achieved.

Obtaining details of each episode of depression also enables patient and clinician to identify triggers or common themes that may be associated with the onset of a depressive episode. For example, through discussion with *Julie* and *Jean* it became apparent that each of their episodes of depression was associated with the loss of an important relationship in their lives. In contrast, each of *Dave's* episodes was associated with a perception of his failing to exert adequate control over a given set of circumstances. On each occasion he attributed this to his sense of not being good enough to meet the demands of the job at hand.

It is also useful to try to gain information regarding recovery from the patient's different episodes of depression. This can be related to the different types of treatment the patient has received over the course of their illness. Relevant treatments include not only prescribed medication but also hospital admissions (including whether the patient has ever been detained involuntarily), electroconvulsive therapy (ECT), psychological therapies and any alternative therapies the patient has utilised. It is useful to try to gain a sense of how helpful the patient has found any treatments they have received and how acceptable these are as interventions. For example, Marion had on one occasion been admitted to hospital on a section of the Mental Health Act and had during this admission received ECT. Although this had helped to alleviate her moribund state, it reinforced her perception that she had little control over her illness and its treatment. She had also talked to a lot of people about her depression over the years and nothing had ever made any lasting difference, so with regard to cognitive therapy Marion was sceptical.

Questions for Assessing the Patient's History of Depression

- How old were you when you first experienced depressive symptoms?
- What was going on in your life around that time?
- How did the illness affect you at the time?
- What treatment did you seek at the time?
- Did you take prescribed medication?
- Did you talk to a professional about your problems?
- Were you admitted to hospital?
- How long did that particular episode last?
- Did you make a full recovery (i.e. symptom and medication free) from the episode?
- How long did you remain well (symptom and medication free) before the next episode occurred?

Social and Environmental Factors in Childhood and Adolescence

The patient's environment, experiences and relationships during childhood and adolescence and their perceptions regarding these are often crucial to understanding chronic depression. This part of the assessment focuses on getting information about traumatic experiences and adverse social circumstances in childhood and also on gaining a broader picture of childhood and adolescence from the patient's perspective. In assessing these areas to develop a formulation, it is worth remembering that some of the information reported may be subject to the negative memory biases discussed earlier. With patients who report unhappy memories of childhood in the absence of overt trauma or deprivation, it is important to consider whether they have always viewed their childhood in such negative terms or whether this has occurred since becoming depressed. Areas to be covered in this aspect of the assessment include: where the patient was raised; parents' occupation; relationships with parents and other carers; how many siblings the patient has; the ages and position of each sibling in the family; any childhood illness and how this was dealt with in the family; illness of significant others in the patient's life; experiences of bereavement in childhood; where the patient was educated; hobbies and extracurricular activities; truanting; friendships during childhood and adolescence; any unwanted sexual experiences; intimate and romantic relationships; unwanted pregnancies; and employment.

Of obvious significance are experiences of abuse, whether sexual, physical or emotional, and neglect from parents, as well as significant losses or illnesses. The psychological impact of any kind of abuse will be influenced by its frequency, severity and duration and also by the degree to which the child experienced any rescue factors that offered protection. Any information on these aspects of any abuse that the patient suffered as a child will help the therapist in building a formulation. However, it is usually neither necessary nor desirable to go into extensive details of abuse at the assessment stage. Some patients are reluctant to discuss these issues at all, and this should be respected. For example, *Catherine* clearly became upset and anxious at the prospect of discussing anything to do with her childhood, which she was very reluctant to do. The way in which she was adamant that there were things that she did not want to talk about suggested to the therapist the possibility of some sort of abuse. This fitted with information available from her medical notes that commented on the unhappy and violent relationship between her parents. Only much later in therapy did she confirm that she had suffered some physical abuse herself, but that her frequently bearing witness to violence between her parents had affected her more deeply. Some patients are reluctant to present their parents or carers in a negative light, and in such cases it can be important actively to inquire about evidence of neglect or criticism. When this is actively raised, many patients describe being excessively criticised or punished for the slightest misdemeanours. Their reluctance to discuss such negative experiences can often make sense, as such patients may well also have been punished for complaining. Experiences of relationships with siblings and peers should also be explicitly considered, as relevant experiences may not be spontaneously reported.

As well as gathering information regarding negative experiences, information regarding positive or rescue factors can also help to guide the formulation. Particular events or specific individuals can act as buffers against noxious aspects of the patient's childhood environment. *Elizabeth*, whose childhood environment was very strict, provided an example of this. From an early age, she was forbidden to play outside with other children. However, once a month she visited her paternal grandmother who believed it was unfair that Elizabeth was not allowed to play with others. Therefore, unbeknown to her mother, her grandmother actively encouraged her to make friends with the neighbour's children. Elizabeth had many happy memories of these playtimes and reported how the kindness of her grandmother was in large contrast to the attitude of her mother whom she described as 'strict' and 'critical'.

The degree to which a patient is able to discuss this type of information is highly variable. It is helpful to warn the patient that you may ask some probing questions and give them permission to stop at any time or to decline to answer certain questions should they wish to do so. Some patients are eager to discuss their background in great detail, and the clinician's job at assessment is gently to guide the patient to cover the different aspects

---

Questions to Elicit Information about Social and Environmental Factors in Childhood and Adolescence

- Where were you born and brought up as a child?
- How many brothers and sisters do you have?
- How would you describe your childhood?
- What do/did your parents do for a living?
- What sort of person is your mother/father? How did you get on with her/him?
- Did you suffer from any serious illness as a child?
- Did you suffer from any abuse or traumas as a child?
- Did you lose any people that were very close to you?
- Where did you go to primary/secondary school?
- What was school like for you? Were you bullied or beaten up?
- Did you ever have any unwanted sexual experiences as a child or adolescent?

of their history in the available time. Once this type of information has been gathered, it can be useful to ask the patient to reflect on how they found discussing their childhood and if they can make any links between childhood experiences, their view of themselves and their current problems. Some patients respond positively to the suggestion that treatment could help them to understand the relationship between childhood experiences, how these may have shaped their view of themselves and current problems. They engage collaboratively at an early stage in developing a formulation of their problems. Other patients are unclear how events from childhood could influence their life now.

Personal and Family Beliefs and Rules

Young (1990) has observed that underlying beliefs are rarely formed in response to single traumatic events, but more often arise in the context of an 'ongoing noxious environment'. In the childhood experiences of patients with chronic depression, the environment often does not seem to have been noxious in an explicit or overt way, nor inherently negative. The culture of the family and community in which patients grew up can exert powerful influences over the formation of beliefs and attitudes. Considering such influences can therefore be important in developing the formulation in persistent depression. The aim of this part of assessment is to try to gain information on the cultural beliefs and rules that provided the context for the formation of the patient's view of themselves and the world. Because these influences are more subtle than those of overt trauma, patients often experience difficulty in making links between aspects of their childhood environment and depression. Areas to be covered in this aspect of assessment include: quality of relationships with parents, siblings, grandparents and members of the extended family; religious affiliation; family rules or mottoes; how children were disciplined at home and by whom; how emotions (pleasant and unpleasant) were shown and dealt with at home; how the patient was treated if they were ill; the 'ethos' of education including the academic, social and disciplinary aspects of school; and attitudes to academic and sporting achievements.

Family systems exert a great deal of influence over an individual's view of themselves, other people and the world. Families tend to have shared value systems and often inculcate a sense of what is right and proper behaviour. As described above, *Elizabeth's* experience was of a strict environment where appearances were emphasised over affection and duty over enjoyment. Elizabeth was well aware of the impact her mother's high standards exerted over her life. She described how her mother had taught her to write with an inkpen with no blots or mistakes. If this was not achieved, her mother would not only be critical but would insist that Elizabeth start again. A family rule was 'If you can't do something properly there is no point in doing it at all'. Many patients describe home environments where there was an emphasis on working hard or doing what was 'right and fair'. Family rules such as 'If you work hard you will be rewarded' or 'If you are fair and honest with others, they will be fair and honest in return' encourage the individual to perceive others' needs as being more important than their own.

In addition to family values about standards, attitudes to emotions in the family can be extremely important. They can have a powerful role in the development of beliefs about emotional control, which can be central to the formulation of persistent depression. Particularly in cultures where material hardship or traumas such as war have been commonplace, families may have little time or sympathy for emotional upsets. Patients may recall oft-repeated sayings such as 'What doesn't kill you makes you stronger'. These attitudes are often presented in a positive light by patients, and it is not uncommon for patients with persistent depression to describe their childhood as happy and normal. It is important to bear in mind that this may be accurate and take this at face value unless evidence comes to light to support an alternative view. In some cases, having been protected from distress as a child may have left the person ill prepared for coping with it in adult life. For example, Margaret, a successful woman in her family and business, became depressed following the death of her father. She described a happy life up until that point, and it emerged in the assessment that she had been protected from upsetting events throughout her life. Whenever Margaret encountered a distressing event in her life, her father had automatically sorted it out for her. Certain patterns of apparently happy developmental experiences would appear to lead to the development of patients' self-perceptions as being competent, capable and in control, which can be shattered by subsequent incidents in adult life.

As well as values expressed within the family, it is also important to pay attention to other institutions within the community that exert an influence over individuals' views of themselves and the world. This includes factors such as school and the culture that predominates within it. The therapist should ascertain the type of school the patient attended: state or public, single sex or co-educational, whether it had a religious affiliation, and the emphasis on academic achievement. The patient's view of themselves in relation to their teachers and peers can usefully be discussed. This area was important for *Dave* who was born and raised in a working-class family in a small village. He was successful in passing the 11+ exam and obtained a place at a local grammar school. Dave recalled feeling inferior throughout his time at the school and perceived the ethos of the school as one of segregation between working-class boys who had won scholarships to the school and those whose parents could afford to pay to send their children. He felt looked down on by some teachers and pupils due to the way he spoke and the fact he could not join in extracurricular activities because his parents could not afford for him to do so. He saw his experiences at school as being central to his sense of not being good enough and his constant efforts to prove himself. Cultural attitudes can shape individuals' attitudes, even when individuals try to resist their influence. For example, *Graham* was raised in a Church of England home and attended a Church of England school and church. As an adolescent he had rebelled against his family and rejected his religious upbringing. However, the value system inherent to his upbringing still resulted in a strong sense of duty to help others more needy than himself. He also related his rule that he must strive to be perfect to a biblical teaching he recalled from school that as humans we are all imperfect and unworthy in the sight of God.

Questions to Elicit Personal and Family Beliefs and Rules

- What type of environment were you raised in?
- What values did your parents emphasise in your childhood?
- How was affection shown in your family?
- How did mother/father/siblings respond when you showed your feelings?
- Who disciplined you as a child?
- What did the discipline consist of?
- How were arguments dealt with during childhood?
- If you were ill as a child, how was this dealt with?
- When a death occurred in the family, how was this handled in the family?
- Were you raised within a particular religion?
- How has your religious upbringing shaped your view of the world?
- What was primary/secondary school like as a child?
- What values did your school emphasise?
- What were your relationships with teachers like at school?
- What aspects of school did you enjoy/dislike?
- What were your reasons for enjoying/disliking these aspects?
- Was there anything you excelled at as a child?

ASSESSING THE PATIENT'S VIEW OF DEPRESSION AND ITS TREATMENT

As discussed in Chapter 1, the ongoing experience of persistent depression can lead patients to develop beliefs about depression itself. As these beliefs about depression will have been shaped by the patient's more general beliefs, considering the patient's view of depression can contribute to understanding their underlying beliefs. In formulating chronic depression, it is important to consider how these beliefs about depression may feed into the key areas of low self-esteem, helplessness and hopelessness. Taking account of the patient's model of depression is also essential in how the therapist attempts to engage the patient in cognitive therapy. As is discussed in detail in the next chapter, engaging the patient in therapy depends on their being able to allow for the possibility that the cognitive model could apply in their case. It is therefore important to assess the patient's view of depression and its treatment. When assessing this, attention needs to be given to:

(1) attitudes to depression as an illness
(2) attitudes to medication
(3) attitudes to psychological therapies.

Attitudes to Depression as an Illness

Although rarely discussed in the context of psychiatric or psychological interventions, most patients have a personal theory or model regarding depression as an illness. A patient's attributions regarding the cause of depression will influence the perceived controllability of the illness and the degree to which particular forms of treatment seem appropriate. An individual's understanding of an illness will be to some extent shaped by ideas predominant in their culture, which in western society is the medical model. This model posits a biological/genetic basis to both physical and psychological illnesses. Perhaps the most commonly encountered belief about persistent depression is the one expressed by *Peter* at the beginning of treatment that 'Depression is all biological'. As this belief indicated that there was little he could do to relieve his depression, it reinforced his helplessness. Moreover, Peter was very clear at assessment that he did not think a psychological treatment could be of any benefit in dealing with his difficulties (this is discussed in more detail below).

Although great strides have been made in reducing the amount of social stigma attached to psychiatric illness, such stigma is still prevalent in many sectors of society. As many patients observe, it seems to be more socially acceptable to have an illness such as cancer than to receive a diagnosis of depression. The degree to which an individual feels stigmatised by depression can reinforce their low self-esteem. In addition, stigma can impact on the degree to which they accept that the diagnosis of depression can be applied to them. Some patients thus seem to 'do battle' with the diagnosis of depression and the implications of this. For example, a number of patients presenting for treatment state that they are not suffering from depression and may refer to their problems as 'stress' or 'exhaustion due to overwork'. One woman, Pauline, attended her first assessment session and declared at the outset that she hoped the therapist was not going to tell her she was depressed. She had seen three psychiatrists who had tried to tell her this and she had never returned to see any of them. It transpired that Pauline's model of her illness was that she was experiencing a stress reaction due to overwork, which had persisted for the last seven years. Information gathered regarding Pauline's family background emphasised achievement and success over all else and viewed psychiatric illness as shameful. This made sense of her insistence on not having a label such as depression applied to her.

Another common belief that seems opposite to those described above is that depression is entirely psychological, so the patient holds themselves responsible for being able to control it. A patient, Tina, held this belief which was manifest in her attitude to relapses of her depression, for which she blamed herself for not 'trying hard enough'. Whenever her illness had started to respond to antidepressant medication, she perceived this as the medication controlling her illness and not herself using her own resources. As a result she would stop taking medication as a 'test' of how much control she had over the depression, generally with poor results. Importantly, many such patients see depression as a sign of their own

---

Questions to Elicit the Patient's Model of Depression

- What is your understanding of depression as an illness?
- What is your understanding of what causes depression generally?
- How did you arrive at this conclusion?
- Have you read anything about depression in books or magazines or watched a television programme?
- What do you consider will be the most effective treatment for your illness?
- Do you know anyone else who has experienced depression? What is your understanding of their illness?

personal or constitutional weakness. Such attitudes often emerge when assessing symptoms, as discussed above, and it can be helpful to explore gently the patient's ideas about the depression to see if views of being weak or pathetic emerge. However, persistent probing regarding emotions will seem intrusive to such patients, who may see themselves as vulnerable, so these beliefs need to be explored with care.

Attitudes to Medication

In attempting to engage the patient in psychological treatment alongside the use of pharmacotherapy, it is important at assessment to consider the patient's attitude to medication as an aspect of treatment. Exploring the patient's view of antidepressant medication can provide additional information on the patient's model of depression. It is important to clarify any reservations regarding the role of medication. For example, many patients believe antidepressant medication to be addictive, while others express concerns regarding potential side-effects. Such individuals often have conditional beliefs around the theme of control and may express concerns that tablets or their side-effects are controlling them rather than them controlling the illness.

It is important that the therapist explores the benefits as well as disadvantages of medication. Some patients will insist that their antidepressant medication is of little benefit. While this may be true in a minority of cases, most patients do derive some benefit from a therapeutic dose of antidepressants. It is worth bearing in mind that the processing biases referred to previously may skew the patient's perceptions. Careful elicitation of the severity of symptoms prior to the commencement of medication in comparison to current severity can help both therapist and patient to recognise the benefits of using antidepressant medication in conjunction with cognitive therapy. The successful identification of a small but significant reduction in symptom severity through taking medication can prove invaluable when it comes to socialising the patient to the cognitive model.

The patient's use of and attitudes to alternative therapies, including herbal remedies and acupuncture, are often relevant. There has been recent interest in the use of St John's Wort as a treatment for depression and some patients find this a more acceptable treatment than conventional antidepressant medication. It is therefore useful to try to make sense of the patient's reasons for endorsing alternative treatments. For some individuals, herbal remedies may be seen to be attached to less stigma or fewer side-effects than taking antidepressant medication. For others, the endorsement of a herbal remedy may reflect a lifestyle choice which seeks to eliminate the introduction of artificial chemicals to the body.

Questions for Eliciting Patient's Perceptions about Prescribed Medication

- What medication are you taking at present?
- What dosage are you taking?
- How do you feel about taking medication?
- How helpful do you find your medication in managing your illness?
- What is your understanding as to how medication to treat depression works?
- Do you have any concerns about taking the medication prescribed for you?
- How often do you take your prescribed medication?
- How many times (if at all) have you missed a dose in the last two weeks?
- Can you describe any troublesome side effects of the medication you have been prescribed?

Attitudes to Psychological Therapy

Eliciting the patient's perceptions of psychological therapy is important at the beginning of treatment. Assessing attitudes to therapy provides a bridge between assessment and subsequently explaining the rationale for cognitive therapy. This is an important step in engaging the patient in cognitive therapy and is described in the following chapter. It is useful to assess the extent to which the patient believes that therapy can be helpful to them and their reasons for this. A high proportion of patients express pessimism regarding the usefulness of a talking therapy as a means of tackling their problems. The generalised hopelessness characteristic of chronic depression undoubtedly reduces patients' optimism regarding any treatment. The formulation should consider the extent to which such hopelessness is reinforced by the past failure of the depression to respond fully to often numerous treatment regimes. With successive treatment failures, the optimism of patients is ground further and further down until they learn not to raise their hopes too high because each disappointment is more difficult to bear.

For example, *Marion's* expectations of therapy represented an extreme, even among patients with chronic depression. At her first assessment, Marion cited a 25-year history of depression. Charting her journey through the psychiatric system provided a historical account of the treatment of depression across three decades. Marion had received myriad interventions, including five admissions to psychiatric wards, ECT, several of each class of antidepressant medication, lithium, mood stabilisers, counselling, psychodynamic psychotherapy, social work support, art therapy, occupational therapy and input from five different community psychiatric nurses. When the therapist asked Marion how helpful she thought cognitive therapy would be, she sighed and simply shrugged her shoulders saying 'It may help for a while but nothing lasts'. She expressed particular sadness that good relationships she had formed with a number of health workers had all ended either because of a lack of improvement in her illness or because a transient improvement led to discharge from the services. Her experience suggested to her that no intervention would provide enduring improvement and that even if she formed a good relationship with her therapist, she would then lose it.

Attitudes about therapy may stem from the patient's model about depression as well as from general hopelessness about treatment. As noted above, the view that depression is 'all biological' is a common factor that limits the perceived appropriateness of psychological treatment. For example, *Peter* informed the therapist at assessment that cognitive therapy would not be of any benefit to him. It became apparent that Peter saw talking about problems as a wholly inadequate solution to his difficulties. He cited the fact that not only had his illness persisted for seven years but that he was taking three different types of medication for his depression, which must be an indication of the severity of his illness. He endorsed a biological explanation of depression, which had been explained to him both by his General Practitioner and his Consultant Psychiatrist as a 'chemical imbalance in his brain'. On enquiring as to whether Peter had any information regarding psychological interventions, he said his wife had given him some articles about depression from a woman's magazine and these had mentioned psychology. He concluded that, as the articles were in a women's magazine and all the case examples were women, then not only must he have a woman's illness (a source of deep shame to him) but the treatments endorsed (talking therapies) must be aimed at women. Thus Peter did not hold talking about his problems (something women do) in high regard as a possible solution.

As well as assessing patients' expectations about the effectiveness of therapy, it is important to elicit patients' views about how therapy might work. A view commonly expressed by patients is that psychological therapies are based simply on talking things over, particularly upsets from childhood. Some patients report that they have tried this, either through previous therapy or informally, and still remain depressed. Other patients recoil from the idea of contemplating past upsets as 'self-indulgent'. Their view of the mechanism of therapy may contribute to their pessimism and, if not addressed, could lead to difficulties in engaging in cognitive therapy.

Some patients talk about therapy as something that will be 'done to' them by an expert. They assume that there are good reasons for what this expert is doing, but do not presume to know what these reasons are or to have an active role in the therapy. They are happy to attend as long as the expert believes it to be worthwhile, but see anything they might do as irrelevant to the process. This kind of attitude reflects helplessness more than hopelessness, as the patient maintains some faith that someone else may do something that will alleviate their problems. Past experiences can contribute to patients' views about how therapy might work, particularly in patients who have been involved in various different forms of psychological treatment. On assessment, Paul described a 10-year history of depression during which time he had spent two years in a therapeutic community and had undergone further extended analytic therapies. It was particularly hard to gauge the effectiveness of these due to the waxing and waning of his symptoms over the extended treatment periods. Paul described the therapies as 'enormously helpful', although he was not sure whether they had resulted in any improvement in his depression. He was very positive about his previous therapists, describing one in particular as 'wonderful'. He believed that the therapy had helped him to understand himself, but was unable to describe any particular understandings or insights. When asked whether he thought cognitive therapy would be of any benefit to him, he responded, 'Well, you would know that better than me'. His helplessness and passivity with regard to the process of psychological treatment was clearly an important issue to be addressed in an active treatment like cognitive therapy.

Questions for Eliciting Patient's Perceptions of Psychological Therapy

- Have you tried any talking therapies in the past?
- How helpful/unhelpful was your previous therapy?
- What changes did you make as a result of previous therapy?
- How optimistic are you that cognitive therapy could help in the management of your depression?
- How do you think cognitive therapy could be of help to you?
- What is your understanding of cognitive therapy as a treatment for depression?
- Do you have any concerns/reservations regarding cognitive therapy?

FITTING THE PIECES TOGETHER

Covering the areas described so far enables an assessment of the extent to which the various factors might contribute to the formulation and of how each factor might influence key cognitions. Having covered these different areas, it is then important for the therapist to integrate the information gained about these different areas into an overall formulation. This 'big picture' can help in understanding how the individual factors that con-tribute to the depression relate to each other. This resulting formulation is important in planning the overall treatment strategy, in implementing particular treatment techniques and in anticipating problems that might arise in therapy.

There are two main aspects to the overall formulation. First, the therapist identifies the links between the different aspects of the patient's current difficulties. The reciprocal relationships between situational, biological, emotional, cognitive and behavioural factors are established. This enables identification of the vicious circles currently involved in maintaining the depression, and of the role of cognitions and behaviours in those circles. These hypotheses on the vicious circles maintaining the depression for that individual patient can be used in 'selling the cognitive model' to the patient (see next chapter). They are also helpful in suggesting the strate-gies that might be most immediately beneficial in achieving some degree of improvement in symptoms. Secondly, the therapist attempts to develop a longitudinal formulation of the factors that have led the patient to be vulnerable to the persistence of depression and of how those factors have been triggered and reinforced over time. This involves constructing pre-liminary hypotheses as to the nature of the patient's underlying beliefs and assumptions. It is rarely possible to gain a firm idea of these beliefs just from information gathered at initial assessment. However, as these beliefs are presumed to lie at the heart of various other aspects of the problems, considering potential links between overt aspects of the com-plaints and history usually gives some clue as to the likely nature of the beliefs.

This process involves identifying potential themes and congruencies be-tween a number of factors:

- the patient's attitude to their depressive symptoms
- overt negative thoughts identified at assessment
- the nature of things that are avoided and the style of avoidance
- the type of events or situations that trigger depression
- the kind of upbringing described
- the nature of any abuse or trauma experienced during development.

Below are two clinical examples of how information gathered during assessment informs the initial formulation that guides therapy in its early stages. These examples also illustrate how this initial formulation needs to be developed further throughout the course of treatment as new information is gathered.

Peter

The main problems identified in Peter's problem list at the outset of therapy were:

- poor sleep, reduced concentration and excessive tiredness
- feelings of shame regarding fact I have become depressed
- loss of purpose and meaning in daily life now I have no work
- avoidance of social activities in case I meet work colleagues
- unpleasant memories of events at work that pop into my mind on a daily basis and make me feel guilty and angry.

A number of aspects of Peter's presentation at assessment have been described above. From Peter's perspective, the main problem was that he had lost his job and, even if he were to recover from his illness, in his fifties in an area of high unemployment the prospects of further work at the same salary were slim. He believed that if he could return to work all his problems would be solved—a cherished but unrealistic ideal. He tended to blame himself for not having handled the circumstances leading up to the loss of his job better. He tried hard not to think about these events, but was subject to frequent intrusive memories and thoughts about them. He interpreted both these memories and the upset they caused as signs that he was not in control of himself as he should be. This was a view that he also applied to other biological symptoms, such as tremor and loss of libido. He tried hard not to let others see his upset or other symptoms, either by trying to exert self-control or by avoiding social situations. In discussing his emotions, he did admit to a sense of shame about being depressed. However, he strongly endorsed a biological view of depression, which had been reinforced by his doctors over the years since the onset of his depression. In discussing his upbringing, he denied any trauma and presented a view of his childhood as happy. He stressed how his parents had always been fair in any discipline and how they had been poor but hard-working.

From the information gained at assessment about his symptoms, problems and his attitudes to them, the therapist hypothesised certain psychological mechanisms as being important in the onset and maintenance of Peter's illness. Specifically these were:

- *A perceived loss of control over events at work.* This had resulted in a loss of his sense of worth, which he defined in terms of work and the respect and status that work conferred. Prior to the changes that occurred at work and the onset of his illness, Peter's view of himself was as capable and master of his own domain.
- *His view that becoming depressed was a sign of weakness.* He viewed the persistence of his illness despite his ongoing attempts to try and 'beat it' (once more highlighting the theme of control) as further evidence of his weakness. This further undermined his self-esteem.
- *His sense of shame at becoming depressed.* Although Peter admitted to feeling ashamed, the concomitant sense of weakness that was hypothesised was not readily articulated by him. Rather, he expressed a strong view that depression was biological in origin, probably as a strategy for 'saving face'.

Because of Peter's sense of shame at becoming depressed and the doubts that he expressed about cognitive therapy, a degree of caution was employed about sharing this formulation. The therapist was concerned that being too explicit with Peter regarding his perceptions of weakness may lead him to disengage from treatment. Therefore the initial formulation shared with Peter was presented very tentatively. On the basis that Peter saw himself as weak and having no control over his illness, it was important that the therapeutic style did not engender in Peter a sense of having his weakness pointed out to him or being out-smarted by his therapist. After two assessment sessions, the initial formulation was introduced in terms of the practical losses that he was confronted with. The meaning of these in terms of additional personal losses were then discussed.

Practical losses I have suffered as a result of becoming depressed:

- loss of job
- loss of ability to be active like I used to be
- financial losses
- loss of retirement plan.

Personal losses I have suffered since becoming depressed and losing my job:

- loss of sense of security
- loss of role in life
- loss of purpose and meaning in life
- loss of status
- loss of respect for self and in eyes of others.

When these losses were written down and discussed with Peter, he could identify strongly with the idea that his external losses had also triggered certain internal changes and losses.

At the beginning of the following session, Peter told the therapist he had been doing a lot of thinking over the week and had concluded that his biggest problem was how ashamed he felt about becoming depressed. The therapist asked what was shameful about becoming depressed, to which Peter replied tearfully, looking at the floor, that he saw it as a weakness. The therapist discussed with Peter the fact that this was a common view held by people who became depressed, particularly among men. Importantly, this helped to confirm the therapist's initial hypotheses and presented an opportunity to discuss the formulation more fully. This formulation was elaborated throughout the course of therapy in discussion of his beliefs and their relation to his upbringing.

A number of important conditional beliefs were hypothesised and were subsequently endorsed by Peter:

- *If you are not in control, it is a sign of weakness.* The theme of control was central to the onset and maintenance of his illness and was formulated as a conditional belief. Peter perceived that he had not taken control of circumstances in a climate of change at work. As a result, he saw it as his fault that others had lost their jobs. He also saw it as his fault that he had then become depressed and failed to control his illness.
- *If you show your emotions, you will be ridiculed and humiliated.* This belief to a large extent reflected a cultural norm. The environment in which he was raised endorsed men not showing any vulnerability i.e. being seen to be emotionally strong and not showing their feelings. Outbursts of emotion would be likely to result in criticism and ridicule and thus entail a loss of respect and social status.
- *If you work hard, you will be rewarded.* Peter saw working hard as a virtue in itself that also conferred a sense of self-worth. Hence his self-esteem was predicated on his work. This belief was a contributory factor in the onset of his depression, as he had always believed that as long as he worked hard he would get both material rewards and respect in the eyes of others. He had found it impossible to adjust to changes in the work place that he couldn't control, and this belief accounted for his feelings of anger and sense of injustice at what occurred. This work ethic had been a strong factor in his upbringing and also represented a cultural norm in the area where he lived. It had been reinforced as Peter 'bettered himself' through his hard work from his humble origins in a poor working-class family.

Formulating his unconditional beliefs presented more of a dilemma for the therapist. Since he had become depressed, he seemed to interpret much of what went on in his life in terms of his own weakness. In contrast, throughout his life prior to his depression, he had viewed himself and been perceived by others as being strong, capable and in control of his life. This was reflected in his sporting success both as a child and an adult (for example, he was captain of the school football team both at primary and secondary school, a source of pride in himself and respect from others). He also drew pride and self-worth from having worked continuously throughout his adult life in an area of high unemployment. Having worked himself to be in a position of leadership, he drew self-respect from others looking to him for help and guidance. Because his view of himself had changed so drastically when he became depressed, neither his prior view of himself as capable nor his current view of himself as weak could be framed as a true unconditional or core belief. Rather than basing the formulation around a negative perception of self (i.e. failure) that had been confirmed by the changes that occurred at work and his subsequent depression, the formulation was based on a positive view of self as strong and capable. This view of himself had been shattered by an inability to control events at work and his subsequent depressive illness. His view of himself as weak related only to having become depressed, rather than representing a completely general view of himself. What distressed him was that, having become depressed, this undermined his certainty in his view of himself as strong ('perhaps I was wrong about myself all these years').

Peter's view of the world was also ambiguous. Prior to his depression, he had believed the world was a fair place. This was closely linked to his belief that if you worked hard you would be rewarded and very much reflected the value system within his family. Until the changes at work, Peter believed the world had always been fair to him and it had been fair because he had worked hard. Following his retirement on grounds of ill health and penalties on his pension, he saw his 25 years of service as not having been fairly rewarded. He felt angry and bitter at his circumstances and saw no means of recompense for this.

The extremity (all or nothing nature) and rigidity with which Peter held his beliefs was formulated as an important contributor to the upheaval in Peter's beliefs about himself and the world. The way in which Peter held his beliefs was thus seen as being fundamental to his vulnerability. This was reflected in his conviction that he should have been able to control events at work to prevent his staff being made redundant, and a difficulty accepting that in reality he had little, if any, control. This rigidity was also evident in relation to his belief 'If you show emotions you will be ridiculed and humiliated'. When asked 'In what situations is it acceptable to show emotions?', after much deliberation Peter said at the funeral of a child on the day of the funeral. Not only did he actively exclude crying after the funeral or at the death of an adult, he also ruled out displaying happiness on receipt of good news, crying at an emotive book or film and any overt displays of anger or excitement whether in public or private. All of these he deemed as evidence of weakness and a lack of appropriate control. He believed that such displays would be judged by others in a negative light, entailing a loss of respect and status.

The beliefs hypothesised in the formulation were manifest in a number of ways in the presenting problems described by Peter. His beliefs about the importance of control accounted for his self-blaming automatic thoughts and feelings of guilt regarding the events at work. They also explained his constant attempts to control his symptoms and memories, and his interpretation of the difficulties in doing so as evidence of weakness. His belief that lack of emotional control would lead to humiliation accounted both for his complete social avoidance since becoming depressed and for his high levels of anxiety whenever he was in the company of others. Peter's beliefs fed his marked cognitive avoidance, as shown in his effort to suppress distressing intrusive thoughts and memories, and behavioural avoidance, as seen in his social avoidance and inactivity. These problems clearly reflected the themes of the chronic cognitive triad: his self-esteem had been shattered by the loss of control over his life and himself; his inability to influence events or his depressive symptoms left him feeling helpless; and his hopelessness regarding his prospects for returning to work was reinforced by the failure of his depression to respond to treatment.

Peter found the development of the formulation to be one of the most helpful aspects of therapy. It played a pivotal role in engaging him in interventions that were often difficult and distressing for him. Making sense of his experience helped him to engage in a psychological intervention despite his biological view of depression, as will be discussed further in the next chapter.

Jean

Jean's initial problem list was sparse and general as follows:

- Being attracted to men who treat me badly
- Irritability on a daily basis, especially with the kids, which leads me to feel guilty
- Disturbed sleep pattern.

By Session 7, her problem list had been refined with the following additions:

- Seeing other people as more important than myself, which means I always put others' needs first and I can get taken advantage of as a result
- Seeing people as always letting me down, which leads to excessive self-reliance
- Avoidance of letting people get close for fear of rejection.

At assessment, Jean described her main problem as being attracted to men who in her words were 'bastards'. She attributed her current problems to the decision of a kind man with whom she had developed a close relationship not to enter into a long-term commitment with her. She described him as the only man who had ever treated her with respect, in contrast to her previous relationships with the two men who fathered her five children. Jean expressed difficulty in understanding how the end of this good relationship had precipitated her depression, when both her previous relationships had been violent and emotionally abusive but at no point had she become depressed. When asked how she made sense of the end of this caring relationship, she replied in a resigned and matter of fact way 'he just didn't love me enough and he didn't want to take on the kids—I can understand that—he could do a lot better than me'. This highlighted two themes of potential importance in terms of how she viewed herself: unlovability and seeing others as better than herself. This possibly accounted for her willingness to remain in relationships with men who were at best unsupportive and often abusive. As Jean put it, 'This is my lot in life—decent men wouldn't want to know me'.

In comparison to her description of this problem, Jean tended to gloss over any other problems or symptoms. In response to questioning, she admitted that her mood was highly variable and that she had spells of quite intense guilt, irritability and anxiety. In addition, she described herself as constantly tired and disinterested in doing anything unless she had to. Assessment suggested that she spent most of her time keeping busy and when able to do this reported little in the way of low mood or negative automatic thoughts. However, if she was prevented from keeping active—such as on one occasion when she sprained her ankle and was forced to rest—her mood dropped dramatically. Jean could readily articulate that keeping busy 'stopped her thinking', which she recognised was associated with a lowering of mood. This was suggestive of an avoidant coping style. When the issue of how she spent her time was examined further, Jean described how she was confidant and problem-solver to a number of friends, always made a tremendous effort for other people's birthdays and would offer help to anyone who asked for it. She did not see any problem in this.

From the outset, it was clear to the therapist that what people thought about Jean really mattered to her. The therapist's initial ideas on formulation therefore revolved around the themes of approval and subjugation. This was manifest in how she consistently put helping others above her own emotional and practical needs. This behaviour was formulated as being driven by a conditional belief 'If you help others, they will like you'. This belief, operating alongside her endorsement of the importance of self-reliance, meant that none of her relationships were in fact reciprocal. She had no real experience of sharing mutual support or of people being there for her when she needed them. Assessment suggested that this may have stemmed back to her family of origin.

In considering early experiences that may have influenced her beliefs, Jean described herself as 'the black sheep of the family'. She recalled her mother as critical and emotionally absent. Her father had a physical disability and required a great deal of home care, which was provided by her mother. As a result, Jean and her siblings were left to look after themselves a good deal of the time. Indeed, Jean recalled looking after her younger siblings from the age of 8 onwards. In addition, Jean felt she had never really fitted in with the family and saw herself as something of an outsider. She saw this as a result of her mother singling her out for criticism of her lifestyle. Jean felt that whenever she had a problem and required support, her family told her it was of her own making and therefore 'having made her bed, she should lie in it'.

The themes identified in Jean's account of her upbringing fitted well with some of the issues potentially contributing to her current situation. The importance of looking after other people's needs (especially her father's and younger siblings') had been drummed into her. This was formulated as a belief that 'Other peoples' needs are more important than my own'. Meanwhile her own needs had at best been unsupported, which led her to develop a strong sense of self-reliance. This was taken to an unhelpful extreme, in that Jean often didn't recognise when she needed to ask for help. When she did consider asking for help, she expected that it would not be forthcoming and experienced this as rejection, leading to extreme sadness and low mood. Her self-reliance seemed to be driven by a conditional belief 'If you don't rely on anyone, you won't get hurt'. The therapist hypothesised that this, along with her view of the importance of other people's needs, reflected deeper unconditional beliefs about herself and others. In particular, unconditional beliefs that 'I am unlovable' and 'People are unreliable' were hypothesised.

This initial formulation regarding her beliefs was refined on the basis of her reactions to therapy as it progressed. Her apparent reluctance to focus on her problems or symptoms became more striking: often at the outset of a session she would present as bright and bubbly, but as she began to work on a particular problem during the session her mood would plummet. This style was also reflected in how Jean approached early homework assignments. Few written examples of automatic thoughts ever materialised on a diary sheet, as Jean would state 'I have been fine all week, there was nothing to write down'. However, talking through the intervening week in the session would often raise a number of situations where her mood had dropped and Jean would give out a stream of pertinent automatic thoughts. When this pattern was drawn to Jean's attention several sessions into therapy, she said that it was important to 'put on a front'. This front consisted of being 'cheerful, bouncy and helpful to others'. When asked what the consequences would be if she did not put on this front, she stated 'people wouldn't like me and wouldn't want anything to do with me'. This helped the formulation of a conditional belief: 'If others knew what I was really like, they would reject me'. A poignant discussion of what Jean was really like revealed two central themes. Firstly, she saw herself as unlovable. Secondly, she was unlovable because there was something intrinsically bad about her and, as a consequence, she did not deserve good things. In discussing 'good things', it transpired that for Jean the most painful area was relationships, as she believed that she did not deserve to be in a decent, mutual relationship. As therapy progressed, it was possible to see that her low moods were invariably triggered by disruptions or breakdowns in relationships. Jean's perception that 'people are unreliable' was key to her reaction, especially as she attributed others' treatment of her to her intrinsic unlovability/badness.

Jean's unconditional beliefs that she was unlovable and that other people were unreliable explained her catastrophic reaction to the end of her first genuinely caring relationship. They also accounted for her avoidance of close relationships, due to the fear of rejection, and her tendency to stay in abusive relationships, as she believed they were what she deserved. Her continuous and exhausting activity level was driven by two factors: avoidance of unpleasant thoughts and her belief about the importance of attending to other people's needs. Jean did not recognise this overactivity as a problem but as a life-long helpful strategy for avoiding painful feelings. Jean's friendly and upbeat way of interacting with the therapist while actively downplaying her problems was hypothesised as being a reflection of her need to hold others at arm's length in order to prevent her true self from being discovered. For Jean, low self-esteem was also manifest in her perpetually putting others first, her acceptance of abuse and her seeming inability to express her needs and have these met. That her beliefs gave her no choice over the overwhelming demands on her fed her sense of helplessness, as did the apparent inevitability of abusive relationships. Because she attributed her problems to her intrinsic character, she could see no possibility of having another satisfying relationship and so also had a strong sense of hopelessness.

This formulation is a good example of the interpersonal context in which much chronic depression has its origin. Interpersonal beliefs are usually formulated as beliefs about self-in-relation-to-others and beliefs about other people and relationships. The formulation usually describes how unconditional beliefs influence conditional beliefs that determine the strategies by which people conduct their relationships. The impact of this belief system on therapy and the therapeutic relationship needs to formulated. This helps in the anticipation of problems arising during therapy and enables the therapy relationship to be used in testing out beliefs. The therapy situation can thus be a useful starting point for constructing behavioural experiments aimed at modifying these important beliefs (see Safran & Segal, 1990).

SUMMARY POINTS

- The volume of information and the guardedness of some patients make it hard to conduct a complete assessment at the start of therapy.
- Enquiring about each domain relevant to the patient's current problems (symptoms, situations, emotions and behaviours) can yield important information about the patient's thinking.
- The therapist should be particularly alert to themes in the patient's thinking, to their thinking processes and reactions to discussing emotional material.
- Discussing past episodes of depression (or lack thereof) can be useful in identifying common triggers for the depression and attitudes that may influence its persistence.
- Information on relatively subtle aspects of the patient's early experiences, such as family and cultural values and rules, can be important in formulating the patient's underlying beliefs.
- Assessing the patient's beliefs about depression and its treatment is essential to subsequently presenting the cognitive model and engaging the patient in therapy.

- Assessment should provide sufficient information to construct a preliminary cognitive formulation: this should account for the patient's current problems and their maintenance in terms of a system of possible underlying beliefs.
- Further information needs to be gathered throughout therapy and the formulation amended accordingly.

Chapter 4

INITIATING THERAPY: SOCIALISATION AND SETTING GOALS

In this chapter, you will find suggestions on:

- Foreseeing obstacles that might prevent patients with persistent depression engaging in cognitive therapy
- Adapting presentation of the cognitive model to facilitate the engagement of patients with firm views on the nature of their depression
- Illustrating the vicious circles that maintain depression
- Discussing underlying beliefs early in therapy
- Identifying targets that will combat the low self-esteem, helplessness and hopelessness of patients with persistent depression
- Setting specific goals for treatment

Before interventions aimed at modifying the patient's problems can be undertaken, a number of important tasks need to be carried out: the engagement of the patient in therapy, their socialisation into the cognitive model guiding therapy and the setting of goals for therapeutic intervention. In acute depression, it is usually possible to convey an understanding of the therapy within the first couple of sessions, over the course of which the patient quite naturally becomes engaged in the process of therapy. As a result of the difficulties we have outlined, in chronic depression these processes take somewhat longer and require more detailed consideration. In this chapter, we consider some factors that require particular attention in the engagement and socialisation of chronically depressed patients into therapy. We then discuss the importance of setting goals in cognitive therapy and describe the process of setting goals with patients with persistent depression. We consider how appropriate goals can target the low self-esteem, helplessness and hopelessness that are central in persistent depression.

PRESENTING THE RATIONALE FOR TREATMENT

A standard feature of all cognitive therapy is explicitly sharing with the patient a cogent treatment rationale. The aim of this is to help patients to consider the possible role that their thoughts and thought processes have in maintaining their problems. Socialisation into the cognitive model is accomplished through discussing the distinctions between thoughts, feelings and other domains of the model and outlining the way that these domains may feed into each other. It is important that the application of these ideas to a patient's problems is then illustrated with reference to specific examples from the patient's own experience. This socialisation process also provides an important example of the collaboration and guided discovery essential to the style of therapy.

Patients with chronic depression tend to express considerable hopelessness and helplessness, and this affects their attitude to starting cognitive therapy. It is 'par for the course' that the therapist will not be working with a highly motivated individual brimming with enthusiasm for the therapy. A number of the other factors we have described in Chapters 1 and 3 also work against the patient readily accepting the cognitive model. Patients may have pre-existing strongly held views about the cause of their depression that conflict with the cognitive model or they may suppress the thoughts and feelings essential to seeing the validity of the model. Working with chronic depression, the therapist needs to be particularly active in addressing these barriers to engaging the patient in treatment. Care needs to be taken to present the cognitive model in a way that the patient can see may be relevant to their individual problems and goes some way to accounting for the difficulties the patient is facing. During this process, it is important that the therapist does not try to persuade the patient that cognitive therapy will help, but rather acknowledges their scepticism and encourages them to test the validity of the model.

Engendering in the patient a sense of hope, however small, that the therapy may be of some help will foster engagement in the therapy. Therefore, an initial attempt to present the cognitive model and discuss its relevance with the patient is usually undertaken by the end of the first session. Initiating the socialisation process with the patient generally requires at least 15–20 minutes. There is often a danger of reaching the end of the first assessment session with insufficient time to implement this important intervention. It is usually preferable to postpone some areas of the assessment so that a start can be made in presenting the cognitive model at the first session.

THE VICIOUS CIRCLE MODEL

In the cognitive model, the vicious circle is viewed as an important mechanism contributing to the maintenance of current problems. An important goal of cognitive therapy is to improve mood and functioning by slowing or breaking the vicious circle. Thus the basis of socialisation to the cognitive model is to work with the patient to construct an idea of how just such a vicious circle relates to their problems. In standard therapy with acute depression, this is usually addressed with reference to negative thoughts and low mood, and the interrelationship between them. Patients often readily endorse the idea that their thinking becomes more negative as their mood becomes lower, and that this then makes them feel even worse, and so on. However, as discussed on page 120, chronically depressed patients often have their own explanations for their persistent depressive symptoms. These may be ideas that the symptoms are all biological in origin, reflect some constitutional defect or result entirely from situational factors. Attempting to explain depression simply in terms of a vicious circle of thoughts and feelings may conflict with the patient's existing ideas. Patients who are certain that they have serious biological malfunctions or are beset by numerous social difficulties can react with outrage to any apparent suggestion that the problems are all 'just the way they are thinking'. When patients have had problems for years and see them as part of their make-up, they may scoff at the idea that changing their thinking will be effective or even possible. Clearly, evoking these reactions risks seriously hindering the patient's engagement in the therapy.

When working with chronic depression, it is therefore preferable to present the cognitive model in broader terms. Using Padesky and Mooney's (1990) generic maintenance model (see Figure 4.1) allows the interrelationships between environment, biology/physiology, thoughts, emotions, and behaviour to be considered. Although this model is undoubtedly more complicated than just considering thoughts and feelings, there are distinct advantages. To ensure that this more complicated model is understood by the patient, it is important that the therapist allows adequate time for discussion and uses both verbal and written methods of presentation.

Encompassing the Patient's Model

The aim is to socialise the patient to the model in such a way that the treatment rationale given encompasses rather than conflicts with their current model of depression. Thus the clinician needs the flexibility to emphasise differing aspects of the treatment rationale (using medication,

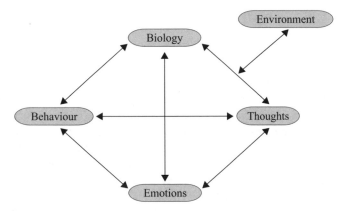

Figure 4.1   The cognitive model showing the vicious circle in persistent depression. Reproduced from Padesky and Mooney, 1990, with permission of the Center for Cognitive Therapy

modifying behaviour or unhelpful cognition etc.) according to the needs of the patient. For patients with many environmental stressors, the therapist can include the importance of these in contributing to depression. The therapist should thus acknowledge the social losses and difficulties that the patient has suffered, which can be considerable. Patients have frequently lost partners, friends, jobs, or homes and suffered increasing strife within relationships before or during their depression. Cognitive and emotional avoidance can make it hard for the therapist and potentially aversive to the patient to empathise fully at an emotional level with any major losses or setbacks. If this is the case, it is sufficient at this stage to engage the patient at an intellectual level with the idea that these factors are important. This can lead to the introduction of some consideration of the role of attributions and interpretations in influencing their effects. The role of cognitive factors can then be discussed within the patient's existing model of depression.

For patients who believe strongly that depression is a biological disorder, the inclusion of biology as one of the elements is vital. This enables the therapist to start from an emphasis on persistent biological symptoms and the role these may play in the maintenance of current distress. Moving within the model to consider thoughts about biological symptoms can often be achieved without invalidating the patient's model. The inclusion of biology as one of the elements also allows the therapist to account for the use of prescribed medication as a treatment intervention alongside cognitive therapy. Where patients perceive the benefits of medication to support a biological model, cognitive therapy is not sold as an alternative to medication but as an additional intervention that may lead to further improvements in mood and functioning. Where patients perceive no tangible benefits of medication, the therapist can help them to make comparisons between symptom severity prior to the commencement of antidepressants and current symptom levels. Identifying any improvements, however slight, can help to illustrate the potential role of negative thinking and serve in engaging patients in the cognitive therapy rationale.

In Chapter 3 (page 124), the example was given of *Peter*, who stated during his first assessment that his problems were biological in nature and therefore he did not think cognitive therapy would be of any benefit. Trying to persuade Peter that this was not the case would be likely to result in a polarised position between therapist and patient. Instead the therapist tried to place Peter's beliefs about biological factors in depression within the above model in order to allow for other influences as well. The therapist first agreed with Peter that, given what his psychiatrist and others had told him, biology was very important in the origin of his depression. The therapist then asked Peter what had made him come to the therapy session, to which the reply was that his psychiatrist had recommended cognitive therapy. The therapist summarised that, although Peter did not think that cognitive therapy would help, his faith in his psychiatrist's recommendation put him in two minds. Peter then agreed to the therapist's suggestion to discuss what cognitive therapy involves in order to see whether it might be of any relevance.

The therapist described the model illustrated above, placing initial emphasis on the biological components and biological interventions. When the therapist said that it sounded like the medication had been extremely helpful in improving the symptoms, Peter replied yes and no, that the symptoms tended to wax and wane. Further discussion identified that his symptoms tended to wax and wane in relation to life events, such as his mother dying and his granddaughter being born. Asking Peter how he made sense of this, he reflected that his mother's death had made him dwell on his childhood and how happy he had been then. When he had looked at his state now by comparison, it had made him feel very depressed for a number of months. In contrast, he had cried with happiness when he first saw his new granddaughter, and the hopeful feelings this triggered had led to some symptomatic improvement in his depression. The therapist asked Peter how he made sense of this experience in relation to a biological explanation. To this Peter replied that he still thought the cause was biological. However, when asked 'Is it possible that all these factors—biology, environment, thoughts, feelings and behaviour—together keep the depression going?', Peter replied 'Yes, possibly'. The therapist then proposed an experiment to test out over the next few weeks the idea that the combination of these factors was keeping the depression going. The possibility was stressed that Peter could call it a day after that if he was still of a mind that cognitive therapy would not help. Peter readily agreed to this proposal. This agreement allowed patient and therapist to engage collaboratively in the initial stages of treatment and to develop a preliminary formulation of his problems.

Breaking Down the Problems

Breaking depression down into five components (thoughts, emotion, behaviour, biology/physiology and environment) can help to combat the global, negative processing biases inherent in persistent depression. Patients have often come to identify themselves with their depression and to see depression as a permanent aspect of their constitution. Presenting the model in terms of these five components requires the patient to consider the distinctions between the different aspects of their depression. Making these distinctions can begin to weaken this tendency of patients to identify themselves completely with the depression. This can also constitute the first step towards enabling the patient to see thoughts as thoughts rather than as immutable facts about self, others, world and future.

It is important to give consideration to which aspects of depression are placed in which domain of the vicious circle, as this can influence the clarity of the rationale underpinning socialisation. A problem standardly addressed during socialisation is the lack of distinction often made between thoughts and feelings. Patients and therapists often refer to thoughts as feelings. Patients commonly make statements such as 'I feel a failure' or 'I feel so useless'. For example, *Julie* described a problem of poor concentration that affected her to the extent that she found it difficult to focus on any task. She described her reaction to her concentration difficulties in terms such as 'I feel stupid', which compounded her low mood and led to her either not starting activities or giving up on them very quickly. In socialising her to the cognitive model, it was helpful to view 'I feel stupid' as a thought rather than an emotional state. In this example, the thought that poor concentration is indicative of stupidity ('I am stupid') resulted in a lowering of mood (emotion). Helping Julie to relabel these 'feelings' as thoughts enabled their role in lowering mood to be seen more clearly. Care also needs to be taken over how to categorise cognitive deficits, such as impaired concentration and memory. These symptoms could be placed in the domain of thoughts on the grounds that they are aspects of cognition.

However, in this case one of the goals of the therapist was to help the patient to make sense of the impact of impaired concentration and memory on their mood. It was therefore important to elicit the patient's attributions regarding these concentration and memory deficits. Viewing these as symptoms in the biology domain made it easier to elicit associated automatic thoughts and examine their impact on mood and behaviour.

How the model is communicated to the patient is important. The cognitive deficits often present in chronic depression may mean that patients find it hard to remember what has been discussed. In addition, patients' rigidly held views can result in subsequent distortion of any conclusions. It is advisable to work with the patients to draw out the vicious circle on a piece of paper, which can be given to them to take home. As discussed in Chapter 2, information regarding the model can be supplemented by providing the patients with a handout (see Appendix 2) and an audiotape of the session. Not only does a tape help the patients to remember what has been discussed, it also provides them with an opportunity to make further observations regarding the relevance of the cognitive model to their illness. For example, one patient repeatedly apologised throughout the first assessment session that she was 'not explaining things well' and 'not making sense'. Despite the therapist's assurances that this was not the case the patient remained unconvinced. However, she listened to a tape of the session as part of her homework and at the next session she observed that she had indeed made sense. She then went on to relate this to the vicious circle discussed the previous week stating 'I guess this is an example of my perceptions being biased'.

ILLUSTRATING THE VICIOUS CIRCLE

It is important that the model is not presented in purely generalised and abstract terms, as this may perpetuate the global and overgeneral processing of information characteristic of chronic depression. Once the elements of the model and relationships between them have been described in general, it is essential that they are illustrated using examples relevant to the patient's experience. The standard examples used in cognitive therapy to share the model with the patient (e.g. you are lying in bed at night and you hear a loud noise) may be less useful in chronic depression. Using an example that is not tailored to the patient's current problems gives the patient more opportunity to disengage from the socialisation process, claiming that the example in the metaphor is not relevant to their particular circumstances. It is particularly important to identify specific examples from the patient's recent experiences.

The therapist should work to identify a *specific, recent* example of a distressing time as the basis for illustrating the model. On many occasions, the patient will spontaneously have recounted during assessment a specific low point that can be used as an example. With other patients, a suitable example may have to be elicited by identifying a recent occasion when the patient felt particularly low. When the patient has difficulty with this, it can help to probe for times when they were most bothered by one of their main concerns, whether this is a physical symptom (e.g. fatigue, pain or difficulty concentrating) or external problem (e.g. debts or disagreements with family). To illustrate the vicious circle, the therapist uses a series of linked questions to identify how each of the elements was affected at the specific time and how each factor affected the others in the circle. Some useful questions for eliciting an example and information related to the factors in the model are provided below.

Socratic Questions to Elicit a Vicious Circle

- Can you recall an occasion during the last week when you felt particularly depressed/anxious/guilty?
- Where were you at the time? What were you doing? Who were you with?
- What happened that was so upsetting?
- How did you feel in your body? Did you notice any bodily sensations at the time?
- At what point in the situation did you feel most depressed/anxious/ guilty?
- At the point where you felt most depressed/anxious/guilty what was going through your mind?
- What was it about what happened that made you depressed/anxious/ guilty?
- What did it say about you as a person?
- What is the worst thing you can imagine happening?
- How did you deal with the situation?
- What did you do as a result?

In many cases, gathering a specific, recent example in the course of the initial assessment is easier said than done. Some patients are so overgeneral or unforthcoming that it is impossible to gain sufficient detail regarding a current difficulty to use as an example. In these circumstances, the most powerful example for illustrating the model can be low mood or anxiety evoked in the session itself. If the patient is interpersonally sensitive, the questioning style of cognitive therapy frequently elicits an anxious or even hostile response. This is usually a result of the patient's perception that they don't know the right answer to the questions or fear that they will make a mistake and look foolish. The patient's view that the therapist is judging or criticising them can be related to their discomfort or anxiety in the session. This can provide a productive example of the model, because the emotional immediacy increases the personal relevance of the example. However, if the therapist were then to leave ambiguity about their actual view of the patient's difficulties, this would be likely to be interpreted as endorsing the negative view and could weaken the therapeutic alliance. Therefore, the therapist should be as direct as possible in countering the patient's perception that they have not reacted in the right way or have been judged as foolish. Rather than simply providing reassurance, this can provide a further example to the patient of how a change in their perception can lead to a change in their emotional state. If using the patient's reaction to the therapy session itself seems too threatening, how the patient felt while they were sitting in the waiting room prior to the session can provide a useful alternative.

For example, at her first session *Catherine* had difficulty identifying any particular times when she felt depressed, as she reported feeling similarly depressed the whole time. When the therapist described the cognitive model in general terms, she was sceptical about it applying to her as she reported that she did not have any thoughts. As she was evidently hopeless in the course of this discussion, the therapist decided to use her reaction in the session to illustrate the model. With Catherine's permission, some of the things she said in the course of discussing how she felt in the session were written down on a sheet of paper. In discussing her complaints of fatigue and aching and her worsening feelings of hopelessness during the session, a number of statements were written down. These included 'I don't have any thoughts', 'This therapy will never work for me', 'It's all too hard', 'Nothing I do makes any difference' and 'I'll always be depressed'. When the therapist showed her the list and asked what she made of it, she said with some surprise 'I guess I do think quite negatively, don't I?'. The therapist then wrote the thoughts in on the sheet describing the model and began to examine the relationships between the aspects of the model (see Figure 4.2).

Using Positive Examples to Illustrate the Model

Where a mood *change* that is evident to the patient can be identified, it can be traced to a specific time and linked to the particular thoughts at that time.

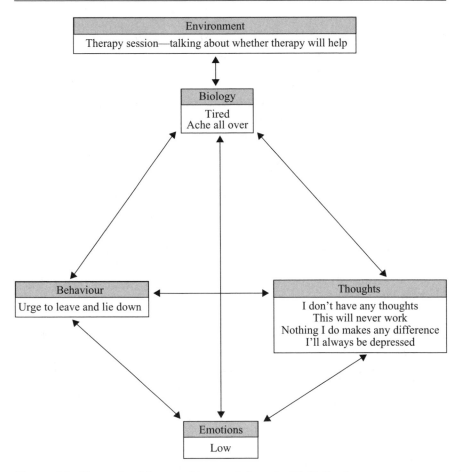

Figure 4.2 Example of the cognitive model used with Catherine

However, many patients with chronic depression describe longstanding and apparently unvarying low mood. This can impede their seeing the relationships between the way they feel and other aspects of the model. Where the patient professes to feel and think the same things all the time, it can be hard for them to see any connection between the thoughts and feelings. In these cases, it can be particularly helpful to contrast recent examples of when them felt or thought differently. If a more positive situation can be identified, this can be of particular benefit in highlighting the relationships between the domains of the model. For example, even when the above model was discussed with *Catherine*, she could not envisage that her feelings could be any different and so could not see any possibility of thinking differently. Somewhat fortuitously, she had mentioned to the therapist that she had recently been to a family party, to which she and her husband had taken some ageing relations. The therapist focused on how she had felt after the party in order to try to elicit some contrast with the model illustrated above. Catherine complained of feeling 'totally shattered' after the party (biology) and of just wanting to go to bed (behaviour). When the therapist asked about her mood and her thoughts, she reported that she had still felt low, but that it was 'a bit different'. On prompting, she said that she had felt somewhat pleased that she had been to the party and reported a thought that 'At least I made it possible for Elsie and Bob to go and they really enjoyed it'. These thoughts and feelings were written on another diagram of the model and contrasted with the previous one. Although she was careful to maintain that she had still felt low, Catherine concluded that her view that she had helped some old people to have a happy time had contributed to her feeling pleased.

The Need for Caution

The danger that some patients may react negatively to a discussion of emotional situations must also be considered. This danger is illustrated by the case of Diane. During the course of assessment, it became apparent that Diane often perceived herself to be a failure. When it came to sharing the model with her, the therapist chose an example where Diane viewed herself as a failure. As the circle was written down, Diane began to cry. When asked what was upsetting her, Diane replied 'It is you talking about these things. I was fine until I came here. If this is what cognitive therapy is about I don't want it.' Diane never attended another session. The therapist had two telephone conversations with Diane's husband (she declined to speak to the therapist) in which he stated that talking to the therapist had upset his wife to such an extent that it had taken her three days to recover and she therefore did not want any further contact. This example shows that the manner in which a patient responds to the sharing of the model will be coloured by their belief system. Many patients do not see their negative thoughts written on the paper; they see 'themselves'. This can escalate feelings of humiliation and hopelessness. In retrospect, it would have been more helpful to choose a more peripheral and specific example that was less strongly related to Diane's core view of herself, perhaps concerning the impairments in daily functioning caused by Diane's depressive symptoms. It is important for the therapist to weigh the likelihood of the example helping the patient to distance themselves from their upsetting thoughts versus their identifying completely with the thoughts discussed in a catastrophic fashion.

FURTHER STEPS IN SOCIALISATION

Processing Biases

For patients who have responded well to the initial presentation of the model, it can be helpful to discuss how their thinking may contribute to the maintenance of their depression in greater detail. Presentation of the model can be expanded to include discussion of mood-dependent processing biases. It can be useful at this point to discuss how depression can bias the interpretation of events or lead to biases in the recall of events. For example, with *Jean* the cognitive model was discussed with reference to a conversation with a friend about how she was going out for the day with another mutual friend. She readily endorsed the idea that her low feelings at this time were related to her thought that 'They don't like me'. The therapist was able to discuss the idea that depression could be biasing the way Jean was interpreting the situation. Further, the idea that depression can bias memory was illustrated by the fact that the event triggered memories of being left out as a child. Elaborating on the model in this way should only be attempted with patients who have readily endorsed the idea that thoughts can contribute to depression. For patients who are not yet ready to assimilate these ideas, further elaborations of the model will seem complicated and confusing.

Double Vicious Circles

Seeing for themselves the role that their thoughts have in maintaining low mood can provide a helpful insight for patients. For many patients, rumination *about* low mood can play a further role in the persistence of low mood. Low mood is initially triggered by a negative response to some particular circumstance, which might be an external event or an internal stimulus or symptom. The occurrence of low mood itself then becomes the focus of attention. Further negative processing about the meaning of low mood then serves to maintain or exacerbate the low mood. The self-perpetuating nature of the cycle set up between low mood and interpretations of low mood can be a factor in explaining how the mood of some patients appears to be divorced from any external trigger. It can be particularly helpful to construct a double vicious circle to illustrate the trap in which patients can find themselves. An illustration of this was provided in discussing the model with *Elizabeth*.

During the assessment session, the therapist noted that Elizabeth frequently berated herself for not doing certain things or for making a mistake. The therapist began to draw this to Elizabeth's attention. Elizabeth subsequently recounted a time when, because she felt tired and lethargic, she decided to buy pizza for the family instead of cooking a meal herself. She saw this as a sign of laziness, and so tried to 'make an effort' by preparing a complicated dessert.

T: Now you say that while making the dessert you missed out an ingredient so the dish didn't turn out as intended?

E: It was a complete disaster. In the past, before any of this happened, I would never have made such a silly mistake.

T: When the dessert went wrong you said you felt really miserable. From what I wrote down, your thoughts went something like this: 'This is pathetic'; 'I'm useless'; 'I never do anything right'; 'I've failed again'. Is that right?

E: (*sighing heavily*) Yes, but its true, I can't do the things I used to be able to do.

T: Then once the dessert had gone wrong you threw it in the bin and then once you had your pizza you went to bed?

E: (*Nods.*)

T: Okay, let's try and add this to our diagram (*shows Elizabeth the diagram in Figure 4.3*).

T: Now one of the things you mentioned is that your mood actually got even worse after that—indeed to such an extent you eventually went to bed at 8.30 p.m.

E: That's right. I felt dreadful.

T: How do you make sense of the fact you felt worse and worse as time progressed?

E: I don't know. It always happens and there is nothing I can do to stop it.

T: Did anything else go wrong that evening?

E: On the contrary. The family came home. They really enjoyed the pizza. They said I deserved a rest. I felt terrible.

T: You said that you recognise as a pattern that once something happens to lower your mood it seems to worsen as time goes on in spite of other things going well?

E: Yes.

T: On Tuesday I wonder—did the dessert going wrong play on your mind?

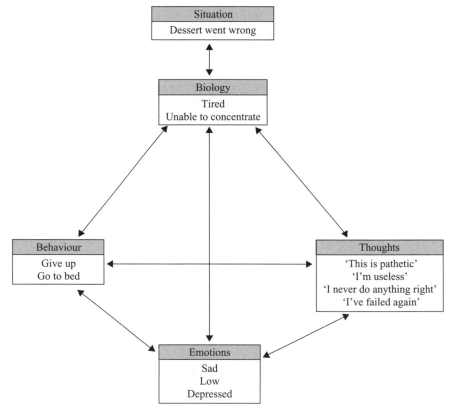

Figure 4.3   Example of the vicious circle used with Elizabeth

E: Definitely. I kept going over in my mind how stupid I was to miss out
   the baking powder. I had wasted all that money buying the ingredients.
   I felt so useless.
T: What is the effect on your mood of going over and over your mistake
   in your mind?
E: I suppose it makes me feel worse.
T: Did that persist the next day?
E: Not as bad, but it was still there, especially when I had to empty the
   bin. This is so trivial isn't it?
T: It doesn't seem to be trivial, it sounds like you were really upset.
E: Yes, but upset over a pudding—now that's pathetic!
T: How are you feeling right now Elizabeth?
E: Annoyed at myself for letting such a small thing get to me.
T: Are those self-critical thoughts resurfacing now?

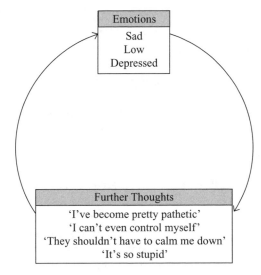

Figure 4.4   Second vicious circle added to Elizabeth's example

E: What do you mean?

T: You seem to be thinking that it was a small or trivial thing to get upset about and that that is pathetic, which makes you annoyed at yourself. Did you get annoyed at yourself on Tuesday for getting upset?

E: Well, I have become pretty pathetic, haven't I?

T: When you think that—that you've become pretty pathetic for being upset—how does it make you feel?

E: It gets even worse doesn't it? I can't even control myself.

T: Let's try and draw another circle (*together Elizabeth and therapist add a further vicious circle to the diagram, see Figure 4.4*)

T: So when you get upset...you think 'I've become pretty pathetic' and 'I can't even control myself'. How do those thoughts affect how you feel?

E: Hmmm. Well, I guess they make me feel even worse.

T: Does it explain why you don't feel any better when your family are kind to you?

E: I just think I should never have got so upset.

T: So even when they are nice to you, you're still thinking that you're pathetic?

E: Yes, they shouldn't have to calm me down about something like making a pudding.

T: It looks like your thoughts about being upset are quite important. (*pointing to diagram*) What do you make of this?

E: I'm just so annoyed with myself for getting so upset—it's so stupid.

T: And what effect does it have on your mood thinking like that?

E: Oh . . . It looks as though thinking I shouldn't be upset is making me worse.

T: Right. So as well as looking at how you criticise yourself for making mistakes, we may also need to look at how you criticise yourself for being upset.

Distinguishing the Person from their Depression

Patients who experience chronic depression often have difficulty distinguishing between their sense of self and depression as an illness. It is not uncommon for the depressed patient to describe having forgotten what they were like as a person prior to the onset of their illness. Some individuals perceive that they have undergone a complete change of personality or that they have become the illness. Relatives and friends of the patient can reinforce this kind of observation. For example, at the first session, *Peter's* wife confided in the therapist that she saw her husband as 'a shadow of his former self'. When asked what changes she had observed she stated with great sadness: 'He used to be lively and sociable, always on the go. Now he is tearful, withdrawn, hardly goes out and doesn't really talk—he is not the man I married.' When patients or their relatives make characterological attributions for the symptoms of depression, it can feed the low self-esteem, helplessness and hopelessness the patient experiences.

Using the model to break down the depression into its different aspects can help to weaken the patient's identification with the depression (see page 142). The therapist can also try more explicitly to help the patient to separate their personality from depression as an illness. As well as being to the patient's benefit, this can help to maintain the therapist's motivation. When socialising the patient into the cognitive model proves difficult, the therapist's automatic thoughts may include: 'she is determined nothing will work', 'he doesn't want to get better', or 'she is being obstructive on purpose'. However, much of the patient's seeming reluctance to engage in cognitive therapy may be explained by the symptoms of the illness itself. The therapist needs to be on guard not to label what may be symptomatic of illness—for example, hopelessness and passivity—as characteristic personality traits. The processing deficits characteristic of chronic depression, such as poor concentration, overgenerality and the difficulties patients have in generalising skills, may all limit the patient's ability to grasp the cognitive model. As these genuine deficits can at times make therapy painstaking, it is important for the therapist to recognise the detrimental influence that these processing deficits can exert over the completion of tasks in therapy and everyday life.

It is helpful for the therapist to acknowledge the difficulties (e.g. hopelessness, poor concentration or lack of energy) the patient has when confronted with a particular task. The patient's tendency to attribute their difficulties to the kind of person they are can then be contrasted with attributing the difficulties to the illness (i.e. seeing the difficulties as symptoms). This technique was used later on in the session with *Elizabeth* described above.

T: If we go back to the example on Tuesday, how do you explain to yourself that the dessert went wrong?

E: Well I didn't take enough care. I should have tried harder.

T: Are there any mitigating circumstances?

E: Like what?

T: Well you said to me that you would not have made the same mistake before you became depressed. Have I got that right?

E: No, I wouldn't.

T: So let's add those two pieces of information together. The dessert went wrong but this is less likely to have happened prior to you becoming depressed. Indeed you say yourself you are a pretty good cook. So what has changed since you became depressed that makes the task of making the dessert more difficult?

E: Well I can't concentrate and I felt so tired. My thinking gets muddled.

T: Right. So if we return to our vicious circle (*pointing to biological component of vicious circle*) what made the task more difficult on Tuesday, the poor concentration, tiredness and muddled thinking which are symptoms of depression or as you state your view that you don't try hard enough and are useless?

E: Well, seeing it written down like that I guess the symptoms play a part. But you know I spend a lot of time thinking I'm not really depressed, that I've just got lazy. Are you telling me these symptoms are real?

T: Most of the people I see describe these types of symptoms.

E: I see.

T: Elizabeth, don't just take my word for it—how about if we try an experiment? How often in the course of a day would poor concentration, tiredness and muddled thinking be particularly problematic when trying to complete a task?

E: At least once or twice a day, sometimes more.

T: Okay, how about if between now and next time we meet you try and collect one example of a time when your poor concentration, tiredness and muddled thinking is particularly noticeable and try and pay attention to how this affects your thoughts, feelings and behaviour. (*The therapist points to each aspect of the vicious circle.*) It may help to try and write it down.

E: I'll try.

Acknowledging Losses

Patients who have been depressed for many months or even years can sometimes be helped in this way to see their difficulties as part of a depressed state rather than inherent to their character. This can raise a fresh difficulty: seeing the depression as potentially treatable can make the suffering that has been endured seem unnecessary. In addition to the obvious external losses the patient may have suffered due to the depression, they have lost months or years of productive or satisfying time to the depression. One patient observed, 'But if I can do something about this depression, it means I've lost the best years of my life for nothing'. Seeing the depression as inevitable, as many persistently depressed patients do, can help them to accept these losses. Coming to see the depression as potentially treatable reminds some patients in a painful fashion of what they have lost. Where this occurs, it is important for the therapist to acknowledge the losses perceived by the patient, including external losses and loss of time. Facilitating some emotional experience associated with this loss can help to consolidate the shift in perspective from seeing the depression as an inevitable consequence of being made that way to seeing it as a potentially changeable state.

DISCUSSING UNDERLYING BELIEFS IN THE EARLY STAGES OF THERAPY

In persistent depression, the patient's underlying beliefs may affect the process of therapy from its earliest stages. The rigid and negative nature of underlying beliefs can hinder engagement in therapy through the processes of avoidance and through undermining acceptance of the cognitive model. It is therefore important that socialisation into the cognitive model includes discussion of the possible existence of longstanding beliefs. This can help to minimise the detrimental influence of those beliefs on the task of engaging the patient. However, as discussed in Chapter 2 (page 91), in the early stages of therapy, the therapist's aim is not to modify the underlying beliefs directly. Questioning core beliefs before the patient has been engaged in therapy or has acquired any skills in tackling more peripheral thoughts can be excessively distressing or unproductive. Identification and modification of beliefs is postponed until a solid working alliance has been established and the patient has some experience of using standard cognitive techniques on more peripheral thoughts. (The benefits of working on automatic thoughts prior to beliefs are discussed in more detail in Chapter 6, page 203.) At this early stage, the nature and effects of beliefs are acknowledged and described in general terms.

Acknowledging the possible existence of underlying beliefs at an early stage of therapy can help patients to make sense of longstanding problems, as well as limiting the adverse effects of those beliefs on engagement. It is helpful to raise the possibility that the patient may be affected by certain patterns of thinking and behaving which are longstanding, but which may be amenable to change. Once a problem list has been elicited in the assessment, summarising the problems back to the patient can provide an opportunity to find out if the patient is able to see any common themes or mechanisms underlying their problems. Asking questions such as 'Seeing all the problems listed together like this, do they seem to have anything in common?' can be useful to help the patient to identify any overall patterns. During the assessment, the therapist will have taken some interest in the patient's history. This can be used to give some idea of how earlier experiences may be influencing the patient's pattern of thinking in their current situation. In using this information, the goal is not to identify the conditional and unconditional beliefs with firm precision. Rather, it is to illustrate the idea that certain fixed patterns of thinking resulting from early experiences may be shaping current experiences.

Explaining the Concept of Schemas

It can be helpful to explain the concept of schemas using a non-emotive example, such as an everyday object. For example, patients can be asked how they knew what to sit on when they entered the room to illustrate how, through experience of many different chairs, people acquire a general idea of what a chair is. They can identify many varied objects as chairs, even if they have not seen that kind of chair before, and when they think about chairs, their various characteristics are automatically brought to mind, such as legs and a seat. Once the patient agrees that they have a concept of what a chair is, it can then be suggested that through their experiences people develop a general idea about themselves, other people, relationships and the outside world. This also automatically includes various characteristics, so just as a chair is expected to have legs, depressed people define themselves in terms of negative attributes. Some people with depression may see failure and worthlessness as being as much a fact about or part of themselves as a seat is a definitive feature of a chair.

Relating Difficulties to Long-Term Patterns

Sometimes patients with persistent depression spontaneously use global negative terms, such as uselessness, to describe themselves or other people. Even though these terms may not precisely describe the patient's actual unconditional beliefs, it can be helpful to adopt them in explaining the idea of long-held, general patterns of negative thinking. Where the patient rarely uses negative labels about themselves, this can be a result of cognitive avoidance, and for such patients, it can be excessively challenging at this stage of therapy for the therapist to confront the patient with their guesses on the precise nature of the core beliefs. It can be helpful here to use terms such as self-confidence, self-image or self-esteem, which refer in vague, general terms to the person's overall view of themselves. Most chronically depressed patients readily endorse the idea that they are suffering from low self-esteem or have little self-confidence. These concepts can be used to tie together the influence of early experiences with patterns in current thinking processes and emotional states. For example, much information was gathered in the assessment with *Elizabeth* about the high standards and constant criticism to which her mother subjected her when she was a child. Having discussed the role of her negative thinking in the cognitive model, she found it helpful to consider that this could be a reflection of longstanding low self-esteem. The idea was floated that, through adopting her mother's tendency to criticise her, she constantly formed a low view of herself. Although her unconditional beliefs were not identified precisely or questioned at this point in therapy, the acknowledgement of their influence helped to engage Elizabeth in the possibility of taking a new perspective on her thoughts about herself.

Helping the patient to consider the possibility that some of their problems may result from longer-term influences of beliefs or low self-esteem can help to limit the potential for these beliefs to have adverse effects on therapy. The therapist can explain that these effects can include emotional sensitivities, for example being highly sensitive to signs of rejection or criticism, or behavioural reactions, such as giving up on things before they have been given a fair trial. The patient can be asked if this has applied to any of their reactions to therapy so far and can be encouraged to see if any subsequent difficulties with therapy might be of this nature. For example, Elizabeth acknowledged with some reluctance that she had felt quite daunted at times during the discussion of the cognitive model and therapy. She wondered if perhaps she was 'not up to being able to do the therapy properly'. At the therapist's prompting, she could relate this to the previous discussion about her low opinion of herself. Understanding her reservations in this way led to some sense of relief, in that she acknowledged that low self-esteem would not necessarily rule someone out of being suitable for therapy. Predicting adverse reactions can help to convey the idea that they are understandable consequences of the beliefs that are a familiar target for therapy. This can help to mitigate some of their more counterproductive effects, such as hostility towards the therapist or premature termination of therapy.

KEY TARGETS IN PERSISTENT DEPRESSION

Once the initial assessment is complete and the process of socialisation has begun, suitable goals for therapy need to be adopted. Before the therapy goals are discussed and agreed collaboratively with the patient, the therapist needs to consider the targets that are most likely to be of benefit. In previous chapters, we have described how low self-esteem, helplessness and hopelessness are key psychological features in the presentation of chronic depression. It is important that the goals of therapy address this chronic cognitive triad. In acute depression, questioning the negative thoughts that arise in relation to particular circumstances often leads to significant improvement in how the patient thinks and feels about themselves, their life and the future. In chronic depression, low self-esteem, helplessness and hopelessness tend to be more generalised and enduring, and simply questioning thoughts related to the chronic triad often results in only minimal improvements. Addressing the chronic cognitive triad demands an integrated therapeutic strategy that takes account of the various factors that maintain it. Considering the different factors contributing to the chronic triad enables the setting of goals for therapy that will systematically undermine low self-esteem, helplessness and hopelessness.

Addressing the Chronic Cognitive Triad

In the cognitive model of chronic depression, low self-esteem, helplessness and hopelessness are reflected at a number of different levels. The chronic cognitive triad is manifest in the patient's global negative thinking, but originates in underlying negative beliefs, is maintained by passivity and avoidance, and becomes entrenched by repeated confirmatory experiences. Eroding the chronic triad in therapy is achieved through addressing these different levels. Thus, the aims of the therapist include not only reducing symptoms, but also combating avoidance and addressing conditional and unconditional beliefs. Helping the patient to engage more fully in activities in their daily life is often central to these aims. Engaging in activities will entail the development of tolerance of emotions and of skills in managing painful emotions. Such engagement then enables negative beliefs to be put to the test and raises the possibility that they may be applied with less rigidity to current experiences.

It is important that the goals of therapy act as guides to foster the engagement of the patient behaviourally in activities and relationships and cognitively in the processing of experiences. Setting useful goals for therapy involves identifying specific activities in which the patient wishes to engage. To achieve the collaboration of the patient with the general aims of therapy, it is vital that these therapy goals are grounded in specific life changes that the patient would like to see. Making progress towards these goals can then be used as a vehicle for combating avoidance, regulating affect and testing out negative beliefs. As these factors are crucial in maintaining the chronic triad, adopting appropriate goals for treatment can specify the means by which low self-esteem, helplessness and hopelessness may simultaneously be relieved.

When setting specific goals, it is important to take account of the longstanding nature of the avoidance and beliefs. Building self-esteem or a view that activities in life can be effective and worthwhile is a long-term venture. Within the short time frame of therapy, the therapy goals constitute the first steps towards these longer-term goals of improving self-esteem and seeing life as worthwhile. It is important that the agreed goals of therapy represent markers of observable progress towards these overall goals. It can be helpful to point out to the patient that taking even these small steps can entail coming to new ways of understanding problems and developing new skills for addressing them. If therapy can equip the patient with a better understanding of their problems and new skills, these can be used in the future to continue to build a greater sense of self-esteem or worth.

SETTING GOALS FOR THERAPY

The therapist's high level aim in the therapy is to tackle the persistent symptoms of depression and the chronic cognitive triad. The overall strategy to be employed is to help the patient to engage in, rather than avoid, activities and relationships, and thereby to help the patient to test out new ways of thinking. In working with each patient, these overall aims and strategies need to be translated into specific individual goals for therapy. To facilitate the engagement of patients in therapy, it is vital that they are involved in the process of generating goals and endorse the goals adopted for therapy. However, the fact that patients believe themselves to be inherently defective and incapable of attaining any worthwhile outcomes and believe that nothing can improve interferes with their being able to specify how they would like things to be different. The chronic triad can thus interfere with the ability of the patient to set goals. Thus, the therapist must work with the patient to help them to set suitable goals and the goals for therapy must be discussed and agreed collaboratively.

The Importance of Collaboration

The process of collaboratively setting explicit goals for therapy has a number of benefits. In view of their urge to avoid negative thoughts and feelings, patients with chronic depression often find it less uncomfortable to discuss positive goals than to engage in many of the other aspects of therapy. Given the reluctance of many patients with persistent depression to engage in therapy, mutually agreeing goals for treatment can help to begin to establish a sense of collaboration between therapist and patient. Having an explicit idea of treatment goals can thus strengthen the patient's fragile motivation for addressing their difficulties through therapy. The goals that have been agreed can then provide a guide for selecting and prioritising the specific issues to be addressed. Particularly where patients are prone to avoid certain issues, relating the progress of therapy back to explicitly agreed goals can prove essential to maintaining collaboration throughout treatment. Importantly, setting goals with the patient can be an effective intervention in itself. In the face of often entrenched negativity and hopelessness, attempting to agree goals with the patient entails their thinking of desired possibilities and beginning to assess how realistic these are. Although most patients remain extremely doubtful that they will attain any of their goals, establishing specific goals can sow seeds of doubt in their conviction that they will not get anywhere. The process may thus begin to erode a previously firm sense of hopelessness.

In acute depression, patients often readily identify goals they wish to pursue. These often relate to restoring a previously satisfactory level of functioning. Because that state was only recently lost, there is usually minimal difficulty in helping the patient to identify personal goals related to the restoration of mood and of social and occupational functioning. In chronic depression, the patient may have little or no memory of times when they functioned at a satisfactory level, or their memory of such times may have become idealised or distorted. The goals adopted usually involve trying to specify some desired ways of functioning that are new to them. Specifying goals that both therapist and patient can see as desirable and realistic can thus involve considerable effort.

General Procedure for Setting Goals

Discussion of goals for therapy usually flows most sensibly from the discussion of a patient's overall problem list. There is rarely time within the first therapy session to elicit problems, present the cognitive model and agree treatment goals. The latter is therefore usually left until the second session. However, if a problem list has been established during the first session, asking the patient to make a short list of goals they would like to work towards in the course of treatment can be a useful homework assignment after the first session. This can involve the patient in the process of therapy from an early stage and helps to establish the patient's participation. Any ideas of goals that the patient identifies as homework can form the basis for negotiating specific treatment targets at the following session. Before discussing the goals of therapy, it is helpful for the therapist to summarise the patient's problem list, including the situational, interpersonal and intrapersonal problems identified in the first assessment session. By doing this, the therapist can ascertain that the problem list is accurate and that nothing has been left out.

Once the problems have been summarised accurately, the therapist can elicit goals for the therapy. Questions such as 'In what ways would you like things to be different?' are useful initial prompts. Because of the difficulties that many of these patients have in accessing specific positive information, it is usually helpful to follow up such questions in a more specific way. The therapist can help the patient to build a more specific picture of what their life would be like in, for example, six months' time if therapy had been successful. A more directive prompt can be helpful, such as 'To help us think what would be the most helpful goals for the therapy, I would like you to think forward to the end of the therapy. Let's suppose that the therapy had worked as well as you could imagine and that things had improved for you as much as they could in six months' time. What would be different for you then?'. Other useful questions for eliciting goals are suggested below.

Questions for Eliciting Goals for Therapy

- What goals would you like to work towards in treatment?
- In what ways would you like things to be different?
- What would you most like to change about your current circumstances?
- What things have you stopped doing since you became depressed which you would like to resume?
- Are there any things you have started doing since you became depressed which you would like to change?
- What would you be doing differently if you were not depressed?

SETTING GOALS TO ADDRESS KEY PROBLEMS

As described above, it is important that goals for therapy are adopted that will entail the reduction of low self-esteem, helplessness and hopelessness. This involves helping the patients to identify how they could engage behaviourally, cognitively and emotionally in desired situations and activities. Considering the problems identified in a patient's problem list can lead to the generation of suitable, specific goals. Goals related to key problem areas of symptoms, situations, interpersonal problems and intrapersonal problems can then be identified.

Goals Related to Symptoms

Reflecting their helpless outlook, patients with chronic depression often see their depression as arising from factors beyond their control. They frequently fail to set goals of reducing certain symptoms because, from their perspective, the depressive symptoms are intractable. In some cases, symptom reduction may seem quite feasible to the therapist who may need to be active in suggesting possible goals. For example, on summarising *Julie's* current problems, the therapist noted that her poor concentration was preventing her engaging in many day-to-day activities. When the therapist asked if she would like help with improving her concentration so that she could get back to some of her previous activities, Julie replied: 'Is that possible? I thought nothing could be done about it and I just had to live with it.' Prioritising this as the first target for change proved crucial in engaging Julie in treatment, especially as she could see that her concentration levels had improved significantly after a few therapy sessions.

Where symptoms are greatly impairing day-to-day functioning, goals of therapy may focus on accomplishment of small activities of daily living. For example, *Marion's* lack of motivation and cognitive impairment were such that on most days she had difficulty even getting dressed. She saw no point in trying any of the strategies of cognitive therapy because she believed that nothing was going to eradicate her depression. In order to reduce the impact of such entrenched pessimism, short-term goals were discussed to help Marion to focus in the here and now and minimise her opportunity to predict weeks, months or even years ahead. One of her agreed therapy goals was thus to plan the day one hour at a time and to include activities such as washing, dressing and cooking. With Marion, given the lack of lasting benefits from previous interventions, it was important to strike a balance between sufficient optimism that some changes could be made and making unrealistic claims regarding what cognitive therapy could achieve.

Patients who subscribe to a biological view of depression may set a goal of feeling less depressed but have no belief that therapy could help them to achieve this goal. For them, only some kind of biological intervention seems to offer any promise of improvement. In cases like this, finding out what a general goal, such as feeling less depressed, means in more specific behavioural terms is particularly important. It can help to ask the patient what they would do if they did feel better. Specific targets, such as social (e.g. 'I would be able to call some of my old friends') or leisure activities (e.g. 'I would do some of the things I used to enjoy, like knitting'), can then be elicited. Again, the important task is to define specific reference points that are apparent to patient and therapist.

Goals Related to Situational Problems

Some patients attribute their depression entirely to external situations. Where patients see their problems exclusively in terms of external causes, they often put forward goals that are outside the scope of therapy. However, even where external situations are identified as the major problem, goals related to the chronic triad can be identified. For example, Reg, a middle-aged man whose depression was precipitated by having been made redundant, proposed that the goal of therapy should be for him to be working again. Clearly, it was beyond the remit of the therapist to fix up a suitable job. Where the patient proposes goals that depend on some external circumstance coming about, they can be prompted to consider goals related to how they could make the desired situation more likely to occur. With Reg, the therapist focused on the internal changes that he might make to improve his chance of getting back to work. The therapist asked: 'Even if you hadn't got a job, what would be a sign that you had made any progress in that area?' Reg replied that he would be reading things to update himself about issues relevant to his work and would be filling out application forms. The therapist then asked what signs would indicate to Reg that he was more ready in himself to go back to work, to which Reg replied that he would have the self-confidence to attend interviews. Generating these more appropriate internal goals helped Reg to acknowledge the possibility that therapy might be relevant to his depression. Standard prompts that are useful in generating goals relevant to external situations, such as getting a job or a partner, are 'What would have to happen inside you for you to stand more of a chance of getting that?' or 'How would you have to think or act differently for that to come about?'.

It can be particularly difficult to set relevant goals where satisfaction and self-esteem have previously been derived entirely from a situation that is no longer available. This is most commonly encountered in patients whose esteem has been largely derived from working or from caring for children who have now grown up and left home. Patients like *Peter*, whose only measure of worth was work, often hold on to a cherished ideal of returning to full-time work and see this as the only worthwhile goal of therapy. Early in treatment, such patients may discount the relevance of other potential sources of self-esteem. Therefore, the early goals of treatment that involve re-engaging in activities of daily living have to be couched as a step towards returning to work. Only once Peter had engaged more fully with treatment were goals established to help him to try to develop a sense of worth in other areas. These included engaging in activities that he had previously put second to work, such as contact with his granddaughter, social activities with his wife and trying to develop hobbies for pleasure in itself.

Low self-esteem, helplessness and hopelessness can result from patients having an exaggerated sense of responsibility for external problems over which, in reality, they can exert little influence. This can result in inappropriate self-blame and excessive guilt. In this case, therapy goals may involve learning to recognise and reassess self-blame. Where the sense of responsibility results in the patient making extreme efforts to sort the problems out, goals related to letting things take their course or allowing other people to sort out some problems are appropriate.

Goals Related to Interpersonal Problems

Low self-esteem, helplessness and hopelessness are frequently associated with the avoidance of particular social interactions or relationships. The therapy goals can usefully specify the kinds of interactions in which the patient would wish to engage. Identifying particular activities that are avoided can lead straight to relevant goals. For example, *Elizabeth* repeatedly avoided putting herself forward for promotion at work, despite being asked by her boss to apply. As she also had some minor financial difficulties that a promotion would help her to solve, being able to apply for promotion was established as a goal of treatment. It is important to establish goals related to avoidance that are realistic in the time frame of therapy. For example, it is unlikely that someone who has avoided the company of the opposite sex over their whole adult life will have started an intimate relationship by the end of a typical course of therapy. Although being in an intimate relationship may be a valuable long-term goal, it is essential that the therapy goals include more realistic subgoals, such as talking to members of the opposite sex at work or at parties.

Other interpersonal problems relate to the nature of the patient's relationships, rather than social avoidance. For example, *Jean* seemed stoically to accept perpetually being overwhelmed by other people's difficulties, as she believed that her role was to meet the needs of others before her own. She was also in a relationship with a man who was at best unsupportive. It was tempting for the therapist to encourage her to set goals aimed at putting her own needs first and disengaging from physically and emotionally abusive relationships. Although these seemed worthy goals, for Jean any previous attempts to free herself from the demands of others had resulted only in criticism and humiliation. In setting goals to combat this kind of problem, developing new activities and relationships outside the existing social network can help to balance the patient's interactions with critical and demeaning others. The experience of interactions that involve support and reciprocity can help to build self-esteem and decrease helplessness. Goals may therefore relate to means of eliciting support, as well as decreasing the sense of responsibility. For Jean, two important goals on her list were:

- To find out about parent support groups at the local community centre
- To recognise when others are making an unreasonable request of me and on some occasions say no.

Goals Related to Intrapersonal Problems

Intrapersonal problems, such as self-criticism, oversensitivity to criticism or low self-worth, can also be translated into useful goals for therapy. For example, *Elizabeth* was always very critical of her perceived mistakes and short-comings, which often lowered her mood considerably. Thus, one of her goals for treatment was to be more tolerant of making mistakes and less harsh with herself when things didn't go as she had planned. In contrast, *Kate* often found herself enraged or distraught when she thought she had been criticised by others, as she saw any criticism as a personal attack on her. When the cognitive model was presented to her, some progress was made in understanding how thoughts and beliefs may have been feeding her explosions of negative feelings. From this, a goal of aiming to understand her sensitivity to any implied criticism and to react in a more balanced way was collaboratively identified. One marker of this was defined as sometimes being able to stay in the situation to find out what degree of criticism was intended.

Many individuals with low self-esteem or little sense of self-worth have a very limited sense of their own wants and needs. This can interfere with their proposing or endorsing appropriate goals for therapy. This is common in patients whose self-esteem has from childhood been built upon meeting the needs of others or who have no intrinsic sense of worth or value. Goals can be agreed that help the person to identify more clearly their own wishes or preferences and then sometimes to act in accordance with those wishes. Elizabeth was always overburdened by attending to the needs and demands of others. One manifestation of this was that she home-cooked every meal for her family from scratch. For her, a goal of sometimes doing what she wanted was linked to sometimes getting a takeaway, rather than doing the cooking herself. As she had little idea which sort of takeaway food she liked, the chance to identify and act on her preference made this goal particularly relevant.

REFINING THE GOALS OF THERAPY

The Importance of Specificity

Goals for addressing the chronic triad in therapy should be realistic and achievable within the scope of therapy. They should be stated in terms that are as specific and concrete as possible, so that both therapist and patient can see when progress towards the goal has been achieved. In setting goals with patients with chronic depression, those initially elicited are frequently idealistic or have no concrete reference points by which to judge any progress. For example, general goals of 'feeling better' or 'having higher self-esteem' are insufficiently elaborated to be helpful in guiding the therapy. Such general goals need to be specified with greater precision. Where a patient's goal is 'to feel better', the therapist needs to ask questions to ascertain what would constitute concrete markers of success. If the patient describes their goal in terms of 'stopping feeling depressed', the therapist might gently point out that aiming never to feel low again would not be realistic. When a more feasible overall goal of feeling less depressed has been articulated, the next step is to define how the patient would know if that had occurred. Sometimes it is possible for the patient to estimate how much of the time or to what extent they are depressed using a percent scale, and then to ask what would constitute a significant reduction. For many patients, however, it is more meaningful or motivating to define the goals in more positive terms. Rather than having a goal of feeling depressed only half the time, for example, it can be more helpful to set goals such as 'to have any time when I could simply enjoy something without feeling the depression hanging over me' or 'to have a day without any suicidal thoughts'.

Setting specific goals for therapy proved useful in the case of Pauline, who insisted that she was not depressed but was suffering a stress reaction due to overwork. Her initial response to questions about how she would like things to be different was:

P: To have less to do, so I wouldn't be so stressed.

T: (smiling ruefully) Much as I would like to, I'm afraid I can't just say you don't have to do lots of the things you have to do. But I wonder, what would it be like for you to have less to do?

P: It's just not likely. There's just so much I've got to do.

T: Right . . . so what would be any sign of being less stressed by all that?

P: If I could just leave work at work sometimes and not take it home. I wouldn't have to keep thinking about it.

T: What would have to happen for you to be able to do that?

P: Someone said to me recently that I ought to lower my standards. (aghast) You're not going to suggest I do that, are you?

T: Are there any things you could leave without lowering your standards?

P: Well, I guess if I have a list of phone calls to make, there are usually some that I could really leave until the next day.

T: So, leaving some of the less vital phone calls until the next day. That sounds a good goal. Are there any other things you could leave so you could just go home?

P: There are some things I could delegate a bit more.

T: You said before that that often results in more work for you because you have to ensure that your colleagues have done things properly. It sounds like a lot of work to go over the things your colleagues have done. Is there anything you could do differently so that you really did end up with less work?

P: I suppose I would just have to leave them to it.

T: Would that actually be a new thing for you then?

P: Well, as head of the department, it's always been down to me to make sure that the work we do is up to the right standard.

T: So what would your new goal be then?

P: Ermm ... I'll just have to hope everything doesn't get done in too slap-dash a way.

T: So am I right thinking that it would be quite a new approach for you to give things to other people to do and let them get on with it without checking the standard of their work as they go?

P: Yes ... sounds a bit ... Hmmm (*looking doubtful*)!

T: Well, if you could do that at all, would that be a good goal for the therapy?

P: If people did the work properly, it would be quite a relief.

T: So, so far we have got two goals—to leave some phone calls until the next day and to leave some of the people in the office to do the things you ask them to. That would mean coming to terms with your worry that they might not do things to the right standard. Is that right? Are there any other things that you would like to be different?

Subsequent discussion focused on what Pauline would do if she were not so overworked. She recognised that she had little time for any interests of her own or for a personal life. Exploration of what interests or friendships she might pursue resulted in her becoming unsure about what things she was really interested in. A goal of therapy was therefore defined as trying some activities outside of work to see which would result in any interest or satisfaction. Pauline agreed to start with getting reacquainted with what was going on in the world of films and cinema, as this was something she had previously enjoyed.

Setting Priorities

Once some suitable goals for therapy have been identified, the order in which to address them can be discussed. Setting the priorities for therapy involves assessing not only the importance of each goal to the patient but also the ease with which it might be achieved. Some problems are more readily tackled than others and patients are more likely to be motivated by therapy if they experience progress early in treatment. With this in mind, it may be that the patient's most pressing problem is not the one that is tackled first. It is best to explain that while a particular problem may be causing the patient a good deal of distress, this may not be the easiest to address first. This was the case for *Julie*, who cited as her biggest problem her difficult relationship with her husband whom she described as 'critical and controlling'. An associated goal of asserting herself, which included sometimes saying what she wanted to do, was identified, but the therapist felt that this would not be an area where it would be easy to effect change. After some negotiation, it was agreed that the first goal to be addressed would be to try to improve Julie's poor concentration on reading and daily activities, followed by resuming some social activities with her friends. Indeed, progress towards these goals provided an important foundation for working on her difficult relationship with her husband.

To help with this prioritisation, it is often useful to break goals down into short term, medium term and long term. Suggested time frames would be:

Short term: the next 2–6 weeks
Medium term: the next 2–6 months
Long term: the next 9–24 months.

This can help patient and therapist to set a realistic time frame in which the patient can address their goals. As discussed above (page 164), it is an important goal for some patients to establish a romantic relationship. This was true of one young woman, Emma, who had never had such a relationship. As she could not see this coming about for many months, if ever, it could be seen to be a long-term goal beyond the remit of therapy. However, it provided a good starting point for negotiating short- and medium-term goals that could help her to work towards this, such as socialising more with men in general and discussing men more with her female friends.

For *Elizabeth*, the first problem to be tackled was poor concentration and excessive tiredness, which was interfering with her ability to mix socially or engage in activities because everything was too much effort. Some of the short-term, medium-term and long-term goals that were agreed in relation to these problems are illustrated below:

Short term

• To improve concentration span from 20 minutes to 30 minutes
• To re-establish a routine for household tasks and work at the office.

Medium term

• To resume embroidery
• To resume attending the Mother's Union once per month
• To be more tolerant of mistakes and less harsh when things don't go according to plan.

Long term

- To resume attending church every week
- To place less demands on myself and on some occasions put my needs first
- To go on holiday in Britain with my husband.

Once goals for the therapy have been identified, it is helpful to go back over the patient's problem list to see if the stated goals adequately address the problems. It is also important for the therapist to consider whether progress towards the goals that have been agreed for therapy would result in the desired improvements in self-esteem, helplessness and hopelessness. If this is not clearly the case, then the goals will have to be revisited as therapy progresses.

Setting clear and specific goals that are grounded in specific changes in thinking and behaviour can reinforce the process of socialising the patient to the cognitive model. This process also acts as a further model of the collaborative nature of therapy, with the therapist acting as a guide to help the patient to see the adverse effects of setting unrealistic or inappropriate goals and helping to amend them accordingly. Socialisation and goal setting can thus increase the patient's motivation for engaging in the use of cognitive and behavioural strategies to address their symptoms and problems.

SUMMARY POINTS

- Negative reactions of patients with persistent depression to simple presentation of the cognitive model can range from disagreement to outrage.
- Including a role for biology and environment in the model presented can help to encompass patients' views that might otherwise conflict with the cognitive model.
- The cognitive model should be illustrated using specific, recent examples from the patient's experience.
- Examples from during the therapy session or of moments of relief from the depression can be useful in illustrating the model where there is difficulty in identifying specific downturns in mood.
- The therapist should be on the alert for the patient's negative thoughts about low mood itself, which often feed into a double vicious circle.
- Helping the patient to distinguish different aspects of depression can help to weaken their global identification of themselves with the depression.

- Early in therapy, it is helpful to describe the possible existence and effects of negative beliefs, and to relate these to any longstanding patterns in the patient's problems.
- Setting specific goals that entail engagement in pursuing desired outcomes is an important first step in helping the patient to counter avoidance.
- The goals of therapy should be such that any progress towards them results in improvements in self-esteem, helplessness and hopelessness.

Chapter 5

USING STANDARD BEHAVIOURAL TECHNIQUES

In this chapter, you will find an account of:

- The use of common behavioural techniques in cognitive therapy for depression
- The benefits to be sought from using these techniques in persistent depression
- Common problems encountered in helping patients to monitor their activities
- Common problems encountered in helping patients to schedule satisfying activities
- Suggested ways to progress in therapy when each kind of difficulty is encountered

Helping patients to regain some satisfaction from activities in their lives is an important aim of cognitive therapy for depression. Cognitive therapy for acute depression (Beck et al., 1979) incorporates a range of behavioural techniques that are used to help patients to re-engage in satisfying activities. Many of these were adapted from more exclusively behavioural approaches to depression (e.g. Lewinsohn, 1974). Behavioural techniques such as monitoring activities, scheduling activities and graded assignment of tasks have come to be seen as standard approaches in cognitive therapy for depression. As we have described, the presentation of patients with persistent depression can be markedly different from that of patients with more acute depression. The implementation of behavioural techniques therefore needs to be adapted to take account of these differences. In this chapter, we review some of the standard behavioural techniques used in cognitive therapy for depression and the rationale underlying their use. We then consider each of the main standard techniques and identify some of the most common problems that are encountered when trying to use them with persistently depressed patients. In each case, we suggest ways of maintaining some benefit from the use of these strategies.

Many of the difficulties in trying to implement behavioural techniques in chronic depression reflect the influence of the chronic cognitive triad of low self-esteem, helplessness and hopelessness. This triad in turn arises from rigid underlying beliefs and longstanding patterns of avoidance. Behavioural changes may thus be extremely hard to institute in therapy. Even when patients do manage to change their behaviour in ways that may be thought to be beneficial, the degree of symptom relief obtained may be limited. Therefore, as well as aiming for symptom reduction, the use of behavioural techniques in chronic depression is undertaken with broader aims. These include helping patients to recognise when and how they are avoiding things, to assess the effects of avoiding and gradually to consider the possibility of engaging with avoided activities or issues.

STANDARD BEHAVIOURAL TECHNIQUES IN DEPRESSION

Rationale for the Use of Behavioural Techniques

Many acutely depressed patients spend significant stretches of time doing little other than sitting thinking about their problems. Inactivity and reduced levels of motivation in acute depression are important targets for cognitive therapy. In the cognitive model of depression (see Chapter 1), reduced levels of activity are assumed to exist in a vicious circle with low mood and negative biases in the patient's thinking. When the patient's mood is low, their thinking about any endeavour becomes dominated by negative expectations, and they are put off from engaging in activities that were previously satisfying. As the patient ceases to do things that they previously found rewarding, the reduction in levels of satisfaction or positive reinforcement directly contributes to low mood. Moreover, reductions in activity can then provide fodder for more negative thinking: as patients reflect on how little they are doing, they criticise themselves for their 'laziness' or worry about their apparent incapacity. The negative thoughts triggered by inactivity can then result in a further lowering of mood and motivation, which limits activity levels still further.

Once a patient has been socialised into the cognitive model, the next stage of cognitive therapy usually involves helping the patient to re-engage in activities in order directly to increase levels of satisfaction. Re-establishing previously rewarding activities can also highlight negative expectations that can then be put to the test. By using the active, questioning style of cognitive therapy (see Chapter 2), the therapist aims to engage the patient in collaboratively identifying activities that might improve the patient's mood. A number of techniques can be used in pursuing this strategy, the most common of which are monitoring of activities, activity scheduling and graded task assignment.

Monitoring Activities

Initially, patients monitor their levels of activity and concomitant satisfaction. They may be asked to record their activities over the course of the day on an hour-by-hour basis, and to rate the degree of mastery (i.e. sense of accomplishment) and pleasure obtained from attempting each activity. Monitoring activities in this fashion often provides a number of benefits in depression. Frequently, patients can see from an activity diary that they have been accomplishing more or obtaining more pleasure than they had realised. Any biases in the depressive thinking that filter out signs of satisfaction or pleasure can thus be countered by actively noting and recording in this fashion. Focusing attention on the satisfaction obtained from any activity in this way frequently leads directly to a lift in mood. When patients realise that engaging in some activities can result in some satisfaction, this can also help to counter the hopelessness that results from thinking that nothing will do them any good.

Scheduling Activities

Monitoring of activities enables identification of those activities that are associated with low mood and those that are most likely to be accompanied by some positive feelings. From this, patients can be helped to plan their days in order to maximise the likelihood of obtaining more satisfaction. This technique, known as activity scheduling, hinges around planning small tasks that it is feasible to accomplish even with depression. Activities and tasks are usually written down on a daily plan for the coming few days, which is initially completed in the session with the therapist's assistance. Depending on the patient's degree of impairment, the plan can be completed for small activities on an hour-by-hour basis (e.g. get dressed, make cup of coffee) or for more general activities (e.g. go shopping) over more extended periods. Where patients are suffering from low levels of energy, it is helpful actively to schedule rests as a reward for small accomplishments. As the patients' levels of activity increase, so does the possibility of their gaining at least some satisfaction from the tasks they have attempted. Planning the time in this way also directly or indirectly limits the time the patients spend sitting ruminating about their perceived shortcomings, which can be beneficial.

Graded Task Assignment

As depression makes attempting most tasks more difficult, many tasks may need to be broken down and attempted in a graded fashion. If the degree of impairment demands it, the graded assignment of tasks may initially need to focus on small everyday activities, such as getting dressed. Gradually the patient may become more able to address more daunting tasks that had previously been avoided, such as more complex work tasks or negotiating the management of household bills or debts. With tasks that are likely to be seen as aversive, helping the patient to focus on any satisfaction obtained from accomplishing any steps is crucial to improving mood. For the patient to address tasks in this gradual fashion can help to counter avoidance. Tackling tasks that had previously been avoided can help the patient to develop more of a sense of control over their problems, which can further erode the hopelessness and helplessness inherent in depression.

BEHAVIOURAL TECHNIQUES IN PERSISTENT DEPRESSION

When attempting to use these behavioural techniques with people suffering from chronic depression, many difficulties can become evident. Monitoring of activities requires gaining reasonably precise information about feelings and behaviours. As was described in the previous chapters, patients with persistent depression often do not wish to think about their experiences or their moods in any detail. They are often poor at providing precise information about their depression. Useful information may therefore be hard to come by during the session, and the patients may also find it hard to complete any kind of diary for monitoring their feelings and activities between sessions. Activity scheduling often focuses directly on increasing activity levels. However, many persistently depressed individuals are already quite active and the strategy of simply fostering re-engagement in previously satisfying activity does not readily apply. In addition, many of the activities that are completed result in little pleasure or mastery, so there is also less scope for simply refocusing the patient's attention on positive feelings that might be available. Further, the avoidance of particularly difficult tasks may be accompanied by such a conviction that, if the therapist even suggests that the task should be considered, it may threaten the therapeutic relationship. Such entrenched avoidance can make graded task assignment difficult.

The Benefits of Persistence

Faced with such difficulties, it can be tempting to abandon these standard behavioural strategies in favour of more complex and sophisticated psychological interventions. The influence of long-held attitudes and beliefs on avoidance in persistent depression is often evident. Therefore, changes in behaviour will indeed be harder to achieve than when working with the inactivity induced by low mood in acute depression. However, it is rarely the case that behavioural techniques for increasing satisfaction cannot work at all. The problem in persistent depression is more usually that patients either decline to engage in activities or dismiss any small benefits that result from them. When patients can be induced to engage in appropriate activities, small benefits can result. The challenge for the therapist is to highlight the patient's avoidance and to foster some engagement from the patient. Rather than abandoning the use of these techniques in the face of the difficulties presented by chronic depression, it can be more helpful to persist with the approach and adapt it to the particular difficulty encountered.

As in acute depression, engagement in appropriate activities can lead to increases in satisfaction and to some alleviation of depressed mood. As changes may be small, they may be overlooked or dismissed by the patient. The therapist needs to be alert to this and to respond enthusiastically to any positive shift. The therapist's response can serve to reinforce the smallest signs of change that the patient has made. It can also make the patient more aware of their tendency to dismiss any progress. Where the patient initially finds it hard to see the utility of such small changes, the training this process provides in attending to small shifts in mood can be a valuable building block in the gradual progress of therapy. The experience of engaging in and attending in detail to specific experiences can help to counter the overgeneral style of thinking common in persistent depression. This training in processing specific, small experiences is essential to the process of addressing behavioural, cognitive and emotional avoidance in a gradual fashion.

Even when behavioural techniques are not successful in directly improving the patient's mood, they are important in the overall therapeutic strategy with persistent depression. Where difficulties are encountered in implementing desired behaviours, blocks to progress can be identified.

This provides an opportunity to build a shared formulation of precisely how the problems affect day-to-day tasks. If the therapist can help the patient to make sense of the difficulties they are encountering, this constitutes an important step in addressing the problems. In particular, the patient can be helped to see that they are avoiding certain activities or issues and the precise ways in which they are doing so. The potential drawbacks of avoidance in specific situations can then be made evident. Difficulties in implementing behavioural techniques can be used to begin to highlight the role that thoughts or beliefs may have in maintaining the depression. Shedding light on how beliefs may be interfering with everyday tasks can be helpful in itself. For example, one young woman was having great difficulty re-instating some of the social activities that she had enjoyed prior to becoming depressed. Discussion of the difficulty suggested that it resulted in large part from a belief that she was worthless and so did not deserve to enjoy herself. Once this had been identified, she made some progress in scheduling activities despite her view that she did not deserve to enjoy herself, even without attempting to modify this belief. Even where such quick change does not occur, highlighting the role of avoidance and beliefs in blocking desired outcomes provides an important foundation for later attempts to identify and modify the underlying beliefs.

PROBLEMS IN MONITORING ACTIVITIES AND LEVELS OF MASTERY AND PLEASURE

Early in therapy, patients with depression are often asked to keep a diary of their daily activities and rate each activity for levels of mastery and pleasure, for example on a ten-point scale. This helps to focus the patient's attention on what they have done and the pleasure or satisfaction that resulted. Countering the negative mental filter imposed by depressive information processing in this way can help directly to lift depressed mood. It is also helpful in identifying factors that might be contributing to low mood and that might serve as possible targets for further intervention. These factors include generally low levels of activity, lack of engagement in previously pleasurable or satisfying activities, and specific triggers of low mood.

Problem: Patients have Great Difficulty Completing a Diary of Activity or do not Complete it at All

We have discussed how avoidance is a common coping response in chronically depressed patients, which is used as a means of reducing perceived stress. It is inevitable that avoidance will impact on the performance of tasks within the therapy as well as those from the patient's everyday life outside. As completing a diary involves both effort and the possibility of having to focus on distressing situations, the patient's habitual response to stress may result in the diary not being completed.

Don't

- Give up on monitoring of activities
- Conclude that the patient is too unmotivated to make progress
- Pressurise or lecture the patient that not doing therapy tasks will prevent them from getting better, as this will likely reinforce conclusions that trying anything makes them feel worse and that failure is the only possible outcome

Do

- Find out more about the reasons for the difficulty
- Simplify the monitoring procedure
- Model the activity monitoring in session
- Frame the task as an experiment to find out more about the difficulties.

Patients typically make negative predictions regarding the perceived catastrophic consequences of engaging in avoided activities, including diary-keeping. The therapist aims to work with the patient to identify these predictions and to establish behavioural experiments to test out their validity. This is often easier said than done. The therapy extract below illustrates how the use of avoidance as a coping strategy interferes with diary-keeping and needs to be actively addressed if progress is to be made. In this example, the therapist attempts to help *Marion* to see the link between her not attempting the diary and her prediction that recording inactivity would make her feel worse. The therapist then tries to help her to begin to question this prediction.

T: So Marion, how did you get on with keeping a record of your activities like we agreed?

M: I haven't done it.

T: What stopped you doing it?

M: I don't do anything so there was nothing to write.

T: I think we discussed that as a possible obstacle last week didn't we and we agreed things like getting up and sitting in the chair, eating, drinking, sleeping are all activities?

M: (*nods*)

T: Sounds like you find the whole idea of writing down what you are doing difficult. Let's talk about that. Did you put the diary on the coffee table as we agreed?

M: I did. I even wrote one thing on it. But then I felt terrible.

T: Did you bring the diary with you?

M: No. It's only got one thing on it.

T: But you did make a start. You said you felt terrible after writing that one thing. Can you remember what you wrote?

M: Got up, had a cup of tea and sat watching TV.

T: Can you recall what it was about writing those things that made you feel so terrible?

M: It just shows how pathetic I am. I do nothing all day. I know that. I don't need to keep a diary to remind me of the fact—I'll just feel worse.

T: So, when you made one entry on the diary sheet this triggered a whole host of thoughts in your mind such as 'I'm pathetic', 'I don't do anything all day' and you thought that completing the diary won't help. In fact you thought it would make you feel worse because it would remind you of how inactive you are.

M: Exactly. Things are better if I try not to think too deeply about them.

T: Well, you said when you made the one record on the diary sheet you felt terrible. Can you describe terrible?

M: What do you mean?

T: Well, when you were filling it in did you notice any physical sensations in your body?

M: I don't think so.

T: Okay, Marion I'd like with your help to try a small experiment here in the session. I've got here a blank diary sheet like the one we used last week. What do you think would happen if you tried now to complete the diary sheet just recording what you have done so far today?

M: What, now?

T: Yes.

M: I'll feel terrible.

T: Would you be willing to have a go? It might help us to find out important information about your problems.

M: Like what?

T: Exactly what feeling terrible is like for you and how this gets in the way of completing the diary (*hands Marion the activity schedule and a pen.*)

M: (*starts to write, hands shaking*) Look at me—I feel terrible. My hands are shaking. I can't write. My writing is just scrawl. You won't be able to read it, it's pointless.

T: Well done for having a go. It didn't look easy. Okay, so having a go right now makes you shake, and all these thoughts crowd your mind. How are you feeling right now?

M: Anxious. It's how I always feel when I try and do anything.

T: Okay so would it be fair to say not keeping the diary stops you getting anxious?

M: If you put it like that then, yes.

T: So one advantage of not keeping the diary is you avoid getting anxious. Any other advantages?

M: Well thinking about it in those terms whenever I try to do anything I always feel awful and give up before I've finished it. Giving up on things always makes me feel really down, so often I think it's best not to start then I don't feel such a failure.

T: So another advantage is you avoid running the risk of failing?

M: Yes.

T: Can I ask if there are any disadvantages to using this avoidance tactic?

M: Yes, as a result I do nothing.

T: What is the effect on your mood of doing nothing?

M: I feel terrible.

T: So it seems the avoidance keeps you stuck between the devil and the deep blue sea. If you try and do things to improve your mood, you feel anxious and so not doing it is your way of reducing your anxiety. However, avoiding doing things makes you feel more depressed.

M: Yes. And so it goes on. Can you see why I try not to think about things? It's the only answer.

T: It's interesting what you say there. You've already talked about avoiding doing certain things when you feel anxious and just then you talked about trying not to think about things. Is that also avoidance?

M: I've never really thought about it. I guess so.

T: Well, we have learned quite a bit about how you might use avoidance to reduce the impact the unpleasant thoughts you experience and those seemingly overwhelming feelings of anxiety and depression have on you. It certainly makes sense of why keeping the diary was difficult.

M: Oh. So, I'm not wasting your time?

T: This is your time Marion. How about if we focused our efforts on trying to find a way of reducing the avoidance?

M: Does that mean I'll have to try and do things?

T: Yes, but gradually.

M: I don't think I can.

T: Let's see how we go. What we need is a starting point. What activities have you enjoyed in the past?

In this extract, the avoidance that has interfered with the diary-keeping is identified and framed as a problem to be addressed collaboratively. Although little progress appears to have been made in terms of getting the patient to record their activity or to agree to schedule specific activities, the focus has been shifted from avoidance as being an obstacle to the therapy to avoidance as being a problem to be addressed. A start has been made in pinpointing how negative evaluations trigger negative feelings, which are then dealt with firstly by avoiding activity and then by avoiding even thinking about what has not been done.

Predictions that lead to the task not being carried out often centre around issues of not doing the task properly. Patients may report concerns such as: 'I won't do it properly and the therapist will be critical' or 'My hand writing is illegible, I'll look foolish'. The high standards of completion that the patient assumes would be necessary to avoid criticism seem impossible when the patient is subject to depressive symptoms, so the patient often avoids the task completely. Helping the patient to understand the reasons for the difficulty and then helping them to simplify the task can be helpful, as was the case with *Elizabeth*. She had returned to her third session with a blank activity schedule. She explained that she had been 'very busy that week doing things for other people' and that the activity schedule had seemed difficult to complete. She reported a stream of automatic negative thoughts including 'I'm lazy' (100%), 'I've let you (the therapist) down' (80%), 'You must be annoyed at me' (50%), 'I should try harder' (95%) and 'I'm useless' (85%). As a result, Elizabeth reported feeling sad (50%), guilty (80%) and anxious (30%). There was no sign of Elizabeth seeing the activity schedule as something to help her. Rather it was an activity open to scrutiny and evaluation by others. Further discussion about the activity schedule suggested that Elizabeth was assuming that 'If I can't do it properly there is no point in doing it at all'. This was explored further in the following extract:

T: What does completing the activity schedule 'properly' entail?
E: Filling every section in for every day.
T: OK, and when would you do that?—every 3 hours or so?
E: Oh no! At the time I was doing it.
T: Is that actually possible?
E: It should be.
T: Right. Anything else in your definition of 'properly'?
E: Not sure.
T: What about the mastery and pleasure ratings?
E: Those do take a while. I sometimes worry I'm not doing it accurately.
T: How do you define 'accurate'?
E: Giving careful consideration and reflection, spending time, not being slapdash.
T: I see. What about your handwriting?
E: (*patient sighs*) It's a mess. My mum is always telling me it's a mess. It takes so long to do it properly.
T: Anything else in your definition of 'properly'?
E: It is important that I finish any task I start.
T: You mean finish it without a break?
E: Yes, if possible.

T: Mmm, that seems pretty crucial then given you've already told me how your lack of concentration and reduced energy levels interfere with activities. Okay, let's summarise. Doing the activity schedule 'properly' means giving consideration to (therapist producing written summary):

—How the schedule is filled in i.e. every section completed
—When the schedule is completed, i.e. at the time the activity is carried out
—Accurate ratings of mastery and pleasure, i.e. careful consideration; not slapdash
—Best handwriting
—Finishing the task all in one go.

T: Have I summarised that properly?—pardon the pun! (*Patient and therapist laugh.*)
E: I think so.
T: That's quite a demand to place on yourself.
E: Is it?
T: Have you ever been able to meet that demand?
E: What demand?
T: The demand of doing things 'properly' to such a high standard?
E: Is it a high standard? It was always expected of me.
T: Yes, it was expected of you. Have you ever achieved it?
E: Sometimes, before I became ill.
T: Has achieving this standard become harder since you became depressed?
E: It's impossible.
T: What makes it impossible?
E: I don't know. I know you are going to say my illness stops me from doing things but I think I've just become lazy.
T: OK. How about if we tried an experiment. What if we simplified the rules for completing the activity schedule? What would be the effects of that?
E: (*sigh*) I don't know.
T: If the task did not place such a high demand on you do you think it would be easier to achieve?
E: In theory it would I suppose.
T: OK. Let's see what would happen if you tried to record just two days of the activity schedule rating mastery and pleasure as we defined them last week?
E: What's the point? I'll only get annoyed because I will know I'm not doing it properly.
T: Perhaps that's exactly what we need to find out—how this demand of doing things properly causes you difficulties in every day situations.

E: I see what you're saying but it won't be easy.

T: No, it won't be easy, but what is there to be learned from trying the experiment?

From this point Elizabeth and the therapist negotiated the details of the behavioural experiment, which was implemented with a degree of success. She did manage to complete the diary sheet for some days, which showed a pattern of frenetically doing things for other people interspersed with periods of exhaustion. Pacing her activities then became a focus for discussion in further sessions.

Problem: Monitoring Reveals that the Patient gets no Mastery or Pleasure from their Activities

When the patient is undertaking various activities, but does not get any satisfaction from them, then monitoring of activities does not result in the desired alleviation of depressed mood. Activities that were previously satisfying may have become less so, either due to depressive symptoms (such as tiredness or anhedonia) or due to the application of discouraging rules, standards or beliefs. In some patients, most activities are dictated by an enhanced sense of duty, so that personal satisfaction is simply not considered. This may result in them not engaging in activities that offer the best prospect of any satisfaction. In some patients, a generalised expectation that nothing will give satisfaction means that they do not do the things most likely to give some satisfaction.

Don't

- Try to persuade the patient that things they are doing are in fact satisfying
- Make numerous suggestions to the patient of activities they may find pleasurable.

Do

- Check that ratings accurately reflect satisfaction gained when performing the activity
- Establish whether previously satisfying activities are being overlooked or have become unsatisfying
- Elicit and highlight thoughts which may deprive the patient of potential satisfaction
- Use graded task assignment to simplify tasks
- Test out the effects on mastery and pleasure of reducing excessive activity levels.

Patients' verbal reports and written ratings of mastery and pleasure may be coloured by information processing biases. Ratings that are made some time after the completion of an activity can be based on the depressive feelings the patient experiences at the time of making the rating and may overlook satisfaction that was there at the time of the activity. It can therefore be helpful to check when the ratings were made. If they were not made at the time of the activity, further information on the patient's actual reaction at the time can be gleaned through 'playing back' the event in detail. Close attention should be paid to details of how other people reacted to the patient at the time of the activity and to the patient's reactions in the session when describing what was done. For example, a young man, Paul, showed the therapist his activity diary, which showed zero satisfaction with any activity over the course of the week. He had mainly been confined to the house by his depressive and anxiety symptoms, but on a rare occasion when he had taken his young son to the local shop he also rated his mastery and pleasure as zero. He explained that he could not take any satisfaction from such a small outing that just showed how pathetic his contribution to family life had become. The therapist's enquiry into how he had felt at the time seemed to confirm this lack of satisfaction until the therapist asked how the little boy had reacted. As Paul described his little boy's excitement at going out with his Dad to buy some sweets, the grim expression on his face seemed to lapse momentarily. The therapist asked about this and Paul actually smiled, saying 'Well, it's good isn't it!'. A discussion about how to catch and build on these flickering positive experiences ensued.

Where patients have become inactive or are gaining little mastery or pleasure from activities that they do undertake, it is important to try to find out about activities they found satisfying prior to becoming depressed. Even in cases of chronic depression, suggesting re-engagement in such activities can sometimes lead to an increase in mastery or satisfaction and help to begin to combat depressive symptoms. More commonly, activities that were previously satisfying now afford little mastery or pleasure. This is often due to a combination of the effect of depressive symptoms and the effects of rigid rules applied to the performance of activity. Often patients set idiosyncratic conditions on what must occur to draw satisfaction from something. Conditional rules such as 'If I am to enjoy an activity then it must be productive/an achievement/competitive' can spoil activities previously found enjoyable, as the symptoms of depression make it extremely difficult for the patient to satisfy the conditions. For example, prior to becoming depressed, *Peter* had derived most pleasure from competitive sports, including swimming and running. He had been a member of a sports club, and the pleasure he derived from sporting activities was governed by the degree to which he could compete with others (i.e. take part in a race) or himself (i.e. run five miles in a faster time than he did last week). The tiredness and lethargy that characterised Peter's depression now prevented him from engaging in the activities in the way that he had prior to the onset of his illness. Peter had little sense of enjoying an activity for its own sake, and his activity schedule revealed that his efforts to engage in some physical activities, for example a swim of five lengths or a 10-minute jog, indeed brought little satisfaction. Following discussion of these issues, although he would still not pursue these activities simply for enjoyment, he could gain a modicum of satisfaction if he saw his activity as 'keeping his hand in' or training for when he started to compete again. Most important was the recognition of his rules and standards, which formed an important focus later in therapy. For patients like Peter, whose sense of enjoyment was linked to achievement or competitiveness, broadening the criteria for what is pleasurable may need to be an overall goal of treatment.

Where patients' depressive symptoms are preventing them from satisfying rigid rules and standards, tasks can be simplified and assigned in a graded fashion. As described above, having to do things properly interfered with *Elizabeth* filling in the activity schedule at all. When she did start to monitor her activities, little mastery or pleasure was recorded in her diary. Discussion of this suggested that she only derived a sense of pleasure from an activity that was productive and viewed activities such as soaking in a hot bath or having a beauty treatment as frivolous. The initial goal of treatment was to try to help Elizabeth to find ways of engaging in previously enjoyed activities. Her poor concentration and memory impaired her ability to engage in activities she had enjoyed prior to becoming depressed, such as reading, watching films, handicrafts and cookery. Elizabeth had tried on a number of occasions to engage in these activities but had found it difficult and given up. The problem was tackled by simplifying the activities. Thus, instead of trying to read works of English literature and watch foreign films with subtitles, a compromise was negotiated. Elizabeth began by reading short, humorous poetry and watching films with simple plots (recommended by her daughters). To her surprise and pleasure, by simplifying the task Elizabeth was able to concentrate and remember what she had read or watched. She then progressed to short stories and by the end of treatment had resumed crosswords and fiction books.

On occasion, patients with persistent depression can return activity schedules that are crammed with activities, none of which is rated as giving significant mastery or pleasure. Their excessive activity can be seen as a form of avoidance, as being so busy may effectively squeeze out of awareness uncomfortable feelings and thoughts. The person simply does not have time to 'feel depressed' or think about things. The consequence of this is often a persistent sense of dissatisfaction, fatigue and even resentment. The initial tack taken in therapy is usually to schedule in rests or other rewards for activities successfully completed, with the suggestion that the patient allows some time to process the sense of success or pleasure. This may have to be accomplished by delegating tasks or sharing responsibilities with others. While this strategy can lead to increases in satisfaction from some activities, the patient is usually reluctant to adopt attitudes to activity that they may view as self-indulgent. Patients are encouraged to test out 'giving themselves a break' on the understanding that their belief that they do not really deserve this is returned to for further discussion in later sessions.

PROBLEMS IN ACTIVITY SCHEDULING AND GRADED TASK ASSIGNMENT

Monitoring of activities and levels of mastery and pleasure often leads on to attempts to schedule particular tasks, which may have to be addressed in a graded fashion. As in acute depression, activity scheduling aims directly to increase levels of satisfaction by combating both general inactivity and disengagement from particular previously rewarding activities. The limitations imposed by depressive symptoms, such as reduced energy levels and poor concentration, are taken into account by breaking complex tasks down and approaching demanding activities through a series of graded steps. Particular tasks that have been avoided due to their perceived difficulty or unpleasantness, such as paying overdue bills, can also be approached in this fashion and progress towards their completion can provide some sense of mastery or relief.

Problem: The Therapist is Confronted by a Barrage of Negative Automatic Thoughts as to why Graded Task Assignment is not Going to Work

The negative thoughts surrounding attempts to plan particular tasks can focus either on low expectations of a positive outcome, leading to hopelessness and pessimism about the task, or high expectations of a negative outcome, leading to anxiety and active avoidance. Low expectations tend to be fed by rigid definitions of what would be required to constitute a favourable outcome, for example that the task would have to be executed completely and perfectly. Negative expectations often focus around the reactions of others, such as criticism, rejection or ridicule.

Don't

- Attempt to modify a barrage of automatic thoughts
- Accept the patient's assertions (e.g. 'This won't work', 'This is pointless') that may lead you to abandon the intervention.

Do

- Remain focused on the task at hand and return to planning its execution
- Draw the patient's attention to the negative thoughts
- Use the TICS/TOCS technique (see below)
- Draw the patient's attention to the consequences of the negative thinking (e.g. using a vicious circle diagram).

When attempting to discuss plans for some activity, a barrage of negative thoughts can be highly distracting both for the patient and the clinician. To attempt to answer or counter the negative thoughts usually takes the discussion even further from the task at hand. It also necessitates the clinician trying to introduce complex interventions simultaneously and reduces the chances of any of them being effective. The likely result is that the patient becomes overwhelmed (and possibly the therapist too), leading him or her to give up and disengage from the therapeutic activity. A more helpful strategy is to try to remain focused on the task while acknowledging the negative thoughts and their effects as a general problem.

The patient's attention can be drawn to the negative thoughts with a statement such as: 'I notice while we are planning this your mind seems to be generating lots of reasons why it's not going to work.' Further questions can be helpful in framing the negative thinking as a problem distracting the patient from their agreed task, such as: 'Does that happen every time you approach a task?'; 'How do you make sense of that?' and 'Has that always happened throughout your life whenever you approached a task or just since you became depressed?' The aim here is to focus the patient's attention on the problem posed by the negativity of their thinking, rather than on the specific problems raised by each individual thought. Phrasing questions and comments carefully can help patients to distance themselves a little from their negativity. For example, in the opening statement above, the therapist does not say 'I notice while we are planning this *you* seem to be generating . . .', but uses the wording *'your mind . . .'*. This avoids implying that the problem is something intrinsic to the patient's personality or an intentional obstruction on their part. Rather it opens up the possibility that when someone experiences depression, this is the way their mind operates, i.e. it more readily generates negatives. Helping the patient to recognise the impact of this negativity on the task at hand can help to lay the foundations of awareness of thoughts as thoughts rather than as facts (or meta-awareness, see Chapter 12).

In helping the patient to pull back from engaging with the specific content of any thoughts about doing a task, it can be useful to discuss the concept of TICS and TOCS (Task Interfering Cognitions and Task Orienting Cognitions; Burns, 1989). This is the idea that certain thoughts (TOCS) are helpful in guiding someone through the task being attempted (e.g. 'I'll give this my best shot'). On the other hand, many thoughts that come to mind when someone is depressed (TICS) are simply obstacles to getting the task done (e.g. 'I'll never be able to do it', 'I'm useless'). It is important to reassure patients that they do not have to remember what the jargon stands for, simply the idea that certain thoughts get in the way of what they are trying to do. It is often somewhat reassuring for patients to realise that their kind of thinking is a familiar phenomenon. It can help them to know that others with this problem have found it useful to put their concerns about doing an activity 'on ice' in order to enable it to be done. This can sometimes lend enough weight to the argument for suspending doubts and giving the task a try.

In discussing the negative thoughts about the task, the emphasis is on the *consequences* of the thinking rather than its validity. The patient is encouraged to test the validity of the thoughts in practice through carrying out the activity. Further questions to reinforce this focus are: 'What is the impact of that negativity on the likelihood of you attempting this task?' and 'If you don't attempt the task what is going to be the impact of that?' The effect of not doing the task on the patient's mood is then questioned (e.g. 'If you don't do this, how will you feel?', 'What is the effect on your mood of giving up?'). It can be helpful to draw out a vicious circle to make explicit the links between thoughts, feelings and behaviour in relation to the graded task assignment. As there is considerable danger of confusion and getting sidetracked in these discussions, a final summary along the following lines is usually essential:

T: Now we have spent some time planning how you might get started on some activities over the next two days. We noticed while we were at this planning stage that your mind was bombarded with lots of negative thoughts—reasons why this plan would not work. I think we both agree that these negative thoughts may stop you getting going with this. How about we try this plan of grading activities and see what happens? It might work or it might not. Next time you come to the session we can review how well the plan worked and how much those thoughts interfered with the plan. Is that okay?

It is desirable where possible to present such assignments as a 'no lose' situation. Thus, even if the assignment is not completed, something can be gained from it. If the patient returns to the next session having not attempted the task, then a predicted obstacle has already been taken into account and the patient's observations regarding this can be discussed. It is par for the course in chronic depression that the assignment and the observation process may need to be repeated a number of times before the patient is able to carry out the assignment as intended.

Problem: Engaging in Tasks Results in a Worsening of Depressive Symptoms

In acute depression, with help from the therapist, the patient can usually engage in some activities that give some satisfaction, and this results in some alleviation of depressive symptoms. In some cases of persistent depression, engaging in any activity can provoke more depressive symptoms, including feelings of exhaustion and lowering of mood.

Don't

- Disbelieve the patient or dispute that they feel worse
- Press on with assigning activities as though everything was going well
- Give up on assigning activities.

Do

- Take the limitations imposed by depressive symptoms fully into account
- Break down tasks into smaller chunks or discuss less demanding tasks
- Draw attention to the effects of deprecatory thoughts about starting with small activities
- Weigh the cons and pros of engaging in small activities.

It is important to emphasise that the cognitive model does not see depressive symptoms as 'all in the mind'. The effects of depressive symptoms on energy levels, concentration and pain levels are all too real and have physical effects that can in many cases be measured. In their approach to tasks or activities that have been agreed, patients with persistent depression often do not acknowledge this and make no allowance for their depressive symptoms. This often has the result that they attempt to carry things out as they would if perfectly well, leading either to a direct worsening of symptoms or to a sense of failure about the impairments in performance. When the therapist suggests re-engagement in activities, the patient may perceive the therapist as endorsing their view that they should be attempting to behave as they did before becoming depressed. It is therefore vital that the therapist works to help the patient to see the adverse consequences of setting goals appropriate to a non-depressed level of functioning. The contrast of the 'pull yourself together' approach with identifying activities that are feasible, even with the depressive symptoms, needs to be highlighted.

The role of the therapist is to help the patient to match the demands of the activity to the constraints imposed by depressive symptoms. This can be done by breaking down tasks into chunks (e.g. sorting bills that have been paid from those that have not; writing the cheques; posting the cheques), limiting the time spent on that activity or limiting the amount of the activity attempted (e.g. hoovering just one room).

Many patients with persistent depression become dismissive or condescending at the suggestion of tailoring activities to their current level. They see such an approach as confirming that they have indeed become weak or pathetic, and may even become angry with the therapist for seeming to endorse this view. The therapist can enquire whether the patient can see any good reasons for adjusting the expectations people place on themselves, including illness, emotional upset or life situations. Patients usually concede that such adjustments are helpful when applied to other people, but deny that such a view is applicable to their own persistent depression. Typical responses are: 'Yes, but I haven't suffered a major trauma like people in that disaster' or 'It's all very well making allowances for depression if you get over it in a couple of weeks, but this has gone on for years.' Rather than focusing on changing the patient's view, attention can again be drawn to the effects of dismissing small activities: 'When you think that how do you feel? Are these thoughts helpful in getting you back to doing the things you used to do?' Again the patient is encouraged to test out the effects of persisting with small activities despite their reservations. If the patient then dismisses any small steps by comparing them to what they would have achieved if they were not depressed, the therapist can draw attention to the drawbacks of 'carrying on as normal' and becoming exhausted and depressed. The benefits of completing the small activity can then be highlighted in relation to the detrimental effects of carrying on as if not depressed. With considerable persistence and repetition of this approach, some patients begin to see its benefit and to apply it more spontaneously in addressing continuing low levels of satisfaction.

At the beginning of therapy, *Elizabeth* had ceased to engage in virtually all household tasks, work and leisure activities, including ironing, cleaning, or going for a walk. Activity scheduling focused on one particularly pressing task, that of ironing. Elizabeth's diary sheet showed that she had on a couple of occasions spent over an hour ironing, but had got no satisfaction at the time and had spent hours afterwards in a state of depressed exhaustion. Discussion of this revealed that tiredness and poor concentration seriously impeded her ability to carry out the ironing, such that by the end of an hour she felt exhausted, found it hard even to hold the iron and kept creasing up the clothes. She compared this to how she had done her ironing prior to becoming depressed: to stand for two hours on a Sunday evening and iron while watching TV. After her hour-long efforts, she not only felt fatigued, but was subject to an onslaught of self-deprecatory thoughts about the shortcomings of her efforts. Through Socratic dialogue, the suggestion emerged that simplifying the task and pacing herself may reduce the likelihood of exhausting herself and feeling worse. A behavioural test was established to see the effects of completing 20 minutes' ironing every other day over the next week. The chances of success were maximised by identifying a 20-minute period during the day when tiredness and concentration levels were exerting a minimal impact. The specific activity and times were scheduled on a blank activity schedule and use of a timer was agreed to remind Elizabeth when she was to stop ironing and have a cup of tea with her husband. Despite great initial scepticism and a continuing sense of failure, Elizabeth was surprised to find that she was a little pleased that she could iron for the allotted time without becoming exhausted and that this did contribute to reducing a large backlog of ironing.

Problem: The Patient's Hopelessness and Avoidance are so Entrenched that Suggesting any Activity Provokes a Hostile Reaction towards the Therapist.

The effect of hopelessness on treatment can be especially pernicious. Through its destructive impact on the patient's perceptions of their ability to complete a task, and on their perceptions of the effectiveness of the strategies of cognitive therapy, it drives much of the inactivity and inertia with which chronically depressed patients respond to therapy. It can be so extreme that any attempts to help by suggesting engagement in some activity are seen as a failure on the part of the therapist to understand the problem. The therapist's suggestions are interpreted as a personal attack, because by suggesting the impossible, the therapist is seen as 'rubbing the patient's nose' in how pathetic they have become.

Don't

- Give up or become quiet and withdrawn
- Insist the patient carry out the suggested task
- Rely solely on questioning
- Retaliate (!) or become angry or critical of the patient.

Do

- Try to maintain activity and structure in the session
- Focus on understanding the patient's reaction

- Make educated guesses about this reaction and share them with the patient
- Return to formulating and socialising the patient to the cognitive model.

Some patients are so convinced of the hopelessness of their situation that any suggestion of making changes is resisted emphatically. They interpret the therapeutic situation in terms of their hopeless outlook. Thus if the therapist becomes quieter or less active, this can be seen as confirming that the therapist is acquiescing to the patient's view that nothing can be done. If the therapist just uses questions, the patient believes that the therapist does not know what is going on and this reinforces the patient's hopelessness. It is therefore important for the therapist to remain somewhat active in the face of the hostile outburst. It can be useful to describe feelings of intense hopelessness and how dispiriting it can be when people do not appear to have understood, then to check if this relates at all to how the patient is feeling. Although this may appear to be providing a further target for the patient's hostility, providing an explanation in this way, even if wrong, can give the patient a chance to say how they are feeling. Using a format of empathic statements followed by questions, the information arising in the therapy session can be fed back into the cognitive model. An example would be: 'Like many of the people I see, it sounds like you have thoughts that not being able to do even small amounts of activity shows that you are beyond help and can never get better. When you think this, how do you feel?' Returning to illustrations of the powerful influence that thoughts can have over people's feelings and actions can be helpful.

The following extract from an early therapy session with *Marion* illustrates a number of the problems that commonly arise in using activity scheduling with patients with persistent depression. At this stage, Marion was engaging in very few activities of daily living (i.e. washing, dressing, housework, shopping and the like) and she was participating in no leisure activities. She was extremely pessimistic regarding any potential benefits cognitive therapy may have to offer. In the extract, the negativity and hopelessness that characterise her thought processes and her passivity are very apparent.

T: So Marion, how about if we try to identify one activity you have previously enjoyed and try to develop a strategy for getting you started on that?
M: (*Shrugs her shoulders and looks down.*)
T: Right. I know you told me that you have been depressed for a large part of the last twenty-five years. But I remember you saying during our first meeting that when the children were younger you were more active.
M: Yes.

T: What sort of things did you do with them?

M: (*shakes her head*) Can't remember.

T: Okay, let's try a different approach. If we tried to think about typical things a mother might do with children, what might they be?

M: I'm not sure.

T: Last week you talked about your friend Marjorie. She has a daughter Lisa and a granddaughter Julie. What does Lisa do with Julie?

M: Takes her to the park, reads to her, takes her swimming.

T: Did you do those things with your daughters?

M: I used to take them to the park and bake with them. Didn't go swimming or read with them, I was useless like that.

T: You said you used to bake with them. Is that something you enjoyed?

M: Yes, but don't ask me to do it now. My mind is too muddled—I can't follow a recipe.

T: So, if you were to have a go at baking what would your prediction be about the outcome?

M: I wouldn't even have a go.

T: Okay. So you used to bake, what else did you do with the children? For example, did you ever make things for school?

M: Sometimes. I used to knit. I taught them both to knit.

T: How long is it since you knitted anything?

M: Years.

T: Did you enjoy knitting?

M: Yes.

T: Were you good at it?

M: Sort of.

T: What sort of things did you knit?

M: The usual things.

T: You'll have to help me here—knitting is not my strong point. What sort of things?

M: Jumpers . . . children's clothes . . . toys.

T: Any particular patterns?

M: I could do most things. 'Knit one, pearl one' is a bit boring. I liked doing Arran patterns.

T: (*smiling*) That's some skill Marion.

M: That's a long time ago. (*looking down*) Couldn't do it now.

T: You say you couldn't do it now, what makes you say that?

M: It would be difficult.

T: What would be difficult?

M: My knitting needles and whatnot are packed away.

T: Where are they?

M: In the loft.

T: Could you get them out of the loft?

M: Look at the size of me, I'm so fat! (*making direct eye contact*) If I could climb the ladder, which I can't, I could never fit through the loft door! (*big sigh*)

T: Could your daughter find them for you?

M: I don't like to ask her.

T: What is putting you off asking your daughter?

M: She's busy. I annoy her. I'm just a burden.

T: OK quite a few obstacles there. It seems that whenever you approach a task, for example the knitting, your mind is bombarded with lots of reasons why you can't do it.

M: I can't do anything. I'm useless.

T: Let's look at this as a vicious circle. (*Draws out connections between thoughts, feelings and inactivity.*) Does this seem to fit?

M: (*sighs*) As I said last week, I understand the circle but it's all too difficult.

T: It seems those negative thoughts have really got a grip at the moment.

M: (*big sigh*) Yeah.

T: Let's try to suspend those negative thoughts and imagine you've managed to get hold of your knitting needles and wool. Can you think of anything you would like to knit?

M: Those thoughts never go away—they are always there.

T: I know it seems that way, particularly when you are feeling low but in an ideal world is there anything you would like to have a go at knitting?

M: Well, actually yes. Marjorie's daughter is expecting another baby in July and I'd like to knit a bonnet and booties.

T: Great! How feasible is that as a project given what you were saying before about your mind being muddled? Would you be able to follow a pattern?

M: I could knit a bonnet and booties without a pattern and they are very small.

T: Right, so let's try to devise a way of getting hold of the knitting needles and wool. What options do you have?

M: What do you mean?

T: How can we tackle the problem of getting the equipment?

M: We can't, they're in the loft.

T: Are there other ways of getting hold of needles and wool?

M: I don't think so.

T: Could you borrow them from, say, Marjorie?

M: That doesn't seem right when I'm knitting for her granddaughter.

T: OK. Is there anyone else you could ask other than your daughter to go into the loft?

M: I'm not sure.

T: What about you daughter's boyfriend?

M: (*looking doubtful*) Possibly.

T: When are your daughter and boyfriend next visiting?

M: This evening.

T: OK. Let's try to practice what you are going to ask.

M: What now?

T: Yes. How will you phrase the request?

M: (*silent; red cheeks, looks embarrassed*) I don't know.

T: How are you feeling right now?

M: (*looking down*) Awkward.

T: Do you think you will feel the same when you ask your daughter or her boyfriend to go into the loft?

M: Yes. I always do. I hate asking for help.

T: What is it about asking for help that is difficult?

M: I can't bear it when people say no.

T: And what is it about people saying no that is so upsetting?

M: I feel completely rejected and humiliated.

T: Do people say no often?

M: I try not to ask for things, then I'm not disappointed.

T: So you deal with the problem of feeling rejected by avoiding putting yourself in a situation where you risk being rejected?

M: Yes.

T: In the situation we have been discussing, which is the most difficult between starting to knit or asking for help to go into the loft to get the needles?

M: Asking for help.

T: Okay, let's draw up a plan for asking your daughter for help and identify your negative predictions and test these out when you go home.

M: This is difficult.

T: Yes. But let's see what we can learn from it. How would it seem if we made the goal of the exercise that you bring the knitting needles and wool to our next session?

M: (*looks puzzled*) Why?

T: Well, the treatment goal we are working on at the moment is increasing your activity levels by starting with something enjoyable, yes?

M: Yes.

T: Today we have identified a number of difficulties that may play a part in stopping you getting going. These include muddled thinking, negative predictions about asking for help and difficulty in finding ways of approaching tasks. Would you agree with that?

M: Yes.

T: So if you bring the needles and wool next week we can spend some time getting you started on the knitting and use that as an experiment in the session to see if there are any negative predictions about the activity itself. If there are we can try to generate some solutions to those here and hopefully that will help you when you are trying to knit at home. Does that make sense?

M: I see. (*shrugs shoulders*) If you like.

T: How optimistic are you that you can carry out this plan?

M: I'm not. I can't do it.

T: Do you have anything to lose by trying?

M: Well my daughter will get annoyed at me.

T: Even if your daughter gets annoyed, will she refuse your request?

M: No, she usually does it—but I feel so awful.

T: I think you are right Marion, it is not going to be easy. You have been ill a long time and you have a number of difficult problems to tackle. At the moment, they all seem impossible to solve and we need to try to find a way of helping you go forward. The goal we are working on at present is trying to restart you on an enjoyable activity. If this plan related to the knitting achieves this goal, is there something to be gained from trying to put the plan into action?

M: I see what you're saying.

T: (*smiling*) Let's try. If it doesn't work we can try to identify the reasons and rethink the plan next week.

Three sessions were devoted to re-engaging Marion in her knitting. When Marion did not carry out the assignment the first week, the next session was spent identifying the difficulties she had encountered and tackling these to increase the likelihood of her carrying out the plan the following week. This involved revisiting her predictions regarding asking for her daughter's help and making clearer the part avoidance played in maintaining her difficulties. It is tempting to view devoting so much therapeutic time and effort to the task of knitting as painstaking and trivial, particularly in the face of the fact that Marion was not washing, dressing or cooking for herself at the time. However, the three sessions devoted to knitting paid off in that she completed her bonnet and booties and a jumper for her daughter, and despite further adverse life events she continued with her knitting. The therapist worked with Marion to develop a written summary of what she had learned from this activity. This is summarised below:

- Negative predictions about what other people think of me put me off trying things
- Starting to knit again has given me some sense of achievement
- If my attention is on my knitting and not on how depressed I feel my mood gets slightly better
- I can control my symptoms a bit on some occasions.

In the example the therapist tried to do several things simultaneously in order to try to address Marion's inactivity. This started by trying to focus

Marion on a specific and concrete activity that she might resume. This was chosen because at this early stage of treatment Marion was doing very little. Most days of the week she did not get washed or dressed but sat in the living room in her night clothes ruminating over how bad she felt and how awful her life was. In addition, the therapist began to try to help Marion to build an awareness of the relationship between her low mood and her negative thought processes. This contributed towards the aim of using concrete examples of everyday activity as a focus for identifying and modifying Marion's negative perceptions of herself and her inability to exert any control over her symptoms of depression.

In summary, the twin aims of using these behavioural techniques in cognitive therapy for depression are, first, to increase the patient's degree of satisfaction gained from engagement in activities and thereby alleviate depressive symptoms and, secondly, to provide concrete experiences that help in identifying the patient's negative thoughts in the situations in which they arise. Use of behavioural techniques in persistent depression is subject to obdurate interference by avoidance and by categorical and rigid negative thinking in the form of the chronic triad. The therapeutic strategy is generally to foster engagement through testing out some practical 'middle way' between the patient's tendency to set unrealistic aspirations or to give up completely. Achieving some degree of satisfaction depends on finding a balance between acknowledging the source of interference and persisting with the task at hand. Paying too much attention to the avoidance or thoughts that interfere with these tasks can result in a loss of task focus and becoming mired in or overwhelmed by negativity. Attempting to ignore these sources of interference tends to result in stalemate and loss of collaboration. An appropriate balance enables even patients with persistent depression to make small degrees of progress in engagement in desired activities or in registering satisfaction. It is vital for the therapist to show their delight when these small steps are made. Importantly, progress can also be made in identifying and recognising significant negative thinking processes that form the focus for subsequent cognitive strategies in therapy.

SUMMARY POINTS

- The aim of behavioural techniques is to help the patient to recognise and engage in activities that afford some satisfaction.
- In persistent depression, avoidance can beset therapeutic tasks intended to counter it.
- Avoidance is often related to extreme, categorical and rigid thoughts about the activity in question.

- Therapists must be wary of patients' tendency to pursue unrealistic goals or give up completely.
- Through attempting to engage in activities, the patient can be helped to recognise and label negative thoughts contributing to their difficulties.
- The best chance of obtaining some degree of satisfaction is usually through engaging in small tasks that are manageable, even with the depressive symptoms.
- The same strategy often needs to be applied in addressing avoidance of tasks related to the therapy as addressing avoidance of tasks in the patient's everyday life.
- The therapist must be at pains to label, reinforce and build on any small signs of progress the patient makes in engaging in everyday tasks or tasks related to therapy.

Chapter 6

WORKING WITH AUTOMATIC THOUGHTS

In this chapter, you will find an account of:

- The use of techniques for identifying and questioning negative automatic thoughts in depression
- How the aims of working with automatic thoughts need to be expanded when treating persistent depression
- Common problems in identifying automatic thoughts in persistent depression
- Common problems in questioning automatic thoughts in persistent depression
- Common problems encountered in helping patients to identify and question their own automatic thoughts
- Suggested ways to progress in therapy when each kind of difficulty is encountered
- The importance of the therapist's identifying and questioning their own thoughts when confronted by difficulties in therapy.

To many clinicians familiar with cognitive therapy for depression, helping patients to modify negative automatic thoughts is seen as its defining feature. Although a number of other aspects of therapy, such as formulation, style and structure, are also important, working to modify negative biases in the patient's overt thinking is an essential part of cognitive therapy (Beck et al., 1979). However, most clinicians who have experience of working with chronic depression will be familiar with the frustration or exasperation that can result from trying to help patients to identify and question negative automatic thoughts. The cognitive model of persistent depression describes a number of factors that may interfere with working with automatic thoughts. Avoidance may render it hard in therapy to identify and focus on specific negative thoughts. Even once identified, the rigidity and longstanding nature of the thoughts may make them hard to modify. Furthermore, patients may have had many experiences that back up their negative thoughts. If the therapist assumes that the thoughts are simply biased by the effects of low mood on thinking and expects to achieve rapid and significant changes in the content of thoughts, frustration is likely to result.

Due to these difficulties, working to identify and question automatic thoughts in persistent depression needs to be undertaken with broader aims. As well as changing the content of thinking, using 'standard' cognitive techniques can result in more subtle benefits from changes in the process of thinking. These include recognising and countering avoidance, recognising patterns of thinking, adopting a questioning stance towards experiences, and viewing thoughts as thoughts rather than as unquestionable facts. These consequences of working with automatic thoughts can be important in themselves by not only combating the rigidity of thinking, but also by providing a foundation for subsequent work on underlying beliefs (see Chapters 7 and 8). Working with automatic thoughts in persistent depression is thus an important step in starting to address the chronic triad of low self-esteem, helplessness and hopelessness. In this chapter, we review the rationale for and use of standard techniques for identifying and questioning automatic thoughts in depression. We then identify some of the most common problems that are encountered when trying to work with the automatic thoughts of persistently depressed patients. As with the behavioural techniques discussed in the previous chapter, we aim to suggest how standard cognitive strategies can be adapted to provide some benefit to patients with persistent depression.

STANDARD COGNITIVE TECHNIQUES IN DEPRESSION

Rationale for Addressing Automatic Thoughts

Within the cognitive model, negative thoughts are an important part of the vicious circle that maintains the patient's depressed mood. The model suggests that the lower the patient's mood, the more likely it is that negative thoughts will come to mind. The patient's interpretation of ongoing events becomes biased and casts things in the worst possible light. The patient's memory may become biased such that they can only remember events that went wrong. In very low mood states, patients are subject to a barrage of global negative thoughts about themselves and their lives, which may have little apparent relation to ongoing events. Negative thoughts occur to patients without conscious effort or reasoning, and are believed strongly. These automatic negative thoughts can lower a patient's mood further and, as the patient's mood drops, the intensity of negative thinking further increases. Thus, low mood and negative automatic thoughts feed each other in a vicious circle.

An essential strategy in cognitive therapy is slowing or halting this vicious circle. This is achieved by helping patients to become aware of their thinking and of the possibility that it is biased in a negative fashion. Therapy therefore aims to teach patients to identify negative automatic thoughts and to assess the validity of these thoughts. In examining the validity of the thoughts, it is important that the therapist does not assume that the patient's thinking is wrong. Even when the therapist believes that the thinking is inaccurate or biased, he or she does not try to persuade the patient of this. Rather, the emphasis is on questioning the basis for the automatic thoughts in order to help patients to assess their validity for themselves. The aim is for patients to learn the principles of this questioning process, so that they can apply it between sessions and after the therapy has finished. As with behavioural techniques, cognitive techniques are used within the active, questioning style of cognitive therapy to assist patients in developing skills to understand and address their own problems.

Identifying Automatic Thoughts

Over the course of the first few sessions, the emphasis in therapy shifts from accomplishing particular activities and processing the satisfaction obtained to identifying specific negative thoughts associated with downturns in mood. Although patients commonly report feeling depressed the whole time, monitoring of daily activities and moods in detail usually reveals dips in mood associated with particular negative thoughts. Such negative thoughts can be about the activity being attempted (e.g. 'I'm just not up to this') or can be unrelated intrusions or self-talk (e.g. 'Nobody cares about me'). The therapist guides the patient in identifying their negative thoughts by pinpointing mood shifts both within and between sessions and asking the patient what was going through their mind. Where the patient has difficulty reporting any specific thoughts in their mind at the time, they are helped to identify the meaning they were attaching to whatever was going on. Through the use of prompts such as 'how did you feel right then?', 'what is going through your mind?' and 'what did you make of that?', a patient can be helped to become more aware of, and to spontaneously identify, their automatic negative thoughts. As patients become able to do this for themselves they are encouraged to practice by recording their negative thoughts on a diary sheet, such as a daily thought record (for excellent examples of thought records, see Greenberger & Padesky, 1995).

Questioning Automatic Thoughts

The negative automatic thoughts that are identified are then questioned in order to establish their effects on the patient's mood and their validity. The patient is first asked to consider what has led them to believe a certain negative thought. They are then asked if there are any factors that do not fit with their negative thought. The therapist may draw attention to things they already know about the patient that may be relevant or may pursue new lines of enquiry. Questioning is used to find out whether the patient's thought was biased. Patients often find it helpful to be given a list of typical depressive biases in thinking (see Appendix 2), as this can help them to stand back from their negative thoughts. Alternative ways of construing the situation are considered in order to assess whether they could be more valid or more helpful. Questions frequently used in helping patients to assess the validity of their negative thoughts are shown below (and see Appendix 2 for a handout for patients to guide them in questioning their thoughts). The intensity of negative feelings and degree of belief in the negative thoughts are often rated before and after the questioning process to help to establish whether any helpful change has resulted. From the modelling of this careful weighing up of the validity of thoughts and the exploration of alternatives provided during therapy sessions, the patient can learn to apply a similar process for themselves to thoughts identified between sessions. Again the patient is often asked to record their efforts using a daily thought record.

Frequently the information needed to know whether or not a particular thought is accurate is not available during the session, or the patient can see that an alternative view is possible but remains largely unconvinced. In these cases, a behavioural experiment can be devised. The patient's negative expectations or predictions about some problem situation are first identified. The patient then confronts the situation in order to test out whether the actual results fit better with the negative thought or some alternative view.

Teaching patients to identify and question their automatic thoughts has a number of benefits. Reducing the degree of belief in negative thoughts and considering plausible alternatives can directly lift depressed mood. In addition, through the repeated experience of monitoring and questioning depressive experiences, the patient can acquire an awareness of negative thoughts as they come to mind (Moore, 1996). This awareness is helpful in itself through helping the patient to identify less with their depressive thoughts and feelings. Importantly, it can also then be used to instigate different cognitive processes or behaviours. Even-handed or even sympathetic forms of thinking can be deployed to counter the self-criticism

Questions to Help Patients to Assess the Validity and Usefulness of their Automatic Thoughts

- What are the facts?
  - What leads you to think that? What supports that way of thinking?
  - Is it possible that this thought contains any of the thinking errors we have discussed? Which ones?
  - Are there any things that would go against that thought?
  - What did people actually say? What is the evidence?
  - If this thought was a charge against you, would it stand up in court?
  - Have you overlooked any more positive aspects of this? Were there any things that go in your favour?
- Are there any other explanations?
  - Can you see any other way of viewing this?
  - If a friend was in this situation, what would you say to them?
  - How would you have viewed this when you were not so depressed?
  - How do you think you will see this situation in a year's time?
- What is the effect of thinking this way?
  - Are you just making yourself more depressed?
  - Are you seeing things as worse than they really are?
  - So what if this really was true? Would it be as bad as you are thinking?
  - Will this view help you to deal with the problem? Would another view be more helpful?
- What can you do about this situation?
  - Is there anything you can do differently?
  - If you were not thinking so negatively, what would you do about this?
  - How could you test out the accuracy of this thought? How would you find out if another view fits better?

and condemnation common in depression. This can prevent some of the depressing effects of negative thinking on mood. Through employing these techniques, the patient may then begin to develop more of a sense of control over their symptoms, which can further erode the hopelessness and helplessness inherent in depression.

AUTOMATIC THOUGHTS IN PERSISTENT DEPRESSION

As was discussed in Chapter 1, negative automatic thoughts can be surprisingly hard to identify in patients with chronic depression. Due to emotional avoidance, ups and downs in mood may not be evident. Alternatively, low moods may have been so catastrophic that the patient does not wish to think about the experience further. Cognitive avoidance may also lead the patient to deny having negative thoughts or to present thoughts that seem incongruent with the cognitive model (e.g. 'I was quite pleased to be made redundant as driving to work was getting to be more and more of a pain'). Even when negative thoughts have successfully been identified, attempts to question them can be similarly problematic. Some negative thoughts are held with such conviction that they are seen as incontrovertible facts. Sometimes the conviction in such thoughts is backed up by a long list of evidence. However, frequently the feeling of conviction is such that assessing the evidence for and against the thought is seen as quite irrelevant.

In view of the central role given in the cognitive model of persistent depression to underlying beliefs, it can be tempting to dispense with working on automatic thoughts and attempt to focus immediately on modification of beliefs. As discussed in Chapter 2 (page 90), it is usually essential to complete some work with automatic thoughts before attempting to address directly the patient's deeper beliefs. Focusing directly on underlying beliefs before the patient has some experience of attempts to identify and question more superficial thoughts can be highly threatening to a chronically depressed patient. Beliefs tend to be so entrenched that attempting to modify them directly at an early stage of therapy can be counterproductive. Targeting the thoughts that are most specific to particular situations will maximise the likelihood of change in the short term.

In the face of the difficulties resulting from avoidance and from the influence of underlying beliefs, identifying and questioning automatic thoughts in persistent depression requires persistence and a slow pace of working, as in the behavioural work discussed in the previous chapter. As changes occurring in the degree of belief in automatic thoughts can be small, the therapist can aim to bring about a number of other beneficial changes. These additional aims of working at the level of specific automatic thoughts include:

- reducing the rigidity of thinking,
- recognising and countering subtle forms of avoidance, and
- building awareness of thoughts as thoughts not facts.

Aims of Questioning Automatic Thoughts

Because of the rigidity and longstanding nature of thinking in persistent depression, changes that result from questioning automatic thoughts are smaller than when working with acutely depressed patients. This often makes it hard for the patient (and for the therapist) to see any progress from questioning thoughts. If patients ignore or dismiss small positive changes resulting from their efforts, then this will reinforce their low self-esteem, helplessness and hopelessness. It is an important part of the process of therapy to train patients to give some attention to positive changes, however small. Therefore, it is particularly important for the therapist to maintain vigilance for the smallest changes, which are sometimes manifest in the degree of belief in automatic thoughts or intensity of affect associated with them. Once any such change has been identified, it can be consolidated through examining how it might be put into practice in terms of changes in behaviour. Any behavioural changes need to be brought to the attention of the patient in order to reinforce the change. Identifying and paying attention to small positive changes can begin to introduce some doubt into global negative thinking styles. Where questioning and behavioural tests result in even small modifications at the level of automatic thoughts, the rigidity of the cognitive system that reinforces the negative thinking can be slightly weakened. Small changes at the level of specific automatic thoughts can help to increase the flexibility with which beliefs at higher levels in the cognitive hierarchy are applied.

Secondly, the model suggests that subtle forms of behavioural, cognitive and emotional avoidance have important negative consequences in patients' lives. These negative consequences, such as disruptions in relationships or impairments in work and social roles, can fuel overt negative thinking and reinforce underlying beliefs. In this way, the chronic cognitive triad of low self-esteem, helplessness and hopelessness becomes entrenched. Helping patients to recognise subtle forms of avoidance is an important step in preventing this reinforcement of the triad. Working with automatic thoughts in the session frequently results in patients' subtle avoidance strategies coming to the fore. This can be used to help the patient to recognise their cognitive and emotional avoidance. If the therapist can guide the patient in focusing on specific thoughts about their life situation, this runs counter to such avoidance. Automatic thoughts that fuel the patient's fear of engaging with thoughts and feelings in this way within the therapy session can also be identified and questioned, as will be described in the following pages. Focusing by degree on specific thoughts and distressing feelings within the relative safety of the therapy setting can begin to increase tolerance of distressing experiences. Although the patient may still believe their well-established negative thoughts, working with specific negative thoughts in therapy may foster their cognitive and emotional engagement in subsequent experiences. Fostering such engagement is an important factor in beginning to erode the chronic cognitive triad.

Thirdly, the process of questioning automatic thoughts provides a model for the patient of standing back from depressive experiences to view them from a more objective perspective. Through working with automatic thoughts using standard techniques, the patient may be helped to recognise patterns in their negative thinking, including commonly occurring thinking errors or biases. External factors that are discrepant from their thoughts may be brought to their attention, as may the possibility of behaving in ways other than those dictated by the thoughts. Even when the resulting changes in the content of thought are limited, questioning repeatedly how thoughts relate to specific situations can result in some recognition of the thoughts as internal events, rather than as simply reflecting external reality. This awareness of thoughts as thoughts may be of benefit in itself (see Chapter 12 for research evidence on this possibility), and may also help in the elucidation (to both therapist and patient) of underlying belief systems. Working on automatic thoughts can be helpful in understanding and formulating beliefs before addressing those beliefs directly.

Although underlying beliefs and schemas are not the direct focus of activity during this stage of therapy, it can nevertheless be very helpful to use the concept to help to explain difficulties that arise in focusing on automatic thoughts. As was discussed in Chapter 4, using the idea of schemas can help to explain why certain behaviours or thoughts seem to arise more automatically and feel more natural or 'right' than others. Acknowledging the role of beliefs at this point can help patients to put certain negative expectations or behaviours 'on hold' for a time in the promise that they will be addressed later. This can sometimes permit change in superficial thoughts or behaviours that would otherwise be constrained by the negative beliefs (see example on page 176).

PROBLEMS IN IDENTIFYING AUTOMATIC NEGATIVE THOUGHTS

Throughout the behavioural tasks of monitoring and scheduling activities, the therapist will have been drawing the patient's attention to the negative thoughts that are triggered by the tasks. The patient is then encouraged to identify negative thoughts occurring within and between sessions, and to examine the potential role such thoughts may have in exacerbating or maintaining low mood. In identifying the links between thoughts and emotions and establishing thoughts as targets that may help in alleviating low mood, it is essential that the thoughts that are identified are 'hot', i.e. associated with the *experiencing* of negative feelings.

Problem: The Therapist has Difficulty Helping the Patient to Identify Automatic Thoughts

It is often assumed, especially by those less familiar with the practice of cognitive therapy, that identifying the crucial 'hot' thoughts is easy and that the hard work lies in the process of questioning them that follows. This is by no means always so. Even when working with acute disorders, identifying with precision the thoughts that are key to the patient's distress can be a considerable challenge.

Don't

- Become abstract and try to describe the definitive features of an automatic thought
- Assume there is necessarily avoidance or resistance at work.

Do

- Consider words, images and meanings
- Persist with standard techniques, including review of upsetting events, mood changes occurring in session, and automatic thought records.

When the patient has difficulty identifying automatic thoughts, do not automatically assume there is necessarily avoidance or resistance at work. Accurately pinpointing the relevant 'hot' thoughts is often the hardest task in cognitive therapy, after which questioning the thoughts and identifying beliefs can flow with less difficulty. Patients with any diagnosis may not be accustomed to making the fine discriminations among different aspects of their mental life demanded by the task of identifying automatic thoughts. Automatic thoughts can occur in words, images and meanings. Images, which are often associated with anxiety, and meanings automatically attached to events are particularly hard for patients spontaneously to recognise and report. Some types of automatic thoughts, such as self-critical thoughts, are habitual and therefore difficult for the individual to recognise or observe.

When working with chronically depressed patients, persistence with standard techniques is particularly important. Occasions where the patient has reported upsetting incidents and has spontaneously reported automatic negative thoughts may be rare so need to be emphasised and welcomed. Standard techniques of discussing affect laden situations, including upsets from between or within sessions, and using prompts such as 'What went through your mind?' and 'What did you make of that?' merit many repetitions. Recording any successes at pinpointing hot thoughts on thought records helps to consolidate the embryonic skill and makes it easy to refer back when examples are needed. When using these standard techniques in cases of persistent depression, a number of particular problems can arise.

Problem: The Patient has Difficulty Experiencing and Labelling Emotions

Avoidance in the form of not engaging in certain activities or situations is common in chronic depression. It is also common for patients to avoid distressing emotions more directly by simply suppressing emotional experience. This often applies not only to negative emotions, such as sadness, anxiety, anger, guilt and shame, but also to positive emotional states such as happiness or excitement. This damping down of affect results in emotional flattening, and difficulty in describing and experiencing emotions. Such patients often seem to intellectualise emotional reactions as opposed to experiencing them. The negative mood experienced by such patients is a persistent, flat gloom that has little relation to ongoing events and presents little by way of variation. The conventional cognitive model whereby 'hot' negative thoughts can precipitate downswings in mood has little currency in such patients. They may present negative thoughts, but these are often repetitive and stereotyped in nature and do not appear to provoke (or be provoked by) acute changes in mood.

Don't

- Intellectualise the problem by having abstract discussions regarding emotions
- Use hypothetical examples
- Engage in intellectual debate about the validity of stereotyped, ruminative thoughts.

Do

- Provoke and focus on discomfort associated with desired behavioural goals
- Encourage articulation and labelling of any flicker of feeling elicited
- Slow the pace of therapy whenever there are signs of emotional experience
- Collaboratively construct behavioural experiments to test catastrophic predictions regarding experiencing and showing emotions
- Work with the patient to formulate beliefs about emotions (see Chapter 9).

For many such patients, intellectual discussions about emotional events or talking about how other people would feel is a safe route out of their own emotional experience. Their lives often consist of well-established cognitive and behavioural routines from which emotional experience has long been drained. They seem to have simply 'got used to' certain negative thoughts, such as 'I am weak or pathetic' and 'Things are never going to change'. Engaging with or disputing these thoughts usually results in a rather sterile debate that is a further enactment of the patient's problems rather than a solution to them. Some evoking of discomfort in the process of therapy is usually essential to the elicitation of emotions and of 'hot' thoughts. There is an obvious danger that a patient will see such discomfort as a sign that therapy is going to be unhelpful or damaging, so presentation of a rationale outlining the benefits of emotions and of finding new ways to deal with unhelpful emotions is important.

Discomfort is most likely to emerge where the patient is subject to new experiences. It is most useful to discuss specific life changes that the patient would like to occur. Patients may be happy to fantasise about idealistic scenarios and so the therapist should try to ground such discussion in the possibility that the patient really will have to undertake specific changes. Sometimes the realistic discussion of potential life changes is enough to evoke some anxiety. In other cases, specific behavioural assignments are most helpful. In discussing the specific experiences of the patient, the therapist must be alert to small signs of emotional arousal, particularly changes in posture and tone of voice. Slowing the pace of the session by asking short, direct questions and waiting patiently for the answers can help to magnify these flickers of arousal. The therapist must resist the temptation to answer their own questions or provide stories or examples, as this may extinguish any such flickers. When even a small degree of acute discomfort has been evoked, it should be noted and labelled. It is important to remember that what may seem to the therapist to be a minimal emotional reaction may seem immensely affecting to the patient. Once the emotion has been labelled, an attempt can be made to identify automatic thoughts using standard questions, such as 'What is going through your mind just now?'.

Helping *Stan* to identify 'hot' automatic thoughts in therapy was a challenge. He could talk impassively about situations that might be assumed to be upsetting, such as having been made redundant. He frequently described himself in self-denigratory terms as being weak or pathetic, but this did not disturb his overall air of passive resignation. The first steps towards acknowledging and experiencing emotions and identifying the associated thoughts were taken through considering new ways he might handle situations. For example, at the fifth session he described in a gloomy tone the prospect of going with his wife to a party held by one of her friends. He did not want to go, but passively accepted that he would go and would not enjoy himself. The therapist asked what he would really like to happen.

After some stalling, Stan figured that he would like to tell his wife that he did not want to go. When asked by the therapist what that would be like, he tensed up visibly and replied that it would be terrible. Further prompting as to what would happen revealed predictions that his wife would get very angry, would overrule him and leave him feeling that he had been ridiculous. These predictions were labelled as negative thoughts and their role in making him feel tense and uncomfortable discussed. This led to further discussion that the predictions might not be wholly accurate, but that while he suppressed his feelings and avoided potentially difficult situations he would not be able to find out.

Any emotional reaction in the session may also provoke a secondary emotional reaction of anxiety or shame about showing emotions. As the suppression of emotions is often driven by beliefs about being weak or about being humiliated by others, the breaking down of such suppression in the session is likely to be accompanied by thoughts of losing control or being ridiculed by the therapist. Pinpointing these feelings and thoughts at the time they occur in the session can be extremely helpful in socialising avoidant patients into the model and training them to recognise what 'hot' thoughts are like. For example, in exchanging feedback about the discussion described above, Stan admitted to feeling embarrassed. On prompting by the therapist, he identified thoughts that the therapist would think he was 'ridiculous' and 'should grow up'. Where possible, these 'hot' thoughts that have been provoked in the session should be questioned using standard reality testing techniques or behavioural experiments. In this example, the therapist helped Stan to label his thoughts as mindreading, before clarifying that they were not true. It can sometimes also be helpful to introduce the idea that emotional suppression is driven by beliefs about emotions. Some patients readily endorse beliefs such as 'Emotions are a sign of weakness' or 'Showing your emotions makes you look ridiculous'. Although detailed exploration of the roots of these beliefs and attempts at modification are best left until later in therapy, asking the patient to consider how such beliefs might be affecting the situations discussed can be helpful.

Problem: The Patient Refuses to Discuss Upsetting Situations

For some patients, cognitive avoidance has become a deliberate strategy used to manage upset. The principle that if events make you feel bad then it is better not to think about them has an obvious appeal. The therapist's suggestion of going over upsetting events from the last week or further in the past is seen as unhelpful and potentially damaging.

Don't

- Insist that the patient discusses the upsetting situation
- Change focus to an unrelated area.

Do

- Identify the patient's thoughts about discussing upsets
- Use these thoughts to illustrate the cognitive model
- Discuss the pros and cons of not thinking about upsetting things
- Approach the discussion of upsetting situations in a graded fashion
- Point to the possibility that particular underlying beliefs may be magnifying upsets.

It is important initially to reassure the patient that their wish not to talk about certain upsets makes some sense and that they will not be forced to talk about things they do not wish to. Patients' thoughts about discussing upsetting situations and their specific predictions should be elicited. These commonly centre on the prospect of feeling extremely upset, losing control and making the depressive symptoms even worse. Fears of being criticised or rejected or of being revealed as some sort of horrible person often emerge. The effects of these thoughts on how the patient is feeling in the session can be identified and can usefully be drawn out in a vicious circle diagram. The possibility that these thoughts may be magnifying the most upsetting aspects of the situation can then be raised.

For example, *Catherine* was quite adamant from the outset of therapy that there were things in her past that were too upsetting to discuss and that she was attending therapy only on the understanding that she would not have to talk about these things. As there seemed to be no shortage of other problems to work on, the therapist agreed. Over the first few sessions, she described her mood as 'up and down'. When the therapist asked what had dragged her down, she would say it was better not to think about it and would refuse to discuss things further. The therapist focused on her thoughts about talking about these downswings. She admitted that she was worried that any such discussion would make her feel worse and put her into a deep depression from which she would take months to emerge, if at all. The links between these thoughts, her anxiety and her reluctance to talk were drawn out on paper. The therapist then gently questioned whether the fear of hitting this 'raw nerve' may have resulted in overestimating the upset. Catherine was asked for examples from her own experience of when an initial impression of an upsetting situation proved to be out of proportion. She was able to recall a time when she had felt anxious for some days after a friend had told her about her unhappy childhood. Her anxiety arose from worrying about whether she should tell her friend about her own unhappy childhood. In the end, she had done so and, far from precipitating a profound depression, found that it gave her quite a sense of relief. She could then acknowledge the possibility that this might also happen if she discussed upsetting incidents in therapy.

It is important for the therapist to help the patient consider the effects of the strategy of not thinking about such upsetting things. Possible negative consequences of not thinking about things are that exaggerated views remain unquestioned and the associated distress remains worse than it need be. The idea of testing out the possible benefits of going over an upsetting situation in order to re-evaluate the upsetting thoughts can then be proposed. It is best to identify a relatively minor problem that the patient would find easiest to discuss first and the automatic thoughts about discussing this problem can then be elicited and tested out. For example, in reply to the therapist's questioning, Catherine acknowledged that the effect of having an ever-lengthening list of things that she could not think about was in itself quite stressful. She then agreed to test out the effects of talking about upsets in the session by describing a minor upset from the previous week. At this time, she had felt low after declining an invitation from a friend to go shopping. With some anxiety (manifest in her fidgeting in her chair), she pinpointed her thought that her friend would have lost all patience with her and would not want anything further to do with her. Almost immediately on saying this, Catherine relaxed and said, 'But I guess it's not likely is it—Lynne is just not like that'. The therapist (with a similar sigh of relief) was able to help her to contrast this outcome with her catastrophic automatic thoughts about feeling worse and worse. Although she remained very reluctant for a long time to go into any of her deeper concerns, interventions such as this did begin to help Catherine to develop some skill at identifying and questioning her automatic thoughts.

Problem: The Patient does not Report Negative Thoughts, but Blanks Out or Volunteers Unrelated or Positive Thoughts

Some patients can talk about the circumstances of an upset quite willingly, but when the therapist tries to home in on their thoughts, they blank out or report thoughts that do not seem to fit the situation or their emotional reaction to it. Some patients report quite deliberately trying not to think negative thoughts or thinking thoughts other than those they know will be upsetting. For other patients this seems to occur with less conscious control.

This is sometimes seen in patients reacting to perceived put-downs by denigrating the other person (e.g. 'She asked me if I had found a boyfriend yet . . . well, actually she is quite ugly and overweight. She could do with losing a few pounds'). Some patients respond to apparently difficult situations by thinking positive thoughts, such as 'I'm a nice person' or 'I don't really mind if . . . '. Sometimes the thoughts reported are negative but just not 'hot', as when one patient consistently reported that she was 'useless' in response to questions about situations where it seemed likely to the therapist that she felt lonely and thought she had been let down or abandoned.

Don't

• Become overly aggressive or persecutory in questioning style
• Allow the patient consistently to change the subject.

Do

• Consistently point out the possibility of cognitive avoidance
• Discuss the pros and cons of avoidance as a coping strategy
• Identify negative predictions about acknowledging negative thoughts
• Conduct behavioural experiments to test out effects of recognising negative thoughts.

Cognitive avoidance is one way that patients with chronic depression cope with information relating to underlying negative beliefs. The avoidance can manifest itself in many different forms. When patients become vague, the therapist may end up feeling confused. When patients report negative thoughts which are not those that are really troubling them, the therapist may pick up an impression that things do not quite fit together. For patients to start expanding on other people's problems or talk as though everything was fine can be quite frustrating for the therapist. The effect of all these forms of avoidance is similar: they prevent the activation of negative beliefs but they also prevent problems, whether in thinking processes or life situations, being addressed. Although this avoidance can be very frustrating, it is important for the therapist not simply to react by becoming more aggressive in questioning. Although this can succeed on occasion, patients often become even more defensive in response. Where vigorous probing does succeed in breaking through to hot thoughts, the patient can become highly distressed or angry, leading to disruption in the therapeutic alliance.

When working with this problem, the therapist needs to be alert for the signs of cognitive avoidance. Key signs are when the discussion shifts off the intended focus, becomes unusually jokey or starts to get combative.

The therapist can raise the possibility that avoidance is going on. It can be helpful to describe how people can see upsetting thoughts coming, so they push the thoughts out of their mind or think other things. The therapist can help the patient to begin to recognise their own avoidance by trying to catch it as consistently as possible when it arises in sessions. The advantages and disadvantages can then be discussed. It is important to acknowledge that avoidance can be highly effective in achieving the goal of minimising the impact of distressing events. The drawbacks of avoidance then need to be carefully considered. These include that by not engaging with the process of trying to solve problems or tackle current difficulties, those problems are more likely to persist. The idea that by not thinking upsetting thoughts they remain unquestioned can be compared to a child's view of a 'bogey man': by never going into the room in which this scary horror exists, the child never discovers that the bogey man is in fact just the shadow of a piece of furniture. Deliberately pushing away negative thoughts can also be self-defeating, as pushing away the thoughts can establish a rebound effect. This leads to a ruminative cycle that, far from ameliorating negative affect, in fact results in its persistence (Wegner et al., 1987).

This was the case for *Peter* whose depressive presentation was characterised by rumination over his depressive symptoms and intrusive memories of unpleasant events in his life. When a negative thought threatened, he would say to himself, 'I should not think those sorts of thoughts', and then deliberately push it from his mind, substituting it with a neutral image, usually of that of a footballer kicking a ball. The first step in addressing his cognitive avoidance was to conduct an in-session behavioural experiment to test out the relationship between his deliberate pushing away of thoughts and the establishment of a ruminative cycle (see Garland, 1996). Through being instructed to try as hard as he could not to think a number of his upsetting thoughts, he recognised that the result was that the thought became more likely to pop into his mind and that a sense of dread of the thought persisted. His worries about not keeping the thoughts at bay were then elicited. Peter perceived these thoughts as evidence of a lack of control over his mind. Apart from seeing this generally as a sign of weakness, he took his 'out of control mind' as evidence of an impending descent into madness, involving complete loss of control of his physical and mental faculties. In further discussion of his negative thoughts, he recognised that while he felt far from comfortable, he was actually gaining in confidence that he would not lose control completely. This helped him gradually to recognise and, with the therapist's help, to counter his tendency to avoid distressing thoughts. Helping him to question and modify these thoughts then became the focus for much therapeutic activity (see below).

Problem: The Patient becomes Highly Distressed when 'Hot' Thoughts are Identified and Blames the Therapist for the Upset

When the patient seems to be avoiding thinking about thoughts that are key to their problems (as described above), the therapist will have to probe to identify the key 'hot' cognitions. Even once the advantages of countering avoidance in this way appear to have been agreed, when the therapist manages to pinpoint 'hot' thoughts, patients can become highly distressed. What seems to the therapist to be a sensible strategy is then seen by the patient as an emotional attack. Patients may therefore become quite angry with the therapist.

Don't

- Become quiet and withdrawn
- Ask too many questions.

Do

- Emphatically acknowledge the patient's upset and anger
- Discuss the idea of activation of underlying beliefs
- Plan with the patient practical strategies for dealing with the explosive affect and begin to implement them in the session
- Work at identifying more peripheral automatic thoughts first.

Where patients have relied excessively on cognitive avoidance for dealing with negative information, they will not have developed other ways of coping with negative thoughts about themselves or negative feelings. If they have not acquired any ability to discriminate between thoughts and facts, the therapist's pinpointing a thought of inadequacy or unlovability may seem as though the therapist had directly described them as inadequate or unlovable. In this case, for the therapist simply to continue asking questions is perceived as persecutory. For the therapist to go quiet, even if intended as a time of empathic reflection, may be interpreted either as a sign of tacit agreement with the patient's extreme negative perceptions or as a sign that the therapist is incompetent and cannot handle the situation.

It usually proves more helpful in these cases for the therapist actively to acknowledge the patient's upset and anger, and to formulate it with the patient in terms of the activation of underlying beliefs. The important ideas to convey are that people can have certain negative beliefs about themselves, and that these beliefs are triggered when events are interpreted in a way consistent with the belief. When these beliefs are triggered, it can cause a huge amount of distress. It can be helpful to relate the patient's current experience in the session to other situations where such high affect has been triggered. Identifying common themes can serve as a guide to the content of important beliefs that can be useful later in therapy. The difference between beliefs and facts must be stressed, and can be illustrated in relation to differences between people's view of themselves and others' views of them. The therapist can point out that the immediate priority is to help the patient to deal with feeling so upset and that discussion of the validity of the upsetting beliefs can be addressed in later sessions. Discussion of how to handle the upset can then be helpful, including helping the patient to plan the time after the therapy session. Planning simple, practical activities like seeing a friend, going for a cup of coffee or going for a walk can help to restore the sense of collaboration. It can be pointed out that the patient has faced one of their very worst thoughts and that learning to catch other thoughts will not be so upsetting.

PROBLEMS IN QUESTIONING AUTOMATIC THOUGHTS

Questioning automatic thoughts is often seen as the central aspect of cognitive therapy for acute depression. Because of the information processing biases operating in low mood, questions that draw the patient's attention to new information or prompt them to interpret things differently can result in different conclusions being drawn. The change in the degree of belief in the negative view is assumed to be associated with the reduction of depressed mood. Some useful standard questions are presented in the box on page 202 and their use is discussed in detail in J. Beck (1995). As with other behavioural and cognitive techniques, when using questioning techniques with persistently depressed patients smaller changes are to be expected. Therefore, persistence and repetition are usually necessary. Particular problems that commonly occur in these patients are described below.

Problem: Questioning one Thought Triggers more Automatic Thoughts and an Increase in Distress, which the Patient Attributes to the Therapist

In therapy with chronically depressed patients, just as avoidance can thwart the completion of behavioural assignments intended to counter it, negative thoughts can beset the very interventions intended to modify them. If this is not addressed, then cognitive interventions such as modifying automatic thoughts may make the patient worse rather than better.

A negative reaction to questioning of negative thoughts is usually driven by the patient's underlying beliefs, typically those concerning inferiority, incompetence and ridicule. Questioning the patient's automatic thoughts can activate beliefs about being incompetent, resulting in responses such as 'I'm so stupid' or 'I'm so useless I don't even think properly'. Where patients hold conditional rules regarding the importance of maintaining control or beliefs that they are inferior to others who might ridicule them, they can perceive the therapist as trying to belittle them in a game of intellectual one-upmanship. Some patients may then engage in the intervention as if it were a wrestling match, and it is not uncommon for such patients to make comments such as 'you're very clever aren't you' or 'you're trying to catch me out'. In the face of this, patients can react in a defensive, hostile fashion or feel browbeaten and defeated. If left unchecked, this could result in patients disengaging from therapy altogether.

Don't

• Give up questioning the patient's negative thoughts
• Question the patient's desire to get better.

Do

• Draw the patient's attention to the negative thoughts triggered by this process and illustrate their role in maintaining low mood
• Make sure the rationale for questioning thoughts is clear to the patient
• Give the patient more control over the questioning process
• Continue the intervention, while drawing the patient's attention to factors contrary to their distortions.

Although both patient and therapist may have concerns that cognitive techniques are making things worse, it is important that the questioning techniques are not abandoned, as this will appear to confirm the negative ideas that have been activated. Rather, the focus of the cognitive intervention is broadened to include the thoughts about the intervention itself. The initial step of this is to identify and label the thoughts triggered by the intervention and use them as a further illustration of the cognitive model. For example, a hostile response to questioning was encountered in an early session with Charlie, whose depression was characterised by irritability and anger. The therapist was exploring a situation where Charlie had become angry because he believed that a stranger had tried to kick his dog while out walking in the local park. The therapist was asking questions to try to clarify what happened.

T: So if I can just clarify. You were walking in the park this morning with your dog and a man tried to kick her?
C: Yes.

T: What exactly did he do?
C: Lifted his foot up as she walked past him.
T: Was it a definite kick?
C: Well, no. But I know that's what he was planning.
T: How did you know?
C: I could tell.
T: Mmm... Are there any other explanations for him lifting his foot?
C: (*leaning forward in his chair and speaking through gritted teeth*) Now listen here. Don't you f•••ing start, I know it happened okay, and I know he meant it.

The therapist apologised and quickly moved onto safer ground by discussing his general activity levels. However, some minutes later Charles interrupted the flow of conversation as follows:

C: Can I say I'm sorry for getting annoyed at you when we were talking about Misty (*his dog*)?
T: (*smiling*) Of course. You did seem quite angry, was it anything I said?
C: You seemed to be questioning my judgement.
T: In what way?
C: By asking all those questions.
T: I see. This seems an important thing for us to talk about. In order to do that I might need to ask more questions. Can I ask another question? If you feel yourself becoming annoyed let me know. Is that okay?
C: Yes, go ahead.
T: Could you tell me a bit more about how it felt when I was asking questions?
C: It felt like you were getting at me.
T: So, when I asked the questions it felt like I was 'questioning your judgement' and 'getting at you'. That must have hurt.
C: Yes. I felt like I was being put down. I realise now you are probably trying to help.
T: How are you feeling about me continuing to ask questions at the moment?
C: Okay.
T: I know you said earlier that since becoming depressed you try to avoid other people's company. I was wondering if there was any connection between feeling got at and put down and withdrawing from people?
C: (*nodding*) Yes, it happens quite a lot. I'm not with people a few minutes before I'm angry and arguing.
T: I'd like to try to use this situation of you feeling annoyed when I was asking questions to try to explain how cognitive therapy might help you in dealing with that problem. In order to do that I'd like to write some things down. Are you happy for me to do that?

The therapist then drew out a vicious circle in relation to the therapeutic interaction and related it to Charlie's more general problem of irritability in social situations. It proved particularly effective to contrast the vicious circle of his perceptions regarding the therapist's initial questioning and a more helpful circle regarding his perceptions during the discussion regarding his reaction to the questioning style.

The likelihood of chronically depressed patients misinterpreting the therapist's intentions in questioning thoughts is increased if the therapist launches into this without any explicit rationale. It is usually preferable to minimise the chances of such misinterpretations by providing the patient with an explicit rationale that describes the process of questioning automatic thoughts as a treatment strategy. In addition, for patients who might see the intervention as a competition, giving them control over the questioning process can reduce the chances of them battling against it. This can be done by incorporating into the rationale some encouragement for them to participate actively in the intervention, as illustrated in the following extract from a session with *Dave*.

T: Okay, Dave, from the sessions and homework assignments over the last three weeks we have established that you experience a number of these automatic negative thoughts associated with feeling depressed, anxious and guilty and that they occur in a variety of situations. What I'd like to do now is to try to introduce to you a strategy for trying to tackle these thoughts when they occur. Basically it involves examining each thought using a series of questions to see how helpful the thoughts are. How does that sound?

D: Seems a bit complicated.

T: It certainly takes practice. But we can have a go at doing this together and spend the next three or four sessions practising it. (*smiling*) And of course there's also the dreaded homework in between!

D: (*chuckling*) How could I forget. This is possibly worse than school!

T: As you might guess we have a diary sheet to fill in. We also have a sheet with the questions on. (*Showing these to Dave and placing them on the table between them both.*) Have you got the automatic thought sheet you completed over the last week?

D: Here—can you read my writing, it's terrible isn't it?

T: Yeah, I can read it. So the situation was yesterday when your father-in-law visited and brought up the subject of your business going bust...

D: (*sigh*) As he always does.

T: ...and you felt angry and the thought there is 'He really enjoys rubbing salt into my wounds'. You felt guilty related to a thought 'It was all my fault' and depressed with a thought 'I'm a failure to my family' which you believed 100%. Are any of those thoughts still bothering you now?

D: Well I'm not so angry—he has always been critical of everyone, it's the way he is. Also I did everything I could to keep the business afloat, it isn't really my fault. But I do think I'm a failure to my family, I've really let them down.

T: Okay, let's take the thought 'I'm a failure to my family'. How much do you believe that right now?

D: The same, 100%.

T: Okay. What I want to do now is to try to examine this thought from a range of viewpoints to see that we have the whole picture or whether there is some information we are overlooking. Let me know how you find this and if you want to stop at any point we can. Just to say, it's not a test—it's hopefully something that with practice will prove helpful to you in managing your depression.

D: I hope so. It looks hard.

T: I understand it might seem that way. Let's have a go at working on it together. We are going to use these sheets as the basis for the exercise. As I said before it's usual that learning to use this technique takes a bit of practice. When we've practised the strategy you can take the sheets away to use at home. So let's have a go and then afterwards we can discuss how you found using the technique.

When patients react negatively to the questioning of negative thoughts by the therapist, actively involving the patient in the questioning process can lead to further negative thoughts. Again, these negative thoughts can be highlighted, incorporated within the cognitive model and themselves questioned or tested out. As these thoughts are generally good examples of ongoing 'hot' negative processing on the part of the patient, actively putting them to the test and drawing the patient's attention to discrepant information during the course of therapy can be especially helpful.

Peter was one patient who reacted negatively to various tacks taken in the course of therapy. He was plagued by feelings of guilt over having made some of his work colleagues redundant when he was still working. He held himself 100% responsible for their redundancies. The therapist chose to use a pie chart (Greenberger & Padesky, 1995) to begin to modify this perception. Peter actively participated in the process but when the exercise was complete he looked very deflated. When the therapist enquired as to how he had found the exercise, he replied: 'I'm really stupid aren't I? I should have thought of those things myself—I might as well give up.' To help him to recognise the unhelpful impact of these thoughts on the current intervention, a diagram of his thoughts and feelings in relation to the exercise was drawn out. It was agreed that Peter would put these negative thoughts to the test by working by himself in the session to modify one further thought from his thought record. He was asked to pay attention to when his mood began to plummet. After a few minutes he reported feeling much worse, as during the exercise his mind was bombarded by more automatic thoughts, such as 'this is ridiculous—I should be able to sort this out myself without having to do this'. He also had many further thoughts regarding the events that contributed to the onset of his illness, including 'I worked hard all my life and look how I was thanked' and 'I've let everyone down'. From this, it was agreed that Peter would try to practice developing the skill of modifying automatic thoughts initially by working on one upsetting thought per week. While doing this Peter was to pay attention to any lowering of mood and try to refocus his attention on the task at hand rather than losing himself in his thoughts. While progress in this endeavour was far from smooth, over a number of weeks Peter had some success at questioning thoughts of self-blame over past actions as well as thoughts of incompetence related to difficulties with therapy tasks. Importantly, he also came to view his negative thoughts as 'something my mind does when I am depressed or anxious', rather than as facts.

Problem: Despite Evidence Against the Negative Thought and Plausible Alternatives, the Patient feels no Better

Most therapists who have worked with chronically depressed patients will be familiar with the disappointment of executing an elegant intervention only to find the patient unmoved. In questioning a particular negative thought, a balance of evidence against the thought may have been elicited and promising alternative conclusions explored. Despite this, patients often respond that their belief in the negative thought has not altered or that although they believe the negative thought less, they still feel just as depressed. Where belief in a negative thought remains unaffected by apparently convincing evidence to the contrary, this suggests that prejudicial processing is operating and that the thought directly reflects a fundamental belief. Where belief in the thought changes but mood does not improve, this is usually for one of two reasons. Firstly, the depressed mood may be being maintained by key thoughts or beliefs that are subtly different to, and possibly more fundamental than, the automatic thought that has been disputed. For example, this commonly occurs where the 'hot' thought is apparently along the lines of 'People will think I am useless'. When convincing evidence that people are not reacting so negatively is considered, the patient responds 'Well, I still think I'm useless'. Secondly, where emotions are suppressed, the usual links between thoughts and feelings do not seem to operate. Thus, if the patient thinks the negative thought it does not have an acute adverse effect on their mood; but, conversely, successfully disputing the thought may bring no relief.

Don't

- Try to convince the patient that they are wrong
- Accept that the strategy has failed and conclude that therapy will not work.

Do

- Draw attention to the smallest changes
- Focus on how the thoughts apply to a specific situation
- Pursue changes in behaviour that might follow from the conclusions drawn and devise relevant behavioural experiments
- Formulate the role of beliefs in maintaining negative thinking.

When the patient's thoughts and feelings fly in the face of the evidence in this fashion, it is tempting for both patient and therapist to conclude that there is something wrong with the patient. Patients frequently see such occurrences as proof that they are inherently depressed, have been irretrievably scarred by depression, are irredeemably bad or unlovable or otherwise ridiculously neurotic and weak. The therapist must remember that, according to the cognitive model, the patient's mind may in fact be behaving in an understandable way. The therapist's task is to convey this understanding in a way that helps the patient to employ their mind in a different fashion.

The rationale for working at the level of automatic thoughts, even though core beliefs are presumed to be central to the model of chronic depression, is that processes at more specific and superficial levels are more amenable to change than those at more general and fundamental levels. Helping the patient to focus on situation-specific appraisals, rather than global generalisations, is a key strategy. As the more general structures will not instantly be modified by superficial changes, it follows that the changes that can be expected through these interventions will be small, partial and easily missed or overturned. The usefulness of standard cognitive interventions in the face of powerful negative beliefs depends on recognising and reinforcing small changes that do occur in reactions to specific situations. For example, patients frequently report feeling just the same when their ratings and reports suggest a very small decrease in their depressed mood. A 5 or 10% decrease in depression may indeed be seen as trivial when the mood rating remains at 90%. However, patients can be asked what difference this change would make if it were maintained consistently over a period of a week or a month. For some patients, it might mean the difference between self-harming and not. Although the patient will not be convinced, the therapist needs to afford such changes some attention and importance.

Changes in thinking which result in only minimal changes in mood can be of some importance. Although they do not change the fundamental belief, changes in superficial automatic thoughts can help to support important conclusions that thoughts are not facts and that change is possible. In her efforts to return to work despite her depression, *Rosemary* was convinced that she had 'made a mess of things' and that her colleagues thought she was 'a useless waste of space'. A review of the evidence of how she had got on in her first few days back at work was used to question these thoughts. This suggested that she did manage to do her job competently and her colleagues had been pleased at her return even on the odd occasion when she had to ask for help. Unfortunately, she felt no better as she still believed that she was totally useless, now based on the facts that she felt tired and depressed at work and that she did need some help on occasion in doing her job. However, she no longer believed that other people thought she was a useless waste of space. When the therapist drew this to her attention, she concluded 'I guess it's just me that thinks I'm useless, isn't it'. In continuing at work, she remained depressed but no longer thought that others saw her as useless, suggesting that there had been some peripheral change in her cognitive system. In addition, seeing clearly that her view of herself persisted in spite of the views of others helped her to conclude that this was her own belief. At this point the therapist simply noted that she did seem to have deeply held beliefs about herself which probably contributed to her depression. The results of this intervention proved useful in subsequent sessions when the idea of beliefs as prejudices was discussed (see Chapter 7).

Identifying behavioural markers of these small changes can be helpful. Even when there is no discernible change during a session in the patient's ratings of their belief in the thoughts, they sometimes subsequently act in different ways. For example, in coming to her fifth session, Rosemary felt extremely guilty because she had been unable to babysit for her daughter and reported that she had let her daughter down. Through questioning this thought it emerged, firstly, that although her daughter had seemed somewhat put out, she had managed to find someone else to babysit and, secondly, that one of Rosemary's friends had reassured her that she had handled the situation appropriately. Despite this, she remained convinced that she had let her daughter down and left the session feeling guilty and despondent. However, she returned to the next session saying that this week she had actively phoned her daughter to say that she would not be able to babysit for her. She still felt very guilty about this and believed that she was letting her daughter down, but also felt some satisfaction that she was not totally at her daughter's beck and call. Although the questioning had not changed the rated degree of belief, it had introduced enough doubt to enable a change of behaviour that lifted her mood a little.

The therapist can actively prompt such changes in behaviour after questioning that has not changed the patient's mood. In this regard, questions such as 'If you were to act on the basis of this evidence we have discussed rather than on how you feel, what would you do differently next time?' are most helpful. These occasions where small changes in belief are not accompanied by changes in emotion can usefully be followed up by a behavioural experiment to test out further the validity of the thought. Behavioural experiments that provide opportunities for experiential learning can be effective in facilitating changes in mood and need to be implemented both during and outside the session.

On a cautionary note, belief in negative thoughts can sometimes rest on specific pieces of evidence that the patient does not readily present, even to the therapist. Where such 'proof' remains undisclosed and undisputed, sometimes no amount of counter-evidence will produce any cognitive or emotional shift. For example, with one young man who had many automatic thoughts about being a horrible person, the therapist worked for several sessions to draw to the patient's attention evidence of his likeable actions and qualities, all to no effect. It seemed that the thoughts constituted a core belief. However, the patient subsequently 'confessed' to once having willingly participated in some sexual experimentation in his early teens with his older sister. When the therapist reacted with relief rather than disgust and helped the patient to consider why this did not constitute evidence of 'horribleness', the patient's belief in his negative thoughts quickly and drastically reduced. Being careful to elicit all the evidence that the patient believes supports their negative thoughts can be crucial.

Problem: The Patient Produces Convincing or Voluminous Evidence in Support of their Automatic Thought

In chronic depression, many of the thoughts reported by patients are unfortunately not just a product of the biasing effects of mood nor of deeply held but prejudicial beliefs. Patients frequently have much evidence to support their negative thoughts. For example, the idea that therapy will not work can be supported by the apparent ineffectiveness of many previous treatments. Evidence of personal weakness can consist of a life history of challenges unconfronted, projects abandoned and abuses tolerated. A string of failed relationships, abuse and abandonment can make a convincing case that such people will always be on their own. In practice, as suggested in the cognitive model, such strings of events rarely represent an independent series of misfortunes. Rather, they are often connected, in that core beliefs can result in strategies that produce or maintain certain negative life situations. For example, perceptions of the inevitability of abuse can trap people in abusive relationships, thus perpetuating the perception.

Don't

- Minimise the evidence the patient holds in support of their thought
- Accept your own negative thoughts about the patient's situation.

Do

- Fully acknowledge the distress associated with the patient's setbacks
- Identify any signs of resilience that have helped the patient to come through past difficulties
- Carefully weigh the evidence and its relation to the negative thought
- Think of the strategy that will best serve the patient from here on.

The cognitive model does not presume that the causes of depression are all in the mind. The overwhelming evidence for the contribution of life events and inadequate social support to the onset and maintenance of depression is well documented (e.g. Brown & Harris, 1978). In addition, people who become depressed may themselves have failings, weaknesses or shortcomings, and it would not be helpful for the therapist to deny or minimise these. Indeed within the cognitive model, cognitive avoidance and suppression of the emotional impact of negative events contributes to the maintenance of depression. It is therefore important for the therapist to acknowledge the impact of the setbacks and traumas the patient has suffered. This may be important in forming an alliance with the patient and also in modelling an adaptive response to distressing situations.

Although it can initially seem dispiriting, time spent considering the evidence for negative thoughts is rarely wasted. On rare occasions, a benign interpretation for facts that the patient had considered damning can be persuasive even to a chronically depressed patient (see final paragraph of previous section). On the majority of occasions, when this does not happen, the procedure can still be somewhat helpful. Careful consideration of facts requires the patient to move out of a way of thinking that is automatic and global to a mode of thinking that is more effortful and specific. Even when no new conclusions are drawn, some of the consequences can be beneficial. Firstly, such consideration directly counters the cognitive and emotional avoidance that characterises many cases of chronic depression. To the extent that this avoidance is involved in maintaining the depression, being able to think about specific distressing facts and situations may be beneficial. In addition, thinking about the relationship between the thoughts and the evidence can result in patients being more able to stand back from their thoughts and recognise them as thoughts, even when supported by facts. The process thus helps in the development of meta-awareness of thoughts as thoughts.

For example, Laura was a single mother who had been feeling particularly low the week preceding her third session, following an argument with her parents. She had spent much time pondering the thought that she was a 'useless' person. When the therapist asked her what made her think this, Laura launched into a long series of difficulties. The argument with her family was over some money which she had failed to pay back, because she was 'skint', which was a result of her not working and being 'crap with money', in turn due to having left school without a single qualification because of having become pregnant . . . This discussion took up the entire session, so it was with some trepidation that the therapist asked her what she concluded from the discussion. She replied only slightly gloomily, 'Well, I guess I'm not *such* a bad person'. The therapist asked what it was about the discussion that had lightened her view of herself, and she observed 'I've got problems—who hasn't? I guess I've got to look after Chrissie (her daughter)—that's the priority'. Although the magnitude of her positive reaction is unusual in this patient group, it nevertheless illustrates the benefits of considering apparently negative evidence from a specific standpoint.

Finally, the specific consideration of facts and situations, even those that have lent support to negative conclusions, is more likely to lead to thoughts and activities directed at solving the problems than does more general abstract thinking (Williams et al., 1997). The therapist can help the patient to consider what different strategy might be useful in addressing the problems by asking questions, such as 'If you had your time again, how would you have handled this differently?' or 'If your good friend X was in this situation, what do you think they would try to do?'. Patients with chronic depression—even when a plan for addressing a difficult situation has been identified—will have little faith in being able to carry it out. The plan should be broken down into the smallest possible steps and the smallest first step set up as a behavioural experiment, if possible. *Kate* was extremely low following the break-up of her latest relationship several sessions into therapy. Her automatic thoughts were 'All he wanted was sex and some fags', 'I shall never have a decent relationship', and 'I will always get trodden on'. The therapist already knew something of her long history of short, broken and abusive relationships with men, and indeed the latest break-up served to remind her of these many past miseries, which in turn reinforced her negative thoughts. Guided by an emerging formulation in which themes of being horrible and being abandoned were central, the therapist gently helped her to explore what she might do differently to improve her chances of getting into a 'decent relationship'. She could see that she would do better if she did not quickly accede to the advances of men she did not know, as she had previously tended to do. Although she worried that 'No one decent is going to stand around waiting for me', she agreed that a strategy of taking her time and being more choosy in her relationships was worth a try. The first step in this was to go out with her best friend for a 'girls only' night in order to catch up and get a bit of sympathy, and to put off any men who approached her. Going out with this intention was something she had rarely done and was something of a relief to her. This strategy was worked on in more detail in subsequent work on her core beliefs.

PROBLEMS WITH HOMEWORK ASSIGNMENTS

The importance of homework generally in cognitive therapy and some guidelines for its implementation with patients with persistent depression were discussed in Chapter 2. To make good progress in therapy, it is particularly helpful for patients to develop their ability to recognise negative thoughts as close as possible to the time when the thoughts come to mind. Engagement in some form of monitoring of automatic thoughts is therefore beneficial. Patients also need to develop skills in standing back from and questioning their automatic thoughts, so some form of practice at this between sessions is highly recommended.

Problem: The Patient has Great Difficulty Identifying or Questioning Automatic Thoughts between Sessions

Patients with persistent depression can find it especially difficult to monitor and question thoughts between sessions due to the urge to avoid distress or due to the deep conviction with which thoughts are held. Patients often believe that they cannot change the way they think and this often interferes with any effort to try. Even when they do make such efforts, without help from the therapist, chronically depressed patients frequently find it extremely difficult to identify specific thoughts and question them.

Don't

- Give up setting assignments on automatic thoughts
- Operate on assumptions: find out the reasons for the difficulties.

Do

- Discuss as collaboratively as possible the purpose of monitoring and questioning thoughts
- Agree tasks that are realistic and achievable
- Specify the assignment precisely and write it down
- Problem solve potential obstacles immediately after the assignment is agreed
- Review homework every session and reinforce the patient's smallest efforts
- Be mindful of your own task-interfering cognitions (e.g. 'There's no point in setting homework, she never does it').

The general guidelines for assigning and reviewing homework presented in Chapter 2 are especially relevant when helping patients to monitor and question their own automatic thoughts between sessions. In particular, it is important that patients can see the purpose of identifying and questioning their own thoughts. The rationale for this should therefore be presented clearly and may need to be repeated in several sessions. It can be helpful for the therapist to find out what the patient has made of any such discussion by asking them what benefit they might get from a given assignment. Rather than just discussing the rationale in the abstract, it is best if assignments on monitoring or questioning thoughts are linked to particular helpful moments during therapy sessions. Times in the session when a specific thought was pinpointed or when questioning led to a change in perspective or feeling can usefully lead on to suggesting monitoring or questioning similar thoughts as homework.

As with working on any task with persistently depressed patients, it is important that assignments are small and specified in detail. Whereas patients with acute disorders may be assigned a general task of recording their automatic thoughts, in persistent depression it is preferable to specify more precisely which thoughts will be monitored and when. It can help to agree the particular type of thought that will be monitored (for example, 'shoulds', self-criticisms or negative predictions) or the number of thoughts (for example, two negative thoughts to be caught in the coming week). It also helps to discuss when the process of reflecting and recording will be carried out. Some patients prefer to carry a diary sheet or notebook with them, whereas others prefer to set aside a few minutes at a specific time for identifying thoughts in a more retrospective fashion. When assignments move to questioning thoughts, a specific initial task can be to question a particular thought that has been identified during a session using a sheet of suggested questions on a handout. It is best to hold back the suggestion of questioning negative thoughts in general until such time as patients have had some experiences of success in questioning particular thoughts within or between sessions.

When reviewing the patient's efforts to monitor or question their automatic thoughts, the smallest signs of any progress should be reinforced enthusiastically. For example, many patients do not manage at first to make a written note of their thoughts, but come to a session able to describe a particular time of upset or a particular thought that had crossed their mind. The therapist can greet this positively ('That's it, just what we wanted, a time when a particular thought dragged your mood down') and put it on the agenda for discussion. The possible benefits of and obstacles to writing down such incidents and thoughts can then be raised.

THE THERAPIST'S AUTOMATIC THOUGHTS

One of the biggest challenges facing the clinician when using these cognitive techniques is the impact the patient's negativity can have on the clinician's own thoughts and feelings. Working with patients suffering from chronic depression can involve much hard work for apparently small gains. If the therapist is not careful about their own thoughts, this can lead to frustration and then irritation or demoralisation. In one session with *Elizabeth* (see Chapter 8), the therapist tried to use problem-solving to help Elizabeth to develop an action plan to feed some guests who were visiting her for the weekend. Elizabeth had high standards and was anxious and distressed due to the fact she had been unable to prepare food in advance. Throughout most of the session, Elizabeth cried and the therapist was bombarded by Elizabeth's automatic thoughts regarding her predictions of her guests' negative reactions and the perceived inadequacy of the action plan. As this was happening, the therapist was mindful of her own automatic negative thoughts and their potential to lead her to abandon the intervention at hand. In this instance, they included 'This will never work', 'It's pointless', 'I don't know what else to do' and 'She will never carry this plan out'. It is important for the clinician to recognise that these thoughts are predictions to be tested out in practice and not facts. The thoughts do not provide a good basis for abandoning the intervention. Even if an intervention is not productive initially, it can be helpful to examine the reasons why it has not worked and modify the strategy accordingly. In this particular instance, the therapist stuck to the task despite these reservations, and the intervention proved extremely beneficial to the progress of therapy. Therapists' use of standard techniques on their own automatic thoughts during the course of therapy can be of great benefit in keeping the therapy moving. The use of supervision to assist this process is discussed in Chapter 11.

In summary, working with automatic thoughts in persistent depression raises many difficulties. Repeated and persistent application of techniques for identifying and questioning thoughts may be necessary. In the course of this, the style and aims of the work need to be adjusted in view of the avoidance and enduring negativity encountered in persistent depression. Focusing on the thoughts motivating avoidance is often more fruitful than focusing on thoughts that are consequences of it. As many of the interventions in therapy may provoke avoidance, thoughts about the interventions themselves can usefully be made a focus of therapy. Rather than just aiming to effect change in the content of thinking, the techniques can be used to modify important aspects of the process of thinking. These include introducing flexibility into negative thinking, increasing the patient's ability to consider and question negative experiences and increasing awareness of thoughts as thoughts and not facts. When used with appropriate aims, the use of standard cognitive techniques can introduce a degree of doubt into a previously rigid cognitive system and can help to prepare the way for addressing important underlying beliefs.

SUMMARY POINTS

- Behavioural, cognitive and emotional avoidance can make it hard to identify 'hot' negative thoughts in persistent depression.
- The therapist can help the patient to recognise their subtle avoidance within everyday activities and in therapy.
- When 'hot' thoughts are absent, the therapist may have to provoke them by gently confronting the patient with issues or tasks that they have previously been avoiding.
- Avoidance of or distress about tasks or interactions in therapy can be used to identify negative thoughts about the therapy itself.
- Negative thoughts about the therapy can provide an excellent model of identifying and testing out 'hot' thoughts.
- When therapy triggers overwhelming emotions, a more directive, problem-solving approach is often needed.
- Negative thoughts in persistent depression often do not respond in large degree to questioning.
- Changes in behaviour can be useful in consolidating small changes in thinking.
- Where negative ideas persist despite the evidence, this can be used to raise the patient's awareness of the role of thinking processes and beliefs.

- Guiding the patient in the consideration of specific thoughts and evidence may be useful in undermining global and rigid thinking processes.
- Small changes in thinking can be valuable and should be reinforced.
- The therapist can usefully be mindful of their own negative thoughts when confronted by difficulties.

Chapter 7

RECOGNISING UNDERLYING BELIEFS AND THEIR EFFECTS

In this chapter, you will find descriptions of:

- The importance of helping patients with persistent depression to recognise their underlying beliefs
- The main ways in which underlying beliefs can be identified
- Problems encountered in helping patients to recognise underlying beliefs
- How patients can be helped to see links between early experiences and their underlying beliefs
- The use of the prejudice model to highlight thinking biases
- Belief maintenance diagrams that illustrate how beliefs are maintained

---

From the outset of therapy, the therapist will be concerned to develop hypotheses regarding the conditional and unconditional beliefs that are central to the formulation of the patient's difficulties. In previous chapters, we have described how these beliefs may affect the engagement of patients with chronic depression in therapy and may undermine the use of standard cognitive and behavioural strategies. We have suggested that these adverse effects of patients' central beliefs can be minimised by formulating and explaining their effects early in therapy, while priority is given to the management of symptoms and questioning of surface level cognitions. Standard behavioural and cognitive techniques can result in helpful symptomatic and cognitive changes. Importantly, they can also highlight to both therapist and patient the role of underlying beliefs, assumptions and associated behavioural strategies. Once therapy is well underway, the focus in therapy shifts to identifying the conditional and unconditional beliefs with greater precision and helping patients to recognise the role beliefs play in maintaining problems. In this chapter, we describe the process of helping patients to identify negative beliefs and to understand how they may contribute to their problems. Helping patients to become aware of the prejudicial nature of their thinking can help in weakening these beliefs and is often a necessary precursor to building alternative views, as discussed in the next chapter.

THE ROLE OF RECOGNISING AND MODIFYING BELIEFS

When working with acute depression, where the patient has good premorbid functioning, considerable symptomatic improvement can be achieved with standard cognitive and behavioural interventions. In acute depression, conditional and unconditional beliefs may be problematic in only a limited set of the patient's life domains and can be outweighed by adaptive views in other life domains. Giving patients strategies to modify automatic thoughts may adequately compensate for continuing adverse effects of negative beliefs. Thus, in acute depression, while work at the level of conditional beliefs is seen as desirable in helping to reduce vulnerability to relapse, work on unconditional beliefs has not been viewed as essential to bring about lasting change.

However, when working with more persistent depression, formulation and intervention at the level of the underlying belief system is more important. Working to modify the belief system becomes an integral part of cognitive therapy, and a prerequisite to effecting any lasting change. It is vital for both therapist and patient to try to develop a working understanding of the relationships between different levels of the belief system and how these are activated in everyday situations. The rigidity and inflexibility of underlying beliefs can result in frequent, intense or chronic activation of negative ideas at different levels of the cognitive system. At times, such activation of the belief system and the concomitant affect can directly contaminate day-to-day activities and interpersonal encounters. At other times, the avoidant coping style that functions to prevent such activation affects the person's activities and relationships, usually in a detrimental way. The patient's beliefs and avoidance can have effects within their social environment that result in the beliefs consistently being confirmed. As well as serving to maintain the disorder, these factors may also serve to frustrate many treatment strategies. In treating persistent depression, the therapist constantly needs to take into consideration the complex relationship between beliefs, behaviour and adverse social circumstances in terms of their effects on the course of the illness.

In persistent depression, because beliefs are rigid and have been reinforced over a long period, the process of modification is often difficult and slow. Helping patients with resistant depression to modify longstanding and rigid beliefs depends on the accomplishment of two prior tasks: identifying the beliefs that are central in contributing to the problems and helping the patient to recognise that these are indeed beliefs. In acute depression, patients often need little prompting to identify the issues that are problems for them and to accept that these are unhelpful beliefs that they can work to re-evaluate. By contrast in more persistent depression, beliefs are often obscured by the processes of avoidance that we have described. When beliefs have been identified, they are usually seen either as incontrovertible facts or as principles that are so essential that they cannot or should not be questioned. In this chapter, we describe ways of helping patients to see their beliefs as beliefs, rather than as reality. This helps them to gain some distance from the beliefs and provides a necessary platform for initiating and consolidating changes in the content of beliefs. (Strategies for modifying the content of beliefs by eroding negative beliefs and working to build more adaptive alternatives are discussed in the next chapter.)

IDENTIFYING UNDERLYING BELIEFS

In persistent depression, from the earliest stages of therapy the therapist will need to be aware of beliefs as they affect the process and tasks of therapy. From the outset, the therapist takes some interest in the patient's history and how earlier experiences may be influencing patterns of thinking in current situations. We have described how it may be helpful at an early stage to discuss with the patient the idea that certain fixed thinking patterns resulting from early experiences may be contaminating their current experiences (see page 155). If the therapist does not have a clear idea of the nature of the underlying beliefs by session 6–8 into therapy, then specific strategies for identifying conditional and unconditional beliefs will usually be employed. As the therapist formulates the nature of these beliefs, this needs to be checked out with the patient, firstly to help to confirm the precise nature of the beliefs and also to help the patient to recognise the beliefs for themselves.

Identifying Themes

A number of approaches to identifying underlying beliefs have been described in standard texts on cognitive therapy (see Beck et al., 1979; J. Beck, 1995). Possible conditional and unconditional beliefs can be hypothesised from a consideration of the themes in the patient's reported thoughts in problem situations. For example, *Elizabeth's* self-critical stance was evident in how she described any activity she had undertaken (e.g. 'I didn't do my diary quite right'; 'As you can see I made a mistake here and here'; 'I could have done a better job if I'd taken more care'), which helped to explain her persistent low mood and despondency. This highlighted to the therapist that Elizabeth perceived the outcome of everything she undertook from a negative position. It was therefore reasonable to propose that she may have a conditional belief around working towards the highest of standards, i.e. 'If I don't do something properly there is no point in doing it at all'.

The Downward Arrow Technique

Use of the 'downward arrow' technique can often lead straight to the identification of unconditional beliefs. Here the therapist takes an automatic thought from a specific upsetting event reported by the patient and elicits the deeper meaning associated with the automatic thought via a process of socratic questioning. Questions such as 'What does that mean to you?', 'If that were true, what does that say about you as a person ?' or 'What is the worst thing about that?' are useful in eliciting deeper meanings. In persistent depression, use of the downward arrow technique may entail a degree of skating from side to side, rather than leading straight down to deeper levels of the patient's belief system as it may do in acute depression. However, this can be useful in exploring the relationship between different aspects of the patient's meaning system. This is illustrated in an extract from a session with *Dave*, who had become depressed following his business folding and his being declared bankrupt. This is a discussion regarding Dave's reluctance to mix socially, which resulted in his avoiding a family gathering the week prior to the session.

T: What was it about the christening that you were particularly not looking forward to?

D: My wife's family. Her dad runs a business and he would have asked me about mine.

T: OK, let's imagine you went to the christening and you began a conversation with your wife's dad. How would you feel?

D: (*looking upset and lowering his head*) Really anxious and embarrassed.

T: What would be the most anxiety provoking thing?

D: Her dad asking how my business is going and my having to say I lost it.

T: For you, what is so difficult about this man knowing the business folded?

D: He will see me as a loser.

T: Can you define what you mean by a loser?

D: Someone like me (*eyes downcast, very sad*).

T: (*very gently*) Can you describe 'someone like me'?

D: (*tremor in his voice*) Someone who has lost his business, his house, his car, his job, his health and his marriage.

T: (*gently*) What does it say about you that your business, house, car, job, marriage and health are no longer as they were?

D: I made mistakes.

T: What sort of person makes mistakes?

D: The sort that doesn't anticipate problems and deal with them effectively.

T: I'm not suggesting this is true or something I think, but let's imagine for a moment that you don't anticipate problems and deal with them effectively. What would that say about you as a person?

D: That I'm doing something wrong.

T: What are the reasons you are doing something wrong?

D: What do you mean?

T: Sorry, let me rephrase the question. Are you doing things wrong because, for example, you have a lack of skills that could perhaps be learned if you did a course?

D: (*giving a cynical chuckle*) Oh, no. No matter how hard I try I'm just not up to it.

T: Not up to it. What do you mean not up to it?

D: (*angry tone*) I don't meet the mark—I'm just not good enough.

T: (*sensitively*) Mmm... you seem very upset, like we've hit a raw nerve.

D: (*sniffs and nods*) Yeah. I've never been good enough. Always second best.

T: I know you are feeling upset at the moment but this seems a really important area to explore. Can I ask you a few more questions?

D: OK.

T: What, for you, are the consequences of always not having been good enough, always second best as you put it?

D: There is always someone better than me, always.

T: Do you lose anything as a result of not being good enough and being second best?

D: I guess status. All those things I mentioned, business, car, job, house, wife... People look up to you when you have those, no one could possibly look up to me now.

T: Right. So you feel you have lost status. Does status confer anything on people?

D: People respect you more when you have those things.

T: So status and respect are related and you have lost these?

D: Yes.

T: Can I just summarise? Two important themes seem to have been identified here: one is this view of yourself as not good enough and also a view that people are in some way better than you. When you say better than you, how would you define that? Do you mean more intelligent, kinder, more likeable?

D: No, more successful. There is always someone more successful.

T: Is everyone more successful than you?

D: No. (*bitter and angry tone*) But there is always bloody someone!

T: Like your wife's dad at the christening?

D: (*through gritted teeth*) Yes!

T: So, to summarise again, you have this view of yourself as not good enough and some other people as more successful than you. This seems related to that rule we discussed two sessions ago where you talked about the idea that 'If I strive to do things properly I will be the best'. What do you think?

D: I'm sorry, I haven't a clue. My mind is a jumble. Can we stop now?

T: Sure. Take a few moments and then we can summarise what we've discovered from what we've discussed.

Through this discussion, the relationships between different factors at different levels in Dave's belief system become clearer. Dave's view of himself as a loser depends on his having lost the things that confer status and respect. He sees this resulting from a constitutional inability to be the most successful person ('no matter how hard I try ... there is always someone more successful'). This in turn confirms a more fundamental view of himself: 'I'm not good enough.'

Labelling the Belief

Once candidates for underlying beliefs have been identified, they should be checked out with the patient to see if they believe that idea does describe how they see themselves or does fit with their view of other people or the world in general. Firm endorsement by the patient is generally necessary for a statement to be considered a good description of one of that patient's central beliefs. Only in exceptional cases would a candidate belief that is denied or given lukewarm endorsement be accepted as an unconditional belief, and only where the denial could be explained well by the formulation in which that belief was integral. As was the case with *Dave*, the patient's emotional response can help to confirm whether an underlying belief has been identified. A high degree of upset to simply the use of certain words or phrases indicates that those words are likely to be descriptive of an important core belief. Where central beliefs are conditional, high levels of affect rarely accompany simply identifying, pointing out or discussing those ideas.

Although the therapist may be instrumental in helping to identify the precise nature of the belief, it is best to use the patient's own words to label the belief. Where the patient has not spontaneously supplied an obvious label during the process of identifying beliefs, this can be done by reminding them of a typical situation or two where their beliefs have been activated and asking them what word or phrase best describes their sense of themselves in that situation. Idiosyncratic or colloquial expressions frequently capture the content of unconditional beliefs better than more conventional psychotherapeutic terms ('I am worthless'). For one patient, the idea 'I am a blob' captured his view of himself both physically and socially. He had always thought of himself as fat, and indeed had been teased for this when he was young. Moreover, the idea of being a blob also summed up for him how he viewed himself as both weak and unable to have much effect on the world around him, which in his view left him at the mercy of others' uncharitable judgements. One young woman adopted the phrase 'I am crap' to describe her self-schema. This encapsulated for her how she saw herself failing at anything that she attempted, how she saw herself frequently failing even to attempt things and also how either way she just felt upset and miserable. Although she would doubtless not have used this word about herself when she was a child, she believed it reflected how she viewed herself even then. Moreover, it also seemed to capture the rather nasty self-critical nature of much of her self-talk.

Beliefs about Other People

As well as negative beliefs about the self, it is important to identify beliefs about other people in persistent depression. These beliefs are often complementary to the beliefs about the self, as can be seen in the above example with *Dave*. Where the self is assumed to be bad, horrible or unacceptable, other people are often expected to be demeaning, critical or rejecting. Where the self is viewed as weak and inadequate, others are often seen as strong and invulnerable. Even though most of the work on beliefs will probably focus on the self-beliefs in such cases, it is usually helpful explicitly to identify such other-referent beliefs. In particular, this helps to clarify the nature of the negative predictions when conducting behavioural experiments. There are cases where the beliefs about other people are more important than self-related beliefs and cannot simply be inferred from them. For example, Doug consistently expressed the view that other people could not be trusted and that they would let him down. Early in therapy, the therapist assumed that this was related to a core belief that he was not worthy (of their respect and effort). As therapy progressed, it became clear that even when his view of himself was positive and he was satisfied with his part in things, Doug still saw other people as a let down. His view of others, which could be traced back to being brought up in a highly protective relationship with his parents in a rough neighbourhood, was an important core belief.

PROBLEMS IN IDENTIFYING UNDERLYING BELIEFS

In general, the patient's conscious endorsement and emotional arousal can help to guide the therapist in identifying central beliefs. However, in persistent depression, behavioural, cognitive and emotional avoidance can interfere with identifying unconditional beliefs. Active endorsement or emotional arousal does not necessarily accompany the identification of central beliefs. Cognitive avoidance may result in denial of underlying beliefs, whereas emotional suppression often enables patients to talk about core beliefs with minimal overt upset, although this is frequently accompanied by a general increase in tension levels. Identification of underlying beliefs in persistent depression relies on careful guided discovery by the therapist over a period of time, along with familiarity with the range of the patient's problems. Quick methods such as the use of questionnaires can often backfire. One patient who was asked to fill in the Dysfunctional Attitude Scale (Weissman & Beck, 1978—a measure of the extent to which patients endorse various attitudes that are supposed to reflect their underlying beliefs) placed all her responses in the most extreme right-hand column and gave it back, clearly believing that she had represented her views in the most negative terms possible. However, she had failed to realise that some of the items are reverse keyed (where strong agreement through use of the rightmost response box is a positive response) so her score overall was quite middling. When the therapist got to know her better, it became clear that this failure to process the detail of apparently negative responses was consistent with her cognitive and emotional avoidance in a variety of situations.

Difficulties due to Behavioural and Cognitive Avoidance

Behavioural avoidance can operate so that crucial issues are simply not considered. Cognitive avoidance results in reluctance to think about certain issues and, when confronted with them, to miss their significance. For example, Pauline (who at the beginning of therapy insisted that she was stressed rather than depressed) had no really intimate relationships and her day-to-day lows concerned her inability to accomplish certain tasks. Over the first few therapy sessions, she came to acknowledge seeing herself as worthless and could relate this to failings in attempting various tasks. However, Pauline's distress when discussing these issues was minimal and inconsistent with the severity and persistence of her depression. If therapy had addressed only those concerns about the day-to-day tasks in which she engaged, then important issues would have been missed. Her more deeply upsetting belief that she would be abandoned by others became apparent only when the therapist raised the possibility of her deepening some of her relationships to elicit more support. Even when discussing these issues, Pauline would use the term 'worthless' about herself in a vague fashion, which made her less upset by obscuring her distressing belief that she would always ultimately be left on her own.

In such cases, where situations or issues are being avoided, mentally or actually confronting the avoided issues helps to elicit the underlying beliefs.

This is usually done in session by asking the patient 'what if?' they were in that situation or, getting them to imagine themselves in the avoided situation. With Pauline, the therapist asked what would happen if she did let particular friends know how low she felt at times—for example, on the anniversary of the untimely death of her sister. She responded that if people knew she was upset, they would lose interest in her. This was followed up by 'downward chaining', posing further 'and what would that mean?' questions. Fighting to contain her upset, Pauline said that she believed she would be left alone, in pain and abandoned. When such high levels of distress accompany global thoughts about self or others, the therapist has taken a significant step in identifying the underlying beliefs. However, some patients may then revert to avoiding the issue and may still not acknowledge the underlying beliefs themselves. The therapist may need to be quite patient in repeatedly highlighting the potential for upset, pointing out the avoidance and suggesting the possible underlying belief.

Difficulties due to Emotional Avoidance

In addition to behavioural and cognitive avoidance, emotional avoidance can also interfere with the identification of core beliefs. In their state of blunted gloom, some patients experience some degree of difficulty in most activities of daily living and fairly readily endorse virtually any negative sounding statement about themselves. The endorsement of all negative content along with minimal acute emotional response to any of it renders it hard to assess what the most central issues are. Familiarity with the problems of patients is helpful, as over time some issues almost always emerge as more important than others. Once patients begin to acknowledge that they keep their feelings 'under wraps', it can be helpful simply to ask them what would happen if they did not keep their feelings at bay. The downward arrow technique can then be used to lead to underlying beliefs. Many patients respond that they would break down or lose control over their feelings, that the therapist would see this, and that would show them to be the weak individuals they truly are. As patients gradually relax their guard over their feelings, content related to the core beliefs can begin to emerge. With some patients this seems more likely to happen when they know the session is coming to an end.

Assessing the Relative Importance of Different Beliefs

Another problem encountered in identifying unconditional beliefs is where several different beliefs are uncovered. There is usually a question of whether one in particular is truly at the core or whether they are equivalent but separate core beliefs. In many cases, trying to identify which belief is 'more core' than the others in order to target the true core belief can be important. Distinguishing beliefs that seem to be driving problematic feelings and behaviours from those that seem to be consequences of the problems can be useful. Examining the historical roots of the beliefs to see which came first can also shed some light on this. From the outset of therapy, *Rosemary* frequently became guilty, resigned and hopeless when she was in situations where she thought she had failed to meet other people's needs or expectations. She reported many negative thoughts about letting other people down. In one session, she reported feeling guilty about having failed to visit an elderly aunt the previous day as she had intended. She reported that she felt bad about having let this old lady down (even though she had not in fact confirmed with her aunt that she would visit). When the therapist asked 'Supposing it was true that you let the old lady down, what would it say about you as a person?', she replied that it showed what a horrible person she was. She went on that the old lady could no longer get around for herself and had few visits from her own children (who were not seen as horrible), which confirmed to her how horrible she was. Rosemary then began to catalogue previous things she had done that seemed to prove this point, including her rather messy divorce some years previously, which she had alluded to several times in sessions but was reluctant to discuss. She described how she had instigated this divorce which had indeed been upsetting to her children and had resulted in divisions within her family. To her, this put the matter of her being horrible beyond debate. Her dismissal of information contrary to her belief and the way she tied disparate events together in a single theme seemed to confirm that her view of herself as horrible was a core belief.

However, it had also become clear to the therapist that for much of the time Rosemary was faced with a daunting set of demands from herself and others which made letting people down inevitable. She took on tasks for others without considering what was possible for her, practically or emotionally. Attempts by the therapist to explore with her the possibility of setting some limits on what she took on for others or to schedule time to rest or do things for herself were met with an aghast expression and assertions that this would prove she was selfish. When the meaning of this was further explored, she said that she believed that if she did not do what others wanted then they would see her as a nuisance. When the therapist asked how she felt about never getting to do anything she herself wanted, she replied that her feelings didn't count. At this point, she had shrunk down into her chair and was speaking even more quietly and apologetically than usual. When the therapist asked what she was thinking about herself, she replied, 'Well that's me isn't it? I don't count.' Her reaction here and the theme that seemed to tie together her behaviour in many situations suggested an alternative core belief that 'I don't count'.

The therapist formulated that the belief that she did not count was driving her tendency to take on anyone else's demands (through her assumption that if she did not she would be seen as a nuisance). The consequence of this was that she was bound to fail to meet them all. When she did fall short of these boundless expectations, she assumed that she had let people down and that she was a horrible person. Her view of herself as a horrible person was a consequence of believing that she did not count, which was a more fundamental belief. This formulation was backed up by examining the roots of the beliefs. She had spent most of her childhood in the care of her grandparents, as her parents were away or busy. Although her grandparents were kind to her, she was always aware that they were doing her a favour to look after her and had often felt that she was in the way when their other children (i.e. her aunts and uncles) came to visit. The sense that she did not really matter to her parents, and the sense of being cared for being a special favour rather than something she deserved, fitted with her fundamental belief that she did not count. To stop herself feeling too much of a nuisance she would take on various chores, but would sometimes get overwhelmed by them and would believe that she had let her grandparents down terribly. This set in train the pattern of events reinforcing her view of herself as horrible.

With Rosemary as with many patients with resistant depression, identifying her underlying beliefs was complex and time-consuming. It involved different techniques, such as identifying themes and downward chaining, and much exploration of the meaning she attached to current and past events. Once the two potential core beliefs had been identified, careful formulation of their precise relation was tested against information gathered through discussion of her early childhood. Working to identify which belief was 'more core' proved valuable to her progress in therapy. It helped to engage her in a process which she had largely seen as an indulgence and helped to give her some understanding of her sense of herself which could be used to build some distance from her beliefs. It also clarified the most important targets for work on modifying her beliefs: for Rosemary, addressing her belief that she did not count would be likely to help with her belief that she was horrible, whereas the reverse was not true. However, in some cases, such consideration does not lead to firm conclusions about which is the 'most core' belief. Rather than getting hung up on theoretical nuances, the most important consideration here is what the patient wishes to achieve. Discussing the different negative beliefs and how the patient would most like to see themselves differently often gives enough sense of which belief it is most important to address in short-term therapy.

DEVELOPING AWARENESS OF UNDERLYING BELIEFS

In acute depression, once conditional beliefs have been identified, patients can often begin to question them immediately. While this is sometimes so in persistent depression, immediate and direct attempts to question or challenge beliefs are usually unsuccessful. This is to be expected. Central beliefs are not generally experienced as beliefs by the patient. Rather, the phenomenal experience of these ideas is as facts—the sky is blue, grass is green and, for example, as *Marion* would define herself, I am unlovable. For many patients, their unconditional beliefs are to them unquestionable truths. Even conditional beliefs or assumptions are held as principles that are essential or fundamental in life. The notion of questioning such ideas makes little sense to many patients. For the average person, it would be like trying to tell them the sky is not blue. Although most people would concede that sometimes the sky can be pink, and that all too often it is grey, they would return to the view that the sky is blue. As many patients have held these beliefs to be true over a long period, starting to question them immediately they have been identified is usually met with incredulity, accompanied by anxiety and defensive resistance. This is understandable, as undermining these beliefs in a direct and forthright manner too early in treatment can leave patients feeling as if they have experienced an onslaught on the core of their identity.

Recognising Beliefs as Beliefs

Within a short-term treatment protocol of around 20 sessions, it is not generally realistic to aim for the patient to adopt completely different fundamental beliefs. Even in longer courses of therapy, the aim of working with beliefs can be seen as one of beginning to create doubt (and tolerance of that doubt) where previously there was certainty. The clinician is attempting to introduce a degree of flexibility into the patient's belief system to facilitate more adaptive interactions with the environment. Before there can be any chance of questioning or modifying underlying beliefs, the patient must be helped to consider the possibility that these beliefs are ideas or perceptions, rather than being unquestionable truths which are etched in stone 'in the world'. Conveying the idea that, while holding these beliefs may be understandable, their content is not necessarily accurate paves the way for any subsequent attempts at modification of those beliefs.

Many of the symptom-based cognitive therapy interventions discussed earlier in this book set a precedent for this aim. Developing formulations of problems, modifying automatic thoughts and establishing behavioural changes can help patients to begin to distance themselves from their thoughts. These approaches can help patients see that many thoughts are not invariant, but that their believability varies according to mood state. When the focus moves on to more fundamental beliefs, this earlier work can improve the likelihood that belief modification will be approached as a collaborative endeavour between patient and clinician, rather than the patient seeing the interventions as something that is done *to* them by the clinician. However, even when progress has been made in developing strategies for addressing symptoms and current problems, some recognition of beliefs as beliefs needs to be developed before work to question beliefs will be accepted. There are three main strategies that can assist with helping patients to see their underlying beliefs as ideas or perceptions rather than as facts. These are: examining the experiences that may have led to the development of the belief; presenting the idea that beliefs are like prejudices; and understanding the mechanisms or cycles by which the belief is maintained. Two or three sessions are often devoted to these strategies before more active attempts to modify the unconditional beliefs are attempted.

Examining the Development of Beliefs

The first step in helping patients to see their beliefs as ideas or perceptions rather than unquestionable truths is often taken through exploring the early experiences that led to their adopting those ideas. Soon after the underlying beliefs have been identified, the aim is to help patients to see that certain prior experiences may be colouring how they see themselves or interpret events in the present. The general impressions they formed during the earlier experiences are highlighted and compared with their current beliefs and expectations. Precise details of any traumatic events and re-experiencing of the associated emotions are not necessary at this point (in contrast to subsequent work which aims at restructuring the meanings associated with traumatic memories). Where patients report evident physical, sexual or verbal abuse during their childhood, the general effects of this on self-image and expectations of others are not usually hard to identify. For example, *Kate* described how her father had constantly criticised every aspect of her behaviour from an early age. This included not only common 'shortcomings' like playing too boisterously or not doing well enough at school, but also that she breathed too loudly and swallowed too loudly when eating. On occasion, her shortcomings had resulted in her being beaten with a belt. Kate recalled feeling constantly discouraged and hiding from her father in her bedroom. She found it easy to see a link between this and her core belief that she was 'horrible', which had been identified from themes in her automatic thoughts about her current personal life. Seeing that her sense of herself had probably been impressed on her by these early experiences helped her to stand back a little whenever she felt judged and rejected like this.

In other cases, the links of current beliefs and childhood experiences are more subtle. The detrimental effects of being brought up in an environment where the noxious influences were more insidious or ongoing can be harder for the patient to recognise. This is often the case where the family background was experienced as positive or where the unhelpful influences were socially or culturally reinforced. Teasing out the historical roots of the belief can be particularly helpful in these cases. For example, during therapy with *Graham*, the themes emerged that he saw himself as inadequate, others as more important than he was, and the need for the world to be fair. In seeking to identify early experiences that may account for this view, Graham reported his childhood as impoverished but reasonably happy. Although he described his parents as strict and not emotionally demonstrative, he felt that his large family had got along well. He recalled disliking his Church of England primary school. At senior school, he was academically able and enjoyed the academic work. This school was strict and Graham recalled trying to be well behaved in order to avoid punishment.

In this fairly ordinary mix of positive and negative experiences, Graham had difficulty identifying experiences that may have contributed to the formation of his belief that he was inadequate. As Graham had disliked his Church of England primary school but had also attended a Church of England Church until he was 16, the therapist asked Graham how religious ideas may influence his view of himself, other people and the world. Graham stated that he had rejected all concepts of God and religion in his adolescence and therefore felt that these ideas did not really impact on his view of himself, the world and relationships. When asked what had led him to reject his religion, Graham said he disliked the dogma and inflexible rules of the Church, which judged people and their actions in black and white terms. He perceived what he termed 'religious people' as often being harshly and unjustly critical of others. Earlier therapy sessions had already identified that Graham was extremely self-critical and that he set rigid and high expectations regarding his own performance, which frequently led to a subjective sense of disappointment. The therapist then asked if it were possible that, while at an intellectual level he rejected religious dogma, at an emotional level he had internalised principles from his religious upbringing as rules for living. Initially Graham was sceptical. For homework, Graham was asked to consider the type of rules that existed in the family and at school regarding how he was expected to conduct himself, and to listen to an audiotape of the session.

At the following session, he brought up further discussion of his upbringing as an agenda item, from which he was able to articulate what he saw as the central message from his childhood, at home, at school and in Church. The principles he identified stressed that a person has to strive to be better, indeed perfect, but according to religious rules, people are at best imperfect and at worst bad. In addition, these principles stressed that it is important always to put others first and to 'know your place' by showing humility in all endeavours. This helped to make sense of Graham's conditional beliefs 'If you are good, kind, fair and hardworking you will be rewarded' and 'I must strive to be perfect in order to be worthwhile'. Graham now recognised that when it came to himself (but not others) he applied these principles harshly and with exacting rigour. He felt he could never live up to the standards dictated by these rules he set himself, and as a result he felt continually disappointed in himself. The implicit message of always being found to be wanting accounted for his view of himself as inadequate. The origins of his view that others were more important than him and that as a principle fairness was of paramount importance were also now recognisable. This articulation of early experiences that may have accounted for Graham's view of himself, others and the world helped him to take the stance that these were indeed perceptions open to further examination, not immutable facts. Seeing that his sense of himself had likely been shaped by these early experiences helped him to stand back a little from applying these rules to himself in such a self-defeating and unforgiving way. Over time this led Graham to begin to tackle some of his longstanding avoidance, particularly in the realm of relationships.

The Prejudice Model

A second strategy for helping patients to see their beliefs as beliefs rather than facts is the prejudice model, which was originally described by Padesky (1990). The idea of prejudice is used as a way to demonstrate the information processing errors that can maintain unconditional beliefs and to suggest to the patient ways for initiating change in those beliefs. Framing negative beliefs as possible prejudices can give patients some distance from those beliefs and begin to lessen their impact. The prejudice model is used once the patient has some familiarity with the process of questioning automatic thoughts. This will usually have resulted in some recognition from the patient of the possibility that not all their perceptions are accurate or true. It helps if the patient and therapist have agreed on a suitable label that describes the patient's underlying view of themselves, others or the world. Using this method generally takes around 30 minutes, but when working with chronic depression, it can take up a full therapy session. The prejudice model was used in *Elizabeth's* twelfth therapy session, as presented below.

T: Can you think of someone you know who has a prejudice with which you disagree?

E: Yes, my friend Bob thinks all women are bad drivers.

T: OK. So when Bob sees a woman who is not making such a good job of driving how does he react?

E: Oh, he gets really annoyed and is really critical.

T: In what way is he critical? What does he say?

E: Things like, 'Isn't that just typical!', 'They're all useless', 'They shouldn't be allowed on the road', 'They are dangerous'.

T: Okay, he'd say it was typical and see them as useless or dangerous. How does Bob react when he sees a woman driving competently?

E: I don't think he would even notice.

T: Right, that seems important he wouldn't notice. Anything else he might do?

E: I'm not sure.

T: Say, for example, you brought to his attention an example of a woman driving well?

E: He would make some excuse.

T: What sort of excuse?

E: Well, like she was an exception to the rule.

T: Right, so Bob might discount the example in some way?

E: Yes.

T: If you were to give Bob a piece of statistical evidence that men are involved in more car accidents than women and that this results in higher insurance premiums for men, what would he say?

E: I've tried this. He will have none of it. He dismisses it as a conspiracy against men by the government because it's politically expedient to favour women. Therefore, government must be putting money in the insurance companies' back pockets to produce such statistics and insurance deals.

T: Wow that's some explanation! Just to summarise then. When encountering an example of a woman driving badly, Bob would immediately notice it and seize upon it as evidence to prove his point—'I told you so'. However, if Bob comes across an example of a woman driving well he may *not even notice* or he'd *discount* it as an exception to the rule. And finally in the face of hard statistical evidence against his prejudice he would *dismiss* the evidence without even giving it any consideration. Does that seem a fair summary?

E: Yes.

T: So, if Bob sees a woman driving well, would it change his view?

E: Not at all, no.

T: So what would happen to the way he thinks—this prejudice of his?

E: Nothing, he carries on thinking the same way.

T: Right, he carries on thinking the same despite the facts.

In this phase of presenting the model, it is important that the patient chooses a prejudice with which they disagree. Only by doing this will the patient be able to see the distortions inherent to the prejudice. Choosing a prejudice with which the patient disagrees helps to convey the message that firmly held beliefs can be ideas or perceptions rather than unquestionable truths. Apart from the prejudice described above, patients have raised a range of issues, including: 'Men are bastards'; 'Southerners are unfriendly'; 'People with tattoos are thugs'. The purpose of this phase of the metaphor is to use socratic dialogue to identify how Bob responds to information that is discrepant with his belief 'Women are bad drivers'. It is important to prompt the patient to identify several information processing biases for dealing with discrepant information, including not noticing, distortion, discounting, and calling the observation an exception to the rule. The next step in presenting the model is to examine how the prejudice might be changed.

T: Then how could you change Bob's prejudice against women drivers?

E: I don't think I could.

T: Let's imagine that it is important for Bob to try to change his prejudice. How might we go about it?

E: Mmm . . . that's difficult. I'm not sure.

T: OK. You said before that one of the things that prevented Bob's prejudice from changing is that when he encounters a woman driving well he either doesn't notice it or discounts it by saying it is the exception to the rule.

E: Uhuh.

T: So, what would happen if we asked Bob to keep a record of how many times each day he saw examples of women driving well?

E: Oh, I see. Yes, that might work.

T: Any other strategies we might use?

E: I guess we could ask him to keep a record of all the times he got annoyed at women drivers and then ask him to try to develop a more balanced view.

T: That seems like a good idea, how might we do that?

E: We could ask him to keep a thought record and help him to examine the evidence for and against his thoughts.

T: You mentioned examining evidence for and against thoughts, which is something we have done in our sessions together. Alongside that we looked at thinking errors. What thinking errors exist in Bob's prejudice?

E: Err... discounting the positive, overgeneralisation, black and white thinking, magnification and minimisation and emotional reasoning.

T: Quite a few thinking errors there. How might we go about tackling some of these?

E: That's a hard thing to do.

T: Yes, it is. What might be the effects of asking Bob to record examples of men driving badly and identify how he minimises their mistakes and magnifies those of women?

E: Yes. That may help him to add in the shades of grey and develop a more balanced view.

T: How often would Bob need to use these strategies?

E: Every day I suppose.

T: Over what time period would he need to keep his record?

E: Mmmm... I think it would be hard to change. Several weeks if not months.

T: Yes, I'd agree with you there.

The degree to which each patient engages in this part of the process is variable. It may be influenced by the extent to which the patient has been able to utilise symptom relief strategies effectively in the early stages of cognitive therapy. If they have been successful in using these strategies and have gained benefit from them, then patients are more likely to advocate their utility in the scenario presented in the prejudice model. The final phase in presenting the prejudice model is to examine with the patient whether their unconditional belief acts as a prejudice.

T: OK, Elizabeth, what do you think is the reason I've been talking about prejudice today?

E: I'm not sure.

T: Since we started our sessions the theme of failure has come up a number of times. Over the last two sessions, we have been talking more about this theme and how it impacts on your life. I wonder if your perception of yourself as a failure is in any way similar to Bob's prejudice that 'All women are bad drivers'?

E: You mean in the way I think?

T: To some extent yes. Can we examine your perception of failure in the same way we examined Bob's prejudice?

E: OK.

T: Let's say that your perception 'I am a failure' is a prejudice you hold against yourself. Do you remember three weeks ago when you inadvertently deleted your report from the computer at work?

E: Oh, yes (sighs).

T: If you get out the diary sheet we recorded your automatic thoughts on when that happened...

E: (*rifles in her therapy folder*) Here it is.

T: What thoughts did you record? (*Elizabeth puts it on table between herself and therapist.*)

E: 'I'm useless.' 'I always make mistakes.' 'I should know better.' 'I've wasted the whole day.' 'I'm such a failure.'

T: How many times have you thought about that incident since it happened?

E: Initially every day for the first week. Now it comes into my mind every time someone mentions that particular report.

T: How do you feel when you remember it?

E: Pretty annoyed. It shouldn't have happened.

T: Right. Let's compare that incident with the time last week when your boss praised your work and told you how the new filing system made his job so much easier. What went through your mind when he said it?

E: I'm not sure.

T: OK, I made a few notes when you were talking about it in the session. (*Elizabeth looks down.*) You said 'anyone could do that, it wasn't difficult and he was probably just trying to be nice because I've been off sick'. If you compare how you responded to deleting the report—which was a mistake in most people's book—versus your boss praising your work, do you notice any differences in how you make sense of the information?

E: Well . . . I guess I pay more heed to the mistake and disregard the praise.

T: Would you say that is something you generally do?

E: (*sighs*) Yes.

T: Would it be fair to say that when you make a mistake, your attention is immediately drawn to it, you turn it over and over in your mind and add it to a long list of evidence you have accumulated to support the idea you are a failure?

E: Mmm . . . .

T: And yet, when you do something well and you receive praise, you dismiss this or try to find reasons which underplay your role in the success or discount it as irrelevant?

E: OK, I see what you are saying.

T: So, similar to Bob's beliefs about women drivers, could this perception 'I'm a failure' be a prejudice you hold against yourself?

E: But it's true, I am a failure.

T: So you seem to view the idea you are a failure as a fact.

E: It is, isn't it?—well, it seems so to me.

T: Mmm . . . would that be an example of something someone with a prejudice might think?

E: How do you mean?

T: If we returned to Bob for a moment, wouldn't Bob say it is a fact 'All women are bad drivers'? Do you agree that is a statement of fact?

E: No, it is his opinion.

T: OK, what would happen if we tried to view this idea 'I am a failure' as an opinion or prejudice you hold about yourself that others may disagree with in exactly the same way you disagree with Bob's opinion of women drivers?

E: (*heavy sigh*) I see what you are getting at but it seems impossible.

T: I appreciate it seems that way right now. I'm reminded of when we began therapy and we started working on breaking tasks down into more manageable chunks. At first you found that pretty difficult as I recall.

E: Gosh, yes.

T: So we worked together on it at first, but now am I right in saying we don't really refer to it in sessions and you pretty much use it on your own?

E: Yes, I use it all the time.

T: So do we have anything to lose by applying the same practice and persistence to working on this perception 'I'm a failure'?

E: I guess not, but I'm not sure it will work.

Attention should be drawn to reactions of the patient that confirm the beliefs, such as 'I told you so' and 'My beliefs are true'. The therapist should ask whether these are things that someone with a prejudice would think. It is particularly important to draw attention to times when the patient discounts, distorts or makes an exception for things that do not fit with their negative self-view. It is helpful for the therapist to be able to bring up examples of this from preceding therapy sessions as well as drawing attention to these processes whenever they occur subsequently in therapy.

Most patients can make some use of the prejudice model, which helps them to see the possibility that their beliefs are beliefs rather than facts or reality. As the negative view of self is pervasive, patients often find questioning of their beliefs or contemplating alternative viewpoints uncomfortable. To begin by viewing this negative self-view as a prejudice is less threatening. Even though the patient still believes it, the prejudice model affords some psychological distance from the negative belief. This paves the way for testing out the prejudice and considering alternative beliefs using a variety of methods outlined in the next chapter.

Belief Maintenance Cycles

In addition to helping people see the historical roots of their beliefs and how their beliefs may be maintained through prejudicial thinking processes, it is also important to explore with patients how acting in accordance with their beliefs may be reinforcing them. The cognitive model proposes that beliefs often drive avoidance and compensatory strategies, and that the effect of these strategies results in experiences that consistently confirm the beliefs. Given this, it is important when working with persistently depressed patients to illustrate how the way they behave may serve to confirm their beliefs. Patients can then see that, although there may be some truth to their beliefs, this truth in part results from their own actions. This opens the possibility of testing whether different courses of action may produce different outcomes and so support different beliefs. This strategy is pursued by focusing on a current problem situation and asking how the conditional and unconditional beliefs influence how the patient handled the situation.

For example, *Stan* arrived at a session mid-way through therapy in a gloomy mood because his family had all arranged to go on a day out the following weekend. Other members of his family had decided where they would go and Stan was not expecting to enjoy the outing. In previous sessions, Stan's view of himself as weak had been identified from themes in his negative thinking and the prejudice model had been discussed. The therapist suggested examining how Stan's belief about himself was affecting how he dealt with things and suggested writing this down on paper (see Figure 7.1). The therapist asked how Stan's view of himself as weak affected how he handled the situation regarding the outing. Stan replied that he had not said where he wanted to go in the discussion of the outing, as he thought that no one would listen to what he wanted anyway. When asked what the effect of this was, he replied that others then took control of the situation and he ended up doing what other people wanted. Stan could then see that he concluded that he had no control over the situation, which made him feel more stressed about it. The therapist asked what the effect of this was on his view of himself, and Stan realised that he saw other people taking control and his feelings of being stressed out as further evidence of weakness. In this session, the belief of weakness, its effects on his behaviour, the interpersonal consequences of this behaviour and the further effects of this on his beliefs were sketched out on paper to illustrate a vicious circle. This is shown on the left-hand side of Figure 7.1. This helped Stan to see that acting and thinking as he did, there was little prospect of seeing himself as anything other than weak. He concluded 'nothing's going to change while I think like this'.

Over the next couple of sessions, Stan's other typical behaviours, and how they tended to reinforce his view of himself as weak, were added to the diagram. For example, he and his wife had given a family party for his daughter's birthday. The party had been greatly enjoyed by his daughter and all

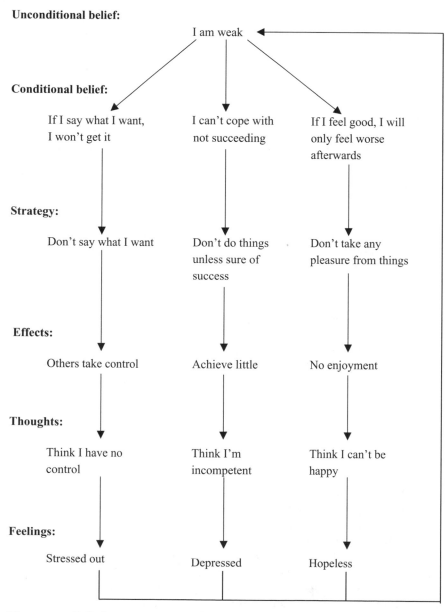

Unconditional belief:

I am weak

Conditional belief:

If I say what I want, I won't get it

I can't cope with not succeeding

If I feel good, I will only feel worse afterwards

Strategy:

Don't say what I want

Don't do things unless sure of success

Don't take any pleasure from things

Effects:

Others take control

Achieve little

No enjoyment

Thoughts:

Think I have no control

Think I'm incompetent

Think I can't be happy

Feelings:

Stressed out

Depressed

Hopeless

Figure 7.1   Belief maintenance diagram for Stan

those present except Stan. He could see that he had kept any potentially pleasurable feelings at a distance for fear that they would disappear and leave him feeling worse afterwards. However, not enjoying a party that everyone else enjoyed resulted in him thinking that he was incapable of being happy, which reinforced his view of himself as weak. In this way, a belief maintenance diagram was built up over several sessions, comprising his core belief, conditional assumptions, resulting behaviours, environmental consequences and further effects on his thoughts and feelings (see Figure 7.1). This is similar to a cognitive conceptualisation diagram, as described by J. Beck (1995), in which the core beliefs, dysfunctional assumptions, compensatory strategies, automatic thoughts and emotions are set out in full.

It is often helpful to use an analogy to reinforce the perspective gained through this kind of discussion of how beliefs are maintained. Various analogies have proved useful, including that of having a bank account that only allows for debits, but not credits. As another example, at Session 10 of therapy, *Elizabeth* rang to cancel her appointment with the therapist in order to go into work to finish a report. When she attended the following session, the therapist had not seen Elizabeth for three weeks due to the Christmas holidays. Elizabeth described herself as 'exhausted' and everything as being 'an effort'. It transpired that Elizabeth had been busy meeting the numerous demands that others made on her time and energy to the detriment of herself. In a tired and exasperated voice, Elizabeth told of how she had agreed at the last minute to decorate Christmas cakes for two friends to whom she felt unable to say no, of how she had also completed all the necessary shopping for the family, of how she had gone into work in order to finish a report that was outstanding instead of taking the three days annual leave she had planned, and of how she had single-handedly cooked meals for 10 people on Christmas Day, Boxing Day and New Year's Day. On top of this, she had made a 30-mile round trip every day for three weeks to visit an elderly uncle in hospital who had broken his leg. She expressed a stream of self-critical automatic negative thoughts, including 'No matter how hard I try, I never get everything done. I haven't done my homework. I really should try harder—I'm so disorganised. I'm useless.' Elizabeth finished her update with a huge sigh. She put her head in her hands and said wearily: 'I feel like one of those hamsters going round in a wheel, running round and round, faster and faster and getting nowhere.'

This seemed an excellent metaphor to characterise the ideas on the maintenance of beliefs that had previously been worked on. The therapist seized the opportunity to ask her: 'What are you chasing in the wheel?' Elizabeth and the therapist agreed that high standards and the approval of others were the two things she was chasing in the wheel. The previous session had focused on drawing out how trying to reach the highest standards and avoiding disapproval were strategies Elizabeth attempted to use to compensate for her view that she was a failure. The conclusion had been reached that these strategies served to reinforce her belief in two ways: firstly, that she could never satisfy the never-ending stream of demands she placed

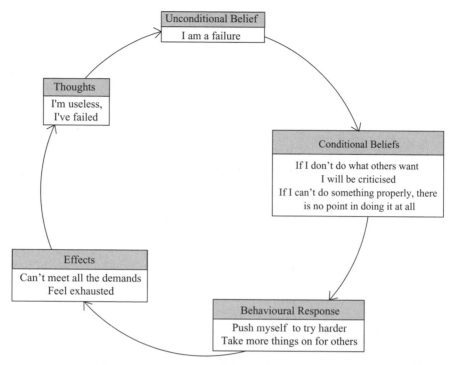

Figure 7.2   Elizabeth's belief maintenance diagram

on herself; and, secondly, that she tended to interpret her constant feelings of exhaustion as an inadequacy that proved that she was a failure. The therapist was thus in a position to ask Elizabeth how the sense of chasing round in the hamster wheel was similar to the belief maintenance diagram drawn up the previous session (see Figure 7.2).

Elizabeth described this as helping her to make sense of the recurring sets of circumstances in her life, but nevertheless remained despondent. She said, 'I've always been like this. It's wrong to put yourself first and I just feel so bad when I try, it's not worth it.' The therapist dealt with this negativity by acknowledging that given that this had been a longstanding pattern in Elizabeth's life it certainly wouldn't change overnight. However, two questions were raised: 'What would help you to slow the wheel down?' and 'What, if anything, would allow you occasionally to temporarily step off the wheel?'. These were posed as questions not to be answered there and then but as the basis for a series of behavioural experiments aimed at collecting evidence to test the validity of her conditional beliefs. The questions were deliberately aimed at questioning the dichotomous nature of Elizabeth's thinking by considering that the wheel could go at variable speeds and that Elizabeth may from time to time step off the wheel.

The procedure of drawing out these belief maintenance cycles involves considering how a specific upsetting situation is affected by beliefs that have previously been identified. The emphasis of questioning focuses on the *consequences* of each step in the cycle. Useful questions in this process are: 'how does this way of thinking affect what you do?'; 'what happens when you do that?'; 'what are the effects of that?'; and 'what are the consequences of all this for how you see yourself?'. In contrast to interventions where specific negative thoughts are questioned, the validity of the thoughts is not questioned here. As with the prejudice model, the aim of illustrating the maintenance cycle of beliefs is to help patients to see their beliefs as part of a system that is self-perpetuating. This has two potential benefits. As in the case of Stan, the process of examining how the beliefs are reinforced can lead to something of a realisation that change is possible. Secondly, once such a diagram has been drawn up, whenever therapy is held up by a belief-related thought or behaviour, the therapist can ask 'where are you on this diagram right now?'. This allows for repeated experiences of helping the patient to go from being *immersed* in a habitual way of seeing things to seeing their habitual way of seeing things as just that. This raises awareness of the beliefs as entities that can potentially be changed, and sets the stage for the possibility of testing out different ways of thinking, feeling and behaving.

SUMMARY POINTS

- Formulation of and intervention in the patient's belief system are essential aspects of therapy with persistent depression.
- Before underlying beliefs can be modified, it is important that the patient is helped to consider the possibility that these are indeed beliefs rather than incontrovertible truths.
- Hypotheses about the patient's beliefs are derived from themes in their thinking, use of the downward arrow technique, and from the things they avoid discussing.
- Where several beliefs are identified, consideration should be given to their relationships within the patient's overall belief system.
- Examining in detail early experiences that contributed to the development of beliefs can help patients to see their firm beliefs as understandable conclusions from particular experiences, rather than as unquestionable truths.

- Comparing the patient's belief to a prejudice that they disagree with can help them to consider the possibility that their belief might bias the way they see their life.
- Drawing a diagram of how the belief is maintained can help patients to see that how they act makes an important contribution to what they believe to be true.
- Helping patients to recognise that their beliefs are beliefs is essential in engaging them in the difficult process of modifying their beliefs.

Chapter 8

MODIFYING UNDERLYING BELIEFS

In this chapter, you will find descriptions of:

- General principles to keep in mind when trying to modify underlying beliefs
- Methods for modifying conditional beliefs, including examining their advantages and disadvantages and carrying out behavioural experiments
- Methods for weakening unconditional beliefs, including scaling, historical review of the evidence and guided imagery
- Methods for building adaptive beliefs, including scaling on the alternative belief, positive belief logs, and initiating new behaviours
- Ways of helping the patient to consolidate changes in beliefs

Having helped the patient to recognise their underlying beliefs and how they are maintained, the therapist has then to help the patient to modify those beliefs. The aim is to foster a greater degree of flexibility in the beliefs and how they are applied in various situations in order to give the patient a greater choice over their responses. The task of modifying underlying beliefs and assumptions is two-fold: to weaken the negative or maladaptive belief and to build a more positive or adaptive alternative. Within the cognitive therapy literature, a range of methods has been described for addressing both of these tasks (see Beck et al., 1990; Padesky, 1994; Young, 1990). In this chapter, we first outline some general principles for modifying longstanding negative beliefs within a time-limited course of cognitive therapy. We then describe in detail the application of specific techniques for modifying conditional beliefs, weakening unconditional beliefs and building adaptive alternative beliefs in persistent depression.

GENERAL PRINCIPLES OF BELIEF MODIFICATION

Underlying beliefs underpin longstanding patterns of thinking, feeling and behaving that have been developed and elaborated over many years. These beliefs represent the individual's core constructs regarding the self, others and the world. As discussed in the previous chapter, patients will not previously have experienced these ideas as beliefs, but rather as unquestionable facts about themselves and their lives. Even when progress has been made in helping them to recognise that their beliefs are just that, mental representations influenced by behavioural and cognitive processes, the prospect of confronting and questioning such long-held certainties is daunting and threatening. In persistent depression, passivity and avoidance will tend to interfere with the task of modifying conditional and unconditional beliefs. Patients are unlikely to believe that change is possible, so their motivation for the sustained effort required is likely to be low to begin with. The prospect of addressing these beliefs can lead to a range of negative responses, including hostility to the idea of examining beliefs; denial or minimisation of the impact that beliefs exert over their life; or a perception that the risk involved in entertaining the possibility of an alternative view of self is too great. The rigidity with which conditional and unconditional beliefs are held also affects the style of therapeutic work.

Achieving any degree of enduring change in underlying beliefs requires systematic and tenacious effort in the application of change methods. Any changes are usually small in degree and occur quite slowly, as with most work in persistent depression. The therapist must therefore be particularly alert to small changes, in order to help the patient to see them. Small changes that do occur are fragile, and new perspectives or behaviours which have helped on one occasion cannot be assumed to 'stick'. The therapist will need to help the patient to consolidate them in order to integrate them into a new perspective. This usually involves considerable repetition of any helpful interventions, with the therapist at first taking much of the initiative. The therapist needs to balance taking enough responsibility for initiating activities that will facilitate change with not allowing the patient to disengage from the attempt to effect change. When any degree of change has been achieved, the issue of how the patient can take responsibility for maintaining it usually has to be addressed explicitly in some way.

The therapeutic change process often has to start at a rational or intellectual level. Abstract discussion may promote insight into the mechanisms that maintain underlying beliefs, but is unlikely to lead to any lasting change that will improve day-to-day functioning. Such change depends on experiential learning derived from consistent attempts to undermine the basis for unhelpful beliefs. It is often helpful if changes are experienced within the therapy setting before they are exported to the less controlled setting of the person's everyday personal life. It is vital for the therapist to ensure that work with beliefs generalises to times when the patient's emotions are activated in real life situations. In practice, this is achieved through specific behavioural experiments aimed at testing out beliefs and from systematic collection of data to build alternative views of self, others and the world. Overall, the therapist and patient are aiming to rehearse different strategies for processing information and acting in the world, and in so doing to build a portfolio of experiences to counterbalance underlying negative beliefs.

It can be helpful for the therapist and patient to be clear about the degree of change that will be most realistic and helpful. In order to accomplish helpful change, it is neither necessary nor advisable to dismantle or destroy the patient's entire belief system. A realistic aim is to work towards introducing some flexibility where previously there has been rigidity or creating a degree of doubt where previously there has been certainty. A metaphor that some patients have found helpful is to compare their belief system to a sculpture hewn out of a block of marble. Although the sculpture may have some undesired features, it is not most helpful to consider pulverising the entire thing. It will be more feasible and helpful to chip away at an individual feature in order to reshape it and change the overall appearance, for example from a frown to a smile.

Clearly there may be a conflict between the sustained and long-term nature of this kind of work and the short-term nature of the cognitive therapy contract. For lasting benefits to be achieved, the patient may need to continue to chip away at their unhelpful beliefs using specific cognitive therapy strategies for many months after therapy has ended. Indeed for some patients with chronic low self-esteem this may be a life-long venture. The goal of therapy is therefore not only to accomplish some degree of belief modification during the course of the sessions, but also to develop a template that the patient will continue to use to consolidate new perspectives after the end of formal therapy. Modifying underlying beliefs is crucial to the patient's progress in the longer term, both in terms of making continued improvements in well-being and social functioning as well as preventing relapse.

MODIFYING CONDITIONAL BELIEFS

Within the cognitive model described in Chapter 1, the patient's belief system comprises both conditional and unconditional beliefs, which feed into each other in an interlocking system. The core or unconditional beliefs drive a range of conditional beliefs, rules and assumptions within the cognitive hierarchy. In intervening at the level of this belief system, the patient's conditional beliefs are generally addressed before unconditional beliefs. The conditional beliefs usually specify a range of behavioural strategies geared at avoiding or compensating for the defects assumed within the unconditional beliefs. These behavioural factors are crucial in maintaining the core beliefs. The conditional belief predicts the negative consequences to be expected if such avoidance or compensation is not successful. Some typical themes in persistent depression involve the importance of maintaining emotional control, of succeeding at any endeavour and of being acceptable to others. Common conditional beliefs are:

- 'Unless I keep control of my feelings at all times, they will run away with me and I will lose control completely.'
- 'It is better not to attempt something than run the risk of failure.'
- 'If I don't do all I can to please people, they will not want anything to do with me.'

These conditional beliefs involve predictions concerning the consequences of failing to adhere to certain rules. Once conditional beliefs have been identified, patients frequently assert that these are helpful or essential principles that should not be questioned. Unless the patient can see some reason for addressing them, motivation for engaging in a potentially painful process of change will be low. Therefore, the advantages and disadvantages to the patient of holding these assumptions often need to be examined before attempts to modify them can be initiated. The main approach to modifying conditional beliefs is that of designing behavioural experiments to help the patient to test out their predictions. Standard approaches to devising behavioural experiments have been well described in previous texts (e.g. J. Beck, 1995).

The Advantages and Disadvantages of Conditional Beliefs

Before these assumptions can be put to the test in behavioural experiments, the detrimental consequences of holding the assumptions may need to be considered. The belief maintenance diagram (see previous chapter) can be used as a prompt to identify the relationship between particular problems and the underlying assumptions. When the patient describes a problem, the therapist can ask 'Where do you think you were on this diagram when this was going on?'. For example, the therapist referred to *Elizabeth's* belief maintenance diagram (see Figure 7.2) whenever she seemed to be going about things in a perfectionistic way or acceded to others' implicit demands that she should do something for them. This helped in consistently making her aware of the conditional belief driving her behaviour in problem situations. Identifying the conditional belief contributing to a particular problem in this way has the advantage of consistently drawing the patient's attention to the negative consequences of adopting this assumption. This helps to raise the patient's awareness of the role of negative beliefs in contributing to their problems and can foster some motivation for change.

The advantages and disadvantages of adopting particular assumptions can then be weighed up more explicitly. This strategy was used with *Graham* who held the belief 'If you show your emotions, it's a sign of weakness'. He held this to be true not only for negative emotions such as anxiety or sadness, but also for positive emotions like love and happiness. Graham managed his fear of showing emotions by avoiding situations where they might be activated. He was able to discuss his emotions in a detached and intellectual way only after the event, but not at the time he was experiencing them. As a result, Graham downplayed his emotional reactions and tried to convince others and himself that he was not becoming anxious or upset. Once this rule had been identified, the therapist helped Graham to weigh up its advantages and disadvantages as follows:

Advantages

- I present an image of being in control which was important in my role at work.
- I avoid the risk of being criticised or humiliated by others.
- I avoid feeling anxious/upset because I avoid situations where there is potential for becoming anxious/upset.

Disadvantages

- Some people see me as cold and aloof, which interferes with relationships.
- I miss out on getting close to others.
- It interferes with therapy because I try to avoid discussing upsetting topics—yet I know this is what therapy is about.
- It annoys some people because it seems I am not bothered about things when I am but can't show it.

This helped Graham to recognise that he missed out on many emotionally rewarding experiences as a result of this belief. It provided some motivation for him to begin to identify situations where the belief became activated and led to a series of behavioural experiments. These started by examining times in the sessions when he felt emotional, through which his catastrophic predictions that the therapist would see him as weak and inadequate were tested out.

Behavioural Experiments

Conditional beliefs lead to predictions about particular situations that patients may encounter. In devising behavioural experiments to help patients to evaluate their conditional beliefs, their predictions about these particular situations are examined. Testing out conditional beliefs begins with identifying the assumptions that are being applied in a particular problem situation. Once the key assumption driving a patient's response to a situation has been identified, the patient can be asked what they predict will happen if they act contrary to that belief. Specific predictions arising from conditional beliefs can thus be pinpointed and examined. These predictions can be evaluated using standard questioning techniques before setting up a behavioural experiment. For example, early in therapy with *Elizabeth*, a conditional belief was identified that if she ever rated herself as competent, others would see this as unjustified and would think she was big-headed. Elizabeth was first asked to bring to mind examples of other people who seemed confident of their own competence and to rate whether they were viewed as big-headed. When she equivocated that some were and some were not, discussion ensued as to what degree of seeing yourself as competent made you appear big-headed to others. This helped Elizabeth to consider the possibility that this was not a great danger for her.

Ways of gradually putting these predictions to the test in practice can then be discussed. Through specific behavioural experiments, changes in patient's expectations about particular situations can sometimes be generated, where directly trying to change the overall belief would not succeed. By conducting a series of behavioural experiments, the validity of the conditional belief can be undermined in a number of situations. In the session with Elizabeth described above, she agreed to test out her belief about rating herself as competent by commenting on something that she knew she had done well at work in the coming week and noting carefully the reactions of those around her. Her first tentative experiments with such 'big-headedness' in fact drew little comment or notice from others. Subsequent discussion of this reaction suggested it was consistent with the possibility that others also saw her as competent, so made little of further evidence of this. Subsequent more forceful assertions of her successes then met with positive reactions from others. As a result of these reactions, Elizabeth started to give some credence to an alternative belief that 'it is sometimes acceptable to see myself as competent'. This helped to introduce the idea that judgements of herself as competent could indeed hold some validity. In this way, the rigidity with which the conditional belief was applied across situations was diminished, thereby increasing the flexibility with which some alternative viewpoints could be applied. As the conditional belief is part of the system maintaining the unconditional belief, any gains in flexibility at this level can subsequently be used in attempts to undermine beliefs at deeper levels.

Subsequent work focused on building on these gains to modify a further conditional belief that unless she did everything to the highest standard, people would disapprove of her. Having examined the role of this belief in contributing to the maintenance of her problems (see page 253), behavioural experiments were used to help Elizabeth to test it out. One such experiment illustrated both the difficulty encountered and the potential gains to be reaped when longstanding and engrained principles are challenged. Elizabeth arrived at one session exhausted and dejected, having fallen prey to her familiar vicious cycle, this time concerning some old friends coming to stay the following day. She had been so busy during the week sorting out the problems of various people at work and home that she did not now have time to prepare the fine feast she thought would be necessary. She also felt so tired that meeting her exacting standards for entertaining these friends would now be impossible. The therapist saw this as an opportunity to try to test out the validity of her conditional belief and pursued the following line of questioning:

T: Elizabeth, do you remember a few weeks ago when you were finding the activity scheduling difficult, how did we overcome those difficulties?

E: (*sighs*) We made it easier by doing less.

T: OK. How could we apply that principle in this situation?

E: I'm not sure.

T: What would make the task easier?

E: Don't suggest I cancel their visit. You can't do that to people. It's wrong.

T: (*gently*). I see you very much want your friends to visit.

E: Yes. It's a long time since I've seen them.

T: Are you looking forward to seeing them?

E: (*more calmly*) Yes. I always have a lovely time with them.

T: That's good to hear. So it's only the dinner arrangements that are proving a problem?

E: I guess.

T: (*drawing Elizabeth's attention to piece of paper with Figure 7.2 on it*) You seem to have got tangled up in a similar sort of vicious cycle again. (*Elizabeth sighs and nods*) The fact you can't produce the food to the standard you want is really upsetting you. Your prediction is that if you don't meet this standard, your friends will be critical or in some way disapprove of you—have I got that right?

E: Yes.

T: Elizabeth, remember last week we talked about testing out predictions like this to see if they are valid? Well, for example, what would happen if you bought pre-prepared food?

E: (*taking a sharp intake of breath and looking aghast*) I can't do that. They would be totally insulted and think me really lazy.

T: Right, so my suggestion has elicited some more predictions. It sounds like it may be quite important to test this out.

E: I can't. I feel awful at the thought of doing it.

T: (*very gently*) Feeling awful is sometimes a sign that testing something out could be helpful. What would be the advantage in doing something you felt comfortable with?

E: (*becoming tearful*) I just simply can't do it.

T: Elizabeth, let's try to plan it to see what the plan looks like. You don't necessarily have to carry it out. Let's take it one step at a time and at least plan it.

E: If you insist.

In the face of Elizabeth's resistance, it was tempting for the therapist to abandon the task. However, this would have colluded with her avoidance and reinforced her belief. In view of the positive therapeutic relationship that had been established, the therapist thought that the best way to begin to address this avoidance was via a process of gentle but persistent confrontation, despite Elizabeth's growing discomfort. The next 40 minutes were spent, with some collaboration from Elizabeth, drawing up a plan of action for purchasing the food, explicitly identifying her negative predictions and rating their likelihood of being realised in percentage terms. As the exercise progressed Elizabeth became more anxious and tearful. The therapist stressed that the task was not punitive, by giving a clear rationale for what was being tested. The therapist was warm and empathic, and persisted in focusing on the task by acknowledging but not directly tackling the numerous automatic thoughts elicited. When the action plan was complete, Elizabeth remained anxious and firm in her view that she would not be attempting the plan. After the session had ended in stalemate, the therapist felt exhausted and rather hopeless regarding the intervention.

At the following session, Elizabeth began by telling the therapist how she had gone home and told her 24-year-old son about the session. She had shown him the action plan and had started to cry. Her son told her this was an excellent idea and immediately bundled Elizabeth into the car and took her to a supermarket. The following day, her son helped her to lay out the food. Elizabeth subsequently wrote down the results from the behavioural test:

- I realise my friends came to see me because they like me not because of what I do for them or how much effort I put in.
- I got to spend more time with my friends.
- I was touched by my son's concern and thoughtfulness.
- I was not so exhausted as on previous occasions.
- I felt happy!

Her conclusion was that putting her belief to the test had been hard to do, but that 'it was worth it'. This was a turning point in therapy for Elizabeth.

She had learned powerfully at an emotional level that the conditional beliefs she had been following all her life did not hold true in this situation. This was used as an example of her stepping off the hamster wheel (see page 254). Via further behavioural tests at work and with friends, Elizabeth went on to learn that her conditional beliefs in fact did not hold true in many situations. This in turn had the effect of 'disempowering' her unconditional belief 'I am a failure'. It is important not to underestimate the role her son had played in increasing the likelihood of the behavioural test being carried out. Actively recruiting the help of significant others in behavioural experiments can greatly increase the chances of ideas discussed in the therapy session being applied in the client's home environment.

In persistent depression, the way in which conditional beliefs are underpinned by cognitive biases and behavioural strategies can serve to undermine the smooth progress of behavioural experiments. Once a suitable behavioural experiment has been set up to evaluate the predictions stemming from a conditional belief, it is common for it to be executed in such a way that it appears to confirm the conditional belief. For example, a conditional belief was identified in therapy with *Stan* that 'If I try to do anything I am not certain of, then I will fail and end up feeling worse'. He agreed to take a first step in putting this to the test by getting a new program to run on his rarely used computer. He attended the following session in a state of marked despondency saying that his worst fears about this task had been confirmed. He had managed to buy the program and had started to install it, only to find that the program would not run properly once he had done so. He saw this as confirmation of his inability and weakness and concluded that he would indeed be safer not to attempt anything. As a result, he had given up on previously hard won progress at keeping himself active and spent the remainder of the week sitting in a chair ruminating on his latest failure. This illustrates how in persistent depression, interventions designed to be therapeutic can in themselves become subject to the effects of avoidance and cognitive biases.

During this session, Stan was helped to identify the way in which he had interpreted the problem with the computer as a failure. He linked this to many previous perceived failures, which had served as fodder for much of his rumination during the week. From an examination of the similarities between these instances a pattern emerged: that as soon as Stan encountered any difficulty, he attributed it to his own weakness and then gave up. His giving up always made it appear as though the difficulty was indeed down to his inadequacy. Some alternative explanations for the current difficulty were then raised, the most likely of which was a problem with the software he had purchased. Stan agreed to test this out by ringing the helpline of the computer company, although he remained convinced that this would only confirm his failure. He returned to the following session a little brighter in mood, as he had been told that the problem that he had encountered was due to an incompatibility of the program with his computer. The company had talked him through how to rectify the problem and had been very apologetic. In contrast to Elizabeth's reaction above, Stan's reaction in finding that his assumption did not in the end apply in this situation was one of some confusion and agitation. This kind of reaction is not uncommon when patients discover that a long-cherished idea might not always be true. With Stan, it was important to discuss with him how some degree of confusion was understandable, before following this up with similar behavioural experiments using different tasks. This was backed up by discussing alternative views, such as that he might be able to handle any difficulties that cropped up. As with much of the work with persistent depression, behavioural experiments can provoke the very beliefs they are intended to modify. In many cases, progress can be made only if the obstacles affecting the intervention itself are identified and addressed. Perseverance is then required to increase the chances that gains made in one situation might be generalised to other situations.

WEAKENING UNCONDITIONAL BELIEFS

Behavioural experiments can result in some increase in the degree of flexibility with which conditional beliefs are applied. Addressing the patient's unconditional beliefs then starts with efforts aimed at weakening the patient's negative or maladaptive beliefs before attempting to build some alternatives. Relatively more rational techniques for examining the validity of beliefs are generally used before more powerful experiential and emotive techniques are introduced.

Examining the Evidence For and Against Unconditional Beliefs

Weakening maladaptive beliefs usually starts with standard techniques for examining objectively the evidence for and against the unconditional belief. As has been described (see page 220), when working with persistent depression, beliefs will usually have emerged at points as automatic thoughts. The first step in questioning unconditional beliefs is to examine the accuracy of the belief as applied to specific current situations. For *Elizabeth*, her perception of herself as a failure was confirmed by constantly being behind with report writing at work. Whenever anything occurred to remind her of this—for example, one of the six people for whom she worked asking how a specific report was progressing—her belief that she was a failure would be activated. She would perceive the enquiry as a direct criticism of her secretarial skills and worry that she was going to 'get into trouble'. This would provoke an escalation of anxiety, with concomitant poor sleep and difficulty concentrating. Elizabeth would stay after work or work at weekends in order to get through her workload, but would then become exhausted and overwhelmed. She would often then phone in sick, at which her mood would crash down further with the conviction that her failure had been proven.

Socratic questioning focused repeatedly on her competent accomplishment of many work tasks and also on her view of a number of her colleagues who were also behind with their reports. Alternative explanations for her never being up to date with her work were discussed, such as that she was not employed a sufficient number of hours per week to meet the demands of the workload of the number of people for whom she worked. Such exchanges usually ended with Elizabeth saying 'yes, I see what you mean but I still feel such a failure'. Although no cognitive shift was apparent, she was nevertheless able to use this questioning to help her to ask her colleagues how they viewed the fact that they too were behind with their report writing (it did not cause undue concern) and to go to her boss to discuss the problem. It transpired that Elizabeth had more work than any of her colleagues. Her boss told her that the reason for this was that she was the most skilled secretary, so the managers liked her to do their work for them. While this information was a revelation to Elizabeth, it still seemed to do little to counter her perception of herself as a failure until it had been acted on in behavioural experiments in further sessions. These involved discussing with her boss a decrease in workload and reorganisation of her role in order to utilise better her considerable administrative abilities. Equipping Elizabeth with the skills to examine objectively her unconditional belief did not lead to immediate belief change but enabled the exploration of changing behaviours, which could then be used in furthering the process of belief modification.

Scaling on the Negative Belief

In patients with chronic depression, categorical or black and white thinking is a common processing bias, which reinforces the negative content of beliefs in a prejudicial way (see page 246–250). For example, Keith believed that he was a completely bad person and tended to focus on any shortcomings or transgressions as proof of this. He took as evidence for his badness

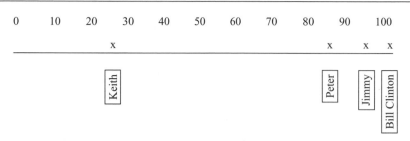

Figure 8.1   Keith's scale of badness

a long history of difficulties in family relationships, including longstand-ing marital conflict and a daughter who was frequently in trouble with the police. Keith had been depressed for the last five years and in his view this pointed towards the fact he was a bad person and was being pun-ished. In cases like that of Keith, using a scale or continuum method to rate degrees of various attributes in self and others can be a powerful way of introducing some flexibility to the way information is processed. This can train patients to process information in a more graded fashion, which interferes with the processes reinforcing the negative belief. One way of doing this is to use the scale to make comparisons between patients' own actions or attributes, which they view as confirming their negative belief, and the actions of others. Towards the end of therapy, Keith disclosed that early in his marriage he had on one occasion had a sexual encounter with another woman. Although this had been opportunistic in the course of his work, had been initiated by the woman and there had been no further contact between them, Keith still felt extreme guilt about this incident. He believed that he was still being punished for it and took it as evidence of his inherent badness. The therapist used a continuum to examine his per-ception, drawing up a scale of badness from 0 to 100% on a piece of paper (see Figure 8.1).

T: Keith, here is a scale of badness from 0%, meaning that something was not bad at all, to 100% meaning that something was as totally bad as could ever be imagined. If you were to rate how bad you are on that scale given what you have just told me, where would you place yourself?

K: As I said, 100%.

T: OK. Do you know anyone else who has ever been unfaithful to their wife?

K: Oh, yes. My friend Jimmy is always being unfaithful.

T: When you say unfaithful can you elaborate?

K: Well he's a salesman, so he gets lots of opportunity when he is travelling, and he takes it.

T: OK. So let's compare your action to Jimmy's for a minute. Where would you put Jimmy on that scale?

K: Well, to be honest, I think what he does is pretty disgusting.

T: In what way is it disgusting?

K: Well, he's been with lots of women—it's unfair on his wife and, you know, not very safe.

T: I see, so how does what you did on one occasion compare to Jimmy's repeated action?

K: Well, putting it like that it's not as bad.

T: So if we were to rate Jimmy's actions on this scale where would you place them?

K: 95%.

T: (*placing a cross on the line and writing Jimmy beside it*) OK, if Jimmy's action is rated at 95% can we rerate yours in the light of that?

K: I suppose.

T: So how badly would you rate your action now?

K: 85%. It's still a bad thing to do.

T: (*placing new rating on scale*) Right, apart from Jimmy can you think of anyone else you know who has been unfaithful?

K: Yes, another friend Peter, who is married and has three lovely children has been having a relationship with a woman at work for the past ten years and has a child by her.

T: Mmm. How do you judge that?

K: I don't talk about it to him. It makes me furious. His wife is fantastic and his children lovely.

T: So on this scale how bad would you rate Peter's actions?

K: I'm not sure which is worst, what Jimmy does or Peter.

T: How would you rate Peter's actions in terms of how bad they are?

K: 85%.

T: Okay, so that is the same rating as you gave yourself. How does your one-off action compare to Peter's?

K: Well, I suppose it's not that bad.

T: So if we were to rerate your action, where would you place yourself on the scale now?

K: 50%.

T: That's some reduction there. I wonder if we can think about other examples of people engaging in types of bad behaviour?

K: Mmm . . . can't really think of any.

T: What about Bill Clinton? He's been in the papers a lot recently. How does your action compare to his?

K: (*sharp intake of breath*) Oh, what he's done is terrible for a man of high office.

T: So on this scale where would you place Bill Clinton's actions?

K: 100%.

T: (*nodding*) Pretty despicable then.

K: Definitely.

T: Then in comparison to Bill Clinton where would you place yourself on the scale?

K: 25%.

T: So in making these comparisons there has been some shift in how you rate the 'badness' of your action. What do you make of that?

K: That's very clever. I've never thought of looking at it this way before. Can I take this away with me to look at?

T: Certainly. One thing I noticed while you were talking is that you saw yourself as a bad person but you talked about Jimmy and Peter as behaving badly. Indeed on the scale, we rated the badness of the actions of the person, not the badness of the person themselves. What makes you define yourself as bad but Jimmy and Peter just as men who do bad things?

K: Mmm...I noticed that. I've never really thought about that before either. A bit stupid really, aren't I?

This last remark from Keith is not untypical of patients with chronic depression. Using any cognitive method can, in patients with chronic low self-esteem, elicit negative thoughts that they are stupid, that they should have been able to reason this out without the aid of the therapist or that the therapist is trying to catch them out. This reflects how even the use of cognitive therapy techniques can be processed in accordance with core beliefs. If this is not actively addressed in the sessions, it can create a serious block to progress. At the very least, the therapist needs to point out such self-criticism and its possible negative effects.

Using a continuum in this way sometimes results in a revelation that most judgements made are relative. This can provide a simple technique to help the patient to move from black and white thinking patterns and begin to introduce more shades of grey when considering schema-related issues. The technique can also help the patient to distinguish between the person and their actions, which undermines global or rigid definitions of self and promotes a more flexible view that can take into consideration potential mitigating factors. What proved particularly powerful for Keith was the fact that he socialised with Peter and Jimmy on a weekly basis and viewed them as good friends. What he disliked was their behaviour in certain circumstances. Asking him to judge himself by these same criteria set in train a process whereby Keith could view himself and his actions in less harsh terms. This use of the scaling method thus works particularly well where patients focus on their own shortcomings in comparison to others' assumed infallibility, using some kind of double standard.

There are some patients for whom drawing comparisons between self and others needs to be approached with caution. Core beliefs are not always associated with straightforward negative comparisons with others. Some patients who seem to see themselves as not good enough, inferior, or weak also see some others in these terms. They may try to bolster their fragile self-esteem by actively scanning their environment for others' shortcomings, which enables them to view themselves as better than those around them. This tendency to demean others or put them down can be formulated as schema compensation (Young, 1990). Patients who hold such beliefs rarely see interactions with others as occurring on equal terms and often hold a hierarchical view of interpersonal encounters where the world is seen as threatening, hostile and competitive. Associated conditional rules often revolve around themes such as 'I must be in control at all times, otherwise people will take advantage of me' or 'If I show any vulnerability, I will be ridiculed and humiliated'. In such instances, teaching patients to use a continuum to compare themselves to others risks reinforcing an already well-established processing bias. However, some progress can be made by using the scale to incorporate vulnerabilities or shortcomings of people previously viewed in idealistic terms and strengths of people previously viewed at the inferior pole. In this way, patients can be helped to move from a rigid categorical system of self-comparison to a more flexible and graded system of self-comparison. By helping the patient to make more reflective, graded judgements, the see-saw effect of judging the self in terms of better or worse may be lessened. This may be achieved by moving on to use the scaling method to build an alternative view of self in relation to others, as described in the latter half of this chapter.

Historical Review of Evidence

As well as considering evidence for and against beliefs from current situations, it can be useful to help patients to re-evaluate the extent to which evidence from their past supports their negative beliefs. Objective evaluation of the overall evidence for and against the unconditional beliefs can be done in the form of a historical review (Padesky, 1994). This involves, firstly, ascertaining the key evidence from events over the course of the patient's life which they consider to prove the validity of their unconditional belief. Then alternative explanations for that evidence are examined, and evidence that could undermine the belief is brought to light. One way of doing this is to focus on specific time periods from the patient's life and to scrutinise it in detail for evidence that does and does not support the underlying belief. Usually the time periods considered move between schools (nursery, infants, junior, senior) and subsequent jobs or relationships. For patients who have moved around a lot during their life, the time period living in each town can make a good division. Patients frequently have a schematic view of how each époque fits with their unconditional belief, supported by one or two 'typical' events from each period. When using this technique, it is therefore most helpful to go into considerable detail for each period. Aspects of each period that do not fit the unconditional belief often reside in details that have been overlooked or forgotten. This technique aims to counter mnemonic biases whereby schema-inconsistent details are unlikely to be recalled spontaneously.

For example, Doug had been depressed since losing his job and believed that this confirmed that he was a weak person, as he had suspected throughout his life. He could list various events and circumstances from different periods of his life that fitted with this view. For example, when primary school age, his mother had not let him go out to play or walk to school by himself, which he considered to be a sign that he must have been weak. An alternative explanation was that his family lived in an area considered rough by his mother and that it was she who was worried about him being picked on, rather than that he was weak in himself. This alternative was supported by the fact that Doug had once helped his older brother to defend himself against a gang of other boys. In conjunction with other more day-to-day examples of being perfectly able to engage in ordinary activities of childhood, such as playing at the park with his friends, Doug could then see that his view of himself as weak was not wholly supported by events of this period.

While this is a useful method for developing counter evidence to undermine the core belief, it does have disadvantages. It is particularly time consuming, and going into a suitable level of detail on each time period can take a full session or more. To cover the person's entire life in this way within a time-limited course of therapy is usually not feasible. One way of addressing this is to deal with just one time period during one session. This can often be sufficiently illustrative to cast doubt on the core belief generally, so that the patient can draw some general conclusions from the exercise. The patient can be asked to repeat the exercise for different time periods as homework. This should be suggested only for patients who have already shown evidence of flexibility, otherwise the patient may just use this as a chance to rehearse schema-consistent information. An alternative strategy is to consider the patient's life as a whole and examine the extent to which the more major events and situations support their unconditional belief. This has the advantage of brevity but, as the events are already a more selected sample, the therapist may have to work harder to counter the patient's interpretative biases. When conducting a historical review of only the more major events and situations in the person's life, it is even more important to consider alternative explanations of events that the patient considers to support the unconditional belief.

Patients vary considerably in their degree of response to this objective reappraisal of current and historical events. For some, these events, their interpretation and the low mood surrounding them seem to have constituted the essence of the unconditional belief. Reappraisal in the context of the general low mood of the patient can have a significant effect on the degree of conviction they lend to the unconditional belief. However, many patients indicate that although their intellectual agreement with the belief has perhaps reduced slightly, they do not really view themselves any differently 'at a gut level'. Such patients often observe 'I know it in my head but I don't believe it in my heart'. This can be due to the influence of affect-laden schema-consistent memories, which can either be of single events (e.g. finding a parent who has committed suicide) or of groups of experiences (e.g. being repeatedly beaten by their father). The historical review method is unlikely to promote significant change where core beliefs are supported by intensely emotional memories.

Modifying Memories using Guided Imagery

Where the influence of affectively charged memories on unconditional beliefs is strong, it is often essential to modify the meanings associated with these memories in the presence of the associated affect (Edwards, 1990). This technique has been termed 'imagery rescripting'. The experience of a cognitive shift in the context of high levels of emotional arousal during the session can provide a powerful prototype for reinterpreting other past and current events that are being processed through the maladaptive schema. There are four phases to the procedure for imagery rescripting. Firstly, an affectively charged schematic memory is identified and replayed in detail to establish the meanings that the person extracted from the event. Secondly, the memory is discussed objectively and new appraisals of the event are established. The event is then replayed in detail to allow these reappraisals to be introduced into the memory in an experiential fashion. Finally, there is a debriefing phase, which allows conclusions from the procedure to be drawn and implications for current and future thoughts and behaviours to be elaborated. As discussed below, some caution is required in implementing such an intervention. Triggering emotionally charged schematic memories is only recommended once the patient has demonstrated some skills in objective reappraisal of situations and has experience of successfully negotiating high levels of emotional arousal in the session. Sufficient time must be allowed to ensure that the patient does not leave the session in a state of excessive distress.

In the first phase, the unconditional belief is reviewed and discussion of a recent event that triggered the belief is used to reactivate emotions associated with it. The patient is then prompted for an early memory of similar thoughts and feelings. This memory may be of the first time the patient felt like this or of a time that typifies the experience of these thoughts and feelings. For example, Susan's self-schema had been labelled as 'silly', which to her was not the relatively innocuous self-view it may sound. For her, it encapsulated a sense of being ridiculous and neurotic, which had been proved by her several bouts of depression, as well as by her perceived incapability in relation to ordinary life tasks, such as keeping a partner, and by her perceived lack of achievements. She described the first of many times she had been made to feel 'silly' by her mother. This was a time when she was very young and returned home from a friend's house in tears, to the disgust of her mother.

Once a memory has been identified, the patient is asked to replay it in their mind's eye and to describe it to the therapist in as much detail as possible. The therapist instructs the patient to try to recapture the situation as though it were happening now and to describe what is going on in the first person, present tense. The therapist guides the patient in re-experiencing the situation through prompts such as 'what is going on?' and 'who is there?'. Susan described, 'I'm walking up the path and opening the front door and going into the hall. Mum comes out of the living room.' The patient can be helped to enter into the memory by recalling concrete details, such as the decoration or furniture in the room, what they and other people are wearing, or what they can see, hear or smell. Once the patient is vividly recalling the memory, they are gently guided through the situation with prompts like 'what happens next?'. Further details relevant to the associated affect are elicited using more specific prompts: 'what do they look like?', 'what are they doing?' and 'what are they saying?'. Susan went on,

> It is quite dark because it was sunny outside, so it seems like she sort of looms up. Her arms are folded and she's asking what I'm doing home already. I know it's not alright and I'm quite frightened and I can feel myself starting to cry again. She asks what am I crying for...she sounds really horrible. I say I don't know and back off into the kitchen. She is shouting at me. She's screaming at me to tell her what happened but I can't really say. Now she's coming at me like she's going to hit me. I sort of hide under the table and she's trying to smack at my legs...She's saying she'll give me something to cry about...it smells of this bleach smell and I want to be sick too. She has another go at me and then shrieks 'you silly girl' and storms out.

At key points of particular significance, the therapist asks the patient what they are feeling and importantly asks 'what is going through your mind right now?'. Other questions can help to tap how the patient is processing the event, such as 'what does this mean to you?' or 'what are you making of this?'. Through this process the meanings taken from the event and which are essential to the core belief are identified. Susan continued,

> I'm left here under the table and I can't stop crying. I've got my head down and my tears are shiny on the lino and I don't even know why I'm crying. I feel like I'm so hopeless, like a real let down ... I'm just so silly.

Once the meaning of the event in terms of the core belief has been identified, the patient is brought back to the present to re-evaluate their beliefs about the event that they have recalled. This maximises the chance that they will be able to re-evaluate the meanings they have attached to the memory using more objective reasoning. Standard questions are posed to help patients to develop alternatives to the negative interpretation contained within their memory. Patients are asked about any aspects of the event that do not fit with their core belief and, more importantly, what other interpretations might be possible. In generating alternative perspectives it can be helpful to ask how they would view the event if it had happened to someone else. The impact of this can be maximised by asking them to bring to mind a child that they care for and asking how they would view it if that child reported to them the same experience. Using these techniques, Susan was able to see that she would handle the situation completely differently if her own daughter came home in tears. She said that she would have comforted her daughter and tried to find out what the matter was. Even if her daughter had not been able to say why she was crying, Susan did not think that this would show irredeemable 'silliness', but rather that it is quite normal for children to get upset sometimes for no apparent reason. It can also be helpful to ask the patient to identify someone with whom they had a positive relationship at the time of the event recalled in the memory and to ask the patient what that person would have said about the event. In the case of patients who have been physically, sexually or emotionally abused by a parent, a kinder aunt or grandparent often fulfils this role.

Having established a different interpretation of events in the present, ways of bringing this new view into the memory are discussed. One way is to ask the patient to picture the benevolent person they have identified entering into the image and intervening to protect or defend the child. Alternatively, the patient can be asked to imagine themselves as an adult entering the image to comfort themselves as a child. In other cases, it can be helpful for the patient to imagine themselves as a child taking some form of action in order to bring about a different outcome in the memory.

Once the best way of introducing the new interpretation into the memory has been agreed, the patient is asked to replay the memory again in detail until the schema-related thoughts and feelings have been reactivated. Once the point in the memory has been reached where the affect is at its highest and the negative view is at its strongest, the therapist guides the patient to introduce the alternative view into the memory. The scene is played through, again in the first person present tense, incorporating the new perspective. This might involve the benevolent messenger helping the child to bring about a different outcome to the situation or simply comforting the child and helping her to see that she is not to blame. For Susan, the positive messenger was the neighbour (Auntie Amy) at whose house she had been playing, and who had often looked after her kindly when she was a child. She replayed her distressing memory up to the point where she was under the table and her mother was trying to slap her. The therapist then prompted her to bring Auntie Amy into the image.

> Mother's shouting that she'll give me something to cry about...but then there's a knock at the door and in comes Auntie Amy. Her face falls and I think she's going to tell me off too. Mother has stopped hitting me and tells her I am having one of my tantrums again. Auntie just says she thought I was crying when I left and she wanted to see if I was alright. Mother says there's no reason for me to be carrying on like this, but Auntie Amy says I am just a little girl.

The therapist can guide the patient in imagining a dialogue between themselves as a child who expresses their negative beliefs and the benevolent messenger who can disconfirm them. The therapist needs to be alert to whether the most negative meanings that the patient has attached to the event are being exposed to re-evaluation and, if not, to bring them into the scene. The image with the more adaptive meanings is played through in the patient's mind's eye until the child in the image experiences some change in their beliefs and a reduction in distress. Susan described the scene unfolding further.

> Mother mutters something about being corrected in her own house and walks out of the room. Auntie Amy bends down and asks me what's wrong. I don't know so I start crying again. She puts her arm round me and it feels all warm...I can see her face and she's not going to tell me off. She just looks nice. I say I'm so silly crying over nothing. She says that all little girls cry like that sometimes and that's what makes them sweet. I ask shouldn't I be given something to cry for and she says no—more like I need cheering up. I don't feel so upset now and I don't think I'm so silly. I want to cuddle Auntie Amy for the rest of the day.

The patient is then brought back to the present again for a 'debriefing'. This involves helping the patient to draw conclusions from this experience that might undermine their negative belief. It is helpful to write these down. Discussion of how these conclusions might be applied to forthcoming situations is usually necessary and action plans can be devised to facilitate this process. For Susan, there was an important realisation that the punitive view about being upset that she had adopted from her mother actually made her upset worse and prevented it from resolving. The experience of imagining Auntie Amy gave her a sense that if she could be a bit kinder to herself when she was upset, then she would not only feel less silly and ridiculous, but would be less upset too. She resolved to put this into practice by letting herself cry sometimes when she felt upset and experimenting with things to comfort herself, including having a long bath or phoning one of her friends. Finally, the therapist helped her to gather herself to leave the session and to plan the next few hours when she might feel especially emotionally raw.

Where used appropriately, the strength of the feelings experienced during the procedure can make it one of the most powerful techniques for modifying long-held unconditional beliefs. However, it should be noted that this rescripting procedure can be emotionally draining, often for both patient and therapist. As stated above, it should only be used once a patient has some confidence in the therapist and process of therapy, and once they have some ability to develop some balanced responses to negative thoughts. The procedure is also time consuming and it is inadvisable to launch into this half-way through a session. It often works best if some preparation is done at the end of one session and the imagery work is started at the beginning of the next. Preparation involves giving a rationale for the procedure and preparing the patient for the likelihood of becoming upset. The therapist can stress that some degree of emotional distress is necessary for the associated beliefs to change and that on this occasion the distress will be put to good use. Patients should be given an opportunity to express their scepticism or fears regarding the intervention. If the efforts of the therapist to counter these meet with no success, patients should not be forced or persuaded reluctantly to proceed.

If the therapist or patient doubt whether the strong feelings can be tolerated, the procedure can be approached in a graded fashion by watering down the likely emotional triggers in the first run through. This can be done by deliberately glossing over details, limiting imagery, talking in general rather than concrete terms or even talking about the event as though it were a story happening to someone else. Once some tolerance to and restructuring from the watered down version have been achieved, successively more emotion can be introduced into further repetitions. Some of the immediacy and impact of the technique may be lost, but it can promote significant change in patients who manifest entrenched cognitive and emotional avoidance.

BUILDING MORE ADAPTIVE BELIEFS

The unconditional belief or schema is likely to have formed an integral part of the patient's identity. It is vital that, rather than simply knocking down this part of the patient's identity, therapy seeks to help the patient to build a new view of self and the world. Padesky (1994) has observed that gradual decreases in the degree of negative belief can be limited in their impact for patients with chronic disorders. By contrast, even a small increase in belief in a desired viewpoint that the patient had previously seen as unattainable can be powerfully rewarding. In cognitive therapy with patients suffering from persistent depression, building more adaptive beliefs does not rely simply on 'trying to think positively'. Rather, patients are helped to initiate and process specific positive experiences that can be linked to the establishment and maintenance of positive beliefs at a deeper level. The aim is not to replace global maladaptive or negative beliefs with global positive ones. It is to afford patients a degree of flexibility and choice in the way that they respond to emotionally charged situations in order to limit chronic distress and allow some fulfilment.

Labelling the Alternative Belief

Once the patient has identified and had a chance to begin to recognise their negative beliefs, therapy must help them to specify alternative views that they wish to build up. Following discussion of the prejudice model is often an opportune time to raise this issue. The therapist asks, 'If you didn't see yourself (or others or the world) as X, how would you like to see yourself (or others or the world)?' In any discussion of behaviours, attributes or traits that the patient sees as desirable, the therapist's aim is for this to be crystallised into a word or phrase that sums up an adaptive new view. This should be an expression that has the most appeal to the patient and should use their language.

There are several considerations to be kept in mind when guiding the patient in the adoption of a new view of self or others to be built up. Many of these have been outlined by Padesky (1994). Most important is that the new belief should be inconsistent with the old. More specifically, information that supports the new belief should contradict the old belief. If a patient has believed that they were unlovable, an appropriate alternative would be that they are lovable. Any evidence of things about them that they consider lovable or evidence that they actually are loved would directly undermine the old belief. Working to strengthen the new belief will therefore weaken the old and reduce vulnerability. (Fortunately, the converse is not true: if the patient is on occasion not loved or behaves in ways that are not lovable, it does not rule out the possibility that they may simultaneously be lovable.) New beliefs that are expressed in terms that are potentially conditional or partial may allow the old belief to be maintained. A new view expressed as 'I am sometimes lovable' is more likely to permit the adoption of the view 'Although I can sometimes be lovable, really and essentially I am unlovable'. Although this may suggest that the pole of the new view should be described as its extreme, common sense of therapists working with depression would suggest caution. For a patient with a negative belief 'I am a failure', a new view expressed as 'I am a success' may take forever to begin to register, as it encourages the black and white thinking common in these patients. A new view that 'I am successful' is both inconsistent with the old belief and encourages attention to small or intermediate successes.

In the examples above, the new belief is opposite in sense to the old belief. This does not have to be the case. Appropriate new beliefs can appear to represent an entirely different dimension to the old belief. For example, *Dave* who had seen himself since childhood as not good enough, chose to work on building up a new belief 'I am content'. The danger that he could continue to view himself as not good enough even in the face of evidence of contentment was raised with him. After discussion, it was clear that this was highly unlikely for Dave and that any possibility of being content with his achievements, or even lack of them, would itself represent a sea change in his view. Another common case where the new view is not simply the opposite of the old is where patients like Stan, with beliefs about weakness, wish to adopt new beliefs about being normal, or in his case 'able'.

Scaling on the Alternative Belief

Once the pole of the new belief has been identified, the task of building up the degree of belief in it commences. In working on this, the patient first needs to be helped to process existing information that fits with the positive belief. They then need to be helped to develop new behaviours that will, in themselves, support the new view and that will help to generate further evidence for the new belief. One of the best ways of helping patients to process new information is through the use of scaling on the adaptive belief (Padesky, 1994). The aim here is to encourage the patient to rate each bit of evidence on the scale of their new belief. This helps to counter black and white thinking, as was described in the above discussion of scaling on the negative belief. In addition, it encourages the processing of bits of information that might previously have been missed completely, using constructs the patient may have used only rarely before.

A scale is drawn up where 100 shows that the new belief describes the patient totally, and 0 shows that the new idea does not describe the patient at all. Physically drawing the scale out on paper or on a whiteboard to use during the discussion in session tends to emphasise any useful points that emerge. As with scaling on the negative belief, it can be helpful to get the patient to rate themselves and others on the new scale. Patients are sometimes surprised to realise that they do not put themselves right down at the zero end of the scale. This may reflect partial success of their attempts to compensate for their negative view, partial satisfaction of assumptions relating to self-worth or a previously unrecognised and rarely acted on element of genuine self-esteem. It is usually possible to identify other people, whether from the patient's personal life or from the media or literature, that the patient will rate at different levels on the scale. Where the patient's view of others has previously been idealistic, this can provide concrete evidence that others are not all clumped at the top end of the scale with a yawning gulf between them and the patient. For *Stan*, who had previously seen himself exclusively as weak in comparison to others since the onset of his depression years previously, a small sense of empowerment came from using this technique. He saw that, while he indeed put himself at the lower end of the scale, he could not rate anyone unequivocally at the top end of the scale and that many people he thought well of were above him only by matters of degree.

Use of Subscales

Patients sometimes have difficulty in placing other people on the scale. Many patients reflect that people can vary in how they come across in different situations. A common distinction is that people often differ in their ability to handle more formal or more casual social situations, with people who are skilled in one situation not necessarily shining in the other. Patients can be encouraged to rate themselves in different situations to see if the position they place themselves on the new belief also varies. The technique can also be used to break down the different attributes that might contribute to the new belief. For example, *Stan* found it hard to put the people he knew in order on his new scale of being 'able'. One of his acquaintances was good at getting things done, but sometimes got into difficulties when things backfired. In comparison, another friend often seemed rather feeble, but always tended to come through in the end. These and other observations were used to identify a number of attributes or subscales that related to the new belief of being able. These included getting things going, seeing things through, getting on with others and being happy with your lot. As recommended by Padesky (1994), these subscales were drawn out from 0 to 100 on a sheet below the 'able' scale and Stan was asked to rate himself on the subscales. On several of the subscales, Stan rated himself higher (at

20–30%) than he had initially rated himself on the overall scale (10%). When his attention was drawn to this, he was able confidently to revise his rating on his 'able' scale up to 15%. Such revisions commonly occur when ratings on subscales are introduced. This probably reflects the establishment of links that may previously have been weak or missing between relatively specific bits of information and higher level beliefs or schemas. Even where such positive revision does not occur with this technique, there is nevertheless some benefit in helping the patient to elaborate their new belief in terms of specific situations or attributes that contribute to it. Helping the patient to elaborate their new belief in this way may also help to counter the rigidity and inflexibility of thinking inherent in chronic depression.

Collecting Evidence for the Adaptive Belief

Having begun to foster processing of some information in terms of the more adaptive new belief, the next major task in therapy is to amass evidence that will help the patient build up their degree of belief on the desired scale. A positive belief log that patients use to note down as many examples as possible of evidence for their new belief is by now a tried and trusted therapeutic technique (J. Beck, 1995; Padesky, 1994). Patients are instructed to keep a record of any events occurring in the period between therapy sessions that fitted with their new belief. This is clearly not without difficulty: the cognitive model suggests that patients with chronic depression lack the cognitive and behavioural processes necessary to register and interpret information in accordance with a positive belief. To the patient, the strategy may make some sense rationally (if any progress has been made so far), but may seem like being asked to go to collect some water in a desert stretching as far as the eye can see. Patients usually need considerable prompting to be able to identify and accept bits of evidence for their new belief. The therapist needs to review the log in some detail with the patient, not only to reinforce what has been written down, but also to cast a net out for things that might have been missed. One strategy is to go through the events of the preceding week in detail to see if any events relate to the new belief. In doing this, it should be stressed that the search is not for things that confirm the new belief at the level of 100%. Rather, it can be helpful to consider any action or event that has even the smallest relevance for the new belief. Patients are therefore asked to rate how much each outcome reflects their new belief, again on a percentage scale. The analogy of 'if you take care of the pennies, the pounds take care of themselves' can be useful in justifying the attention to small details.

With help from the therapist, *Elizabeth* agreed to begin to construct a view of herself as being competent, as an alternative to her previous view of herself as a failure. The homework task to begin building this alternative view was to collect any evidence of competence over the week. On her diary sheet, Elizabeth managed to record one example where she had succeeded in completing a piece of embroidery that was especially complex. After praising her for catching this example, the therapist asked if there were any other areas where Elizabeth had demonstrated competence over the preceding week. Elizabeth believed that there were no other examples. The therapist asked how Elizabeth had got on at work and what she had been doing that week. Elizabeth was able to list several things she had accomplished during the week, but discounted these as being 'part of my job'. The therapist nevertheless asked Elizabeth to rate each activity on the 0–100 scale of competence and then to rate her week's work overall. Each individual task was given a low rating (10–20%) on the scale and the week overall a little higher (20%). The conclusion Elizabeth eventually reached was that each task provided some small evidence of competence that did cumulatively result in viewing herself a little differently in relation to her week's work. She agreed to pay more attention to everyday activities in the forthcoming week as evidence of competence.

Patients may initially have great difficulty linking specific bits of positive information with the higher level concept or belief. Patients therefore need to be helped to recognise specific bits of evidence that support their new belief. One way of doing this is to elaborate different kinds or categories of evidence that fit with the new belief. The categories may represent different kinds of information from external sources and different kinds of new behaviour. For example, *Rosemary*, who had a core belief that she did not count, chose to work towards a more adaptive self-view of 'I matter (like other people)'. A range of different categories of information were identified that could provide evidence to support this new belief. Some would begin to take account of behaviours that she had done all along, such as 'I helped someone out', and reactions she had always tried to elicit, as in 'Someone was grateful to me'. Others were new behaviours, such as 'I accepted a compliment with good grace' and 'I disagreed with someone', and previously uncharted events, such as 'I shared an enjoyable time with someone'. Rosemary found it considerably easier to recognise events that fitted these categories than to look for evidence for the overall belief. Once she had identified events using the categories as prompts, she rated each event on her 0–100 scale of 'I matter'. These categories were incorporated as prompts in her daily log, in order to help her to identify relevant events on a daily basis (see Figure 8.2). It is helpful if the patient does not simply record the events, but also rates the believability of their new belief in relation to the events.

As noted above, this is at least initially an apparently impossible task and it is important for the therapist to forewarn patients that progress may at

DAILY BELIEF LOG		
Category	*Example*	%
I helped someone out		
Someone was grateful to me		
I accepted a compliment with good grace		
I did something I wanted to do		
I looked after myself		
I shared an enjoyable time with someone		
Overall belief: I matter (like other people)	--	

Figure 8.2 Rosemary's Daily Belief Log, including categories of evidence as prompts

first appear slow. Otherwise, the patient may see slow progress as evidence that they cannot change rather than as an inevitable characteristic of the task at hand. For Rosemary, ratings on the new scale were initially made reluctantly and were associated with considerable discomfort, as she perceived this as a selfish way of viewing herself. Through perseverance over several sessions, the process became more acceptable to her and her new belief did start to consolidate. For some patients, when working on apparently small minutiae, particular events can take on a welcome significance. For example, *Stan*, who had such an entrenched view of himself as weak, addressed the task of identifying signs of being 'able' for some weeks with little apparent success. He then arrived at one session in a state verging on excitement (which was itself a new experience for him). He proudly described how he had bought some new shoes (which was something of an achievement in itself), but on returning home realised they were faulty. With some trepidation, he realised this was a chance to act in accordance with his new belief ('I am able') and drove back to return them. On leaving the shop again, he realised that he had not been refunded the full amount and went back again. By the end of this episode, his initial trepidation had been supplanted by a sense of confidence that he had never experienced before. Not only could he confidently place this particular outcome at 60% on his scale, but it also provided a prototype that motivated and guided him in further situations.

Behavioural Changes and Experiments

As will be clear from the above, belief modification is not a purely cognitive procedure of processing information that has previously been ignored or dismissed. As with work on conditional beliefs, changes in behaviour are generally essential in developing new unconditional beliefs. Changes in behaviour can help to strengthen the new belief in two ways. Firstly, the new belief can be enacted in the execution of any new behaviour. For *Rosemary*, disagreeing with someone demanded of her that she adopt a view that she and her opinion mattered enough to do so. Secondly, new behaviours can generate further information consistent with the new belief. Thus, when Rosemary disagreed with someone, it gave her a chance to see if her view was afforded any acknowledgement or consideration. If the main behaviours that have reinforced the negative belief have been identified (see page 251), then alternative behaviours that might strengthen the new belief are usually apparent. To maximise the possibility of change at this deepest level, any changes in assumptions, rules, strategies and behaviours can be processed using the new unconditional belief. For example, *Graham* saw himself as inadequate and therefore actively avoided doing anything novel for fear it would go disastrously wrong. As a result, he led a restricted lifestyle where he avoided taking any risks. For him, important new behaviours involved acting in a way that was consistent with the more adaptive view of self he was seeking to develop, namely 'I am capable'. For Graham, initiating any new activity enabled him to examine whether there was any evidence that he was capable. New activities were tackled in a graded fashion, directed at his pace and on any occasions where he managed to start any planned activity, this was then rated between 0 and 100% on his 'I am capable' scale.

In initiating behaviours that might provide evidence for the new belief, care needs to be taken that these behaviours are not just the patient's much practised compensatory strategies. For example, to Rosemary, the most obvious sign supporting her new belief of 'I matter' was being useful to other people, as evidenced by helping them out or by them being grateful. For her to pay attention to these things would therefore seem to hold promise for building the desired new belief. However, consideration of the maintenance of her negative belief 'I don't count' suggested that assumptions such as 'If someone has a problem, it's up to me to put it right' and rules such as 'I should always help other people whenever they need it' were crucial. Her need to be useful to others was thus an element of the very system maintaining her negative belief. To base her new belief on seeing herself as useful to others would result in little fundamental change. For Rosemary, it was vital to pursue the line of enquiry, 'If you really believe that you matter in the same way as other people, how will it affect what you do?' Through considering examples of other people who seemed to Rosemary to really believe that they mattered, she recognised that truly believing that she mattered was not simply a question of being useful to others. It would mean that she would sometimes be able to disagree with people, to set aside time to do something enjoyable or to refuse a request if she really thought it was unreasonable. These types of behaviour are manifestly at odds with both the old core belief and with the assumptions and strategies maintaining it. Processing even small successes connected with these outcomes resulted in a degree of fundamental change.

Once some degree of elaboration of the adaptive alternative belief has started to occur, the new belief can be used directly as a guide in generating new ways of behaving. Patients can be helped to consider how someone who believed the new belief would behave. Enacting the new belief in practice can then help it to seem more realistic, rather than being a purely rational possibility. *Kate's* core belief that she was 'horrible' led her to think that unless she was always nice to others and did whatever they wanted, they would 'see through her' and reject her. She wished to build up a new view of herself as 'alright' (in the somewhat 'hip' sense of being a good thing). A short time into working on her core beliefs, an ideal opportunity to put her new view of herself into practice presented itself. She had recently befriended someone in the same block of flats, who was assuming that Kate would look after her cat while she was on holiday. In fact, Kate was highly allergic to cats and was very concerned about the prospect. However, she predicted that if she did not agree to her friend's request, they would be so annoyed that they would not want anything further to do with her. In session, an objective appraisal of her friend's likely reaction was attempted: although Kate did not yet know her well, unlike many of her previous friends, this woman seemed quite reasonable. Kate revised her prediction and conceded that her friend would most probably be disappointed and perhaps a bit annoyed, but would get over it. This was followed by a consideration of what an 'alright' person would do. An 'alright' person would balance their own well-being with their wish to help, and would assume that other people would be able to accept this. Discussing this new view increased Kate's resolve to explain that she could not look after the cat. At the next session, Kate reported that her friend had been very understanding and they had mutually agreed to go out socially on her friend's return. The therapist was careful to draw attention not only to her friend's reaction but also the role of her own action when rating this incident on the 'I am alright' scale.

On occasion, patients have great difficulty specifying new ways they might act. Years of behavioural and cognitive avoidance can impoverish the mental structures required to think about situations and take actions in areas that have rarely been physically or mentally encountered. Emma was a young woman who had a profound view of herself as someone who could not fit in with other people. She had never remotely considered the possibility of having a romantic relationship, seeing it as out of the question. A new view of herself as 'like other people' had been identified. Further discussion suggested that being able to have a relationship would make a huge difference on this new belief. Emma's inability even to imagine this seemed to be contributing to her negative view of herself. Some time was therefore spent in therapy and in homework assignments getting her to think about what kind of relationship she would like and with what kind of partner. Despite not being in a relationship by the end of therapy, she had made progress in thinking about this and had begun to talk more about relationships with her female friends. Her prediction that this would prove that she was not the sort of person who could have a relationship was not confirmed. Her thoughts and discussions actually made her 'feel' more like other people, and resulted in her seeing a possibility of having a relationship in future, although the prospect provoked some anxiety. In cases like this, carrying out the behavioural experiment in the patient's mind is a necessary precursor to actual behaviour changes in the world. Caution is needed in using this kind of approach, as encouraging avoidant patients to indulge in fantasy runs the risk of simply reinforcing their avoidance. Where fantasy acts as a substitute for any intention of carrying out a new behaviour it is likely to be therapeutically unhelpful. However, where it results in an increase in intention to act differently, it is likely to be helpful. Even where the target behaviour (here being in a romantic relationship) is not being carried out, helpful fantasy may be reflected in changes in associated small behaviours (here discussing relationships openly with her friends and interacting more comfortably with men).

The therapy relationship itself often provides a valuable setting for experimenting with new behaviours. In Emma's case, when the therapist asked for feedback after these relationship issues were raised, Emma admitted that she felt quite uncomfortable discussing them. She believed it showed her to be ridiculous and that therapy would become an uncomfortable charade, as the therapist would be unable to take her seriously after that.

She seemed relieved that the therapist did not dismiss this possibility but warmly encouraged her to note the balance of apparently genuine versus false seeming responses during therapy. After engaging in further detailed discussion of her potential to have a relationship, Emma reflected that she had found the therapist respectful and caring, and did believe this was at least somewhat genuine. Patients' feelings and predictions about the therapeutic relationship can thus provide powerful opportunities for them to test out their beliefs. In providing a relationship where patients' beliefs will be put to the test, it is important for the therapist genuinely to exhibit a degree of care, as discussed in Chapter 2. Most commonly, use of the therapeutic relationship in this way involves identifying the patient's expectations of ridicule or criticism within the therapy sessions, either through obtaining feedback routinely or through vigilance for patients' emotional reactions to the session. In contrasting these negative expectations with the therapist's more caring response, care needs to be taken that any signs of caring are not dismissed by the patient as just professionalism.

The beliefs of many patients lead them to behave in placatory or deferential ways in therapy. Changes in these behaviours during sessions can be used to test the patient's negative predictions and to reinforce more positive beliefs. For example, Rosemary's belief that she did not count had been reflected in her keeping up a rather guarded, but prickly, style of interacting throughout therapy. It was also reflected in her having worn rather sober, nondescript clothes to every session. One session close to the end of therapy, she arrived in brightly coloured, stylish new clothes. The therapist expressed genuine pleasure at this change of tone and the change was used in discussing how changes in everyday behaviour can be used to test and reinforce new beliefs.

CONSOLIDATING CHANGES IN BELIEFS

Negative beliefs will have been maintained over periods of many years and reinforced by the patient's own habits and interpretations as well as by feedback from the environment. Therefore, changes in the balance between the negative and more adaptive beliefs are inevitably fragile. Even once some progress in building the new belief has been achieved, the patient will need to reinforce it through continuing efforts. Analogies with planting seeds and having to water them regularly or with getting fit and then maintaining fitness through regular exercise can be helpful. Various ways of helping the patient to integrate rehearsal of thoughts and actions which support the new belief into their lifestyle can be used. The therapist can help regular completion of the positive belief log by making sure that as far as possible it becomes part of the routine of the therapy sessions by the end of therapy. Devising a personalised checklist of the new belief and the categories of behaviour that will reinforce it can help to facilitate regular self-help. The patient can use this to note behaviours and do percentage ratings on a daily basis.

Flashcards can provide further support for any new belief. Many patients find it helpful to write their new belief on a card which they can carry with them or have somewhere they will see it regularly (e.g. by their mirror in the bathroom). If the card has some key bits of evidence supporting the new belief, it can be read at times of stress to counter the effects of negative thoughts. If there has been one particular time when the patient realised that their new view really had some basis, they can use an image associated with this time as a reminder of the new belief. For example, one young man, Don, had since infancy had a sense of himself falling apart when people he loved abandoned him. One day, after a major argument with his mother, he realised with some sense of relief and achievement that he was not disintegrating. To him this was the first time he had experienced any genuine belief in his new view 'I am whole'. Don had a vivid image of looking up at the clouds in the sky at this time, which he was able to use thereafter to call up the new belief and the feelings associated with it.

In consolidating embryonic developments in new adaptive beliefs, environmental factors also need to be taken into consideration. The cognitive model suggests that in chronic depression, negative beliefs may have been enacted over many years leading to contingencies in the patient's environment which serve to reinforce the old beliefs. On occasion, some of these factors can easily be reversed. One middle-aged businesswoman had a core belief about herself as helpless. One factor contributing to this was a long-term pattern of being perpetually overwhelmed by a long list of uncompleted tasks at work. In the course of discussions of her working habits, it emerged that not only did she take work home with her, but that she had piles of work in every room in her house. She believed that this was necessary as, given that she was always behind, she ought always to be ready to do some work. Thus, if she woke in the night, there was a pile of work waiting to be done next to her bed. The effects of this in maintaining a level of constant anxiety, a consistent sense of defeat and her fundamental view of herself as helpless were not hard to see. It was an important boost to her new view of herself as an effective person to set up an office area at home, so that all her work could be done and left there. The other rooms in her home could then be used for their proper designation of sleeping, eating or relaxing.

Other environmental factors are harder to modify. Chronic emotional and behavioural avoidance often leaves patients with a restricted lifestyle affording few opportunities for socialisation or satisfaction. Building up new activities and relationships is evidently a long-term project. Patients' negative views of themselves can become entwined with their difficulties in marital (or equivalent) relationships. For example, it is not uncommon for patients who view themselves as worthless to find themselves in long-term relationships with partners who are persistently critical and demeaning of their achievements. Any work aimed at modifying this self-view needs to be implemented giving due consideration to this environmental contingency. Beliefs about self need to be formulated in relation to beliefs about relationships, and how any new belief will accommodate external criticism will need to be addressed. The therapist may also need actively to explore the viability of working with the patient and his or her partner in order to address the impact their interactions have on the patient's negative view of self. Changes in lifestyle that can support new beliefs after therapy has ended are discussed further in Chapter 10.

SUMMARY POINTS

- Modifying longstanding beliefs in persistent depression requires consistent and systematic effort to initiate changes and foster their generalisation.
- When working with a patient's belief system, the effort needs to be shared between modifying conditional beliefs, weakening negative beliefs and building up positive or adaptive beliefs.
- Procedures intended to help modify beliefs will be successful to the extent that they provide meaningful new experiences for the patient.
- Before patients will question cherished conditional beliefs or assumptions, they may need to be helped to consider any negative consequences of those beliefs.
- Behavioural experiments are particularly helpful for patients in testing out predictions from their conditional beliefs.
- Detailed and balanced examination of the evidence, scaling and guided imagery can introduce doubt into long-held, unconditional beliefs.
- Patients can be guided to process small bits of information in terms of a new belief through use of scaling, prompts and belief logs.
- Patients with persistent depression often react to any difficulties in belief modification with avoidance or biased processing.
- Difficulties in implementing belief modification procedures can be addressed by persistence, breaking the task down, labelling biased thinking and eliciting more balanced perspectives.

- Any changes achieved will need to be consolidated through behavioural changes, repeated practice of cognitive strategies, use of flashcards, and addressing environmental factors.
- The magnitude of belief change during short-term therapy may be less important than the extent to which the patient adopts new behavioural and cognitive routines.

Chapter 9

WORKING WITH SOME TYPICAL THEMES IN PERSISTENT DEPRESSION

In this chapter, you will find illustrations of overall therapeutic strategies in patients with prominent beliefs about:

- Depression
- Weakness and emotional control
- Insignificance and responsibility
- Unacceptability
- Achievement and approval
- Work

From the preceding chapters on the cognitive model and different stages of intervention in cognitive therapy, it will be clear that the cognitive 'psychopathology' of persistent depression has to be considered at a number of different levels of processing. The patient's behavioural strategies, conscious thoughts, conditional beliefs and unconditional beliefs form a complex system of interlocking factors, each of which reinforces the others. So far, we have described how the focus of intervention falls successively on different levels of the system and illustrated the different techniques best suited for targeting each level. However, we hope it has become clear that these different levels cannot be considered or treated in isolation. As a result of the persistence of depression, the unconditional and conditional beliefs, avoidance and automatic thoughts become closely entwined. Because the different aspects of the cognitive system are interdependent, they cannot be worked on independently. Intervention in cognitive therapy is not guided just by considering which technique to use to target a particular level in the cognitive hierarchy; rather, interventions are part of an overall therapeutic strategy that is guided by the individual case formulation. In this chapter, we draw together some themes often encountered in working with chronic depression. By dividing the material according to these themes in the concerns presented by patients rather than by the techniques of therapy, we illustrate how interventions at different levels can be integrated into an overall therapeutic strategy related to each theme. The intention is not to imply that these are independent and separate themes that can be clearly delineated; rather, the aim is to show how the issues relating to any theme at different levels can successively be addressed in a course of cognitive therapy.

BELIEFS ABOUT DEPRESSION

Beliefs about depression as an illness are common among patients who have suffered repeated or persistent episodes of depression. Earlier chapters have described some typical beliefs about depression (i.e. 'depression is a biological problem' or 'my depression is untreatable') and their effects on cognitive therapy. Such beliefs about depression are not core, unconditional beliefs in the usual sense. Nevertheless, in many cases depression becomes incorporated into the patients' core view of themselves in a way similar to other unconditional beliefs. Thus, some patients define themselves as depressed, gloomy and negative and back this up with a history of always having been like this. Other patients have not always seen themselves as depressed at the core, but see a later onset of depression as a sign of having changed irrevocably. They see having succumbed to depression as proof that they are now pathetic or inadequate. Negative thinking is seen as a mark of the person's gloomy or inadequate character, so tends to be accepted or indulged. As the beliefs indicate that there is no point trying to be any different, patients tend to behave in an extremely passive fashion reflected either in inactivity or compliance with any activity suggested to them.

As discussed in Chapter 1, patients may have been told on many occasions that a particular treatment will work for them, only to find that it was of limited benefit. Therefore, presenting conventional arguments that depression is an illness that is treatable or questioning how the patient views others who are depressed rarely results in much of a cognitive shift in patients with persistent depression. However, the therapist's interest and persistence can be of benefit even to chronic patients who are often weary of treatment and therapists. Many patients have experienced an array of treatments and of comings and goings of therapists and, sadly, explaining clearly the expectations of treatment is not always the norm. In cognitive therapy, the aim is to set out the expected duration of treatment from the outset to minimise the likelihood of the patient attributing termination to untreatability. The therapist provides a model of giving greater relative interest to signs of change rather than to evidence of chronicity and of being keen to use the failure of one strategy as a signal to try something different.

Although the patient will remain sceptical, the therapist's efforts make it harder for them to disregard this purely as professionalism. Importantly, rather than trying to persuade the patient as to the causation of depression or reassure the patient that their depression is treatable, the therapist relates both the patient's view and the therapist's view to the cognitive model and proposes testing things out to get the evidence.

As discussed in Chapter 4, bringing an acknowledgement of biological factors into the cognitive model can be crucial (see pages 140–142). Many chronic patients deny that their thinking has any influence on their depression, seeing depression entirely in biological or characterological terms. Early in therapy the effects of biology on mood and thinking are discussed. Many patients readily agree that their biological symptoms, such as fatigue, can drag them down or can make it hard for them to think about or do anything positive. The reverse influences of thinking on symptoms perceived as biological can then be examined, usually through outlining negative influences first. Useful tests can be of the influence of thinking about an upset or setback on tiredness or muscle aches. For example, *Catherine* viewed her depression as an intractable biological illness that had been visited on her and about which she could do nothing. As discussed on page 145, when she denied that her thoughts had any role in contributing to her depression, the therapist did not dispute this but asked her permission to write down some of the things she said during the first session. A lengthy list of statements was compiled over the course of the session, such as 'I'll always be depressed', 'Nothing I do makes any difference' and 'This therapy will never work for me'. This list was subsequently used in a mini-experiment. Catherine was asked to read the list back and focus on the thoughts to find out how this affected her. She found that reading the list did make her feel considerably more worn out, although she still doubted that such thoughts really contributed to her depression.

The therapist then works to clarify further the role of negative thinking and passivity in maintaining the depression. The patient is encouraged to monitor their mood using mood diaries or mood 'thermometers' (i.e. ratings of mood on a 0 to 100 scale). The therapist needs to be particularly vigilant for evidence of shifts of any direction or magnitude that the patient is likely to have missed. Any shift in mood, whether spontaneously occurring or from an experiment to test different thoughts or behaviours, is used to compare the characterological with the cognitive-behavioural view of depression. Specific downswings can sometimes be welcomed as evidence that the patient has explicable depressive reactions to setbacks. Any improvements, particularly those that result from the patient's efforts, are related to the cognitive model. Catherine started to complete mood diaries over the first few sessions of therapy, much of which indeed confirmed that her mood was flat most of the time. However, there were also not infrequently 'chinks' when she visited friends or walked briefly in the country. She acknowledged that what she did could affect her mood, but, as this was only temporary, she maintained her belief that there was nothing she could do about her depression. This was subsequently used in discussions exploring her beliefs and their prejudicial nature.

These experiments in examining the effects of thoughts and behaviours on mood rarely have a large impact on long-held beliefs about depression. However, as well as providing brief periods of relief, they can be useful in making those beliefs explicit and clarifying the basis for them. On occasion, patients are found to have overly simplistic models of depression derived from particular past experiences. This is often the case where close family members were depressed while the patient was growing up. It can be very helpful to re-evaluate such experiences in terms of differences between the patient and their depressed relatives. For example, Robert was a middle-aged man whose mother had been depressed throughout his childhood and killed herself when he was 12. He had been well looked after by his father and other relatives but had experienced bouts of depression during adolescence and early adulthood. He had suffered from a further episode of depression over about the previous five years and was convinced that this showed that he was doomed to the same fate as his mother. He was resistant to simple reassurance to the contrary. Several sessions into therapy, a more detailed comparison of his mother's life course and character with his own proved extremely helpful. However, Robert remained quite depressed, believing that although he used to be different to his mother, he had now become the same as her. Particularly convincing in this regard was that when he made great efforts to engage in previously satisfying activities at work and at home, he now got little satisfaction from his efforts. Further discussion suggested that he now tended to do things with the attitude of a condemned man. Robert engaged with the possibility that seeing his continuing decline as inevitable drained his activities of any value. He started to recognise that this negative view was constantly in the back of his mind. In session, he worked with the therapist to flesh out alternative possibilities for the course of the rest of his life and as homework he experimented with the effects of conducting everyday activities with different 'mental hats' on. He found that this did make a difference and on occasion recognised glimmers of his previous satisfaction. From that point, he started to believe that he had turned a corner, which further dented his absolutistic view of depression and gave added momentum to his improvement.

The therapeutic strategy involves helping the patient to consider the view that depression is not fundamental but is a variable state. In the course of this, it often becomes clear that negative beliefs serve a self-protective purpose for the patient. Patients often believe that if they let themselves experience any improvement, any setbacks or upsets would then be impossible to bear. There is a firm belief that while being continually depressed is bad, improving only to crash back down again would be even worse. This is a plausible idea to many people that has some currency in our culture (viz. 'The higher you climb, the further you fall'). This can be tested out against the idea that being less depressed makes it easier to cope with both the demands of normal life and with setbacks or disappointments. This idea can be examined through analogy with physical illness and whether illnesses are easier to cope with if you are generally run down and unhealthy. It can also be helpful to discuss different people the patient knows and whether the more depressed people cope better with disappointment. It is important to remember that the aim is not to convince the patient of what is in any case a contentious issue, but to introduce enough flexibility to render actual tests of the patient's experience possible. These generally take the form of scheduling activities that have previously given satisfaction or pleasure, and examining in detail what happens when these end. At times, spontaneously occurring upsets can be put to use in shedding light on these issues. For example, after discussing these issues over several sessions, one patient was involved in a minor car accident. He reflected that although on this occasion he had felt devastated for a couple of days, a similar accident previously had provoked a serious suicide attempt. His conclusion was that allowing himself to feel better had helped him to cope with this setback.

In many cases, identifying and examining with the patient the basis of their beliefs specifically about depression can result in significant progress in itself. In other cases, although some progress is made at this level, these interventions suggest that beliefs about depression reflect just one aspect of even more fundamental beliefs about self, others and the world. The most common are seeing depression as a sign of weakness that should be kept under control; seeing depression as a sign of being more generally unlovable that should be kept hidden; or seeing depression as resulting from an intrinsic lack of worth that needs to be made up for by looking after others. These are discussed below.

BELIEFS ABOUT WEAKNESS AND EMOTIONAL CONTROL

In many cases of chronic depression, the central beliefs revolve around themes of weakness. Such patients tend to view other people as paragons of normality who are unaffected by upsets and manage to continue competently with any task in any situation. The unconditional beliefs are supported by a range of conditional beliefs that configure around the theme of control, inadequacy and ridicule. Some commonly encountered examples are:

- If I can't control my feelings, it is a sign of weakness
- If I am depressed, then it means I am weak
- If I show my emotions, I will be ridiculed and humiliated
- If I lose control even slightly, I will become totally overwhelmed.

These conditional beliefs are often held in an extremely black and white fashion, resulting for example in an expectation that any consequence of losing control will be catastrophic. Patients who hold such beliefs frequently use emotional suppression as a means of trying to deal with emotions and typically find it hard to tolerate experiencing and expressing any emotions. However, the very act of trying to suppress emotions may in fact heighten the fear of losing control. This is likely to drive the patient to even greater lengths to try to contain their emotions in order to avert the feared consequences. Although the emotions may never actually rise to the surface, the continual effort to suppress them can be experienced subjectively as a constant potential for humiliation. This can manifest in feelings of shame, which are taken as further evidence of intrinsic weakness or inadequacy, thus confirming the patient's negative view of themselves.

These patients often initially report feeling fine and may have been persuaded that they are depressed by family or professionals. When they do admit to negative feelings, they often report feeling low with no finer discrimination. Although cognitive therapy is frequently misconceived as a rather intellectual process by therapists from other approaches, unless the therapist is able to elicit and maintain some emotional arousal in the patient then the strategies of cognitive therapy are likely to be of limited value. For any patient who holds beliefs about the need to control emotions in order to avoid dire consequences, talking about potentially distressing material can be aversive in itself. Beliefs about emotions and their expression can block the therapist's first attempts to engage such patients in cognitive therapy. Working with patients who hold these beliefs involves enabling them to recognise and express emotion more adaptively, alongside helping them to adopt more flexible rules regarding the experiencing and expression of emotion.

For some patients, it can be important early in therapy, either explicitly or implicitly, to help them to recognise and differentiate between a range of different emotional states. This can be approached in a number of ways. Patients can sometimes be helped to discriminate differing emotional states using images, commonly of colours (red for anger or anxiety and blue for sadness) or common situations (a funeral for sadness, a driving test for anxiety, a fight for anger). For many patients who have difficulty identifying and labelling emotions, a good starting point is to pay particular attention to bodily changes, as these can provide a first step to emotional recognition. This was the starting point for Matthew. From the first assessment session, he could speak eloquently about the complex and longstanding set of problems that had brought him to therapy, but whenever the therapist enquired about his current emotional state and attendant negative automatic thoughts he would reply 'I don't know'. After three sessions Matthew was able to make a link between upsetting events and a feeling of 'heaviness' in his stomach or head. This was used as a cue to make links between his sensation of 'heaviness' and negative automatic thoughts. By Session 7, Matthew's 'heaviness in his head' had been defined as feeling sad or depressed and the 'heaviness in his stomach' as anxiety. Over time Matthew was encouraged to pay attention to varying degrees of emotion by rating his mood in session or during the day on a 'mood thermometer'. Gradually he started to acquire concepts of variability of and discrimination between specific mood states. This helped to counter his perception of his negative mood state as invariant and unremitting.

As well as helping the patient to identify emotions, the therapist needs to investigate what the patient is doing to keep his/her emotions under control. Patients can often identify with terms such as clamping down or battening down their feelings. Particular strategies or safety behaviours that patients use to control their emotions can be identified, including clenching their teeth, tensing their stomach or blanking their mind. The patient can then be asked what they predict would happen if they did not maintain control over their emotions. Predictions tend to have two themes: that the feelings would overwhelm them and result in permanent loss of control or damage and that others (including the therapist) would humiliate them in thought or deed. These predictions can then be tested out by encouraging the patients to let go by degree some of their safety behaviours and engage in some form of emotional expression. On some occasions when discussing a potentially upsetting situation, the therapist's asking 'are you doing anything just now to keep your feelings down?' can prompt a release of emotions. This can prove extremely helpful in decatastrophising emotional experience and expression.

Beliefs about emotional expression often predict negative consequences of expressing positive feelings. Where this is so, it can be less threatening for the patient for their first experiments with allowing some emotional experience to focus on positive rather than negative emotions. Ideas that it is foolish to look happy and that any good feelings will result in an even more painful fall are common in chronic depression. Thus, there is often suppression of any positive emotion due to its perceived transience and the predicted devastation when the grinding feelings of depression return. An example of this was provided when *Stan* described his daughter's recent birthday party (see page 251). He talked about how the party had gone very well, but in a flat monotone. When asked how he felt about the party, he replied flatly 'okay'. In response to the therapist's questioning, he conceded that his lack of positive feeling was noteworthy. He revealed that he thought he would look foolish if he acted too pleased about this and he believed that such foolishness would be confirmed when the positive feelings departed, leaving him as low as ever. With considerable difficulty, and much prompting, he was able to describe some of the things he had found really good about the party, such as the pleasure in his daughter's face when she opened her presents. With further encouragement from the therapist, he was able to use this specific memory to kindle some happy feelings during the session. In 'debriefing' from this experience, he could accept that the therapist's pleasure at this was genuine and not concealing some disparagement, and at the next session he reported that the feeling had just gradually drifted away with no ill effects. This apparently innocuous experience provided some motivation for subsequently expressing some pleasure at home, which met with significant positive results. When the conclusions of this were examined in terms of his core beliefs, he was surprised to find that he saw himself as less weak and more 'able'.

Once patients have made some progress in experiencing positive feelings, they can be helped to test their beliefs in relation to negative feelings. This can take advantage of upsets that occur in the course of therapy or can use discussion of significant past upsets. The predicted consequences of such discussion are compared with the actual outcome, usually focusing on the patient's degree of control and the therapist's reaction during the discussion. This strategy was used in the case of *Peter*, whose previous view of himself as a capable man in control of his life had clearly been shattered by the experience of becoming depressed. During therapy, it emerged that he believed 'If I can't control my emotions (depression) then it's a sign of weakness'. As a consequence, Peter dealt with his illness using a range of tactics to control his emotions and feared that if he lost this battle, he would suffer a loss of his mental faculties and public humiliation. His tactics included suppressing any distressing thoughts and images that came into his mind and distracting himself from negative affect through physical exercise. In the short term this was reasonably effective, but over the years it had led to a sense of the feelings becoming increasingly powerful. Trying so hard to control his negative affect maintained his perceptions that he could not do so, which he took as further evidence of his intrinsic weakness. In therapy, his beliefs about the need for emotional control were formulated and a series of behavioural experiments to test the consequences of relinquishing some degree of emotional control were planned.

One such behavioural experiment focused on discussion of the circumstances leading to the onset of his depression (which he had initially forbidden). Initially, Peter was asked to rate how upsetting he thought it would be to discuss the incident, which he rated at 95%, and his more specific predictions were identified. These were that he would start to cry and not be able to stop (80%); that he would not be able to get to the end of the story (100%); and that the therapist would think he was weak (95%). Peter was allowed to dictate how the discussion progressed. The therapist encouraged Peter to talk about the incident that led to the onset of his depression, which involved making people at work redundant. After two minutes, his voice quivered, he became tearful and began to shake. He stopped talking and began to take deep breaths, stiffening his entire body to try to hold back his tears. The therapist encouraged Peter to continue talking, while asking him to drop his safety behaviours of taking deep breaths and tensing his body. Peter continued to speak for 10 minutes, wiping his eyes and pausing from time to time to compose himself. In re-rating how distressing he found the discussion, he was surprised to realise that it was not as bad as he anticipated (60%). In reviewing his predictions, he noted that although he did cry, even on dropping his safety behaviours this did not overwhelm him and to his surprise he got to the end of his story. He re-rated his first two predictions at 20% and 0%. The final prediction that the therapist viewed him as weak was more difficult to disconfirm. While Peter could not identify any objective evidence for this view, he found it difficult to accept that this was not the case. He re-rated this prediction at 70%, commenting that 'As a therapist you get paid to be nice, so you won't tell me the truth'. From this it was clear that more work needed to be carried out to generalise the conclusions from this experience in therapy to other situations and people in his life. This was accomplished through a range of further tests carried out as homework assignments.

After (or sometimes in tandem with) such behavioural experiments, work on unconditional beliefs about weakness becomes a major focus of therapy. Labelling the beliefs and drawing out how they are maintained (see page 250) can help to highlight to the patient how attempting to avoid or restrict emotion is integral to the problem. Discussion of the early experiences that may have contributed to the adoption of these beliefs can be very useful, even though suppression of emotions renders 'rescripting' of emotional memories unworkable. The early experiences that are crucial can be quite subtle and so have often eluded the patient's efforts to understand their problems. This reinforces the patient's idea that any problems must be attributable to their inherent weakness rather than external influences. One patient who believed wholeheartedly that she was a weak person found it impossible to identify any early experiences that she thought could have contributed to her sense of weakness. She described both parents as kind people with whom she got on well. The atmosphere in the house always seemed to be calm and unruffled, the only exception being when she was herself upset. Her parents were never unkind to her, but told her that there was nothing to be upset about. When she was worried or upset about anything, she tended to go to her room and try to work it out by herself. By the time it came to taking exams in her teens, she was convinced that there was something strange about her inability to get rid of anxieties that were so clearly at odds with the way other family members behaved. For her, describing this situation and viewing it more objectively helped her to see it as understandable that she came to view being upset as a sign of weakness. This understanding was then used as a stepping stone to building up an alternative view of herself as normal.

For patients with beliefs about weakness, the most common adaptive alternatives are ideas of being normal or able. Patients may initially focus on evidence of ability to control emotion as a sign of normality. However, if this were to be the sole focus of efforts to build the new belief, it would also reinforce the assumptions about the importance of keeping control that in the long-term reinforce the belief. It is vital that evidence used to build the new belief encompasses some activities that are at odds with old patterns of avoidance and suppression. Including evidence of emotional expression or tolerance is important in laying the foundations for a new view of self. Black and white thinking may mean that the patient starts off with a rather extravagant view of what emotional experience entails, for example that feeling sad necessarily means sobbing uncontrollably. The patient may therefore need considerable help with recognising, acknowledging and valuing suitably small degrees of emotion.

In working with patients who have very restricted emotions, it can be enormously difficult to begin to get any apparent shift in behaviours or beliefs. It can help to bear two things in mind. One is that, for these patients, structured cognitive therapy is a vastly different experience to anything they have ever participated in before. For them, experiences barely discernible to the therapist represent a transformation. What seems to the therapist like a gentle and rather intellectual discussion of a situation can seem to these patients like an emotional whirlwind. As noted on page 70, *Catherine* described her initial cognitive therapy sessions as like being 'pinned to the ground' and this was consistently her experience of therapy. Therefore, it can be helpful to consider the patient's experience of the therapy itself as possible evidence of ability to tolerate or benefit from emotional experience and expression. Secondly, stability tends to be a hallmark of these patients.

Although this makes it hard to initiate any change, once any small shifts have been achieved, they are more likely to be maintained than in more labile patients.

BELIEFS ABOUT INSIGNIFICANCE AND RESPONSIBILITY

It can be helpful to discriminate between two types of belief that may both be described in terms of worthlessness. For dependent or sociotropic patients, worthlessness is defined in terms of social unacceptability to others, as described in the next section. For autonomous patients, worthlessness seems to be a more moral or existential concept, reflecting a perceived lack of some essential worth that others are assumed to have. The self-concept is often of being insignificant or unimportant. The patient may see themselves as being a nuisance or as being in the way by virtue of their very existence. Such patients tend to suppress their own emotions and wishes. Their conditional beliefs and assumptions tend to revolve around taking responsibility for others and their welfare. Typical beliefs are:

- If I do anything for my own benefit, I am being selfish.
- If someone needs help, I must give it.
- If someone has a problem, it is up to me to sort it out.
- If I put others first, I will be accepted.

To meet the demands of these conditional rules, patients make excessive efforts always to put the needs of others before their own. They often sort out other people's problems at the expense of their own priorities, needs and well-being. In cases of extreme subjugation, patients may actually have little concept of the fact that they have wants, needs and priorities that persistently go unmet. Not expressing their own wishes curtails any chance for the patient's own existence to be valued or validated by others, thus reinforcing the belief of insignificance. Constant vigilance for other people's negative states results in anxiety when all seems well and guilt when it does not. When these emotions or other depressive symptoms interfere with the task of meeting the perceived needs of others, this is seen as further proof of worthlessness.

A further factor that can maintain these beliefs is that individuals in the patient's family and social network are often well served by the patient's slavishly meeting their needs. Behavioural experiments intended to modify the patient's rules usually involve the patient doing less for others in the family and social circle. The negative consequences of this can include not only a marked increase in levels of anxiety and guilt, but also negative reactions from others, such as withdrawal of affection or, in extremes, physical violence. If family relationships change or friendships come to an end, the rewards of modifying such beliefs can therefore be hard for the patient to see. Such external contingencies can serve to confirm the patient's view of their intrinsic worthlessness and their belief that others' needs are more important than their own.

Patients with these beliefs tend to prize their self-reliance, as they are not supposed to make demands on others. Being in the position of needing help in the form of therapy contravenes one of their fundamental principles. This can pose a major barrier to engagement in therapy. Further, their neglect of their own needs in favour of the needs of others can result in therapy sessions receiving a low priority in a long list of demands on the patient's time. Attendance and compliance can therefore initially be a problem. The therapist may at first have little choice than to emphasise the importance of attending and engaging in therapy as satisfying an external responsibility towards the therapist (rather than viewing therapy as attending internally to the patient's own welfare). Early in therapy, the emphasis tends to fall on decreasing the negative consequences of the perceived responsibility for others, through 'decatastrophisation' of not meeting demands and reattribution of blame. It is only later in therapy that building up some idea of the patient taking responsibility for their own well-being becomes possible. This is then used to help the patient to try to establish some degree of belief in their own significance or value.

Work with automatic thoughts of self-blame and letting others down is addressed through standard cognitive techniques. Pie charts (see Greenberger & Padesky, 1995) are helpful in drawing attention to factors that contribute to outcomes and are not the patient's responsibility. The idea that other people will feel let down if the patient does not meet their perceived demands can usefully be put to the test. Although such interventions often result in little change in belief in chronic patients, they help to highlight the possibility that the patient's beliefs and attitudes contribute to their problems. This can help the patient to become more amenable to examination of their beliefs, which were previously seen as completely inconsequential. The prejudice model and belief maintenance diagram (see Chapter 7) can then be crucial in helping patients see the possibility of reducing responsibility *internally*, rather than externally through satisfying others.

Predictions from conditional beliefs about attending to others' needs can be tested by examining what happens when patients resist the urge to sort things out or keep people happy. The intense discomfort patients feel when faced with such a possibility can make such tests hard to set up. The concept of 'toughing out' guilt can be useful. The power of the therapeutic relationship can also be exploited, as the therapist's giving permission not to respond to guilty feelings can provide a counter to the perceived external demands. The patient's attention can then be drawn to any evidence that others sometimes do cope independently and don't always blame the patient. This is then referred back to ratings on the responsibility belief. When some perceived demand has not been acted on, it is also important to note if guilty feelings decrease of their own accord. Strategies for handling actual negative outcomes—such as when others do blame the patient or when others truly are reliant on the patient—may need to be developed, such as helping people to find other sources of help.

Such behavioural changes were crucial in the case of *Julie*, who spent much of her time meeting the needs of her four children, three grandchildren and a number of relatives in her extended family for whom she acted as confidant and problem solver. She rarely saw it as appropriate to refuse the demands of others or ask for help. Unsurprisingly, Julie experienced herself as constantly 'at the mercy' of others in terms of the demands they made on her time and resources. Indeed she was prone to cancelling therapy sessions in order to meet the constant demands placed upon her by her family and friends. Early in therapy, Julie identified her problems as existing in her environment: 'If people didn't make demands of me I wouldn't have this problem.' However, she also blamed herself when she thought she had let others down. There was some benefit in helping her question thoughts that blamed her entirely for failing to meet some of the excessive demands on her. In early sessions, some blame for various problems was re-apportioned to others, including her rather critical husband. Through this work, she was helped to recognise the role of her own thoughts and behaviour in maintaining the problems she described. The therapist needed to be careful that she did not just blame herself further for the difficulties she was experiencing. Simply identifying her beliefs was an important part of this process. By several sessions into therapy, she recognised and endorsed her conditional belief: 'If I put myself first I will be criticised and humiliated' and her unconditional beliefs that: 'I am worthless', 'Other people are more important than me' and 'The world is uncontrollable'. The consequences of these beliefs in terms of her tendency to take on an unreasonable level of demands were illustrated in a belief maintenance diagram. This also helped her to see that it would be inevitable that she would not meet all the demands on her and thus that she would interpret the resulting fatigue and depression as further evidence of her worthlessness.

In seeking to help Julie to build a more adaptive view of herself in relation to others, efforts at belief modification focused around twin goals of helping her not to take sole responsibility for the well-being of others and to recognise and meet her own needs when necessary. Work on this was started through considering a new conditional rule: 'In order to take care of other people, I need to take care of myself.' This enabled her to test out the strategy of looking after herself without first questioning the overriding importance of caring for others. With much encouragement, she was able to test the effects of small aspects of caring for herself, such as having a rest when she felt exhausted before getting on with addressing the next demand on her. Although she felt quite guilty about this, she was surprised to find that no external criticism was thrown at her and that she did feel more able to tackle things. This helped to cast some doubt on her belief that if she put herself first, she would be criticised and humiliated. Furthermore, this enabled her on a number of occasions to resist urges to sort things out for friends and family when she had not been asked to do so. Other interventions helped Julie to take responsibility for tasks for which she was realistically responsible, which had previously received insufficient priority compared to the demands of others. Specific tasks, such as making a dentist's appointment, were used to test out predictions stemming from her belief that she was worthless and that others were more important than she was. Her progress in improving self-care and combating procrastination was related to a new view of herself as being worthwhile and of equal value to others.

Progress from using behavioural experiments to modify conditional beliefs can be used to begin to address core, unconditional beliefs related to worthlessness or insignificance. This can be done by relating the outcomes of behavioural experiments back to ratings on those beliefs, to see whether changes in behaviour lead to changes in belief. It can also help to discuss in some detail the genesis of the underlying beliefs. Formative experiences for these patients often include a pattern of childhood neglect, often in a family background of marital friction, violence, alcoholism, overwork or mental ill health. The patient as a child will often have taken on the role of caregiver either for adults within the family who themselves have problems or for other siblings. The patient may quite realistically have helped to sort out others' difficulties or helped to contribute to a fragile peace in the home by doing practical or emotional tasks for others. The child may rarely have experienced a model of being looked after or having their needs acknowledged and met. Reviewing such details of their childhood from an objective standpoint can help patients to make sense of their view that other people's needs are more important than their own. Identifying any person who did genuinely help to care for or look after the patient when they were a child can cast doubt on the universal applicability of the negative beliefs. Imagery rescripting (Edwards, 1990) can be used to activate particular emotional memories of being held responsible or failing to meet external demands. The benevolent person can then be brought into the image to counter the sense of blame and responsibility, which can be very helpful in these cases.

Examples of adaptive beliefs which patients have found it helpful to work to build up are 'I matter like other people' and 'I am a worthwhile human being'. Patients may initially only see evidence of being useful to others as supporting these concepts. Therefore, they usually need some encouragement to consider things they do for themselves as reflective of their human value. It can be useful to frame the work on the new belief as 'treating yourself as you treat others'. The patient can then begin to direct towards themselves skills of nurturing and problem-solving which they usually reserve for others. If genuine progress has been made in behavioural experiments and in recognising how the negative beliefs are maintained, then patients will start to accept that actions such as refusing unreasonable requests can be a sign of being worthwhile. Giving some priority to other aspects of self-care, including necessary rest or recuperation and things that are pursued for interest or enjoyment, are vital in building beliefs of being as worth while as others. For these patients, their spontaneously reporting that they enjoyed some new or long-neglected activity for its own sake is a sign that the new belief has begun to take root.

BELIEFS ABOUT UNACCEPTABILITY

For many patients, underlying beliefs revolve around the theme of being unacceptable to others. Patients who believe that they are bad, horrible or unlovable usually exhibit marked cognitive and behavioural avoidance. Much of the time, patients who hold these types of belief implement strategies aimed at preventing others from discovering the perceived depth of their badness or unlovability. Conditional beliefs around themes of approval and rejection can often be formulated, as in:

- If people know what I am really like, they reject me.
- If I don't do what others ask, I will be criticised.
- If I let myself get upset, it proves how horrible I am.

It is in the patient's social relationships that these beliefs are likely to be most strongly manifest. The anticipation of rejection means that the patient may have few significant relationships or that the relationships are characterised by compliance, self-deprivation, and even acceptance of exploitation or abuse. As the conditional and unconditional beliefs can be easily activated across a broad range of social interactions, the avoidance often seems frantic or chaotic. Emotions tend to be changeable and extreme, varying from extremes of anger when some small slight is interpreted in terms of outright condemnation, to anxiety when rejection is anticipated, to self-hatred when perceived past rejections are contemplated. Both external factors (e.g. instability of relationships) and internal factors (e.g. instability of emotions) are interpreted as evidence of underlying unacceptability or badness. The avoidance that is motivated by the underlying beliefs thus serves to reinforce those very beliefs.

In therapy, patients may actively try to dissuade the therapist from raising certain issues and may be very reluctant to continue therapy if these issues are touched on. Before underlying beliefs can be addressed, therapy must first help the patient to contain and then cope with the emotional arousal, often generalised self-hatred, when the patient's beliefs are activated. Working to improve patients' tolerance and management of affect is thus a prerequisite to helping patients to test beliefs about their badness. Standard techniques for management of intense emotions and for the planning and execution of challenging activities are useful. In view of the black and white thinking of these patients, grading or breaking down difficult tasks and using time off, self-reward and pleasure following even partial accomplishments can be particularly helpful. The idea of getting help and support from people before things get to a crisis can usefully be suggested. In the early stages of therapy, the therapist has to provide a strong model of these strategies and may have to implement them in a didactic fashion. Only once some flexibility has been introduced into the belief system do patients usually become more able to implement self-regulation strategies for themselves. The initial aim is therefore to provide a context where the predictions from underlying beliefs can more safely be tested.

Therapy then needs to help the patient to test out the predictions inherent in their conditional beliefs. The difficulties in therapy usually arise when fear of extreme emotions prevents the patient from entering situations where beliefs might be tested and change might occur. Once sufficient affective regulation has been achieved to enable patients to confront some situations where they fear the potential for rejection, strategies to process information in a more even-handed way can be implemented. Issues of badness and unlovability typically affect both achievement-related and more intimate social situations. The former type of situation is usually more peripheral and can often be addressed more easily first. Tasks that have been avoided at home and at work will often evoke expectations of criticism or rejection. Standard cognitive techniques can be used to identify and question negative thoughts, which often involve thinking errors such as mindreading and all-or-nothing thinking. These are often effective in producing changes in degree of belief once a patient has been helped to engage with a particular problem. A prediction log for comparing the expected with the actual outcome of successively more daunting tasks can also be useful. However, in some patients with these beliefs, the tendency to deprive or punish themselves can prevent them from readily taking in any positive information.

For example, therapy with *Kate* aimed to help her to develop strategies for self-regulation and used cognitive-behavioural techniques to address successive tasks that activated her negative beliefs. As described previously (see page 34), she initially denied having any problems she wished to discuss in therapy. With only a little prompting, a catalogue of occupational, financial and social problems flooded out leaving her so upset that she ran from the first therapy session. It emerged that she believed that her many problems were proof that she was a 'horrible' person. Judicious use of supervision enabled the therapist to develop a strategy for handling the upset or avoidance in subsequent sessions. This involved a plan that interventions should tackle issues in a graded fashion, so that only easier or more superficial issues were addressed initially. The strategy also involved prefacing each intervention with some discussion of how and why it might be upsetting and following each intervention with some discussion of how to cope with any upset that had indeed been aroused. Early in therapy, the issue of contacting the social security office to sort out problems with her unemployment benefit payments was addressed. The therapist pre-empted her concern about this by explaining that such situations can make people feel bad if they trigger a negative view of themselves. Kate agreed that her 'worst thoughts' about herself made her feel anxious and guilty, even when only discussing claiming benefit and that these feelings would get worse when she actually contacted the benefit office. Through just alluding to her belief of being horrible, specific negative thoughts about this task (e.g. 'They'll look down on me', 'They'll tell me where to get off') were identified and questioned. Mainly by considering how she would view the situation if it were happening to someone else, she agreed to test her prediction that the people at the office would treat her with contempt and tell her that her application had been refused. Following the session, she managed to contact the office and her claim then proceeded with minimal difficulty. Kate was pleased with the way she overcame this problem, although in subsequent sessions it became clear how little this success generalised to other situations where her beliefs became activated.

Achieving such generalisation usually involves explicitly acknowledging, labelling and examining the effects of unconditional beliefs about the self and others. This is often a highly distressing process for these patients. The therapeutic relationship can be a testing ground for the unconditional beliefs, as during sessions the therapist is often witness to things the patient considers unacceptable. Examples may include the patient being upset, avoiding tasks outside the session or confessing 'bad' things that have happened outside therapy. The patient may become overtly anxious about the therapist's reaction and often anticipates disapproval, rejection or the termination of therapy. They may cope by seeking reassurance from the therapist or trying to end therapy themselves. Clear expressions of the therapist's wish to continue trying to help are often discounted as the therapist 'being professional'. In contrast, patients can take great note of the slightest sign of any negative reaction from the therapist. It can be helpful for the therapist carefully to acknowledge their negative reactions, particularly in relation to the patient's attempts to avoid things. The therapist must be quick to contrast these with their more positive reactions when the patient is engaging in therapy. The possibility that it is the patient's avoidance rather than inherent badness that evokes negative reactions can then be discussed.

The historical antecedents of beliefs about unacceptability are often fairly clear, and often involve some degree of physical or emotional abuse. These can be explored once patients have acquired some tolerance for experiencing negative feelings associated with their underlying beliefs and have built up some degree of trust in the therapist. Discussing with the patient the role these early experiences had in the formation of their view of themselves can help them to identify less completely with their negative view. The imagery rescripting technique (see Chapter 8) can then be very powerful in producing significant belief change in a short time. The main focus of such belief change is around the interpretations of badness and unacceptability the patient formed at the time of the abuse. While the upsetting schema is activated within the image, the patient's more rational adult thinking or their memories of a benevolent influence at the time of the abuse is used to introduce fundamentally different interpretations. This experience can provide an important prototype for attributing other people's negative actions and reactions to factors other than the patient's perceived unacceptability. It is also important in doing this work to focus on the therapy relationship. The patient's upset in discussing traumatic experiences often triggers thoughts of being rejected by the therapist. Being alert to this provides another opportunity to disconfirm the negative beliefs when they are at their most accessible. The patient's predictions that result from their unconditional beliefs are made explicit and then compared to the therapist's actual reactions. The therapist should be as clear and unambiguous as possible about caring in a genuine human way for the patient's suffering during any past traumatic events.

Where the patient sees the therapist's reaction as positive, this can be used as a step towards testing reactions of other people in the patient's life. Important new behaviours, such as assertion of wishes, requesting help and appropriate self-disclosure, provide opportunities to test out the underlying beliefs. An initial focus on testing predictions about the reactions of others may in time give way to work on helping the patient to value their own wishes and efforts. This is usually done with reference to adopting an alternative view of self as being okay, or a lovable or good person who can be accepted by others even when upset or when failing to live up to expectations.

In therapy with Kate, discussion of the effects of her apparently quite privileged background helped to set in train changes in the way she related to people around her. The dominant figure in her early life had been her father. He was a very successful businessman who seemed to be extremely popular outside the home. This was in stark contrast to how he seemed at home, where his moodiness and violent temper were a constant threat. Kate described having to monitor herself constantly for anything about herself that might send him into a rage. Being too noisy or too quiet, too happy or upset could all lead to her being banished to her room by her mother for upsetting her father, or to her being beaten with a leather belt by her father. Her younger brother did not get this treatment, but any complaints from Kate about the unfairness of this just led to further punishment. Her father left the family home when she was 9, and made little effort to stay in contact. After this, her mother had told Kate that her father did not love her. She believed that if she had been different somehow, he would not have left. Discussion of these experiences suggested that it was not only the constant punishment that led Kate to see herself as horrible, but also the fact that her father seemed so universally admired and that he did not treat her brother in the same way.

Following an initial fear about being seen to be 'whingeing', Kate began to accept that the therapist's concern to help her to understand and come to terms with her upbringing was genuine. Imagery rescripting was attempted around a number of specific incidents. One was when, on her brother's birthday, she had tried to ride on his new tricycle. This had resulted in her being punished with a belt and her father barely speaking to her for some days. Memories of a kindly neighbour who had looked after her when her parents were out were used to bring into the image information to counter her conviction that she was just a horrible girl. The view that she was an ordinary little girl who was not surprisingly upset at being so out of favour with her father was used to build up a small but significant degree of doubt about her 'horribleness'. This was then exploited in testing her negative view and building up a new view of herself as 'alright' in relation to various ongoing situations. One example was that of her smoking, which she had previously seen as a sign of being horrible. This led to her setting up a (not entirely successful) pact with a friend to give up smoking.

She was also able to 'confess' her urges to cut or burn herself to another friend, with the effect of greatly deepening the friendship and providing an important support at times of emotional distress.

Progress in working with these beliefs is usually more erratic than when working with beliefs about weakness and emotional control. Cognitive and behavioural avoidance make the activation of different unconditional beliefs more dependent on the particular context. Great progress in building new beliefs from some behavioural experiments in which the patient receives positive feedback can be undermined by a subsequent experience of failure or criticism. It is helpful to prepare the patient for this in advance and to help them to devise a plan for dealing with negative outcomes. It is important that patient and therapist gauge change from the overall strength of negative and positive beliefs across a range of different situations, rather than at any particular instant.

BELIEFS ABOUT ACHIEVEMENT AND APPROVAL

Many patients' beliefs about their deficiencies relate mainly to the areas of accomplishment and achievement. Such patients tend to see themselves in terms such as 'a failure', 'no good' or 'useless'. They see others as superior and likely to be critical. Typical conditional beliefs are:

- Unless I succeed at everything I attempt, I am useless.
- If I fail at anything, people will look down on me.
- I must be sure of success before I try to do anything.
- Unless I criticise myself, I will not do things properly.

These beliefs commonly provoke constant self-criticism in relation to endeavours that have been completed and intense preparatory worry about tasks that have yet to be faced. Avoidance is frequently in the form of procrastination, which then forms the focus for further self-criticism. This then feeds into the patient's negative beliefs, leading to more intense worry, self-criticism and urges to avoid, thus reinforcing a vicious circle. However, these patients are often saved from more generalised views of worthlessness or badness by having some faith in their ability to relate to their peers or intimates.

Standard cognitive techniques can usefully address issues such as black and white thinking and mindreading, which are associated with the patient's difficulties in addressing work or personal tasks. For such patients, cognitive therapy tasks themselves can form the focus for worry, procrastination or self-criticism. This provides a useful microcosm of the patient's life, where identifying and questioning negative thoughts and testing out negative predictions about the therapist's reaction, for example to homework assignments, can occur. As has been suggested in relation to the preceding themes, in patients with chronic depression such techniques frequently do not lead to significant cognitive and emotional shifts but rather can be used to highlight to the patient the constantly biased nature of their appraisals. The focus then falls on modifying the biases in these processes and on the beliefs that underlie them.

In subsequent work on underlying beliefs, it can help to put the issue of self-criticism directly in the frame. This can draw together not only the patient's overt negative thoughts about failure and disapproval, but also their intensive thinking, planning and preparation that focuses on trying to get everything right. It may also include ruminating about why they are depressed and failing to find satisfying answers. These thinking patterns and processes can be formulated as attempts to compensate for the unconditional beliefs and illustrated in a belief maintenance diagram. The idea of attempting tasks in a different fashion to test predictions from conditional beliefs can then be suggested. For example, the idea of 'just doing' tasks with minimal preparation or forethought can be explored. This can be rehearsed in session with therapy-related or external tasks in order to practise switching from 'task-interfering cognitions' to 'task-orienting cognition' (see page 187). It can also be helpful to guide the patient in thinking through possible failures, to explore how they would cope.

For example, Joe was a middle-aged man whose life had almost ground to a halt since he had been depressed. His two most common descriptions of himself were 'useless' and 'a failure' and he spent much of his time sitting pondering the various tasks that he thought he was unable to do. His thoughts often centred on everyday household tasks, such as making meals (he had previously worked as a chef) or paying bills, or on the difficulties of finding work. Very often his thoughts focused on his depression and he would spend hours reflecting on why he had become depressed and on his inability to get out of it. Simple activity scheduling had not proved effective and questioning suggested that this was because of his belief that he needed to understand why he was depressed before he could do anything about it. Discussion of the consequences of this belief suggested that, far from helping him out of his depression, it strongly reinforced his sense of failure through his inability to find any explanation that would satisfy him. When small activities were suggested as tests of this belief, Joe was surprised to find that doing things resulted in more of an improvement in his mood than pondering the reasons for his depression.

The impetus of this behavioural test was then used to test out his more general assumption that he needed to be sure of success before attempting any task. Some months previously, Joe had bought some new units to fit in his kitchen but had not started to do so because he was uncertain of some of the steps in the assembly instructions. He was convinced that his uncertainty showed that he would fail if he tried, but also interpreted his not having started as a sign of failure. After some mental rehearsal in session and with the backup that he could call up a friend to help if he got stuck, Joe agreed to try an experiment of having a go at fitting one of the easier units with minimal preparation. He found that he was able to get going surprisingly well and, although at one point he got stuck and nearly gave up, he managed to finish the job. Although he remained critical of the job, with prompting he could also see it as showing some sign of competence, particularly as his wife had been unreservedly delighted with his efforts. He managed to use this as a model to try his new strategy of doing things despite his doubts with a number of other stalled activities.

Alternative views of self can often be built up around ideas of being able or competent. In view of the black and white thinking common in these patients, it is important that they are helped to process evidence of even partial achievement through scaling it on the new belief (see pages 279–284). The therapist will also need to be sensitive to the patient's tendency to dwell at great length on the slightest suggestion of failure, while glossing over many signs of success, continually pointing this out and asking them to try out a different attitude. This work is often made easier once the origins of the unconditional beliefs of failure, associated conditional beliefs and high standards have been clarified.

Frequently the beliefs have been adopted in an ongoing family culture of extremely high standards, rather than in response to specific traumatic events. In contrast to many patients who experienced the circumstances contributing to their underlying beliefs as aversive or traumatic, patients with beliefs about failure may see the formative experiences in positive terms. They see the problem as their own failure to live up to expectations and often continue to view their caregivers, and the extreme high standards they espoused, in an idealistically positive fashion. Joe, for example, continued to believe in the many sayings and aphorisms of his father, who had been a minister, such as 'only your best is good enough', 'if it's worth doing, it's worth doing well' and 'what doesn't kill you makes you stronger'. Therapy scarcely dented the conviction with which he seemed to apply these principles, but through making him more aware of them enabled him sometimes to suspend them in order to apply more helpful strategies in situations where he was having difficulties. This in turn helped him to acknowledge small degrees of credit or success that enabled him to begin to build some motivation and confidence.

BELIEFS ABOUT WORK

Some patients have had a lifelong tendency to derive their self-esteem almost entirely from their work and become depressed in the face of a life event in the work arena. Most frequently this follows redundancy, where harsh reality may mean the individuals' chances of re-establishing stable employment are severely limited not only by their age, but also by depressive illness. Changes in working practices driven by the prevailing economic climate can also trigger episodes of depression. Such changes can be particularly problematic for people in middle age, for whom the requirement to develop new skills in a changing work culture is very anxiety provoking.

For those whose self-esteem is derived from work, their preoccupation with this measure of worth is usually evident from the beginning of therapy. Typically at assessment the patient will cite their lack of employment as their most pressing problem and see returning to work as the solution to their depression. These patients may recount numerous examples of their accomplishments during their working life and be completely preoccupied with the question of whether they will ever find another job. For some patients, such rumination can be so all-consuming that it interferes with their ability to engage in the tasks of cognitive therapy. For example, at every session *Peter* would refer to the fact that if he could return to work he was sure that his problems would be solved. Interventions from the therapist often met with the response 'This is terrible—will I ever work again?'.

In addressing problems in this arena it is important to give consideration to the cultural norms that influence the development of an individual's belief system. British culture places a strong emphasis on the work ethic and many people at some level would subscribe to the rule 'If you work hard you will be rewarded'. The perceived rewards of working may not only be financial or material but may also include self-worth and self-respect. Furthermore, the protestant work ethic stresses the importance of working hard for work's own sake. For many people, working hard is seen as an unquestionable virtue. It is also important to consider subcultural rules concerning gender and class. For example, in the traditional working-class culture in the north of England, stereotypical gender roles are the norm. Not only do they dictate rules regarding expression of emotion (see page 296), but also of a man fulfilling the role of breadwinner and provider for their family. By these rules, working confers status within the family and within the wider social arena, and so is a source of considerable pride. Stigma is attached to not working or living on state benefits, and unemployed men can experience deep shame at not earning a wage. Particularly difficult from a therapeutic point of view is that the spouses of these men often share the same belief system, viewing their partner's role within their relationship as one of earning a living to provide for the family. For example, *Dave*, whose business had gone into receivership during a period of economic recession, worked as a part-time security officer. His marriage came under severe strain when he decided to scale down his ambitions to establish another business and simply look to increasing his hours in his current job. His wife viewed this as dereliction of his duty to provide for his family and was persistently critical of his decision, undermining his self-esteem and setting back some of the progress made in therapy.

These cultural rules provide social encouragement for people to place great value on work. Where the chance to work is then removed by society, it could be argued that the cause of depression should not be located in the individual. It would indeed be inappropriate to blame such patients for the attitudes they endorse. Nevertheless, while respecting those attitudes, the therapist can help the patient to gain some benefit from applying them a little more flexibly. It is the breaking down of the monolith of work and seeing its value in more detail, rather than exhorting other values, that seems to be of most help to these patients.

Patients with problems related to redundancy or inability to adapt to changing working practices tend to see themselves as useless and their lives as lacking any value or worth. As the patient may not have seen themselves in these terms when they were working successfully, these are not unconditional beliefs in the sense of having been held as fundamental tenets about the self in every circumstance. However, once such people become depressed, these beliefs function as unconditional beliefs with similarly pervasive effects on information processing and a similar degree of rigidity and inflexibility. A number of related conditional beliefs can often be identified, along the lines of:

- If I work hard, then I will be rewarded.
- I cannot get over my depression unless I get back to work.
- If I don't work, my life is pointless.
- If I don't work, I am worthless.

In terms of the aims of therapy, the therapist may see their role as one of helping the patient to engage in and value aspects of their life other than work as a means to building some alternative sense of self-esteem or acceptance. In contrast, the patient is likely to see the role of therapy, if any, as one of helping them get back to work. It is often tempting for the therapist to use strategies to undermine the link between work and self-esteem, such as questioning whether the patient sees other unemployed people as worthless. However, early use of interventions which directly challenge the patient's beliefs about work are usually of limited impact. To minimise the potential conflict between the patient's view and the view the therapist is espousing, some validation of the patient's view of the importance of work is usually an essential first step in therapy. Then, rather than presenting competing views or alternatives, it is often better to begin to modify the beliefs by breaking down the concept of work in order to explore more specifically the value of its subcomponents.

Many patients have been so focused on the issue of whether they will get back to work that they have not fully recognised what they have lost or how this contributes to their depression. It is important that the therapist is explicit in acknowledging the reality of the patient's losses in relation to work, in order to help the patient to recognise the extent of their losses and even to grieve for them. Many of these losses are tangible and external, whereas others are more symbolic or internal. Working with the patient to validate these can be a useful step in recognising and understanding how thoughts and beliefs, as well as external circumstances, can be contributing to the depression. For example, both *Peter* and *Dave* had led extremely successful lives by following the principle of 'work hard and you will be rewarded'. They had earned salaries that afforded a high level of material well-being for themselves and their families, and had commanded a great deal of respect and praise for their work. As described in Chapter 3, formulating the theme of loss, both external and internal, was vital in engaging Peter in therapy. The company for whom he had worked for many years retired him on grounds of ill health, and as well as losing his job he had to cash in his pension early in order to meet his mortgage payments, incurring severe financial penalties. His standard of living now and in the future was considerably lower than he had anticipated, and his plans for his retirement were greatly compromised. Losses that it can be important to consider include:

- *External:* my job; my health; my social life; structure to my day; my standard of living; my retirement plan; my pension entitlement.
- *Internal:* my role; my purpose in life; my sense of self-respect; perceived respect in eyes of family/friends/work colleagues; my principles.

For both Peter and Dave, validating their experience by articulating these losses formed an important step in formulating a shared understanding and an agreed focus for therapy.

Developing a shared understanding in this way can facilitate subsequent efforts to examine the patient's perceptions about unemployment. These include perceptions regarding loss of self-worth, entailing loss of motivation and guilt, and cognitive themes of unfairness and injustice, leading to emotions including anger and bitterness. The chronic cognitive triad can provide a template for identifying crucial perceptions. In the case of Peter, important thoughts in the three areas were as follows:

- *Low self-esteem:* 'I'm useless'; 'It's my fault'; 'I should have seen it coming'.
- *Helplessness:* 'I've been robbed of my future'; 'After 25 years of hard work, it's not fair'; 'There's nothing I can do now'.
- *Hopelessness:* 'Things will never be right again'; 'Everything is uncertain'; 'It's all pointless'.

At this stage, standard interventions to modify automatic thoughts can prove useful. For Peter, a pie chart was used to examine his self-blame regarding how he had handled the incident that led him to take time off sick from work. This was followed up by a mini-survey to ascertain how others may have dealt with a similar situation. In addition, Peter had many thoughts about how not working meant a loss of status and respect within the community, which entailed chronic feelings of shame. These were tackled by developing scales for rating degrees of respect and by experiments to collect more information on the attitudes of others to redundancy. Although these techniques tended to result in only transient or small degrees of change in the content of Peter's thinking, the fact of his considering different perspectives reflected the introduction of a new degree of flexibility into his thinking.

Early in treatment, returning to work can be framed as a long-term goal. It can then be helpful to identify the short-term (2–6 weeks) and medium-term (3–12 months) goals that form the intervening steps in achieving this long-term goal. Patients can sometimes see a benefit in strategies they have hitherto eschewed as pointless, such as engaging in pleasurable activities or voluntary work, if they see these initially as 'working towards working'. The degree to which the patient is able to engage with such a plan is variable. For example, at assessment Dave was already engaged in ad hoc work, for which he received an irregular wage. While this was a far cry from running his own business as he had done previously, he drew some satisfaction from generating some income even while depressed. As treatment progressed, he obtained a part-time position as a security officer and readily saw the advantages of a graded approach to a return to work. For some patients, the belief that anything other than work is pointless interferes with tasks related to finding employment, such as updating CVs or scanning job adverts. The consequences of this for the likelihood of gaining employment and for self-worth need to be elucidated. Behavioural tests of engaging in these tasks can then be set up, using graded task assignment if necessary. Patients may initially find engaging in these tasks humiliating, and the relevant 'hot' negative thoughts can usefully be identified and questioned. The potential benefits of sticking at these tasks can be compared with the effects of rumination about not working.

Engaging some patients in the idea of a graded return to work can prove difficult. For example, one idea raised in treatment with Peter was to find some voluntary work as a stepping stone back into paid employment. Peter was unable to contemplate this, as he conceived voluntary work to be entirely lacking in status as it was unpaid. His all-or-nothing stance dictated that if he couldn't get back to the type of job he had, and on the same salary scale, then he was not going to lower his sights. The extremity of his attitude that his value depended entirely on his work status also led to the exclusion of many other activities. An attempt was made to erode the rigidity of this view by asking Peter to identify the components of work that contributed to his sense of self-worth. With the therapist, he identified a number of factors, including financial remuneration, gaining the respect of others, social interaction at and after work, completing tasks that he saw as valuable, and benefiting the community. He was then asked to rate the importance of these components to the overall worth he derived from working. Discussion then focused around how he could increase the level of any activities that would confer any of these benefits. As the formulation highlighted the fact that Peter liked to be in control, he and his therapist worked together to devise small projects that he could plan and execute himself. This included initially building a pond in his garden, and helping his son-in-law to build a patio. To take account of his depressive symptoms, this was balanced with periods of rest and enjoyable activities, such as playing with his granddaughter and day trips to places of interest with his wife. As would be anticipated, this triggered numerous automatic thoughts regarding how unproductive he was being, which were modified using standard interventions.

Re-engagement in previously valued activities usually has to be motivated initially through rating the value of those activities in terms of their potential relevance to working. Once some re-engagement is occurring, then gentle exploration of whether these things have any value other than simply through their relevance to work can be helpful. Some way into therapy many patients can acknowledge, if only at a rational level, that aspects of life such as looking after others or enjoying other things in life, such as friendships and hobbies, could have some value to them. They may then need help in putting those values into practice through identifying and scheduling relevant activities and noting the benefits of engagement in those activities. For many men whose depression is associated with work-related issues, it is not uncommon for them to have given no thought to retirement even though they are in their mid- to late-fifties. A further intervention is to try to use the model of a retirement plan as a means to helping the patient to rebuild their life on different foundations. Although for some patients this can help in normalising the need to adapt their value system, for others it could accentuate thoughts of redundancy and pointlessness. This intervention therefore needs to be used with care.

It is helpful for the therapist not to set themselves over-ambitious targets in modifying beliefs about the value of work. The beliefs have usually been strongly ingrained by close influences of family during childhood, and may have been reinforced by the whole culture in which the patient has grown up and lived. The previous lifelong external validation of their beliefs and values can make these patients particularly hard to work with in cognitive therapy. Therefore, introducing a degree of flexibility into the application of the beliefs, rather than aiming at wholesale modification of the beliefs, seems to be a more feasible and helpful goal for therapy. This can permit both a more sympathetic understanding by the patient of their own predicament and a degree of engagement in life with the restoration of some sense of value and meaning.

SUMMARY POINTS

- Beliefs that depression is part of the patient's character can be weighed against experiences that it is a variable state influenced by what the patient does and thinks.
- Beliefs that emotions confirm a patient's inherent weakness can be weighed against experiences of positive and negative emotions not resulting in total loss of control or humiliation.
- Beliefs that a patient's only value is in meeting the needs of others can be weighed against experiences of the patient caring for themselves as well as others.
- Beliefs that a patient is fundamentally unacceptable can be weighed against experiences of engaging openly with others and being accepted.
- Beliefs that a patient has failed to live up to the highest standards can be weighed against experiences of the benefit of doing worthwhile things at all.
- Beliefs that a patient's worth derives entirely from work can be weighed against experiences of value that occur outside a formal working environment.

Chapter 10

BEYOND THERAPY: PREVENTING RELAPSE AND FURTHERING PROGRESS

In this chapter, you will find suggestions on helping patients to:

- Create a framework for continuing the practice of therapy after sessions with the therapist have ended
- Devise a plan for anticipating and coping with setbacks
- Devise a plan for continuing to develop confidence and self-esteem
- Plan changes to their life situation that can lessen vulnerability
- Cope with therapy ending

Cognitive therapy does not aim simply to effect in-session changes in the patient's troublesome thoughts and beliefs, but also aims to equip the patient with a set of skills that can be used in problematic situations in everyday life. Throughout therapy, the use of behavioural and cognitive techniques to alleviate depressive symptoms helps the patient to develop self-help skills. This is an important aspect of relapse prevention. Later in therapy, addressing underlying beliefs that might contribute to the patient's ongoing vulnerability may also contribute to preventing subsequent relapse. Over the course of therapy, interventions are delivered in a manner that provides for the patient a template through which current and future problems can be addressed. In the sessions leading up to the termination of therapy, the focus shifts more explicitly to how the patient might maintain and further the gains that have been made during the course of therapy. These final sessions assist the patient in developing a plan for continuing to tackle their problems independently of the therapist once formal therapy sessions have come to an end.

In this chapter, we present a framework that can help to engage the patient in continuing to practise and consolidate, in the months and years ahead, what has been learned during therapy. There are two main aspects to this work. One essential element is to help the patient to draw up plans for tackling future setbacks, downturns or crises. This involves their learning to anticipate future stressors, to recognise signs and symptoms that may be warnings of potential relapse and to develop a specific action plan for managing these should the situation arise. The second important aspect is to develop a plan for continuing to erode psychological vulnerability to persistent depression. This is approached through continued efforts to modify underlying beliefs and to build confidence or self-esteem, and through making changes in life situations that could promote well-being. How much emphasis is placed on these various aspects depends on the individual patient. For those patients whose illness is characterised by prominent biological symptoms, a focus on early identification and management of symptoms may be particularly helpful. For those where long-standing low self-esteem is a central issue, then continued work on tackling this area of psychological vulnerability would be indicated.

CREATING A FRAMEWORK FOR CONTINUED PRACTICE

This final phase of treatment aims to prepare the patient to use the skills that have been acquired once contact with the therapist has ended. Discharge from treatment is often very anxiety-provoking for patients and the prospect of having to develop skills to cope without the therapist's guidance is usually daunting. In tandem with planning particular strategies and skills to be used beyond the end of therapy, it is therefore important to help the patient to develop supports and practical procedures for their continued practise of self-help. This can include scheduling booster sessions, identifying times for the regular practise of self-help activities and developing a personal therapy folder.

Scheduling of Therapy Sessions to Foster Self-help

An explicit focus on maintaining progress beyond the end of therapy is usually adopted from about five sessions from the ending of regular sessions. As the end of therapy approaches, the interval between sessions is usually extended. By this stage it would be unusual to be meeting with the patient on a weekly basis and sessions are more usually at fortnightly or three-weekly intervals. Once regular sessions have ended, intermittent follow-up or booster sessions can be scheduled over the longer-term as a means of supporting the patient in their use of relapse prevention strategies. Such sessions would typically be at intervals of two or three months. This extended contact can provide the patient with a safety net during which time they can work with the clinician to detect signs of relapse at an early stage and practise implementing action plans at a point where they will be of value. Supporting the patient in this way can build the necessary skill and confidence in managing and recovering from setbacks.

This kind of extended follow-up can be discouraged within some services within which therapy is provided. However, to the extent that it may help in prevention of relapse, it can be both beneficial and cost effective to the individual patient and also cost effective (see Chapter 11).

It is important in the final phase of therapy, and in any follow-up sessions, that the focus is placed on helping patients to develop their skills at helping themselves. At times when the patient encounters difficulties or when their symptoms worsen, they may look to the therapist to sort things out or expect the therapist to instigate any helpful strategies. It is often tempting for the therapist to do what seems to be expected. However, the therapist will be of most help in the long-term if they can maximise the extent to which the patient addresses any difficulties for themselves. This is most likely if the increasing role of self-help in therapy is discussed explicitly. Practical ways for the patient to engage in practising self-therapy skills should be discussed in a collaborative fashion. It can be helpful to review the patient's therapy goals, so that the goals of their efforts at self-help can be clarified. The content of sessions at this stage of therapy can then routinely be based on reviewing particular targets of the patient's self-help efforts and their progress towards them.

Use of Self-therapy Sessions

With many patients, the idea of 'becoming your own cognitive therapist' is a helpful way to frame the role of self-help in maintaining progress. An analogy comparing therapy with learning to drive can be useful in engaging the patient in the self-help model. In the case of driving, it is not until a person passes their driving test and they are on the road alone that the real independent learning begins. Only then do they really begin to develop skills and confidence in driving. Similarly, during therapy sessions the patient learns new skills in collaboration with the therapist. However, only when the patient practises these independently in everyday life does change really take root. It can be useful to ask the patient to draw parallels between their early attempts at driving a car and their struggles with learning new cognitive therapy skills.

It is desirable to discuss the practicalities of when and how the patient will put their efforts at self-help into practice. The idea of conducting regular self-therapy sessions can form the basis for implementing relapse prevention strategies once therapy itself is completed. Throughout therapy, the therapist will have encouraged the patient to set time aside outside of the session in order to work on particular self-help tasks. In conducting their own self-therapy sessions, the patient takes more responsibility for deciding what kind of self-help tasks will be pursued. Introducing the use of self-therapy sessions before the end of therapy provides the patient with an opportunity to practise them while still in contact with the therapist. Any problems can then be identified and addressed while some therapy time still remains.

The patient is encouraged to identify a specific day and time each week that is to be devoted to the self-therapy session. Ideally, this needs to be time alone free from interruption. How much time is set aside and how frequently needs to be negotiated with the patient. This should take into consideration the particular self-help tasks on which the patient is likely to work, such as reviewing each day for any particular upsets or successes, filling out negative thought records or planning how to put new behaviours into practice. Factors such as work or family commitments that may interfere with this activity also need to be considered, so that the allocation of time is as realistic as possible.

Ideally, the patient would structure the use of the time in self-therapy sessions in the same way as a standard cognitive therapy session. Although this is likely to be too demanding for the majority of patients, they are encouraged adopt some of the structure that has been modelled during their sessions with the therapist. Any of the therapist's usual ways of structuring the time can be suggested, including setting an agenda or planning the time, reviewing mood and any ups or downs, reviewing progress on particular issues and planning how to tackle particular problems. At the end of the self-therapy session, it is best if the patient reviews what has been gained from the session and how this can be applied in everyday situations. Patients vary greatly in how much they are willing and able to adopt a formal structure for their self-help efforts. Some patients have gone as far as devising computerised proformas for self-therapy sessions, which incorporate 'menus' of self-help activities, monitoring sheets and rating scales for mood and beliefs. For the majority, it is necessary to work with a somewhat less rigorous idea of what self-therapy will involve. For patients who regularly use a diary or personal organiser, this can be used as a basis for planning self-therapy sessions. To increase the chances of self-help being carried out, the therapist needs to pitch any suggestions at the patient's level. Setting unrealistically daunting targets for self-help may decrease the likelihood of the patient engaging in any regular self-help activities at all.

Use of a Therapy Folder

Written materials are used regularly in therapy. Handouts are given out when particular new tasks are introduced and a handout covering the idea of 'Becoming your own cognitive therapist' has proved useful (see Appendix 2). In addition, summaries of interventions made during therapy sessions are often written down and thought records are often completed in the session. This helps to reinforce the content of each session and provides the patient with guidelines for practising the intervention outside of the session. The patient's thought records that have been completed as homework and other notes also add to the written account of the progress of therapy. As was discussed in Chapter 2, early in therapy the patient is encouraged to keep all of these materials in one place using a therapy folder. The patient is asked to bring this to each session, so the therapist can encourage the use of the folder by referring to and using its contents actively throughout treatment. By the end of treatment, the patient will have acquired a range of materials in their therapy folder, which can be used in their self-therapy sessions. Their folder constitutes a package of resources tailored to the patient's own problems and goals that can continue to be used for self-help once formal sessions have ended.

Reviewing Therapy Goals

The therapy goals that were negotiated near the outset of therapy are important guides throughout therapy. The direction they provide can also extend beyond the termination of therapy sessions. As the end of therapy approaches, reviewing the patient's goals and clarifying how self-therapy may promote further progress towards them can facilitate their engagement in the practice of self-help. As outlined in Chapter 4, treatment targets can be broken down into short-term, medium-term and long-term goals, where long-term goals may cover the next 12–24 months. In this way, it is made explicit from early on that therapy may not address all of the patient's problems while they are in contact with the therapist. The problems that still need to be addressed once contact with the therapist has finished then need to be clarified. For example, low self-esteem often plays a central role in the persistence of low mood, and improving self-esteem is often a goal in therapy. It is unrealistic to anticipate that low self-esteem is going to be fully resolved within an intervention of 18–20 sessions, particularly where it has been a lifelong problem. Thus, it is more helpful to view improving self-esteem as a life goal involving a long road on which therapy may be seen as the first step.

As therapy nears its end, the original goals that were agreed can serve as a basis for devising with the patient a plan for how they will continue to put what has been learned into practice. It can be helpful to spend some time

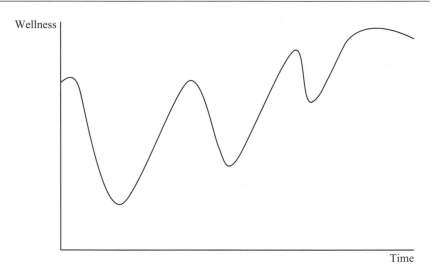

Figure 10.1 Expected course of well-being after the end of therapy

in a session explicitly reviewing the therapy goals (hence it helps if these were written clearly on a sheet of paper). Such a review can usefully occur around four sessions from the end of a 16–20 session course of therapy. This enables an assessment of the progress that has been made towards these goals during the course of therapy and what needs to be done to maintain and further any progress. Reviewing any short- or medium-term goals that have been achieved can provide motivation for the patient to continue working on longer-term goals.

It can be helpful to discuss the likelihood that progress on issues related to therapy tends to be characterised by taking some steps forward, but often with setbacks and backward steps. A diagram of a wiggly line with a general upward trend can illustrate the course that the patient's well-being might be expected to follow after the end of therapy (see Figure 10.1). This can help to convey that the aim of the patient's continued efforts after the end of therapy needs to be two-fold. One aim is to limit the damage during setbacks or downturns by making them less deep or pulling out of them sooner. The other is to improve the overall level of well-being. The emphasis of the final three or four sessions of therapy is often on helping the patient to devise an action plan for coping with setbacks and on helping them to plan how they might continue to decrease areas of vulnerability and build up resilience or confidence. The balance between these two aims is often dictated by the relative lability or flatness of the patient's mood over the course of therapy.

COPING WITH SETBACKS

Detecting Early Warning Signs of Relapse

At times of potential relapse, cognitive and emotional avoidance may lead patients to ignore or actively suppress signs that their depression is worsening. The factors contributing to the worsening symptoms may then go on unchecked and the depression continue to worsen until a relapse into a full depressive episode is inevitable. Helping patients with persistent depression to monitor their emotional state and catch any signs of worsening at an early stage can be an important part of relapse prevention. Ideas such as 'forewarned is forearmed' or 'nipping things in the bud' can be helpful in 'selling' the concept of intervening early to prevent dips becoming disasters.

It can be helpful to identify what kinds of stressful situations will be particularly likely to cause problems for the patient. The patient's experience over the course of therapy can be reviewed to identify the kinds of situations that they find particularly difficult. Events that are known to be forthcoming in the months ahead can then be used in anticipating when difficulties are most likely to occur and when particular coping strategies will be most needed. For example, patients who have been particularly susceptible to downturns in mood following setbacks at work or stresses in their marital relationship can scan through the months ahead to anticipate any likely danger times.

Patients can also be helped to monitor their symptomatic state to alert them to early signs of relapse. For some patients, monitoring overall mood is the best indicator. In such cases, regular use of percentage ratings or ratings on a 0–10 mood scale can be incorporated into the self-help plan. For other patients, a pattern of certain key symptoms, sometimes referred to as an 'individual relapse signature', regularly precedes any major worsening. Either mood ratings or key symptoms can be used in discussing guidelines as to when specific action plans need to be instigated to fend off impending relapse. With *Elizabeth*, three symptoms were identified as important indicators of potential relapse (see Table 10.1). These were used in developing an action plan for managing early warning signs of relapse.

Action Plans for Tackling Setbacks

Having identified the symptoms or situations that warn of the danger of relapse, the action plan can include strategies for managing symptoms and for problem-solving. For many patients, the action plan comprises a

Table 10.1   Elizabeth's action plan for managing early warning signs of relapse

---

Action plan

Which symptoms indicate that I may be slipping into depression?

The following symptoms, if they have persisted for more than 2 weeks:

• Feeling fuzzy in my head, tired and difficulty concentrating.
• Putting things off.
• Getting wound up.

What strategies can I use to manage these symptoms?

1. *Make allowances:* Make an allowance for symptoms (e.g. tiredness, fuzzy head, etc.) and set realistic goals each day.
2. *Activity schedule:* Use the activity schedule to plan my time in advance. Build in breaks for meals and rest periods.
3. *Enjoyable activities:* Use the schedule to keep a balance between things I have to do and enjoyable activities. Use the list from the therapy folder to generate ideas. Enjoyable activities with someone else are the most helpful to me.
4. *Catch putting things off:* Watch out for thoughts that lead me to put things off. Ask myself:

   — what are the reasons for putting off this activity?
   — am I predicting that I will fail?
   — am I looking for an IDEAL way to complete the task?
   — are my HIGH STANDARDS getting in the way?

5. *Solutions to putting things off:* Break the task down into steps and spread the steps over the week. Answer negative thoughts and test them out by doing the activity I'm putting off.
6. *Practice:* Practise doing things to different standards (e.g. half complete a task), but can leave this until I feel better.

---

summary of general behavioural and cognitive techniques that the patient has previously used in therapy for combating low mood. For example, *Elizabeth's* action plan focused mainly on scheduling pleasant activities to combat low mood and breaking tasks down to combat procrastination (see Table 10.1). By contrast, with patients for whom previous escalations of symptoms have been triggered by life events or crises, a focus on specific plans for anticipating and handling such crises is more useful. For *Jean*, discussions in therapy had clarified the danger that particular adverse events could reinforce her perceptions of helplessness, which would then preclude her taking action to resolve any crisis. Her high levels of helplessness had previously resulted in her catastrophising situations and acting impulsively in ways that worsened the situation. On a number of occasions during therapy, managing a crisis by using problem-solving and appropriate support seeking had proved a productive line of action. It was

Table 10.2   Jean's action plan for managing crisis situations

Action plan

What future crises may arise that I need a plan for dealing with?
1. Tracie truanting from school.
2. Rob coming home drunk and becoming aggressive.

What is my usual first reaction to a crisis?
1. I ignore warning letters until the truancy officer comes round, then I get very angry and shout abuse. This worsens the situation and I get into trouble.
2. I get angry at Rob, lock him out of the house and shout at him from the bedroom window. When he eventually shows his face again, I take the huff for several days and don't speak.

What are the potential pitfalls?
- Avoiding things or pretending there isn't a problem means that I don't sort things out and prolongs the problem.
- Getting angry often makes the situation worse.
- Withdrawing into myself means that I start blaming myself for what has happened and so my mood spirals down.

What have I learned in treatment about dealing with these crises?
1. *Tracie:* My own bad experiences of school colour my judgement and make me turn a blind eye. I can make things different for Tracie by trying to get her to school. Although I find it very anxiety provoking, I need to take action and not ignore the problem. It is best to speak to Tracie about her truanting and visit school with her.
2. *Rob:* So far my plan for dealing with this has worked well. When Rob goes on a bender with his mates, give him the keys to his flat and take my keys off him. Then me and the kids don't see him when he's had a drink. We are now arguing much less and things are generally better between us.

What action can I take to manage these and other situations?
1. *Follow the plan:* Check that I have followed each part of my plan and that there is not an issue I am avoiding tackling.
2. *Ask for help:* Practise asking for help and support from friends to tackle the crisis. If necessary, involve outside agencies (i.e. the police, social worker).
3. *Keep myself going:* Watch out for giving up and my mood spiralling. Do small simple tasks at home (tidy sitting room, clean bathroom), then give myself a treat.
4. *Question negative thoughts:* Ask if I'm blaming myself for something over which I have little or no control. Use examples and handouts in therapy folder to help me.

When the crisis has passed what can I do?
1. Review what I have managed successfully and give myself credit.
2. Note what didn't go so well and think what to do differently in future situations.

therefore essential that Jean's action plan contained strategies for dealing with the life crises that would inevitably arise. Table 10.2 outlines two of the potential crises that were identified and the action plan that Jean devised with the therapist's help.

DEVELOPING CONFIDENCE

During sessions with the therapist, time will certainly have been spent in formulating how low self-esteem and poor self-confidence are maintained. Some progress will usually have been made in identifying the beliefs, both conditional and unconditional, and avoidance or compensatory strategies that contribute to low self-esteem or vulnerability. By the end of therapy, the patient is likely to have had some experience of interventions aimed at modifying unhelpful beliefs with varying degrees of success. In the termination phase of therapy, it is important to build on any progress that has been made and build activities specifically aimed at further undermining chronic low self-esteem into the plan for continued self-help. These activities fall broadly into two camps: trying out particular behaviours with a view to putting conditional beliefs to the test and consistently collecting evidence that can undermine prejudicial unconditional beliefs.

Planning New Behaviours to Undermine Underlying Beliefs

In persistent depression, low self-esteem is often associated with high levels of avoidance related to important underlying beliefs. The patient's unconditional beliefs (e.g. 'I am useless') influence the conditional beliefs (e.g. 'If I try anything new, I shall fail') that guide the patient's behaviour. During therapy, changes in behaviour are used to help the patient to test out the validity of their conditional beliefs. In the final stages of therapy, the therapist can help the patient to plan how to continue such behavioural experiments and changes on a more or less formal basis once the therapy sessions have ended. For example, *Elizabeth* engaged in marked behavioural avoidance at work whenever she was asked to express her opinion, use her initiative or take on new tasks. When faced with these situations, Elizabeth would become highly anxious and report thoughts such as 'I'll make a mess of it', 'I'll lose the company business' or 'My ideas are stupid'. During the final stages of treatment (when sessions were spaced at three-weekly intervals), the following discussion took place while developing the relapse prevention plan.

T: During our sessions we've identified some recurring themes about your view of yourself as a failure and the rule related to that about doing things properly. And as we talked about last week, given how long you've been operating on the principle of doing things properly, it'll take some time and practice to make changes.

E: (*nods*) Mmmm.

T: We talked a bit about ways to undermine this view of yourself as a failure, and one of the areas we identified was avoidance, particularly at work in the area of taking on new tasks.

E: Funny you should mention that. My boss has just asked me if I'd like to take on a new role.

T: (*smiling*) Really. What will it involve?

E: He wants me to take on responsibility for organising conferences. It would mean visiting venues and managing the budget.

T: Have you decided whether to take it on yet?

E: I said I would like time to think about it. We agreed to discuss it again tomorrow.

T: It sounds like something has changed for you. In the past wouldn't you have turned him down immediately?

E: Yes, I would. But I feel very anxious about what to say tomorrow. I can't make up my mind. Part of me thinks I might enjoy the chance to use my initiative at work. My boss also said he thought I would be good in this role ... and perhaps I would. I think I will probably give it a try.

T: (*smiling*) Sounds like you have come further than you give yourself credit for. That is a big change in how you see yourself at work.

E: (*slightly embarrassed*) I guess so.

T: What's made you think you would give it a try?

E: I've been thinking I'm 55 years old and I've never dared to take any risks for fear of failing ... so I've missed out on a lot. Now I've been taking some risks and some good things have come from that ... But then, this might all go wrong. I might not be able to do it. Oh, I don't know what to do! (*looks sad*).

T: It does sound like it's raised some hope and some worries. But you haven't let the worries put you off completely, so overall what have been the effects of not just ruling yourself out of taking on this new role?

E: Well, I'm really scared. But actually I'm a bit pleased with myself. And like I said, it would make my job more interesting.

T: It's good to hear that. So it looks like considering this new job has meant that you've been anxious, but also pleased with yourself and there's a chance of it making your work more interesting. I suppose I'm wondering if there might be other ways of adding to these benefits in the future.

E: I'm not sure.

T: Coming back to this idea of a self-therapy plan, could you make trying new things like this one of your goals to keep working on once the sessions have finished?

E: I'm not sure. I don't think I'd be up to it if I kept having to do new things.

T: Yes, it could be stressful if you had to keep doing new things just for the sake of it. I suppose the idea is more to keep an eye on this habit of ruling yourself out of things and when you catch it, to consider what the benefits might be of giving it a try. Can you think of any other things that would apply to?

E: Well, I'm still thinking about whether to go to these painting classes.

T: That's a really good example. So in your self-therapy time, you might look out for things like that that you haven't done, whether they are work activities or activities for yourself outside of work. Then, if they are things you are anxious about, you could look at the pros and cons of doing them or answer your negative thoughts about them. When you have done anything that fits the bill, whether it's big or small, you could see if this view of yourself as a failure is stronger or weaker as a result.

E: I'm not quite clear what it is I have to do.

T: Well, shall we write it down so you can keep it as part of the self-help plan?

Following from this, Elizabeth decided to discuss with her boss the idea of her trying out the role for a while to see how it worked out both for her and the company. A trial period of six months was agreed at the end of which Elizabeth was to review her position regarding this new role. This decision was used as an example of how she could take a particular course of action, 'trying new things', in order to put her negative beliefs to the test.

Worksheets for Modifying Conditional Beliefs

It can take months of consistent and active practice to modify one conditional belief. Given that many chronically depressed patients are grappling with two or three such beliefs simultaneously, a brief course of treatment can only begin the process of modification. Flashcards or worksheets for modifying underlying beliefs can help patients to continue this process after the end of treatment, and are an important aspect of relapse prevention. Such a worksheet can bring together important points covered during treatment in one written summary. It can also contain prompts to aid the patient in carrying out an action plan for further modifying the conditional belief on a medium- to long-term basis.

The form of worksheet illustrated here is based on that suggested by Fennell (personal communication, 1992). Much of the information contained in the worksheet will already have been discussed during therapy sessions. Some patients who have engaged particularly well in the process of modifying their beliefs are able to summarise these discussions on the worksheet for homework. For example, *Elizabeth* was able to use the prompts on the worksheet to summarise accurately and comprehensively the gains she had made in understanding how an important belief contributed to her problems (see Table 10.3). Her plan for continuing to modify the belief was then worked on during the next session. With other patients, it is necessary to complete the whole sheet during therapy, which can take one to two sessions. Given the time constraints within therapy, it may not be realistic to attempt to construct a worksheet for every relevant conditional belief in session. Instead, one example can be worked out in session and the patient can be encouraged to use this as a template for developing others. As with other work on the patient's beliefs, it is important to ensure that the wording used to express the underlying beliefs and adaptive alternatives is generated by or meaningful to the patient.

Positive Diaries for Modifying Unconditional Beliefs

Positive diaries or data logs for helping patients to identify and accumulate evidence in support of their new belief are described in Chapter 8. Their sustained use is an essential part of eroding the beliefs that contribute to vulnerability to persistent depression. The use of these diaries can be presented from the outset as a long-term venture that is of most help when used over a period of months or years. Consistent use of data logs during therapy sessions, and as homework between sessions, can equip the patient to be able to use them successfully beyond the end of formal therapy. As was described in Chapter 8, the beauty of a well-designed belief log is that it can prompt the patient to become aware of a range of different categories of information. These can include new kinds of behaviour initiated by the patient (e.g. I disagreed with someone), as well as particular outcomes or situations (e.g. Someone complimented me). It is important that the instances of each type are related back to the overall new belief through rating the new belief each time a new bit of information is processed. The belief log, with prompts tailored specifically to the key adaptive belief to be developed, can

Table 10.3   Elizabeth's worksheet for modifying conditional beliefs

Modifying Beliefs

I hold the belief that . . .
I must avoid making mistakes otherwise others will criticise me.

It is understandable that I hold this belief because . . .
- My mother set excessively high standards for me (e.g. told me off for every mistake, often stood over me).
- The emphasis at school was on being perfect (e.g. awards for 'tip top girls', often humiliated in front of the class).
- As a child, I used to pray that I wouldn't make mistakes (e.g. reading in assembly).

The advantages of holding this belief are . . .
- My high standards mean that I'm very organised and efficient in my job.
- Doing things to a high standard means that I get a lot of praise from others (e.g. cake decorating and embroidery).
- I avoid the potential for criticism and humiliation at the hands of others.

However, this belief is unreasonable because . . .
- These standards are impossible to meet—it is unrealistic to expect myself to do this.
- These standards are absolute and black and white. I have no shades of grey.
- I would not expect any one else to live by these standards.

The belief is also unhelpful because . . .
- I avoid activities where I would have to run the risk of making mistakes. As a result I've missed out on important things in my life.
- The effort I put into avoiding mistakes is time consuming and exhausting (e.g. repeatedly checking my typing at work).
- I constantly worry about mistakes I might make and live with a sense of constant disappointment about mistakes I have made.

A more helpful belief is . . .
Mistakes are part of living and I can learn from them. If I make a mistake then I will show tolerance towards myself and deal with criticism if and when it arises.

As I have held this belief for a long time, it is going to take time and practice to change. My plan is . . .
1. Use self-therapy sessions (Tuesday afternoon 2–3 p.m.) to keep working on modifying this belief.
2. Catch times I avoid things or criticise myself in every day life where the rule is activated.
3. Deliberately give a piece of work to my boss containing a mistake and test out his reaction (i.e. does he criticise me?).
4. Not to be so excessive in adhering to the 'rules' of cake decorating and observe the impact on myself (thoughts/feelings/behaviour) and on the recipients of the cake (how pleased they are).

Table 10.3 (*Continued*)

---

5. To try out a new role in my job and examine the first six months in terms of what went well, what didn't go so well and the effects on how I view myself.
6. To plan what tactics I'm going to use to deal with mother's criticism (e.g. enrol in assertiveness course at college on a Thursday evening).
7. To give myself a reward every time I carry out an activity related to modifying this rule.
8. To read *A Woman in Your Own Right* by Anne Dickson (1982) and *Overcoming Low Self-Esteem* by Melanie Fennell (1999).

---

usually be carried forward into the self-therapy phase with little additional modification.

Discussion of the continued use of belief diaries in the final sessions of therapy usually centres around practical issues of how often the diary needs to be completed and what medium to use. The therapist can stress that brief but frequent (i.e. 5 or 10 minutes a day) use of the log is more likely to capture relevant information than more extended but less frequent efforts (e.g. 30 minutes each week or month). Different schedules for using the log can be tested out as the idea of a self-therapy plan is developed over the final sessions of therapy. Several computer literate patients have devised for themselves a diary sheet on their computer that incorporates relevant prompts and ratings. Other patients have made good use of hand- or typewritten 'proformas' developed during therapy sessions, which can be photocopied as needed. Others write relevant prompts onto a 'divider' in their personal organiser, which can be moved from week to week in the diary section. With less well-organised patients, any use of odd scraps of paper (even, in one case, the lids of cigarette packets) needs to be enthusiastically reinforced by the therapist.

By this stage of therapy, some patients recognise the benefits brought by taking on the challenge of modifying beliefs. However, for many patients, life-long avoidant coping strategies block their initiating their own efforts at belief modification. Some of these patients can use the structure provided by the therapist to begin to initiate efforts at self-help. The therapist's efforts at comprehensively going through sheets such as that in Table 10.3 prime such patients to continue the work. Other patients respond to the therapist's efforts with passivity, so that greater efforts on the therapist's part in session are not followed by self-help by the patients. The therapist needs to be particularly alert to this when using highly structured materials at this stage of therapy. In such cases, the goals and the self-help tasks aimed at achieving them then need to be simplified until some collaboration with the patient is achieved.

MAKING CHANGES IN LIFE SITUATIONS

The cognitive model of persistent depression describes how negative beliefs in the patient's mind exist in relation to negative situations in the patient's life. In many cases, it is hard to discern 'which is chicken and which is egg' between the patient's negative way of viewing themselves and their world, and the unfulfilling social and occupational circumstances in which they find themselves. As has been emphasised, it is not generally possible to change patterns of thinking in persistent depression without paying attention to the behaviours and environmental contingencies that may sustain them. In the final stages of therapy, it can be helpful to assist the patient to review their life situation and identify any factors that may increase the future risk of the persistence of depression. At the beginning of therapy, the patient is likely to have seen any external negative situations as impossible to change, so may have ruled out the possibility of making any helpful changes in their life situation. As the end of therapy approaches, if any improvements in self-esteem, helplessness and hopelessness have occurred, the patient may begin to glimpse the feasibility of making changes in such situations.

Addressing Occupational Problems

Work-related problems are frequently an important factor in persistent depression. Plans for addressing occupational difficulties may usefully be drawn up in the final phase of therapy. Difficulties can be divided into those of overwork (in both paid and unpaid capacities) versus those of unemployment or underemployment. Overwork usually results from beliefs about failure or responsibility and can lead to fatigue, stress and a lack of personal pleasure or satisfaction. Once some doubt or flexibility has been introduced into the underlying beliefs, the patient may benefit from guidance and support in adopting and maintaining new working practices. This might involve using time during the last few therapy sessions to devise a specific new plan (e.g. having at least every other weekend off) and to discuss how the patient will actually follow it. Planning regular contact with others who have previously encouraged the patient to work less can also be of benefit. Where unemployment is the problem, therapy time can be spent in devising specific plans for getting back into work. This might involve scanning newspapers for relevant job adverts, writing a CV, making applications and practising interview techniques. Alternatively, the emphasis of therapy may be on reviewing resources that patients could access to help with formal employment or their less formal use of time once therapy has finished. This might involve helping them to plan to contact careers advice organisations, skills training agencies or voluntary work organisations. One patient decided, as the end of therapy approached, that his job in the police force would always reinforce his tendency to compare himself with others in a hierarchical fashion. He decided to set up his own small shop and needed little help from the therapist in contacting the various agencies that could provide information and support to him in setting up his own business.

Addressing Social Problems

Social isolation is also frequently a factor in the maintenance of persistent depression. Once patients have made some progress in undermining the negative beliefs that have resulted in their social withdrawal, attention to strategies for eliciting and sustaining a more supportive network can be beneficial. Plans for social engagement and yardsticks to help patients to assess how they are putting their plans into practice can be incorporated into each patient's self-therapy plan. One patient who had previously considered himself a 'loner' unsuited to social contact came to realise that regular informal socialising did in fact improve his mood. His self-help plan included a goal of going out socially on a weekly basis, with a range of options to choose from on his social 'menu'. He was to use his regular self-help time to monitor this and, if he realised that he had not been out for three weeks, to take immediate remedial action.

As well as addressing changes in current occupational or social situations, there is sometimes scope for the patient to change longstanding family situations that may have contributed to the depression. In therapy with Joe, pressure imposed by implicit and explicit criticisms from his parents as he grew up was identified as an important factor in the initial development of his view of himself as a failure. He had tried dutifully throughout his life to live up to the expectations imposed by his parents' standards. This currently involved his making frequent and regular contact with his now ageing parents to ensure their physical and mental well-being. Their continued lack of any expression of pleasure and tendency to criticise his efforts had been noted consistently in therapy as a factor contributing to Joe's low mood. As therapy neared its end, Joe came to realise that, sadly, his efforts made little difference to his parents' attitude towards him and served only to make him feel worse. In the closing sessions of therapy, he discussed new rules for setting limits on the extent of contact with his parents. This involved decreasing the frequency with which he put himself 'in the firing line' in terms of face-to-face and phone contact. He experienced considerable sadness and regret about making this decision, which he planned to cope with by gradually building up more of a sense of solidarity with his brother over handling any difficulties posed by their parents.

DEVISING AN OVERALL BLUEPRINT FOR CHANGE

These areas of identifying warning signs, devising an action plan for set-backs, planning to continue to build self-esteem and planning life changes can be covered in as much detail as needed in the final sessions of therapy. For many patients, particularly those who have derived significant benefit from therapy in a number of areas, putting all these plans together into an overall masterplan or 'blueprint for change' can be of benefit. A blueprint for change serves the useful purpose of summarising what gains have been made in treatment and acting as a guide to future areas of work. This blueprint can summarise the formulation, indicate areas that the patient might consistently benefit from working on, as well as predicting potential pitfalls and outlining the plan for dealing with them. Putting together such an overall blueprint involves a significant amount of time and effort and is often best completed bit by bit as homework by the patient between the final few sessions. The blueprint illustrated in Table 10.4 was developed with *Dave* and incorporates much therapeutic work aimed at undermining his low self-esteem.

ENDING THERAPY

In many research and service settings, a fixed number of therapy sessions will have been agreed at the beginning of therapy. Where this is not the case, a decision needs to be made as to when therapy ends. In some cases where the patient has improved considerably and has developed some confidence in their own use of therapy skills, the decision to end contact presents little difficulty. More usually in persistent depression, further improvement is still to be desired, which makes the decision to end therapy more complex. A number of factors usually have to be considered. How much the patient is continuing to improve in therapy must be balanced against how well they may be expected to cope with any remaining problems by themselves. The patient's desire to continue therapy and their commitment to using therapy to acquire self-help skills may also be factored into the decision. Where the patient is continuing to experience significant difficulties, the availability of other forms of support is an important consideration. Finally,

Table 10.4   Dave's overall blueprint for change

Blueprint for change

What have I learned in my cognitive therapy sessions?
I have learned that I have always measured my worth in terms of how much
I earn, the type of work I do, how big my house is, what type of car I drive,
etc. I've always pushed myself relentlessly to do better. I realise now this is
not a very solid foundation on which to base my life and I have paid a heavy
price in terms of my health. Cognitive therapy helped me to get out of my
depression and to realise that deep down I have always seen myself as not
good enough. I've spent a lot of time, energy and effort trying to prove to
myself and other people that I can cut the mustard. I now realise that I don't
have to prove anything and I can live my life more as I want.

How do I plan to build on what I have learned in everyday life?
1. Fortnightly self-therapy sessions (Tuesday 9.30–10.30 when children are
   at school and wife is at work).
2. Work part-time (22 hours per week) and spend more time with my
   young sons.
3. Choose the work I want to do rather than feel compelled to chase big
   money.
4. Develop hobbies (woodwork; swimming; football team) and be average
   at them!
5. Practise putting my wants/needs on the agenda at home—things have
   got to change!

What obstacles may there be to building on my gains?
1. Feelings of guilt that I am letting myself and my family down by not
   providing for them.
2. My wife placing demands on me to work harder in order to make
   material gains.
3. Finding it hard to get any sense of enjoyment from something that is not
   achievement orientated.
4. Falling back into old ways and pushing myself relentlessly.

How am I going to overcome these?
1. To be on my guard for the signs I am pushing myself (i.e. continuous
   activity, no meal breaks, becoming withdrawn).
2. To use my CT skills and my therapy folder to modify negative thoughts
   and get the situation in perspective.
3. To recall the day when my business collapsed and I contemplated suicide.
   This was a bad time and I'm so glad I never did it. I have survived and I
   now know there are much more important things in life than work.
4. To remind myself of the things that really matter, i.e. my sons, my health,
   watering my tomatoes and being content.

What might lead to a setback for me? (future stressors)
1. Pressure to provide the best lifestyle for my wife and sons at times when
   money is tight (e.g. wife complaining that she doesn't have stuff for
   herself that all her friends have or if I can't buy my sons the latest toy at
   Christmas). I will be tempted to take on extra work or borrow money
   and then push myself to pay off the loan.

(Continued)

Table 10.4   *(Continued)*

2. Any situation where someone compares my achievements with someone else's (e.g. mixing with my wife's family, especially my father-in-law).
3. Comparing myself to other men who earn more (e.g. old business associates contacting me to ask me to go into business with them and challenging me when I say no).

If I did have a setback what would I do about it?
1. Accept that I will have setbacks and not be too hard on myself.
2. Try to view it as a temporary setback and not a failure. Watch out for black and white thinking.
3. Try to identify what led me to fall into the trap and use this as an opportunity to learn so that next time I am more prepared.
4. Make sure I carry on doing things for my own pleasure.
5. Use my skills at questioning thoughts whenever I need them, especially 'How much do I really need their approval?' (use therapy folder for ideas).

competing demands on the therapist's time will also have to be weighed against the needs of the individual patient.

Whether the timing of the end of therapy was decided at the outset or towards the end of therapy, ending can be difficult for both patient and therapist. Consistent with the passivity of many patients in their initial presentation, it is surprisingly uncommon for patients with persistent depression to complain actively of distress at ending therapy. The therapist may gently have to elicit any worries or distress about termination. Many issues about the patient's continuing problems and how to address them using self-help strategies can be dealt with using the framework presented in this chapter. It is also important to assess the patient's thoughts and feelings about finishing therapy itself. For many patients, the therapist will have become an important figure in their life, and some degree of distress at ending contact is often quite appropriate. The therapist can guide the patient in anticipating and acknowledging the loss and the feelings that result. Helping the patient to accept and work through some of this upset can help to provide a model for dealing with any upset that occurs after therapy has finished. Where beliefs about the shamefulness of emotions have been an important aspect of therapy, upset about termination can provide a useful opportunity for the patient to put new beliefs into practice. If the patient's degree of distress about ending seems excessive, the therapist can prompt the patient to identify and question any automatic thoughts about ending using standard cognitive techniques.

Ending therapy may also be difficult for the therapist when working with patients with persistent depression. The personal investment required from the therapist in working with these patients is often greater than with patients with more acute difficulties. Combined with uncertainty about the prognosis of many patients, this can make it tempting to keep the patient in treatment or follow-up. Some therapists may feel a weight of responsibility if patients are still symptomatic when the therapy contract is nearing the end, and so choose to extend the contract. Particularly where the therapist has beliefs about doing things properly, there may be an urge to keep the patients in treatment longer 'to try just a little harder to change their beliefs'. Supervision (see Chapter 11) is particularly important in helping therapists to juggle the issues that termination can raise. Good supervision can help therapists to maintain a perspective on how best to facilitate the patient's overall well-being and how to balance this against the needs of other patients. In facing this decision with patients with persistent depression, it can help to remember that both clinical experience and research data (reviewed in the final chapter) suggest that it is hard to predict how patients will fare after the end of therapy. Some patients in whose coping skills the therapist had considerable confidence have fared worse than expected, whereas many for whom the therapist ended treatment with trepidation have been found to do well. Just as therapy often focuses on helping patients to increase their tolerance for doubt, so tolerating doubt is essential for therapists when ending therapy with patients with persistent depressive symptoms.

SUMMARY POINTS

- In the final sessions of therapy, the emphasis is on helping the patient to continue to put into practice for themselves the strategies that have been learned.
- Tapering the frequency of therapy sessions can give patients the opportunity to practice self-help strategies while still receiving guidance from the therapist.
- Planning the details of 'what, where, when and how' the patient will put self-help into practice can increase the likelihood of the patient doing so.
- Identifying likely stressors and typical symptoms can help patients to anticipate possible setbacks and take preventive action.
- An action plan for tackling setbacks should include the main cognitive, behavioural and social strategies that the patient has found helpful in addressing low mood during therapy.

- Developing confidence and self-esteem depends on the patient developing a routine for consistently practising new cognitive and behavioural strategies.
- Patients can use the gains made in therapy to address work, social and family related problems that could feed future depression.
- The therapist can help to guide patients through any emotional difficulties in ending therapy.
- Good supervision can help therapists to reach balanced decisions about when to end therapy with an appropriate degree of confidence.

Chapter 11

DELIVERING TREATMENT

In this chapter, you will find discussion of:

- Practicalities of therapy, such as number, duration and spacing of sessions
- The management of non-attendance
- Working with the partners of patients
- The importance of liaison with other professionals involved in the patient's care
- Therapist's training, experience and supervision
- Patient suitability and outcome

The preceding chapters have focused on the formulation and strategies employed by the therapist in sessions of individual therapy with patients with persistent depression. In this chapter, we consider some more general issues concerning the provision of therapy with these patients. Due to the difficulties presented by chronically depressed patients, issues about how the therapy is best delivered are frequently encountered. First, we consider some of the practicalities of implementing therapy with individual patients. We discuss issues relating to the management of the therapy contract, such as the timing and duration of appointments and dealing with non-compliance. We then discuss the importance of integrating therapy into the patient's overall treatment package, including liaising with other professionals and with the patient's partner or family. Finally, we consider some issues related to the service context in which therapy is delivered. The importance of support for the therapist in their delivery of therapy, including management of caseloads and provision of training and supervision, is stressed. We also consider suitability of patients for cognitive therapy and the assessment of outcomes.

PRACTICALITIES OF PROVIDING THERAPY

Duration of Sessions

In cognitive therapy, as in most psychotherapies, it is generally recommended to set a duration for the sessions and stick to it firmly. In cognitive therapy, this is usually one hour. Setting a fixed duration for sessions behoves patients to bring up things they wish to discuss during that hour, which may mean that they give this some consideration beforehand. It encourages patients to share the responsibility for the content of sessions, thus fostering collaboration during sessions and self-help between sessions. These advantages of setting boundaries on session duration apply in persistent depression, but must be balanced against the disadvantages of adhering too rigidly to fixed session times. These disadvantages result from the nature of avoidance and beliefs in persistent depression.

Patients with beliefs about the overriding importance of emotional control are highly adept at avoiding issues or emotions that are central to progress in therapy. Knowing that sessions last an hour, their defences can remain firm for much of this time. It is not uncommon that important issues can be thrown up or feelings become more exposed towards the end of a session. Allowing a little extra time to pick up on such issues or feelings can bring them more clearly into the focus of therapy so they can be raised at the next meeting, whereas timely ending of the session may mean starting from scratch next time. Where this happens consistently in sessions with a particular patient, it can be helpful to draw the patient's attention to the pattern and formulate it along with other avoidance strategies. Over the course of several sessions, actively addressing emotional issues in sessions can then form the basis for behavioural experiments aimed at helping patients to re-evaluate their beliefs about emotional experience.

Where an upset has been triggered during the session, patients' difficulties regulating their emotions may make it hard for any satisfactory resolution to be reached by the end of the session. With patients who hold prominent beliefs about unacceptability, timely ending by the therapist is often seen as rejection. If this is done without adequate explanation, it can disrupt the therapeutic relationship and confirm the patient's belief that their emotions prove how unacceptable they are. Clearly this is a major issue that would need to be brought into the focus of therapy. It can be helpful to do this in a less confrontational fashion by allowing extra time to help the patients to plan how to deal with an upset after the session. Allowing extra time here can not only make some allowance for upsets in a non-punitive fashion, but can increase trust and foster future focus on emotional issues.

A balance needs to be struck between, on the one hand, the demands of clinic schedules and the benefits of structure and, on the other, taking advantage of opportunities for appropriate emotional regulation. The decision over whether to be flexible will often be in the hands of circumstances. With some experience of the patient, the therapist may have some idea of when building in some flexibility may be advantageous. For very emotionally flat patients, unwitting disclosures seem unlikely to occur in the first few sessions and the control or safety that rigid timings provide can help to foster their engagement. In contrast, for highly labile patients, it is precisely in the first couple of sessions that a flexible response to an outburst may prove crucial. Later in the course of therapy, when there may be a shared plan to confront particularly sensitive issues or to use highly emotive techniques, such as imagery rescripting, it may be possible to schedule the extra time in advance.

Number and Spacing of Sessions

Conventional cognitive therapy has usually been based on courses of therapy lasting from 12 to 20 sessions. In the outcome study in which the approach described here was evaluated, a course of 18 sessions was used, with 16 sessions during a five-month period followed by two booster sessions at more extended intervals (see Chapter 12). In routine clinical work, there are many patients with persistent depression who will derive significant benefit from this duration of therapy. Although there is little firm evidence on the issue, experience suggests that it would be difficult to treat any patients with persistent depression in much less time than this. Significantly shortening the therapy would render it likely that essential aspects of the therapy or important issues were missed. Even when patients seem to have made exceptionally good progress early in therapy, this can disguise the likelihood of continuing vulnerability, particularly in patients with a known variable course of depression.

Experience also suggests that many patients may benefit from longer courses of therapy. In a standard course of four to six months of therapy, some patients with chronic depression may have improved and then worsened again and others may be just starting to improve after a slow start. In view of this, in the small literature on cognitive therapy with chronic depression, extending the course of therapy, for example to 30 sessions, has been recommended (e.g. Scott, 1998). Where constraints on resources permit, extending the course of therapy in such cases may be well worth while. Where therapy is to be extended, this should rarely be done on an ad hoc or session by session basis, as this tends to focus the patient's attention on their perceived need for therapy to continue. It is better as far as possible to plan the estimated time course of therapy in advance with the patient. This enables goals to be set that are realistic in relation to the time available. The sequence and structure with which goals and tasks are addressed across the course of sessions can then be maintained. Where therapy is to be extended, it can be helpful to conduct the therapy in blocks of half a dozen or 10 sessions. This can provide a framework for periodically reviewing progress and setting or revising goals, as well as collaboratively deciding on the continuation of treatment.

Whatever the length of therapy, it is generally advisable to start with sessions on at least a weekly basis. There are many tasks that need to be accomplished at the beginning of therapy, including assessment, socialisation, formulation and setting goals, alongside engaging the patient in therapy. To begin to gain some familiarity with the patient and gain some momentum for accomplishing change, frequent sessions are preferable. Later in therapy, many patients have begun to acquire some notion of what is contributing to their problems, what needs to change and what actions they can take to further their aims in therapy. Spacing out the sessions at this time not only makes judicious use of limited therapists' time, but also fosters the patients' efforts to implement some therapeutic changes in their daily lives. Gaps of two to four weeks often seem to suit the pace of therapeutic change once therapy has got well underway. Such gaps serve to focus attention on realistic changes occurring over a timescale of months, rather than fostering potentially unrealistic expectations of significant changes occurring each week.

Whether the length of therapy is standard or more extended, many patients benefit from intermittent follow-up sessions after the end of regular therapy, as discussed in Chapter 10. Sessions can usefully be provided at intervals of every two or three months to help the patient consolidate any changes that have been made. Clearly, this kind of follow-up extends the actual duration of contact by some months. In following up patients in this way, therapists may find themselves at odds with the short-term constraints under which many mental health services are provided. After discharge, the constraints on some services may demand that patients have to relapse fully, undergo reassessment and wait for several months before re-accessing treatment. If patients who have gained some benefit from therapy are forced to wait several months for treatment at the point of incipient relapse, their depression may have become entrenched again and the benefits of therapy may be undone. Attempting to limit follow-up may therefore not work to the benefit of chronically depressed patients who are vulnerable to relapse. Having eventually to deal with a full depressive relapse of some months' duration is likely to be more time consuming than providing follow-up, so may prove more costly in the longer term.

Offering sustained support to some patients over the medium to long term may benefit the patient and the service overall.

Addressing Non-compliance

The term 'non-compliance' implies that a certain course of action has been agreed between patient and therapist, and that the patient is not following this agreement. In standard therapy, compliance and non-compliance can be relatively clearly differentiated. In working with persistent depression, difficulties in pursuing the goals of therapy are to be expected as the rule rather than the exception, due to patients' avoidance strategies and entrenched beliefs. Such difficulties are continuously anticipated and therapy adapted to address them. Addressing the potential for non-compliance is thus woven into the framework of therapy, by continuously adapting the style, process and content of therapy.

Non-compliance within sessions is often manifested in hostility towards the therapist, withdrawal or avoiding important discussion. Between sessions, non-compliance is manifested in the patient's not attempting agreed tasks, whether these were written assignments, such as monitoring thoughts, or behavioural experiments. The first step in addressing these problems is to identify and label the problem. Then an attempt is made to formulate the avoidance in terms of thoughts or beliefs and to specify predictions from these beliefs that can be tested out. The therapy task that is being avoided can then be broken down and a smaller scale version attempted, often in session with the therapist's help, as a test of the patient's negative predictions.

The greatest obstacle to this is when non-compliance takes the form of non-attendance. The therapist's response can be informed by their formulation of the nature of the patient's beliefs and avoidance. Patients who tend towards excessive emotional control can find the whole notion of therapy highly threatening and are often openly averse to the idea of therapy. They will often give some sign or advance notice of their intention not to attend. It can then be helpful to give the patient as much control over the timing and frequency of their attendance as possible, to refrain from pressurising the patient and to adopt a welcoming but somewhat businesslike stance. In contrast, in more labile patients, non-attendance tends to be of a more erratic nature and usually results from more momentary feelings or interpretations on the part of the patient. Non-attendance most frequently results from concerns about being overwhelmed by feelings or being rejected by the therapist. In such cases, the therapist usually has to take a much more active role in addressing non-attendance. This takes the form of taking the initiative to contact the patient by phone or letter, 'second guessing' the nature of the problem, asserting ways that it might be addressed and actively suggesting appointment times. In a phone conversation immediately after *Kate* had missed an appointment, her therapist intervened as follows:

K: I'm sorry I missed it today, but I'm too upset to come and see you, okay.
T: I know you're very upset right now and that's why it would be helpful to meet up sooner rather than later. Then we can see what's making you so upset and how you can come through it. In fact, I have a slot free at 3 o'clock tomorrow—is there any chance at all that you can make it?
K: Well, I couldn't find someone to take the children by tomorrow.
T: I can give you the number of the hospital creche—they take children under 11. That way we'll still be able to meet.
K: (*sounding slightly more reassured*) Oh okay then, what time did you say?

Where many patients would have found such an approach overly intrusive and threatening, Kate was somewhat calmed by the therapist's proposing a specific plan. The problem then becomes that the therapist cannot always step in when the patient is upset, so the therapy needs actively to focus on training the patient in strategies for keeping going when upset, including the management of unpleasant emotions and problem-solving.

INTEGRATING THERAPY INTO THE TREATMENT PACKAGE

Working with Partners

Persistent depression often occurs in the context of a lack of social support. Where patients are in a close relationship, reactions of spouses or partners often range from being mystified by the patient's depression to outright criticism or abuse. Although the therapist's prime focus remains on individual sessions with the patient, consideration of whether to include the partner in the therapy can be helpful. Where the partner is essentially supportive, there can be a number of benefits in encouraging the patient to attend with their partner for a session or two. Much can be achieved through helping the partner to gain a clearer understanding of the nature of depression. A lack of understanding can result in the partner exerting undue pressure on the patient to maintain normal activities. Conversely, some partners unwittingly reinforce depressive behaviour by being completely accommodating to the patient's avoidance of activities. By clarifying what level of expectations are most realistic, a helpful level of encouragement from the partner is more likely. The therapist can also prompt some discussion of ways that the partner might be able to help the patient with self-help strategies. This can include helping the patient to make time for self-help tasks or prompting the patient to undertake monitoring tasks. Obviously care needs to be taken that the partner is prompting the patient to use and develop self-help skills, rather than the partner being trapped in a role of being 'the carer' for the patient. It is not recommended that the partner attends the majority of sessions, as the presence of a partner tends to inhibit emotional experience and disclosure in the sessions.

Where there is more overt marital discord or criticism, the cognitive therapist can sometimes broker an agreement for the couple to seek appropriate help. For obvious reasons, it is rarely helpful for a therapist to see the individual patient and the couple. However, where patients are being seen in the context of a treatment team, such as on a ward, it can be very helpful for the cognitive therapist to see the patient while another member of the team conducts work with the couple. Where depression occurs in the context of significant marital problems, there is evidence that marital therapy is particularly effective as a treatment (Jacobson et al., 1991; Jacobson & Gurman, 1986). Where there is reason to believe that the patient is being emotionally or physically abused, an important focus of therapy is how the patient can protect themselves both physically and mentally from the effect of the abuse. The patient may also need help in considering whether to end the abusive relationship.

Working with Other Professionals

In most cases of persistent depression, the cognitive therapist will not be the only professional working with the patient. Most patients will have gained at least some benefit from medication, and cognitive therapy will best be undertaken in combination with pursuing pharmacological treatment. It is important to ensure that the patient does not receive mixed messages about which treatments will work and how they do so. As discussed in Chapter 4, some patients have received a rationale for treatment with medication that has presented depression in purely biological terms. This can undermine acceptance of the rationale for cognitive therapy and hamper the patient's engagement. It is important that the therapist does not present cognitive therapy in a way that could undermine the patient's compliance with their medical treatment. Rather, as discussed in Chapter 4, a model of persistent depression should be presented that can encompass both biological and psychosocial treatments. Further, the potential for such conflicts can be minimised by good communication between the different professionals involved.

If the other professionals involved in the treatment have some idea of the goals and strategies to be employed in the therapy, it is more likely that their interventions will be consistent with it. Good practice would generally involve writing a brief letter to any professionals simultaneously involved in treating the depression on commencing therapy. This should outline briefly the therapist's assessment of the problems and anticipated treatment strategy. Additionally, there are several reasons why intermittent phone contact or meetings between the therapist and the other professionals involved in the treatment can be extremely helpful. Phone contact or face-to-face meetings assist in the sharing of useful information and can help to integrate different aspects of treatment. Many cases with persistent depression have become well known to their doctor over an extended period. The doctor may have a very good idea of the nature of the patient's problems and can provide much useful information to the therapist. Conversely, because of the patient's cognitive and emotional avoidance, it is sometimes possible for the patient's psychiatrist or GP to have had contact with a patient over an extended period without getting much idea of what is bothering the patient. While being careful to respect the patient's confidentiality, the therapist can convey ideas that can inform the advice and support given by the patient's doctor. On some occasions, the therapist can exert a useful influence over other aspects of the patient's treatment. For example, where a doctor believes that insufficient progress is being made, they may be preparing to discharge the patient or pass on the patient's care. Although there are many occasions where this is justified, there are others where it may have a detrimental effect for the patient. Here the therapist can advocate continuation or consistency of care for the patient.

Good liaison with other professionals involved in treatment can be particularly important when the therapy focuses on addressing the patient's avoidance of difficult issues or situations, as is so often the case in persistent depression. Therapy sessions can be experienced as upsetting and can seem to make the patient worse before they get better. Other professionals may not be aware that this can be a sign of therapeutic progress rather than lack of it. They may then undermine the patient's confidence in the therapy or reinforce the patient's desire to terminate prematurely. If the therapist forewarns other professionals of the likelihood and even desirability of therapy provoking upset, then it is more likely that those others will support the therapeutic goals and encourage the patient to stay with it. Where the therapist is confident that other people involved in the case will provide appropriate support with such upsets, this can enable therapy to proceed a little less cautiously and means that important therapeutic issues can be addressed a little more speedily. This can happen to good effect where the therapist is a member of a treating team, for example on a ward, where the different roles of different members of the team are well established.

For patients with particularly severe chronic depression, intensive inpatient programmes have been advocated (see Wright et al., 1993, for a full description of such therapy programmes). Usually such programmes afford an opportunity to combine complex or aggressive regimes of pharmacotherapy with intensive psychotherapeutic input. 'Cognitive milieu' packages have been used, where all the members of the team have received some training in cognitive techniques, so that cognitive therapy principles can be extended beyond individual therapy sessions. As well as individual and group cognitive therapy sessions, such packages often involve a ward programme based on cognitive principles. In addition, assistance and encouragement with self-help tasks such as behavioural assignments and questioning thoughts is available 'on tap' from staff.

THE SERVICE CONTEXT OF THERAPY

Therapists' Training and Experience

Working effectively with patients with persistent depression is in most therapists' estimation difficult. Such cases do not make good 'learning experiences' for novice therapists. Due to the greater complexity involved in formulating these cases and the difficulty often encountered in implementing interventions, therapists who are not already highly familiar with the basic conceptual and technical aspects of cognitive therapy are likely to become overwhelmed. Ideally, cognitive therapy for patients with persistent depression should be conducted by well-trained, experienced cognitive therapists. Although there has been little systematic research, such evidence as exists suggests that patients treated by more experienced cognitive therapists are less likely to drop out of treatment and more likely to improve (Burns & Nolen-Hoeksema, 1992). A therapist's level of expertise is likely to prove particularly crucial with more difficult cases such as these. Some mastery of basic cognitive therapy techniques is essential for the therapist to be able to detect and understand ways in which the desired outcome may be thwarted. Similarly, only once the basics have become somewhat automatic will the therapist be able to focus on adapting therapy to address the complexities of patients with particularly difficult problems. As a rough guideline, patients with persistent depression are probably best seen by therapists who have undergone specialised cognitive therapy training beyond that provided in a basic professional qualification. Therapists should have successfully treated a number of cases of acute depression with cognitive therapy before progressing to treating longer-term cases. Where cases with persistent depression are treated by less experienced therapists, it is vital that particularly close clinical supervision is provided, ideally by a trained cognitive therapist, to safeguard the well-being of both patient and therapist.

Supervision and Caseload

All therapists, whether novice or expert, are likely to encounter significant difficulties when treating patients with persistent depression. It is therefore important that therapists working with such cases have access to regular clinical supervision, which can help to address a number of areas of difficulty. Problems of formulation, therapeutic relationship and technique can all be addressed in good clinical supervision. Where a supervisor is not specifically trained and experienced in cognitive therapy, that person's ability to help the therapist with problems in drawing up a cognitive formulation or in implementing cognitive techniques will be limited. Therefore, it is important that supervision of cognitive therapy for cases of persistent depression is provided by supervisors who are themselves trained and experienced in cognitive therapy (Padesky, 1996; Shaw et al., 1999).

There are a number of areas in which supervision may be particularly helpful when working with persistent depression. Emotional and cognitive avoidance on the part of the patient can make it easy for the therapist to miss issues that may be important in arriving at a helpful formulation. Supervision can provide an objective viewpoint that helps any 'blank spots' to be identified. The passivity of many of these patients can render it hard to maintain the collaborative nature of the therapeutic relationship. When patients are passive in therapy, this often draws the therapist into becoming overactive and taking excessive responsibility for the progression of therapy. This runs the risk of reinforcing the patient's passivity and avoidance, and of the therapist's becoming 'burnt out' when their excessive efforts bear little reward. Alternatively, there may be occasions when the therapist reacts to the patient's passivity by giving up on the patient. Supervision can help the therapist to recognise the potential for either of these reactions and to maintain an appropriate balance between under- and over-involvement. When the therapist becomes confused or tired in working with a particular patient, supervision can often help in identifying practical techniques to provide a way forward.

In addition to helping to identify and remedy difficulties connected directly with the application of therapy, supervision can also usefully address the effects of the therapy on the therapist. When confronted by a consistently hopeless patient who seems to be making no progress, it is not unnatural for the therapist's own motivation to be dimmed. Less experienced therapists may find that it is particularly demoralising to work with these cases. Where this occurs, it is an important part of supervision to help the therapist to restore some sense of enthusiasm for working with the patient. This may occur through taking a renewed interest in the conceptualisation of the patient's difficulties, identifying practical techniques that could be useful or directing the therapist's attention to foibles of the patient for which a degree of affection could be developed (see Chapter 2). Where appropriate, supervision can also help therapists to identify and question their own negative thoughts about the course of therapy (see page 228). In this way, supervision can help to mitigate the effects of any lowering of the therapist's motivation or self-esteem on the course of therapy with the patient. If the therapist's self-esteem is consistently threatened when working with these patients, other options may need to be considered, such as the therapist working in some different capacity or receiving some personal therapy.

Working with a number of patients with persistent depression can help a therapist to build up familiarity and expertise with such patients. However, because of the level of difficulties encountered, it is not recommended that therapists, even those experienced with these patients, work exclusively with patients with persistent depression. To do so would be to court fatigue or loss of motivation sooner or later. Some variety in a therapist's caseload is usually desirable to provide some 'light relief'. This is probably more important for less experienced therapists.

Suitability for Cognitive Therapy

The majority of patients with persistent depression are not those classically thought of as suitable for cognitive therapy. Early studies of the efficacy of cognitive therapy for depression excluded patients with known poor response to medication (Rush et al., 1977). In other studies, duration of episode or chronicity has been found to be associated with poor response to cognitive therapy (e.g. Blackburn et al., 1981). It might be concluded that chronic patients or non-responders to medication are not suitable candidates for cognitive therapy. However, such patients are less likely to respond to any treatment. Therefore, it is response relative to other forms of treatment rather than absolute levels of response that is crucial in making decisions about whether cognitive therapy is appropriate.

When confronted with patients with persistent depression in clinical settings, the most relevant question is usually that of whether cognitive therapy might be of significant benefit for that patient compared to the other treatment options. In the following chapter, we describe a study showing that cognitive therapy can be of significant benefit in patients with residual depressive symptoms, many of whom would not ordinarily be considered good candidates for therapy. When combined with the evidence from the small scale studies described in the Introduction, this suggests that cognitive therapy is a worthwhile addition to treatment for patients with persistent depression, who are unlikely to fare particularly well with any of the other treatment options. Thus, even though patients with acute depression may improve more in absolute terms, the benefits of cognitive therapy relative to other treatments may be greater in patients with persistent depression. Where the other options are limited, cognitive therapy should not be ruled out for patients who are unmotivated or believe that therapy will not work. Nevertheless, it is clearly best to try to treat patients as early as possible in the course of their depression. In the majority of cases with persistent depression, therapy should be used in combination with medication rather than as an alternative to it.

Assessing Outcome of Therapy

There are a number of standard outcome measures, such as the Beck Depression Inventory (Beck et al., 1961) and Hopelessness Scale (Beck et al., 1974), that are of use in assessing the response of patients to cognitive therapy. Scores on such measures in patients with persistent depression need to be viewed with some caution. Cognitive and emotional avoidance in persistent depression may result in under-reporting of depressive symptoms on self-report measures. Occasionally, agreement between the therapist, patient and others that good progress has been made in therapy is associated with an increase in self-rated depression scores. More generally, evidence is presented in Chapter 12 that, even when the immediate benefits from therapy are modest, more significant benefits in the longer-term may still result. While patients' self-reports on measures of depression taken at the time of therapy are of interest, a broader and more long-term view can be helpful in assessing both the progress of individual patients and the impact of cognitive therapy services. Such a broad assessment of outcome might include the views of relatives or other professionals on the patient's progress, evidence of the patient's social and occupational functioning and their use of health care resources. To gain a true picture of the effect of therapy in persistent depression, these outcomes should be considered over a period of months or years from the provision of therapy, rather than simply at termination of therapy.

SUMMARY POINTS

- Although sticking to a set session duration is generally recommended, there are benefits to being flexible when emotions need to be stimulated or contained.
- Longer than usual courses of cognitive therapy are likely to be beneficial when treating persistent depression.
- Sessions should be frequent at the beginning of therapy and spaced out towards the end.
- The therapist's response to non-attendance can usefully be geared to the formulation of the patient's difficulties.
- It can sometimes be helpful to bring the patient's partner into some sessions, although a clear distinction needs to be maintained between individual and marital therapy.
- Close liaison with other professionals is essential, particularly at times when therapy may provoke distress.
- It is best if patients with persistent depression are treated by cognitive therapists who have gained supervised experience following specialist training in cognitive therapy.
- Supervision from a well-trained and experienced cognitive therapist is recommended when treating cases with persistent depression.
- Patients with persistent depression may often be judged as unsuitable for cognitive therapy, but may derive worthwhile benefits.
- Assessments of outcomes of therapy should take account of a range of measures over a period of months or years.

Chapter 12

OUTCOMES AND PROCESSES OF THERAPY

In this chapter, you will find discussion of:

- The Cambridge–Newcastle (CN) Depression Study of cognitive therapy for residual depressive symptoms, for which this approach was developed
- Results of the CN study concerning outcomes and mechanisms of treatment
- Other recent advances in cognitive approaches to the treatment of depression
- Research into basic cognitive processes of importance in therapy
- Clinical implications of research findings
- Recurring themes in cognitive therapy for persistent depression

One of the strengths of cognitive therapy has been its strong empirical basis. The use of cognitive therapy in acute depression is empirically well supported (Hollon et al., 1993). As reviewed in the Introduction, evidence for the use of cognitive therapy in patients with persistent depression is promising, but the studies conducted to date lack rigour. In addition, developments in cognitive therapy that place greater emphasis on modifying unconditional beliefs or schemas in chronic disorders have received little rigorous evaluation. The approach to therapy described in this book was first developed for use in a rigorous, randomised-controlled trial of cognitive therapy for persistent depression. In this chapter, we present the results from this outcome study, the Cambridge–Newcastle Depression Study. We describe the overall outcomes of therapy and then describe some research that investigated the mechanisms underlying the effects of therapy. Some other recent developments in the field of cognitive approaches to depression are then discussed. We outline some novel therapeutic approaches and the evidence for their effectiveness, and then briefly relate the findings on therapy to recent basic research into cognitive processes in depression. The implications of this research for the practice of therapy for persistent depression are discussed. Finally, we draw together some of the recurring themes in this book that pervade work with persistent depression and so merit particular attention either in individual therapy or in further research.

THE CAMBRIDGE–NEWCASTLE DEPRESSION STUDY

The Cambridge–Newcastle (CN) Depression Study was conducted to evaluate the efficacy of the adapted form of cognitive therapy described here in patients with a particular form of persistent depression. The study examined the treatment of residual depressive symptoms following an episode of major depressive disorder. Patients with significant residual depressive symptoms have been shown not only to suffer continuing distress and disability, but also to be at particularly high risk of relapse into full major depression (Paykel et al., 1995). In these patients, the CN study examined whether the addition of cognitive therapy to an adequate regime of medication and clinical management would result in further symptomatic improvement. Importantly, given the high levels of relapse observed even when such patients are maintained on adequate antidepressant medication, the study examined whether cognitive therapy could reduce relapse over and above the effects of continued medication. The study also provided an opportunity to examine the mechanisms through which cognitive therapy achieves its effects. In particular, the issue of what kinds of cognitive changes mediate the clinical benefits of cognitive therapy was examined.

Study Design

The 158 patients with residual depression included in the study had suffered an episode of major depression within the last 18 months and had been treated with adequate doses of medication (on average equivalent to 185 mg/day of amitriptyline or 33 mg/day of fluoxetine). Although they no longer met criteria for major depression, their residual symptoms were at clinically significant levels, in that patients had to score at least 8 on the Hamilton Rating Scale for Depression (HRSD; Hamilton, 1960) and at least 9 on the Beck Depression Inventory (BDI; Beck et al., 1961). All patients received clinical management including at least adequate levels of medication throughout a 20-week acute treatment phase and a one-year follow-up phase. Patients were randomly allocated to receive this clinical management alone or clinical management plus cognitive therapy. Cognitive therapy consisted of 16 sessions during the acute phase of treatment with two subsequent booster sessions during the follow-up phase. Patients were assessed regularly throughout the study on a battery of clinical, social and cognitive measures.

As expected, the sample presented quite a different picture from those included in studies of acute depression. The mean age was 43 years, and around 50% were male. They were suffering from moderate but subsyndromal levels of symptoms, with initial mean scores on the HRSD of 12 and on the BDI of 22. Their current depressive episodes had typically lasted over a year (with a median of 14 months), and over half the sample merited a diagnosis of severe depression at the worst point of the episode. Around a third of the patients were in their first depressive episode and over a third of the patients had had three or more episodes. A quarter of the sample also received a diagnosis of dysthymia. In terms of current DSM-IV diagnoses, the sample thus included patients with Major Depressive Episode, in partial remission; Major Depressive Disorder, recurrent, without full inter-episode recovery; and Dysthymic Disorder (with prior history of Major Depressive Disorder). To be eligible for inclusion, patients had to have been on at least an adequate dose of medication for no less than 8 weeks, but most patients were on doses exceeding the minimum requirements (see above).

Effects of Treatment on Symptoms, Social Functioning and Relapse

The rate of full remission in the overall sample over the 20 weeks of acute treatment was low. Patients treated with cognitive therapy had a significantly higher rate of remission (26%) than the clinical management alone group (12%). On four different measures of depressive symptoms, the scores of both groups decreased over the 20-week acute treatment phase and continued to decrease slightly over the one-year follow-up. Over the course of the study, the addition of cognitive therapy produced significantly greater decreases in overall severity of depression on two out of the four measures. Interestingly, cognitive therapy also had a significant impact on two specific psychological symptoms: self-esteem and hopelessness. Improvements in social functioning (including dependency, interpersonal behaviour and friction) were also significantly greater in the patients treated with cognitive therapy. It should be noted that the additional improvements in levels of symptoms and social functioning due to cognitive therapy, while statistically significant in several analyses, were modest. The differential improvement in patients treated with cognitive therapy tended to be greatest at the end of acute treatment or early in follow-up. (For a full description of these results, see Scott et al., 2000.)

As expected in this kind of sample, there was a steady flow of relapses into full major depression during the 20-week acute and one-year follow-up phases, despite all patients being on continuing treatment with medication. Relapse rates showed a consistent and significant reduction in the patients treated with cognitive therapy. By the end of the year's follow-up, 49% of patients in the clinical management alone group had relapsed, compared to 30% of those who had also received cognitive therapy. This reduction of about 40% in the relapse rate occurred despite the cognitive therapy patients receiving fewer clinical management sessions over the course of the study. The clinical significance of this substantial reduction in relapse is underlined by the fact that it was achieved over and above any preventive effect of continued medication. (For a full description of results concerning relapse prevention, see Paykel et al., 1999.)

Psychological Mechanisms of Relapse Prevention

The theory behind cognitive therapy proposes that it achieves its effects by producing cognitive changes in patients that then result in symptom reduction or lowered vulnerability to relapse. For example, cognitive therapy might reduce patients' levels of belief in certain dysfunctional assumptions, attitudes or attributions and thereby lower their susceptibility to continued depressive symptoms. However, previous studies have found little evidence that successful cognitive therapy produces any more change in measures of these variables than successful treatment with medication (Barber & DeRubeis, 1989). The CN study examined whether the effects of cognitive therapy in preventing relapse were mediated by a number of cognitive measures. These included a number of commonly used measures of the negative content of cognition, including the Dysfunctional Attitude Scale (DAS; Weissman & Beck, 1978) and the Attributional Style Questionnaire (ASQ; Peterson et al., 1982). Evidence for mediation of the effects of therapy on relapse was also examined using some novel cognitive measures, including a measure of meta-awareness (see below).

Using conventional scoring procedures (i.e. based on degree of agreement with item content), scores on five questionnaires of depression-related cognition, including the DAS and ASQ, provided no evidence for cognitive mediation of relapse prevention. A measure of the extremity of responses to those questionnaires was devised, indicating the number of times patients used extreme response categories ('totally agree' and 'totally disagree'). There was convincing evidence that this measure of extremity of responding helped to mediate the relapse preventive effects of therapy. Firstly, extreme responding significantly predicted relapse in the sample as a whole. Furthermore, treatment with cognitive therapy resulted in a differential reduction of extreme responses compared to clinical management alone. In addition, this reduction of extremity statistically accounted for some of the relapse preventive effects of cognitive therapy. The extremity measure included extreme positive as well as extreme negative responses to questionnaire items. This suggests that cognitive therapy reduced relapse through reductions in an absolute, dichotomous thinking style, rather than simply through reducing the negativity of cognition. (For a full account of prediction of relapse from questionnaire measures, see Teasdale et al., 2001.)

Meta-awareness and Relapse

Clinical experience suggests that cognitive therapy, as well as helping patients to question the negative content of their thoughts, can help patients to stand back from their thoughts and experience them as thoughts rather than as reality. If someone is having thoughts, for example of failure, which feed into a global, high-level sense of inadequacy, then those thoughts will undoubtedly be depressing. However, if at some level, they simultaneously have a sense that these are just thoughts that might or might not be true, the thoughts may have less of a depressing effect. Meta-awareness refers to this sense of awareness of thoughts as thoughts rather than reality, which is associated with an ability to identify less completely with those thoughts or to see them in a wider perspective (Moore, 1996). If cognitive therapy helps patients to develop this kind of awareness of their thinking, the depressogenic effect of situations or emotions that trigger negative thoughts could be reduced. The development of meta-awareness could thus help to prevent relapse in depression and could also account for some of the relapse preventive effect of cognitive therapy.

To examine this possibility within the CN study, a new measure of meta-awareness was developed, the Measure of Awareness and Coping in Autobiographical Memory (MACAM; Moore, Hayhurst & Teasdale, 1996). When they are not distressed, patients are often well aware that their thoughts at times of distress are not realistic and can retrospectively appraise their negative thoughts as 'irrational'. However, this does not usually translate into awareness of that possibility when the thoughts actually come to mind during an upset. To take account of this, any useful measure of awareness must tap the way patients experience their thoughts *during* upsetting situations, rather than assessing their general meta-cognitive beliefs about the accuracy of their thoughts. A questionnaire measure would be more likely to capture the latter, more general beliefs than to assess the former, 'on-line' awareness. Therefore, an autobiographical memory-based measure was devised. Patients were prompted by listening to audiotaped vignettes of mildly upsetting situations to recall memories of times when they had had a similar feeling. Patients were then asked to describe their thoughts and feelings at these times of initially mild upset. A semistructured interview format was used to enable the interviewer to rate the patient's degree of meta-awareness at the time of the upsetting memory according to a standardised rating system. Eight prompts were used at each time of testing to elicit a range of memories associated with mild upsets, so that each patient's mean meta-awareness score could be used in the analysis.

In patients with residual depression in the CN study, there was some evidence that meta-awareness mediated the relapse preventive effects of cognitive therapy. Meta-awareness scores at baseline significantly predicted relapse during the study. In addition, cognitive therapy resulted in a significantly greater increase in meta-awareness than clinical management alone. These results are consistent with the possibility that cognitive therapy prevents relapse by increasing levels of meta-awareness. Unfortunately, by the time the post-therapy assessment of meta-awareness was carried out, there were insufficient subsequent relapses to test adequately whether the increase in meta-awareness accounted for the reduction in subsequent relapse. (For full details of the meta-awareness measure and results, see Teasdale et al., 2002.)

Summary of Findings from the CN Study

In patients with residual depression, the results of the CN study showed that the form of cognitive therapy described here produced significant but modest additional improvements in remission rates, overall symptom levels and social functioning when added to good clinical management and medication. Cognitive therapy also produced specific improvements in the key symptoms of hopelessness and self-esteem. Most importantly, it achieved a worthwhile reduction in the rate of relapse into full major depression, which was over and above the effect of continued medication. Consistent with previous studies, analyses of the mechanism whereby cognitive therapy prevented relapse found little evidence that this occurred through changes in the content of cognition. By contrast, substantial evidence was found that cognitive therapy may prevent relapse by training patients to change the way that they process depression-related material rather than by changing thought content. Cognitive therapy produced a reduction in the extremity of emotionally relevant thinking and an increase in patients' ability to experience upsetting thoughts as thoughts rather than reality as those thoughts come to mind. Both these types of change were associated with reduced rates of relapse. Taken together, they suggest that cognitive therapy may help to move patients from a mode of thinking where emotionally relevant information is processed automatically in a dichotomous fashion to a mode where emotional information can be held in awareness and responded to more reflectively.

RECENT DEVELOPMENTS IN COGNITIVE APPROACHES TO THERAPY

The Cognitive Behavioral Analysis System of Psychotherapy

The most impressive results published to date on the treatment of chronic depression have been in a large study comparing the effects of one of the newer medications, nefazodone, with a new therapy, the Cognitive Behavioral Analysis System of Psychotherapy (CBASP; McCullough, 2000). The CBASP model proposes that the thinking of patients with chronic depression has become arrested at or returned to a primitive developmental level, corresponding to Piagetian pre-operational thought. The nature of such thinking renders patients insensitive to feedback from the social environment, resulting in the perception that they are unable to influence any of the situations in their lives. This closed style of thinking results in the passivity and helplessness typical of chronically depressed patients. The strategy behind the therapy is to show patients that their actions do indeed have important consequences, so that patients can begin to initiate behaviours that will be rewarded. Such reward of new behaviours, which comes predominantly from social reinforcement, serves to lift mood and restore motivation. A number of techniques are used in pursuing this strategy including:

- Provision of consistent feedback from the therapist on the interpersonal effects of the patient's actions.
- Teaching patients to discriminate between aversive or abusive past interpersonal situations where they could not affect outcomes and current situations where they can.
- Teaching patients to evaluate systematically whether their actions are assisting them in achieving desired outcomes.

A sample of 519 patients suffering from chronic major depressive disorder was included in the CBASP study (Keller et al., 2000). They were randomly assigned to treatment with nefazodone, CBASP or a combination of both. After 12 weeks of treatment, rates of response (including partial response) were 55% in patients treated with nefazodone alone, 52% in patients treated with CBASP alone and 85% in patients receiving the combination of nefazodone and CBASP. The rate of full remission with this combination treatment was 48%. Given the degree of chronicity of depression in the sample, this result is extremely impressive.

This study provided compelling evidence that CBASP is highly beneficial in the treatment of chronic depression. The rate of full remission with the combination of CBASP and medication in that study was nearly double the rate of full remission of patients treated with cognitive therapy and medication in the CN study. It is quite possible that CBASP will prove to be the most effective treatment yet for chronic forms of depression. This cannot yet be concluded with any certainty, as the rate of response to medication alone was also considerably higher than in the CN study. Although the patients included in the CBASP study seem to be a more chronic sample than in the CN study, it is also likely that they were less treatment resistant.

Cognitive Therapy and Relapse Prevention

The most impressive aspect of the CN study—namely, the relapse preventive effect of cognitive therapy—has also been reflected in a number of other recent developments in the field of cognitive therapy for depression. A study conducted by Fava and colleagues (1994) also addressed the treatment of residual symptoms of depression following treatment with medication. After the withdrawal of medication, patients' residual symptoms were treated with cognitive therapy or with clinical management. Patients treated with cognitive therapy were found to have a lower rate of subsequent relapse than those who received clinical management (Fava et al., 1996). In this study, the residual symptoms were at a low level that would usually be considered as full remission, and did not represent clinically significant persistent or chronic symptoms. This study showed that treating low-level residual symptoms in patients who have responded to medication reduced the rate of subsequent relapse. Thus, these promising results lend support to other evidence suggesting that cognitive therapy is a viable alternative to maintenance medication for preventing relapse in patients who have made a good recovery with pharmacological treatment of an acute episode or recurrence (Blackburn & Moore, 1997).

Mindfulness-Based Cognitive Therapy

Relapse preventive effects have also been shown using other therapeutic developments of cognitive therapy. Segal, Williams and Teasdale (2002) developed Mindfulness-Based Cognitive Therapy (MBCT) which integrates some standard cognitive therapy principles with mindfulness practices. MBCT is administered in a group format with patients who have recovered from a depressive episode. This therapy was designed specifically with the aim of increasing meta-cognitive awareness in recovered patients who are at high risk of further episodes. Through mindfulness training, MBCT aims to develop a mental 'set' of meta-cognitive awareness that is more general than the meta-awareness related just to specific negative thoughts developed in standard cognitive therapy. In vulnerable patients, it was predicted that being able to access such a cognitive set at times of potential relapse would render negative thoughts and feelings less likely to trigger relapse into major depression. MBCT was shown significantly to reduce rates of relapse in patients who had suffered from recurrent depressive episodes (Teasdale et al., 2000). Interestingly, MBCT was also found to result in increases in meta-awareness as measured by the MACAM measure (Teasdale et al., 2002). The reduction of relapse using a version of cognitive therapy that does not aim to change negative cognitive content lends further support to the notion that relapse preventive effects may be at least in part due to the development of meta-awareness.

Well-Being Therapy

A further development of cognitive therapy for depression is that of well-being therapy (Fava, 1999). This therapy uses many standard cognitive and behavioural techniques. However, rather than focusing the use of these techniques on negative occurrences or symptoms, this approach focuses on the occurrence of episodes of well-being. The strategy is to enhance patients' awareness of episodes of well-being and to combat thoughts and behaviours that inhibit or curtail well-being. Patients are then helped to identify and enhance six particular dimensions of well-being according to the theoretical framework behind the therapy. The effectiveness of the therapy was evaluated in a group of 20 patients with low-level residual symptoms following successful treatment of depression or anxiety disorders (Fava et al., 1998a). Patients were randomly assigned to either well-being therapy or cognitive behavioural therapy. Both treatments were associated with a significant reduction in residual symptoms and an increase in well-being. The improvements were significantly greater in the patients treated with well-being therapy. Well-being therapy was then incorporated into a cognitive-behavioural package that was used to treat a sample of 40 patients who had recovered from at least their third episode of depression (Fava et al., 1998b). The patients treated with the cognitive therapy plus well-being therapy package had a significantly lower relapse rate over two years of follow-up than patients treated with clinical management alone. Although the differential contributions of well-being therapy and standard cognitive therapy to reducing residual symptoms and preventing relapse cannot be determined from these studies, well-being therapy does appear to be a highly promising development.

Summary of Recent Developments in Cognitive Approaches to Depression

Overall, the relapse preventive effects of cognitive therapy have been shown consistently in a number of studies. The results of the CN study show that these can be achieved over and above the effects of continued medication in patients suffering from significant persistent depressive symptoms. Results of other studies have demonstrated that treating lower level residual symptoms has relapse preventive effects in patients who have recovered more fully from a depressive episode. Studies of MBCT and well-being therapy suggest that relapse prevention can be achieved using adaptations of cognitive therapy more suited to patients whose symptoms have remitted but who remain at high risk of relapse. In terms of lowering ongoing levels of residual symptoms, the CN study also adds weight to the evidence that cognitive therapy can be significantly effective in treating persistent depression. In addition, the results of the CBASP study are particularly impressive in terms of the degree of improvement achieved in a short duration of treatment in patients with very chronic disorders. There are areas of great theoretical and technical overlap between cognitive therapy as described here and CBASP, but there are also differences. Whereas we have rooted our approach in the well-established tradition of cognitive therapy, CBASP is a more novel, hybrid approach. Further research is needed to ascertain whether there are benefits that are exclusive to the CBASP approach or whether there are particular aspects of CBASP that might usefully be imported into conventionally based cognitive therapy.

RESEARCH ON BASIC PROCESSES IN DEPRESSION

The Role of Avoidance

The cognitive model we have described proposes an important role for different kinds of avoidance in interaction with underlying beliefs. In addition to the usual role for behavioural avoidance, we have suggested that cognitive and emotional avoidance have important psychological and social consequences. These consequences, including reduced tolerance of emotional arousal and impoverishment of social contacts, serve to confirm underlying beliefs and to maintain the persistence of depression. The effect of avoidance on social adjustment generally in persistent depression has been confirmed (Hellerstein et al., 2000). A number of studies have begun to examine more specifically the role of avoidance in outcome of cognitive therapy for depression and in the processes underlying the persistence of depression.

The importance of avoidance in the outcome of cognitive therapy for depression was confirmed in a study by Kuyken et al. (2001). In a naturalistic study of 'real world' cognitive therapy, depressed patients who also had avoidant personality disorder were more symptomatic before therapy and had higher levels of residual symptoms afterwards. The degree of endorsement of avoidant beliefs predicted poorer outcome in cognitive therapy. Although causal inferences cannot be drawn from such a naturalistic study, the results are consistent with the possibility that avoidance is associated with persistence of depression in therapy and that cognitive therapy could be adapted to address avoidance and avoidant beliefs. The relative benefits of cognitive therapy in depressed patients with avoidant personality were suggested in an analysis of data from the large NIMH study (Elkin et al., 1989) of the treatment of depression. This study compared cognitive therapy, medication and interpersonal psychotherapy in the treatment of acute depression. In their analysis of data from the NIMH study, Barber and Muenz (1996) found that cognitive therapy tended to be more effective for avoidant patients whereas interpersonal therapy was more effective for obsessive patients.

Overgeneral Memory

A number of studies in the growing literature on basic psychological processes underlying the persistence of depression are consistent with these data on avoidance and the outcome of therapy. One factor that has attracted increasing attention in research in depression is overgeneral memory. Early studies (e.g. Moore et al., 1987) found that depressed patients have difficulty reporting memories for specific episodes when prompted to do so, and instead tend to recall more generic memories of kinds of event (e.g. whenever I go on holiday) or periods of time (e.g. when I was at college). Subsequent research has found that overgeneral memory predicts the persistence of depressive symptoms, both in naturalistic (Dalgleish et al., 2001) and therapeutic situations (e.g. Brittlebank et al., 1993). There is also evidence that cognitive therapy (Williams et al., 2000) and specific cognitive techniques (Watkins et al., 2000) can reduce levels of overgeneral memory. We argued in Chapter 1 that overgeneral memory should not be seen as a direct form of cognitive or emotional avoidance because it does not appear to be under conscious control. However, there is evidence that overgenerality is associated with avoidant processing styles generally and may specifically be associated with the avoidance of particularly upsetting memories, such as those of physical or sexual abuse (Kuyken & Brewin, 1996).

Rumination

Rumination is another factor that is emerging as central in the persistence of depression. Studies have found that rumination predicts the persistence of depressive symptoms in both clinical and non-clinical samples (e.g. Kuehner & Weber, 1999). Interestingly, rumination is also associated with overgeneral memory (Watkins & Teasdale, 2001). Ruminating over negative moods, characteristics or events may appear to represent the very opposite of cognitive avoidance. However, rumination may be a result of unsuccessful efforts that are intended to control or suppress unwanted thoughts or emotional activation. Clearly, more research is needed on the way that effortful cognitive strategies are used to try to suppress unpleasant emotions and how these strategies may in fact exert detrimental influences, for example through overgeneral memory and extreme dichotomous thinking. We may then be able to specify how people might use conscious awareness to facilitate rather than hinder the emotional processing of unpleasant information, both in therapy sessions and in patients' lives outside those sessions.

Positive Cognition and Well-Being

One further factor that is starting to receive more attention in research on persistence of depression is the role of positive experience (MacLeod and Moore, 2000). This builds on evidence that positive life events are associated with recovery from episodes of depression (Brown et al., 1992). However, it is not just the occurrence of positive events that is important, but also the way they are interpreted. For example, Johnson et al. (1998) found that reductions in depression and hopelessness in depressed patients were predicted by attributing positive events to internal, stable, global factors. Furthermore, Ilardi et al. (1997) found that adaptive attributions for positive events predicted lower likelihood of relapse in depressed patients, whereas attributions for negative events did not. This emerging evidence suggests the importance of considering the processing of positive information in combating the persistence of depression. Recent clinical models of chronic disorders have emphasised the importance of the weakness of schemas for processing positive information as well as the dominance of negative schemas. Recent developments in cognitive therapy, which we have incorporated in the approach described in this book, have recognised the importance in therapy of developing positive beliefs rather than just combating negative ones. Well-being therapy as described above is also consistent with this approach.

CLINICAL IMPLICATIONS OF RESEARCH FINDINGS

Cognitive therapy is now an established treatment for depression. The evidence from the approach described in this book lends further weight to its application in persistent depression. Cognitive therapy can promote further improvements in residual symptoms and can significantly lower the chances of relapse into full major depression. It is notable from a number of studies that the relapse preventive effects do not depend on cognitive therapy being the means whereby symptom reduction was obtained. In the CN study, the effects of therapy on relapse prevention were of greater magnitude than the effects on symptoms. A number of studies have demonstrated the relapse preventive effects of various forms of cognitive therapy in remitted patients who were free of significant levels of symptoms. One important implication of these findings is that the longer-term benefits of cognitive therapy do not necessarily depend on symptom reduction in therapy.

In the CN study, relapse prevention in cognitive therapy was associated with specific cognitive changes. However, these were not changes in patients' reported levels of negative cognitions. Rather, relapse prevention was associated with more subtle changes in the way patients processed information. Reductions in the extremity of patients' thinking and increases in their awareness of negative thoughts as thoughts were associated with reductions in the risk of relapse. A further implication of the findings is therefore that the long-term benefits of cognitive therapy may depend on subtle changes in the process of thinking rather than more obvious changes in its content. Refining our ideas of what kinds of cognitive change promote clinical benefits may help in identifying which aspects of therapy are most helpful in bringing those changes about. However, this is not an argument for abandoning standard techniques that were initially developed to help patients to change the negative content of their thinking. Paradoxically, it may yet be that techniques originally intended to bring about change in the content of cognition prove powerful in changing the process of cognition.

Tolerance of Uncertainty

These findings suggest that it might be difficult to detect readily when cognitive therapy is being beneficial and when it is not. Over the course of a number of sessions, a lack of apparent improvement in moderate levels of symptoms may disguise gradual and subtle benefits. Even during the course of a session, the apparent intransigence of a patient's thinking in the face of the therapist's best technical efforts may not mean that the patient has not benefited from the intervention. Some benefits of therapy may only become clear in the longer-term or may never become clear at all: it is impossible to know whether an individual patient would have done worse without therapy. This means that it is vital for therapists working with persistent depression to be able to tolerate uncertainty. Under these uncertain conditions, they must also be able to foster engagement from their patients. In a field previously proud of reducing uncertainty through a strong evidence base, these conclusions may seem to represent a backward step. However, it should be remembered that, in chronic depression, uncertainty is a step forward from hopelessness, and can be a precursor of engagement and satisfaction.

The approach to cognitive therapy described here included a number of adaptations of the standard approach first used to treat acute depression. The style and techniques of therapy are adapted to address the obstacles presented by enduring negative beliefs. It seems likely that other therapeutic approaches, such as CBASP, may also be of considerable benefit in persistent depression. Further research will be needed to identify the factors that may be common to the beneficial effects of different therapies in persistent depression and to ascertain whether particular approaches have unique benefits. The data currently available suggest that cognitive and emotional avoidance may be a particularly fruitful focus for cognitive therapy. The benefits of CBASP with particularly chronic patients and of interpersonal psychotherapy with patients with obsessive personalities suggests that an interpersonal focus might help to 'dislodge' the problems of particularly stuck or rigid patients. Whether it will ultimately be possible to adapt cognitive therapy to incorporate the benefits of alternative approaches remains an interesting question worthy of future investigation.

CONCLUSIONS

Throughout this book, we have characterised persistent depression according to the 'chronic cognitive triad' of low self-esteem, helplessness and hopelessness. The cognitive model suggests that these themes are manifested in the overt thoughts and behaviour of patients with persistent depression, but are also reflections of their underlying conditional and unconditional beliefs. These beliefs tend to be refractory to contradictory information. Furthermore, processes of behavioural, cognitive and emotional avoidance have both psychological and social effects that tend to confirm and entrench such beliefs. We have described how cognitive therapy attempts to address the overt thoughts, avoidance processes and beliefs of patients with persistent depression in order to progress towards goals of reducing symptoms, improving social functioning and decreasing vulnerability. The treatment of persistent depression requires consideration of a complex array of interacting factors. A number of factors emerge throughout the book as requiring such consideration, and we highlight some of these in this concluding section.

Gender

It is important when working with persistent depression to have some idea of the variety of different kinds of presentation. The gender of the patient can have important influences on a number of other variables. Female patients tend to be younger and experience more impairment in marital and social relations, whereas male patients tend to be older with more impairment in the realm of work (Kornstein et al., 2000). Clinical experience suggests that women with persistent depression tend to have more prominent concerns about inherent unacceptability, whereas concerns in men are more likely to revolve around weakness and the importance of emotional control. Familiarity with gender differences in presentation can be helpful, although some female patients can present in ways more typical of men, and vice versa.

Emotional Regulation

In working with acutely depressed patients, the use of standard cognitive therapy techniques within a satisfactory therapeutic relationship is usually sufficient to achieve adequate regulation of the patient's emotion. With persistent depression, regulation of emotion demands more of an explicit focus in order to engage the patient and to further therapeutic goals. It is an important early step to determine the relative contributions of emotional under- and over-regulation to the patient's problems and to conceptualise how these might relate to the patient's avoidance strategies and beliefs. The therapist may need actively to adjust the style of therapy, sometimes being more probing and at other times more directive, in order to turn up or down the emotional 'heat'. Helping the patient to identify and work towards levels of emotional experience that will help them to achieve their goals in therapy is often an implicit or explicit goal of therapy.

Interpersonal Focus

In adjusting the style of therapy, the therapist adjusts the role they adopt in relation to the patient within the therapeutic relationship. The therapist can usefully pay attention to the effect the patient is having on him or her, and draw the patient's attention to these effects. The negative effects, for example of the patient's passivity in the interpersonal relationship, can then be made part of therapy and related to the formulation of the depression. The positive reactions of the therapist, for example to emotionally laden disclosures by the patient, can be highlighted and compared to the negative expectations of the patient in either formal or spontaneous behavioural experiments. Focusing attention on interactions in the therapy session in this way can provide an immediacy of experience for the patient that can circumvent the operation of their habitual avoidance strategies. The therapist is then in a good position to provide immediate reinforcement of any signs of changes the patient makes that promote the goals of therapy. This approach is more personal than the collaborative but somewhat businesslike style that characterises the therapeutic interactions in acute depression, with its focus on problems outside the therapy session. The research described above tentatively suggests that an interpersonal focus in therapy may be particularly helpful in working with patients with rigid or obsessive personalities.

Importance of Therapists' Personal Qualities

The need to combine trusted therapeutic procedures with attention to the interpersonal relationship places extra demands on the therapist. The patient's belief that therapy will not work, their passivity and the resilience of their negative thinking can also be personally frustrating to the therapist whose remit is to facilitate change. Providing cognitive therapy for patients with persistent depression can therefore demand not only a high degree of technical competence, but also considerable reserves of patience, benevolence and tenacity on the part of the therapist. It is particularly important that the therapist's own resources in this respect are supplemented by appropriate professional support and clinical supervision.

Developing Positive Experiences

Another counterbalance to the frustration of working with entrenched negative beliefs is to bring the focus onto the development of positive experiences. The balance in therapy between countering negative experiences and fostering positive experiences needs frequent monitoring and revision. Whereas in acute depression, combating depressive symptoms can be expected to result in the re-emergence of positive experiences, in persistent depression kindling positive experiences usually requires more active intervention. Early in therapy, techniques with a positive focus, such as mastery and pleasure ratings, may be minimally successful. It often appears that some framework for managing negative experience has to have been negotiated before patients will allow themselves significant experience of positive emotions.

Adopting Appropriate Expectations for Outcomes

The unremittingly hopeless outlook of many patients with persistent depression, who often seem impervious to the therapist's efforts or to any sign that things can improve, can be contagious. If the therapist also becomes demoralised and hopeless, the chances of therapy making any impact are lessened. Some patients can be carried along for a while by the enthusiasm of the therapist, but become even more disillusioned when promised gains in therapy do not seem to materialise. In the face of the patient's hopelessness, it is important for the therapist to balance the respective dangers of expecting too much and expecting too little (Scott, 1998). As described above, the benefits of therapy in any particular case are likely to be uncertain. Any benefits of therapy emerge from engaging in the process of therapy despite this uncertainty. If the therapist can help the patient to move from a position of hopelessness to one of uncertainty, an important step has been taken. This can provide the basis for the patient subsequently considering the possibility of gaining some satisfaction in life.

Rising to the Challenge

We suspect that some of the frustration of working with this group of patients is evident on most, if not every, page of this book. We hope that another theme will also have emerged in the midst of all the frustration and hopelessness—that is, the joys of working with patients with persistent depression. The sheer complexity of patients' problems can spark curiosity. Even amidst the patients' protestations of complete unacceptability, a certain affection for them can emerge. In a background of bleak hopelessness, some small sign of progress can be truly satisfying. The outcome of cognitive therapy for patients with persistent depression still leaves much room for improvement. We hope that our descriptions of this work will provide some inspiration for therapists in carrying out their therapy. We also hope we will stimulate further improvements in our understanding of what will help patients with persistent depression. Thereby, these patients, and the therapists treating them, may be helped in realising greater fulfilment in their lives.

SUMMARY POINTS

- In the CN study of the treatment of residual depression, cognitive therapy resulted in some small improvements in symptoms and social functioning, over and above the effects of continued medication.
- Over a year's follow-up, cognitive therapy resulted in worthwhile reductions in the rate of relapse into full major depression.
- There was no evidence that standard measures of cognitive content mediated the reduction in relapse due to cognitive therapy.
- There was some evidence that cognitive therapy reduces extremity of thinking and increases meta-awareness of negative thinking, and that these changes are associated with the reduced rate of relapse.
- The Cognitive Behavioral Analysis System of Psychotherapy has produced particularly impressive results in a major study of the treatment of chronic depression.
- Other developments of cognitive therapy, including Mindfulness-Based Cognitive Therapy and Well-Being Therapy, have shown promising results, especially in the reduction of rates of relapse.
- A number of cognitive factors, including avoidance, overgeneral memory, rumination and positive cognition, merit further theoretical and therapeutic attention.
- The benefits of therapy may not always be easily or immediately discernible.
- In adapting standard cognitive therapy, we have ascribed particular importance to gender differences, emotional regulation, interpersonal focus, therapists' personal qualities and developing positive experiences.
- For patients and therapists, moving from hopelessness to uncertainty may represent an important step forward.

Appendix 1

MEET THE PATIENTS

Included here are brief biographies of each of the patients whose cases are discussed more than twice in the main text, where they are identified by their names being in italic. They are presented here in alphabetical order. For reasons of confidentiality, certain details have been changed and each patient described comprises features common to several different real people. However, we believe they remain typical of the range of patients presenting with persistent depression.

Catherine

Catherine is a 45-year-old married housewife. She has a 23-year-old son who lives at home and a 21-year-old daughter who has left home. She has been depressed since suffering a 'nervous collapse' five years ago, when she was unable to move for a day. At that time, she was investigated in hospital, and then transferred to a psychiatric ward for a few days when no physical pathology was identified. Since then she has suffered from at least moderate levels of depressive symptoms and has been treated by various mental health professionals. She complains of depressive symptoms including low mood, extreme fatigue, aching muscles, total loss of interest and inability to concentrate.

Catherine was reluctant to discuss details of her upbringing from the outset, as she believed it would be unnecessarily painful. As she believed her depression was due to some sort of damage to her brain or nerves, she thought that such discussion would serve no purpose. Some details of her background were available in her notes, and later in therapy she did discuss her background. Most important in this was the extremely unhappy marriage of her parents, which often involved violence. Catherine and her brother would cower in fear at their parents' fighting. Both parents were hostile and critical to the children, although reserved most of their physical violence for each other. Her mother left the home when Catherine was 9, which Catherine found terrifying, and came back several days later to collect the children. She described her adolescence as somewhat calmer. She continued to live with her mother and brother, and saw her father intermittently. Relationships with both parents improved, but she remained very wary of them and could not wait to leave home. She left school at 16 to work as a shop assistant, whereupon she also left home and went to live with some older friends. These friends introduced her to her husband, with whom she has a stable marriage. The stresses that seemed to contribute to the onset of her depression were some financial difficulties and her son getting into trouble for vandalism. Since she has become depressed, she has not worked and her husband does the vast majority of tasks around the home.

Dave

Dave is a 46-year-old married man with three children. He presents as a quietly spoken and reserved man, who first came into contact with psychiatric services four years ago, having seriously contemplated suicide. The trigger for this was the collapse of his business due to a recession, as a consequence of which his house had been repossessed and he had been declared bankrupt. At assessment, he described his main problems as low mood, anger and irritability, a loss of confidence in his abilities and marital disharmony. On the Beck Depression Inventory, Dave scored 24.

Dave was the eldest of six children born and raised in a mining village. He described a happy childhood with plenty of friends and lots of fun, particularly up to the age of 12. His family were not financially well off, but he described a caring and supportive relationship with both his parents and close bonds with his siblings. His father worked as a miner and his mother was a housewife who worked from home as a seamstress. Dave was academically able and was the only boy in his year at school to pass the 11+ and go to the Grammar School in a nearby town. This was seen as a great achievement in his family and he was encouraged to pursue this course. However, Dave found mixing with children from a more middle-class background daunting and perceived that he suffered discrimination at the hands of teachers as well as fellow pupils. His parents were unable to finance the extracurricular activities in which the other boys participated. He was also very conscious of his accent and made attempts to change this. Unfortunately, this backfired because at home in the village he would be ridiculed for being well spoken, so that Dave felt he didn't fit in anywhere. In addition, his academic performance was not as outstanding as it had been in the village school. This led to a loss of confidence and was the beginning of Dave seeing himself as not good enough. Dave left school at 16 with some academic qualifications. At first, he had no real direction in terms of career and over the next 10 years worked in a variety of jobs. At the age of 26, he set up his own business, which after 15 years of graft became very profitable. At the age of 30, Dave married and the couple had three children. He described being happy with his life until his business was hit by recession.

Elizabeth

Elizabeth is a 55-year-old married woman with three grown up children, who works as a secretary. She relates the onset of her difficulties to an incident at work three years ago, when she was ostracised for following company procedures that others flouted. She describes being depressed for much of the time since. At assessment, she described her main symptoms as low mood, disturbed sleep and impaired thinking, as shown by an inability to get all her work completed. Elizabeth scored 28 on the Beck Depression Inventory.

Elizabeth was an only child born and raised in a semi-rural village. Her father was a manager in a local company and her mother was a housewife. The family were financially comfortable compared to others in the village. Elizabeth described her childhood as lacking affection and very strict, with a strong emphasis on duty. Her mother in particular set high standards for Elizabeth in terms of decorum, dress and practical tasks. If Elizabeth failed to meet these standards, she would be chastised and often publicly shamed. Elizabeth passed the 11+ and attended the local Grammar School where she performed well. She had an ambition to train as a teacher. However, her mother forbade her to leave home, so she reluctantly attended secretarial college instead. Her mother also exerted control over her social life: she selected Elizabeth's friends, would not allow her to wear make-up or attend local dances and Elizabeth did not try alcohol until she was in her mid-thirties. At the age of 23, Elizabeth married a solicitor with whom she had been friendly for some years. From her mother's perspective she had done something right for once in her life. Elizabeth described her marriage as caring and supportive. She had three children, worked part-time as a secretary and became involved in charitable work. However, she had always felt unfulfilled in life. Although she believed that she had done all that was expected of her, she also continued to have difficulties dealing with her now elderly mother.

Graham

Graham is a 44-year-old, divorced man who has been retired from his career as a teacher on grounds of ill health. He first presented to mental health services six years ago, describing a problem of stress due to difficulty in adapting to changes in his role at work. He describes his main problems as tiredness, lack of structure to his day and a loss of direction in his life. He presents as a reserved but pleasant and thoughtful man, but also as bitter about being retired after years of devoted service to his job. At assessment for cognitive therapy, he scored 20 on the Beck Depression Inventory.

Graham was born and brought up in an affluent part of a city. He was an only child raised in a strict Church of England family. His father worked as a schoolteacher and his mother was a housewife who engaged in much charitable work for the local church. He described his childhood in positive terms but recognised there was a lack of overt affection, with an emphasis on giving time and thought to those less fortunate than himself. He described himself as a shy child who was easily embarrassed. Graham performed well at junior school and passed the 11+ in order to attend the local all boys Church of England Grammar School. Despite his shyness, Graham was able to make and sustain meaningful friendships with boys at school. At the age of 14, Graham rejected his religious upbringing and declared to himself that he was an atheist. However, he continued to attend church and church-based activities, as he felt unable to tell his parents of his decision. He achieved well academically and attended teacher training college. This was not a career he wished to pursue but was a decision taken on his behalf by his parents. From a sense of duty, Graham invested his self-esteem in this career. Graham had always been shy in the company of women and found mixing with them very difficult. He had his first relationship with a woman at age 25, and they married a year later. After they had been married for only two months, his wife left him. From this point onwards, Graham avoided relationships with women and devoted himself to his work until he encountered the difficulties leading to his depression.

Jean

Jean is a 30-year-old unmarried woman with four children, aged 13, 11, 8 and 5. She is currently in a relationship with a man who is not the father of her children and has a history of violence and criminality. She has been depressed and receiving treatment for the last two years, since the end of her previous, more satisfactory relationship. Jean describes her main symptoms as tiredness, lack of motivation and low mood. She presents as talkative, eager to please and, to a large degree, downplays her problems. Her Beck Depression Inventory score on assessment was 25.

Jean was born and raised in an inner city area and was the older of two children. Her father was disabled as a result of an industrial accident when Jean was 3 years old. As a result of his disability, Jean's mother worked full time in a local factory. Jean described her early childhood as happy, achieving normal milestones and performing well at school. She reported no difficulties until the age of 12, when her mother expected Jean to take on responsibility for the physical care of her father and certain household tasks. At this time, her performance at school deteriorated and Jean began to play truant. At the age of 15, she became involved in a relationship with an older man, who was renowned in the area for his violence and criminal activity. After six months, she became pregnant and by the age of 18 had two children. Her relationship with her partner was characterised by physical violence towards herself but not their children, and she left him when she was 19. Over the next five years Jean then had two further relationships with men with antisocial tendencies having a child with each of them. When she was 27, Jean embarked on a relationship with a man who ran his own business and was reliable, caring and supportive. They were together for a year before he ended the relationship because he felt unable to take on her children. It was at this point in her life that Jean became depressed and presented to psychiatric services.

Julie

Julie is a 42-year-old married woman with five children from a previous marriage. She has been treated for depression for much of the last seven years. Prior to this, she experienced two serious life events, her divorce and a serious illness requiring surgery. At assessment, she was tearful and angry, and identified her only problem as things going wrong in her life. On the Beck Depression Inventory, she scored 38.

Julie was the youngest of 10 siblings born and raised in an inner city area. Her father worked sporadically, drank heavily and was physically violent towards her mother and the older siblings. Julie recalls her parents as largely absent in her life and she was raised by her eldest sister. Her sister was resentful of this responsibility and left Julie to her own devices, so that she was forced to fend for herself most of the time. She had one or two close friends, but described herself as a shy and quiet child who disliked school. She experienced teachers as critical and judgemental and was bullied by her peers, all of which she attributed to her father's bad reputation. She played truant a good deal of the time from the age of 13 and left school at the age of 15 without any qualifications. She worked in a local shop and soon became involved with a man 15 years her senior. After they were married, he soon became physically violent, but she stayed in the marriage at her mother's insistence. Despite physical and sexual violence, Julie stayed with her husband for 15 years and had five children. At the age of 33, with some difficulty Julie divorced her husband, shortly after which she required surgery for bowel problems. It was at age 35 that Julie first became depressed and came into contact with psychiatric services. Around this time, Julie met and married her current husband. While he was not physically abusive, he soon took responsibility for all household tasks and insisted that Julie spend all her time in his company. Her depression worsened as she continued to experience various life events, culminating in the repossession of her house and her 14-year-old son being detained in a remand centre.

Kate

Kate is a 29-year-old single mother with two children, aged 6 and 3. She is un-employed, having had a succession of different jobs, and is not in a relationship, having had a succession of relationships, some of them abusive. She describes hav-ing had spells of depression for as long as she can remember. From her account and her medical records, at least six depressive episodes could be identified since her first contact with psychiatric services at 16. She has been depressed for most of the last two years, with only brief spells of feeling better. Although when she was seen for her cognitive therapy assessment she reported only minimal symptoms, only two weeks earlier she had reported a 'full house' of depressive symptoms to her psychiatrist. When depressed, her symptoms include low mood, anxiety, fatigue, loss of interest, guilt, poor concentration and urges to self-harm.

Kate was born to parents who were financially well off and has one younger brother. Her father was a successful businessman, who she described as moody and unpredictable at home. She remembers him as highly critical of her, especially in comparison to her younger brother who was clearly his favourite. She received occasional beatings, sometimes with a belt. She got on better with her mother, who nevertheless often chided her for upsetting her father. Her father left home when she was 9 for another woman, after which Kate was told by her mother that her father did not love her. In the following years, Kate described her mother as often 'being in a state' and felt that she often got the blame for upsetting her. Her mother had become very upset over Kate's first boyfriend when she was 15, and had been to see the boy's parents in outrage at the possibility of some sexual activity. Kate did well at school until the age of 15, and got good grades in her 'O' levels despite prob-ably suffering from her first episode of depression. However, she left school just before taking her 'A' levels, probably due to her depression. After leaving school, she had a range of jobs, mainly as a secretary or in hotels, the longest of which was for two years. Most of her relationships with men were also short-lived, and she remembered none of them with any affection. The longest of these was with the father of her children, with whom she lived for two separate periods. During each of these times, she became pregnant and had to move out after the birth of each child due to her partner's violence towards her. Since the second of these occasions two years ago, she has had intermittent relationships with men friends and has not worked.

Marion

Marion is a 54-year-old divorced woman who describes having been depressed over much of the last 30 years. Her depressive symptoms have worsened over the past 12 months in response to her eldest son leaving home. As a result, she has become unable to continue in her job as a cleaner. At assessment, Marion presented as anxious and utterly hopeless. Her mood was flat and answers to questions were monosyllabic. She had no structure to her day and no social contact. Marion scored 40 on the Beck Depression Inventory.

Marion was born and raised in a seaside town. She was the youngest of three children in a family characterised by physical and emotional abuse. Her father was a labourer in the building trade and had longstanding problems of drinking and gambling. As a consequence, the family was often in debt and Marion had vivid memories of the family hiding from debtors who came to the door. On occasions, they had to go without food due to lack of money. When her father was at home, he was often drunk and physically violent towards her mother and her elder two brothers, although not to Marion herself. Her mother would keep Marion with her at all times and would frequently use Marion to protect herself from her husband's rage. Marion recalls her mother being depressed during most of her childhood. She often had to care for her mother emotionally, as well as performing household tasks. Marion's education was disrupted as a result. She had few friends and found it difficult to mix with others. Her erratic school attendance meant that she did not perform well academically and left at age 15 without any qualifications. She secured work in a local factory. At the age of 17, Marion became involved with an older man and married him in order to escape her home life. She stated that she never really cared for him but saw him as her only chance of escaping her parents. She had two children with this man, who several months into their marriage had become physically and sexually abusive. At the age of 25, Marion left her husband. It was at this point in her life that she first sought help from mental health services. Over the course of the next 25 years, Marion experienced repeated episodes of depression. Treatment involved numerous antidepressants, electroconvulsive therapy, social work input, assessment for Formal Psychotherapy (for which her problems were deemed unsuitable) and long-term support from Community Psychiatric Nurses. Over this time, Marion felt that she had never made a complete recovery from her illness. She had one further relationship with a man who was controlling and sexually abusive.

Peter

Peter is a 54-year-old married man. His problems started some eight years ago, when the local company for whom he worked was taken over by a large multinational. This led to redundancies, which Peter had to implement. He found this unbearable and took sick leave with anxiety and depression. Four years later, after two attempts at returning to work, Peter was retired against his wishes on the grounds of ill health. Following this, his depression worsened significantly and has barely improved since. At assessment, he described his main problems as social withdrawal, anxiety when going out during the day, loss of purpose to his life and a deep sense of shame that he has become depressed. He experienced a great deal of difficulty talking about his problems. He attributed this to the humiliation he felt about crying, which occurred whenever he attempted to discuss his illness. Peter scored 32 on the Beck Depression Inventory.

Peter was born and raised in Scotland. His father worked in a factory, his mother was a housewife and he had two younger sisters. He described his childhood as normal for the area, in that he was raised to work hard and respect his elders. He described his father as his main role model in life. Peter mixed well socially both at home and at school, and was above average in his academic performance.

However, he saw his real achievements as being his many prizes and accolades in sports, including athletics, football and cricket. When he left school at 15, Peter was given the opportunity to undergo trials for a professional football team, but saw this as an unreliable source of income. Instead, he secured an apprenticeship in a local company where he remained for 30 years. During this time, Peter worked his way up the ranks from the shop floor to a management position, an achievement in which he took great pride. He got married in his early twenties and the couple had four children. He took his responsibilities as husband and father very seriously and believed it was his role to provide materially for the family. He was also heavily involved in social activities, including a running club and football team. When he reached 40, Peter decided to make financial provision to retire early and implemented a plan that would enable him to stop work at the age of 55. This plan was curtailed by his depression.

Rosemary

Rosemary is a 48-year-old woman in her second marriage. She has three children who have all now left home and are doing well. She has been on sick leave from her job as an administrator for nearly a year. She has had two previous episodes of depression, both of which responded to treatment. On this occasion, she has been depressed for about two years, since one of her daughters was seriously ill in hospital. Although the daughter made a full recovery, Rosemary has remained depressed ever since. She presents as reluctant to talk about her depression, but admits to low mood, prominent guilt, and suicidal thoughts. Her Beck Depression Inventory score at assessment was 30.

Rosemary was an only child from a middle-class background. From her account, because her father had problems with drinking and gambling, her mother worked full time as a nurse. She did not get on well with her mother, who was strict and bad-tempered, but was closer to her father. She spent most of her childhood in the care of her grandparents, as her mother was often working and her father unreliable. She described her grandparents as kind to her, but she always knew that they were doing her a favour to look after her. As a result, she always felt obliged to help them in any way she could with various chores. Rosemary also worked hard at school, but did not have close friends, as she felt unable to invite anyone home. She went to college, where she suffered her first depressive episode, and since then has worked in various administrative positions. She got married in her early twenties, had three children and was happy for some years. However, her marriage deteriorated due to her husband's heavy drinking, which left the family on the brink of financial ruin. After she divorced her husband, she became depressed but managed to return to work and provide for her family. She has since married again to a man she finds kind and reliable, and is confused by her inability to pull herself out of her depression.

Stan

Stan is a 58-year-old married man who was made redundant from his job as an office worker two years ago. He has two daughters, who are both married with children. He finds it hard to say how long he has been depressed, as he describes having had some feelings of depression for most of his life. He has received treatment for depression over the last four years. His main symptoms are lack of interest, tiredness, aching muscles and poor memory. At assessment for cognitive therapy, his score on the Beck Depression Inventory was 20.

Stan was the youngest of three children born to a poor family in a small town. His father worked in a factory and his mother was a housewife. He described both his parents as kind, but was not close to them. Although the family did not have much money, there were never any difficulties at home, as everyone just got on with what they had to do. At school, Stan had some friends, but also remembered being teased a great deal. He pretended not to be bothered by this and did not talk about it. He performed averagely at school and left at the age of 16 for a job in the offices of the local council. He believed this was expected of him (as it had been of his older siblings), so that he would not continue to place a financial burden on his parents. He married his first serious girlfriend at the age of 19, and described his marriage as satisfactory, although he admitted to finding his wife rather bossy. He could report little incident in his life since then until being made redundant from his job.

Appendix 2

HANDOUTS FOR PATIENTS

These handouts are copyright © 2003 Richard G. Moore and Anne Garland but may be photocopied without permission for use in therapy

Handout 1

COGNITIVE THERAPY

Using Cognitive Therapy to Treat Your Depression

What is depression?

Most of us suffer from spells of low mood from time to time when things are not going our way. However, clinical depression is different from these ordinary low spells. Firstly, the low mood is usually much more *intense* in clinical depression. Secondly, these feelings go on for *longer* than an ordinary low patch, sometimes for months at a time. Finally, depression does not just affect your mood. The physical *symptoms* of depression include difficulty sleeping, feeling tired all the time, changes in weight or appetite, and becoming physically slowed down or agitated.

Thinking in depression

The basic principle of cognitive therapy is that our emotional reactions such as sadness, anxiety, guilt and anger result, not only from situations in themselves, but also from the view we take of them. People who are depressed tend to see themselves and their lives in a very *negative* way. For example, imagine that two men, John and Peter, who have both been doing the same job at the same place, are made redundant.

John may think:

'Oh dear! How am I going to fill my time? I must have a job. Life has no purpose without one. Now there's no point getting out of bed in the mornings.'

After a time John may start to feel quite depressed as he contemplates his predicament.

Meanwhile, Peter on receiving his redundancy notice may think:

'Thank goodness! I never have to go to that place again and do that boring job. What a relief to get away.'

Peter may feel relieved and quite happy with his new found circumstances.

John and Peter are experiencing the same event or situation but have reacted differently. What is the reason for their differing reactions? To simplify a complex process, it is to do with our thoughts about ourselves, other people and the world in general. If people get depressed, negative thoughts can come to mind in everyday situations.

The cognitive model of depression

The basic idea can be illustrated using the model in Figure A.1. This was devised by a cognitive therapist called Christine Padesky and is a way to try and understand problems like depression.

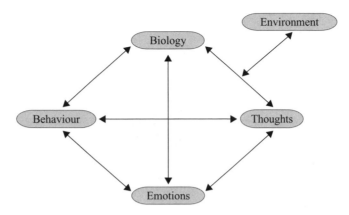

Figure A.1

There are four aspects to ourselves, which are inter-related: thoughts, behaviour, biology and emotions. In addition we live in and interact with the world around us, the environment. The environment we live in includes our family or the people around us, our work situation and the community. We are all affected by both our current environment (e.g. work stress, family tensions) and our past environment (e.g. childhood experiences).

Because all these areas are inter-related, even small changes in any one of them will produce changes in other areas. To try and illustrate this further, let's return to John and Peter.

When John wakes up, he no longer has a job to go to, his ENVIRONMENT has changed.

He lies in bed feeling tired and lethargic, he seemingly has no energy. (BIOLOGY)

He feels sad and despondent. (EMOTION)

As John dwells on his predicament he thinks: 'There is no point in getting up, there is nothing to do, no job to go to, life is meaningless.' (THOUGHT)

John may as a result stay in bed. (BEHAVIOUR)

Several hours later John's further thoughts may be: 'Look at me, I'm still in bed. This is terrible. I'm just being lazy. I should be working. Perhaps if I'd tried harder I'd still have a job. It's all my fault, I'm pretty useless really, I've let everyone down.' (THOUGHT)

John may continue to be inactive and stay in bed (BEHAVIOUR) paralysed by thoughts of how hopeless his situation is and how worthless he seems.

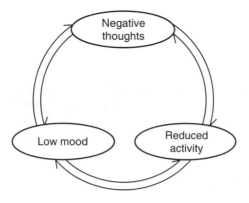

Figure A.2

The downward spiral

A vicious circle can be established which can drag your mood right down. The worse you feel, the more likely it is that negative thoughts will come to mind and the more believable they will seem. The more you believe this bleak way of seeing things, the worse you feel. Further, the worse you feel, the less likely it is that you will do things that might help you to feel better. As you find it harder to do things, you may see this as further evidence of laziness and inadequacy, so cranking the vicious circle round a further turn, as shown in Figure A.2.

Types of negative thinking

To break these vicious circles, we have to find out which negative thoughts are feeding them. Many negative thoughts are *automatic* and just pop up into your mind with no reason. Many such *negative automatic thoughts* (NATs) relate to the particular situation you are in at the time. Other thoughts in depression are more general *beliefs* which you may have held for some time. These beliefs may maintain the

	Types of negative thinking	Example: John
NEGATIVE AUTOMATIC THOUGHTS	Occur in specific situations. Pop into your head without any effort on your part. Often exaggerated and you don't think to question them.	'There's no point in getting up.' 'Life is meaningless.' 'I'm useless.' 'I've let everyone down.'
BELIEFS	Rules we develop as individuals that govern our behaviour in a variety of situations.	'Unless I am productive, then I won't be respected and people will reject me.'
	Fundamental beliefs about ourselves or others, which we accept as facts.	'I am worthless.' 'Other people are critical.'

depression and show up in how you think, how you feel and how you behave in different situations.

The aims of cognitive therapy

Cognitive therapy is a talking therapy which aims to help you to identify and question the negative thoughts contributing to your depression. These negative thoughts tend to *seem* completely believable. But plausible though they seem, they can be unrealistic and unhelpful. By identifying negative thoughts in particular situations and then trying to tackle behaviours and thoughts it is possible to improve how you feel.

Usually we just accept that what we think is true, but in depression it is important to catch the negative thoughts. To see how accurate each thought is, it is helpful to look at the *evidence* for that idea. When depressed, you tend to see only the facts which support a negative view (e.g. the mistake) and overlook any positive things about you or what you have. It is important also to examine any facts which would support a more positive view (e.g. the times you did it right). When this balance is introduced, the negative thought may seem less powerful and a *less negative conclusion* may seem more probable (e.g. Everyone makes mistakes when they are in a hurry). This approach can suggest different ways of handling the upsetting situation: there may be a course of action which would improve your mood or start to solve the problem.

Don't worry if these ideas seem complicated at first. An important part of treatment is to try and understand your depression, where it comes from and how it affects you at the present time. Your therapist will work with you over a number of weeks at trying to identify these patterns—this handout is just the initial introduction that you and your therapist will continue to build on.

The practicalities of receiving cognitive therapy

There are usually about 16–20 sessions of therapy over a period of about six months. It is helpful if sessions are weekly at the start of therapy and then spaced out nearer the end of therapy. Each session will last an hour. As the therapy aims to look at ways you can help yourself, what you do between sessions is very important. Your therapist will discuss with you things that it might be helpful for you to do, for example, making a note of things you have done or what went through your mind at the times you felt at your worst. You are also encouraged to let your therapist know how you are finding therapy, so that together you can find out which things are most helpful to you.

Handout 2

AUTOMATIC THOUGHTS

How to Become Aware of Your Automatic Thoughts

The aim in cognitive therapy is to reduce the effect of your negative thoughts on how you feel. The first step is to recognise these thoughts.

What are negative automatic thoughts (NATs)? Negative automatic thoughts are:

1. *Negative:* they make you feel even worse about yourself (e.g. I'm useless) and your life (e.g. It's all hopeless). They also stop you from helping yourself (e.g. There's no point).
2. *Automatic:* they just pop up into your mind, you don't decide to think them. In fact, you may find it hard not to think them, as they are like a habit.
3. *Believable:* they seem to be right. They seem to be facts and you will tend to accept them.
4. *Biased:* although they seem right, they are likely to be distorted or inaccurate. They may have some support from how you feel or things that have happened, but ignore many other facts which do not fit such a negative view.

How to catch NATs. This will be quite hard at first. They may have become a habit or you may think that they are not thoughts but reality. To learn to catch these thoughts:

1. *Use your feelings* as a cue. Whenever you notice feeling upset or your mood takes a downturn, ask yourself 'What was going through my mind just then?'
2. Look out for *pictures* as well as words. Sometimes the NATs take the form of pictures or images in your mind's eye. It is important to watch out for these images.
3. If you seem to be upset by an *event* rather than a thought, ask 'How did I view this situation?' or 'What did this mean to me?'

Counting NATs. With breaking any habit, catching yourself at it is the first hurdle. Counting the thoughts is one way of doing this. At first, 'tuning in' to the negative things you are saying to yourself can make you feel bad. However, you will soon find that you are more able to *stand back* from them. Try to catch and observe them as they come to mind. You might try putting *ticks* on a piece of paper or card, or counting them using a golf or knitting *counter*. Then you can easily see how many you had that day. At first, the daily tally will go up as you get better at catching them.

Writing down your NATs. The best way to become aware of your NATs is to write them down. It is best to do this as soon as you notice your mood going down. However, sometimes it may be necessary just to make a mental note and jot it down later. You may find that some thoughts come to mind over and again. Sometimes, just catching them and jotting them down can take out some of the sting or help you see things differently. At other times, you will need to use the ways of answering back these thoughts that you will learn during therapy.

Beware:... There are a number of *reasons or excuses* for not catching or writing down your thoughts. It may seem like a lot of *effort* when you are already finding it hard to cope. You may worry that writing the thoughts will only make you feel worse. You may think that it is *stupid* having such thoughts. Although identifying NATs may involve effort and upset at first, remember that *it will get easier with practice*. On the other hand, not tackling these thoughts leaves them free to bother you just as much in the future. There is no pain free way of overcoming depression, but as your skills improve, *your efforts will help you to feel better*.

How to Question Your Automatic Thoughts

Negative thoughts will come to mind when you feel low and will make you feel worse. However, the more you practise standing back and questioning your thoughts, the less they will affect the way you feel. Catching and answering these thoughts in your head is the eventual goal. However, to begin with, most people find that the negative thoughts come back and wipe out the 'answers'. If you **write your answers down,** they are there in black and white even if the automatic thought does come back. The more practice you get at answering your thoughts on paper, the easier you will find it to talk back to them. Try the following steps:

- Was your thinking **biased** in a negative way? Which of the **thinking errors** (all-or-nothing thinking, overgeneralising, etc.) did you make?

- What is the **evidence** for the thought? What are the facts? Is the thought based on facts? Are there any facts which go against it? Would it stand up in court?

- What are the **alternative explanations?** How would someone else see the situation? How would you see it if it was someone else? Or in a year's time? Taking into account all the facts, would another viewpoint fit better?

- What is the **effect** of thinking this way? Are you just making yourself more depressed? Will this view help you to overcome the problems you are facing? Would another way of seeing things help you to act in the way you would like?

- How can you **test out** the accuracy of this thought? How did/would the situation actually turn out? What further information could help you find out which view fits best?

- To the extent the thought is true, what **action** can you take? What can you do to improve things? How could you change the situation? Could you make it less of a problem for yourself? How could you improve your skill at dealing with it?

Remember: Finding convincing answers to your negative thoughts will be difficult at first. The more **practice** you give yourself, the better. Sometimes you may be too upset to find answers to negative thoughts. If so, write the thoughts down and come back to them later on when you are feeling calmer. Beware of finding excuses for not bothering with all this. If you ignore the thoughts, they will continue to upset you just the same. By putting in the effort to question them, you will gradually help yourself feel better.

What Thinking Errors Are You Making?

When you are depressed, your thoughts about yourself, your life and the future may all contain negative biases or errors. These biases distort your thinking and make you feel worse.

1. All-or-nothing thinking You see things as black or white with nothing in between. If what you do is not perfect, it is a failure, e.g. 'I made two mistakes in that letter—it was a total failure', 'I didn't get all the shopping I wanted—it was a waste of time'.

2. Mental filter You single out anything negative and dwell on it, ignoring any positive factors. You see only your shortcomings, e.g. You make a nice dinner but overcook one vegetable and conclude the whole dinner is a disaster. You think only about the mistakes you have made and so see your life as a string of failures.

3. Overgeneralisation Having singled out one or more negatives, you see them as a general pattern of disaster, e.g. 'I made a mistake—I can never do a thing right', 'This argument proves nobody likes me'.

4. Labelling You call yourself unpleasant names which seem to sum you up. These are based on one or two negative occurrences, ignore everything else about you and may imply many faults you don't have, e.g. 'I'm a failure' or 'I'm a wimp'.

5. Disqualifying the positive Even if you do become aware of positive facts, you find a way to discount them, e.g. 'I did manage to get some things done, but anyone would have done it', 'I enjoyed going out, but I only felt down again afterwards'.

6. Exaggeration or **Catastrophisation** You magnify any shortcomings until they seem like unforgivable faults and magnify any mishaps until they seem like total disasters, e.g. after making a stupid sounding comment at a meeting, you think you made a complete fool of yourself and it was awful/terrible.

7. Jumping to conclusions You see things as negative whether or not you have any facts. You assume special powers to tell how badly people are thinking of you **(mind reading)** or what is going to go wrong in the future **(crystal ball gazing/ fortune telling)**, e.g. 'If I go to that party, no-one will like me', 'I'm going to be sacked'.

8. Personalisation If something bad happens, you assume that it was your fault, ignoring other more likely causes, e.g. 'The kids were behaving badly today—I must be a bad mother', 'It was all my fault that mum was upset'.

9. Should statements You make rules for yourself which you have little chance of sticking to, especially when you are low, and make you feel guilty. These reflect high standards for yourself which you would not expect of others—a double standard, e.g. 'I ought to have achieved more than this', 'I should not upset people'.

10. Emotional reasoning Because you feel bad, you assume that things really are bad. Your negative feelings lead you to confuse your thoughts with facts, e.g. 'I feel guilty so I must have done something wrong'.

Handout 3

RELAPSE PREVENTION

Becoming Your Own Cognitive Therapist

As the end of therapy approaches, you are likely to have some worries about finishing the sessions. If you have found the sessions very helpful, you may start to worry about coping without your therapist's help or about the possibility of the depression returning. If you are still facing significant problems or symptoms, the prospect of being left to face those problems without your therapist's help can be distressing. An important aim of the therapy sessions in the closing stages of treatment is to help you to cope once treatment has ended. Most people who are recovering from depression will face some unpleasant situations or experience some depressive symptoms in the months after therapy ends. By practising the techniques discussed in therapy, you can learn to cope better with these problems. Managing to get through these setbacks can even help to give you more confidence that you can gradually learn to overcome the depression.

To put into practice the things you have learned in the therapy sessions, you will need to become your own cognitive therapist. To do this, there are four main areas to work on:

  (i) Making time regularly to put therapy into practice.
 (ii) Identifying danger signs.
(iii) Developing a plan for coping with setbacks.
(iv) Continuing to improve your confidence and self-esteem.

Regular Practice

Why?

As with any new skill, the skills you have learned in coping with depression will need to be practised regularly. Regular practice can help to build up good habits (e.g. in the way you think or the things you do) that can lessen the chances of depression. It can also make you more confident that you have some tools for dealing with the depression whenever it starts to arise. During times you feel well, it may be tempting to 'shelve' the therapy as you may think that you don't need to do it. During times you feel depressed, it may be tempting to 'shelve' the therapy as you may think you are unable to face it. It is better to get into the habit of regularly making use of the skills you have developed, even when things are going well. That way, you will be better able to use these techniques when difficulties come up.

What?

The biggest question is that of what skills it is most important to practise. The answer is often found through reviewing the therapy sessions and homework tasks to find out which techniques were the most helpful. The most common things are:

- Catching potential downturns either before they occur or as soon as possible
- Using strategies for dealing with low mood or difficult situations
- Working to develop your confidence and self-esteem

These will be considered in detail below. Remember that it is often best to practice what you have learned on minor, even trivial, upsets or problems rather than waiting for something major to come up where you need to use the therapy.

When?

It is most helpful to set aside a regular time to think about therapy. Many people are put off by thinking this must be a major enterprise. Remember that it is much better to do a little often. Five minutes a day (or even two) is in most cases more helpful than half an hour a week. It can help to link this to an activity that you do regularly, so that you don't forget, e.g. a mealtime or before you clean your teeth. Once you have got into this habit, you may find that there are things you want to spend more time on. You can then set aside a time for a longer self-therapy session. Many factors, such as children or work commitments, can thwart the best intentions to practice the therapy. Therefore, it is important for you to identify a time when you will be free to do your self-therapy and are unlikely to be interrupted.

Where?

It can be helpful to plan where you will actually do your self-therapy practice. Most people find it best to do it in their own space at home (e.g. their favourite armchair or in their bedroom). Some people find it best to use some of the techniques in the situation where they are most useful. For example, one man found it really helpful to write down answers to his negative thoughts about his work whilst actually sitting at his desk.

Identifying Danger Signs

To prevent the depression returning, try to take action before it has taken a hold. This way, a spell of major depression can be 'nipped in the bud'. Sometimes it is possible to spot a situation where you may be at risk of taking a downturn before it happens. At other times, you can catch the earliest signs or symptoms of the depression beginning to come back. You can then take steps to limit the damage.

Identifying and preparing for high-risk situations

If you are prepared for particular difficult situations, they are less likely to drag you right down. Forewarned is forearmed! It can be helpful to think back over times in the past when your mood has gone down. Use these to try and identify what might be high-risk situations for you. For some people, the worst situations might be arguments at home, for others it might be things piling up at work and so on. Look at the coming weeks and months to see when you are most likely to be at risk from similar situations cropping up. Try asking yourself:

- What can I do, if anything, to prevent this from happening?
- Did I do anything that helped me to cope with this when it happened before?
- What can I do to cope next time this happens?

Identifying early warning symptoms

Occasional spells of low mood are part of ordinary life for most people. It is important to notice when an ordinary dip is in danger of becoming a more serious depression. From considering past spells of depression, it is often possible to recognise the early signs of depression. Some typical early signs are:

- excessive tiredness or disrupted sleep
- starting to put off tasks, such as paying bills
- avoiding people that you usually like to see.

Try to identify if there are any telltale signs that you need to be alert to. You can then take steps to prevent a dip becoming a relapse.

Coping with Setbacks

In recovering from depression, things are unlikely to go smoothly all the time. Hopefully, you will have periods of feeling much better. You may also have times when the depression strikes back and leaves you wondering if it was all worth it. Although it may be tempting to give up the fight, remember that these setbacks are a normal part of recovering from depression. It is possible to overcome these setbacks and to see that your ability to deal with them is gradually increasing. You can use your experiences in therapy to develop a plan for how to handle them. This *action plan* may include some of the following guidelines.

(i) Catch thoughts and behaviours that may make you feel worse

In therapy, you will have talked about how vicious circles can make your depression spiral downwards. Try to stop yourself from:

- *Catastrophising any dips:* When you have a setback it is common to think that this is the start of things going badly wrong. The chances are it will be a minor dip or 'blip' followed by a return to your previous level of coping.
- *Blaming yourself:* When people are depressed, they often become very critical of themselves. Remind yourself that self-criticism will only make you feel even worse. Instead of calling yourself weak or pathetic, try to view this setback with a bit of sympathy and help yourself through it.
- *Giving up:* When you feel depressed it can be tempting to put off things you have to do or give up even trying to help yourself feel better. You may just feel like staying in bed, or brooding over how bad you feel or how badly you have handled things. Again, catch yourself before this gets too much of a hold and remind yourself that this will only make you feel worse. Sure, give yourself a rest if you need it, but then see if you can try any of the following suggestions for getting going with the therapy again.

(ii) Try to keep busy... but not too busy

Inactivity and the brooding that goes with it will make you feel worse. Therefore try to keep going with some of the easier things you were going to do. If it helps, use an hour by hour diary sheet to plan your day. Watch out too for going to the other extreme of overdoing it. Keeping so busy that you have no time to think or feel can be tempting, but in the end will make you feel exhausted and low. So allow for the fact that things take more effort when you are depressed and make sure to plan some rest or relaxation.

(iii) Make plans for getting some pleasure

You may think that you don't deserve anything good until you have done all the things you have to do. This will make you feel more overwhelmed. By making a point of doing some things that you enjoy and noting any pleasure you get, you can help lift your mood a little. You will then be more able to face things you have to do.

(iv) If it's too much... break it down

When you are depressed many things can seem too much to face, even things you normally do without difficulty. It may be possible to put some of these off until you feel better. For the things that you have to do, try to break them down into small steps. Then attempt just one step at a time, giving yourself a break or reward when you have managed each step.

(v) Catch and question your negative automatic thoughts

Sometimes it is tempting to try not to think about things and to block out unpleasant thoughts. It is often more helpful to identify and catch negative thoughts. You can watch out for any familiar culprits that you discussed during therapy sessions. Remind yourself these are thoughts and not gospel truth. It can help to imagine what your therapist would say about them or what a friend would say. Thoughts are often easier to answer once you have written them down. Use thought sheets or handouts from your therapy sessions to see if you can get any new angles on the situation.

(vi) Have your old beliefs been triggered... what would your new ones say?

Dips in mood are often a sign that negative beliefs have been triggered, perhaps even ones you have held since you were little. You may well have discussed these in therapy sessions. If so, see if you can recognise which of your beliefs have been set off. If you have started to work on new beliefs, ask yourself what they would have to say about this latest setback.

(vii) Get some support or help

Feeling depressed can itself make you feel alone or isolated. Worse, you may become reluctant to contact people. You may be surprised how well some people react if you ask them for some support or help. This may be of a practical kind (looking after your children for an hour; advising you on a work problem) or may be emotional support (listening to how you have been feeling). Either way, support is one of the things that has been shown to help people through depression.

(viii) Give it time

Helping yourself may seem daunting and you may want to just flake out for a time first. Even when you start, the things you try will seem difficult and improvements may be small at first. Remember that, given time and effort, setbacks can gradually be overcome.

Improving Your Confidence and Self-esteem

Even when the main symptoms of the depression have improved, many people are left not feeling very good about themselves. General lack of confidence or low self-esteem can provide fertile ground for the seeds of depression. Therefore, it is important to carry on working to improve how you feel about yourself once therapy has finished. This often involves recognising some of your characteristic ways of thinking and behaving. In therapy, you may have discussed how these can feed on negative beliefs about yourself and your life. Trying very gradually to test out new patterns of thinking and acting can over the weeks and months help you to build new beliefs. The main ways of doing this are:

(i) Noticing things that fit a new view

If you have held a negative belief (e.g. I am incompetent) for a long time, you have probably stopped noticing things that do not fit with it (e.g. things you did okay). It can be helpful actively to look out for any signs, however small, that fit with a different view (e.g. I am capable). These can be written in a daily diary or 'belief log'. In this way, you can build up a body of evidence to support your new view. You will also get into the habit of noting the better things about you and your life, where before you only paid attention to shortcomings.

(ii) Doing things to test out a new view or put it into practice

Certain ways of acting can prevent you from developing new views about yourself. For example, if you want to see yourself as likeable you may try to achieve this by being nice to people all the time (e.g. always agreeing with the views of others or doing what they want you to do). People will indeed like you, but you may come to think that they like you only because you do what they want. This can undermine your confidence that they like you for who you really are. Testing out new ways of acting can help you to build up a new view. In this case, sometimes doing or saying what you want could help you to realise that some people do still like you. This could help you to believe that you really are likeable. As another example, doing some things without overpreparing for them can help you to see that you really are competent. You can discuss with your therapist what kinds of new activity might gradually help you to build up a more positive view of yourself. Once the therapy has finished, it is important that you keep putting these new activities into practice.

Develop Your Own Plan

This handout contains some ideas on how to cope once the therapy sessions end. Some of this may be confusing or unclear at the moment. If you have any questions, make sure to discuss them with your therapist. He or she can then help you to develop an individual plan. This can be tailor-made to address your particular problems and fit in with your lifestyle. The more you can remember to put the therapy into practice, the more it will become second nature and the less chance the depression will have of gaining the upper hand. Good luck!

REFERENCES

Akiskal, H.S., Hirschfeld, R.M.A. & Yerevanian, B.I. (1983). The relationship of personality to affective disorders: a critical review. *Archives of General Psychiatry*, **40**, 801–810.

American Psychiatric Association (1987). *Diagnostic and Statistical Manual of Mental Disorders, Third Edition, Revised*. Washington, DC: American Psychiatric Association.

American Psychiatric Association (1994). *Diagnostic and Statistical Manual of Mental Disorders, Fourth Edition*. Washington, DC: American Psychiatric Association.

Amsterdam, J.D., Hornig, M. & Nierenberg, A.A. (Eds) (2001). *Treatment-Resistant Mood Disorders*. Cambridge, UK: Cambridge University Press.

Barber, J.P. & DeRubeis, R.J. (1989). On second thought: where the action is in cognitive therapy for depression. *Cognitive Therapy and Research*, **13**, 441–457.

Barber, J.P. & Muenz, L.R. (1996). The role of avoidance and obsessiveness in matching patients to cognitive and interpersonal psychotherapy: empirical findings from the Treatment for Depression Collaborative Research Program. *Journal of Consulting and Clinical Psychology*, **64**, 951–958.

Beck, A.T. (1976). *Cognitive Therapy and the Emotional Disorders*. New York: International Universities Press.

Beck, A.T., Freeman, A. & Associates (1990). *Cognitive Therapy of Personality Disorders*. New York: Guilford Press.

Beck, A.T., Rush, A.J., Shaw, B.F. & Emery, G. (1979). *Cognitive Therapy of Depression*. New York: Guilford Press.

Beck, A.T., Ward, C.H., Mendelson, M., Mock, J.E. & Erbaugh, J.K. (1961). An inventory for measuring depression. *Archives of General Psychiatry*, **4**, 561–571.

Beck, A.T., Weissman, A., Lester, D. & Trexler, L. (1974). The measurement of pessimism: the hopelessness scale. *Journal of Consulting and Clinical Psychology*, **42**, 861–865.

Beck, J.S. (1995). *Cognitive Therapy: Basics and Beyond*. New York: Guilford Press.

Berti Ceroni, G.B., Neri, C. & Pezzoli, A. (1984). Chronicity in major depression: a naturalistic prospective study. *Journal of Affective Disorders*, **7**, 123–132.

Blackburn, I.M., Bishop, S., Glen, A.I.M., Whalley, L.J. & Christie, J.E. (1981). The efficacy of cognitive therapy in depression: a treatment trial using cognitive therapy and pharmacotherapy, each alone and in combination. *British Journal of Psychiatry*, **139**, 181–189.

Blackburn, I.M. & Davidson, K.M. (1990). *Cognitive Therapy for Depression and Anxiety: A Practitioner's Guide*. Oxford: Blackwell Science.

Blackburn, I.M. & Moore, R.G. (1997). Controlled acute and follow-up trial of cognitive therapy and pharmacotherapy in out-patients with recurrent depression. *British Journal of Psychiatry*, **171**, 328–334.

Borkovec, T.D. & Inz, J. (1990). The nature of worry in generalised anxiety disorder: a predominance of thought activity. *Behaviour, Research and Therapy*, **2**, 153–158.

Bowers, W. (1990). Treatment of depressed inpatients: cognitive therapy plus medication, relaxation plus medication and medication alone. *British Journal of Psychiatry*, **156**, 73–78.

Brittlebank, A.D., Scott, J., Williams, J.M.G. & Ferrier, I.N. (1993). Autobiographical memory in depression: state or trait marker? *British Journal of Psychiatry*, **162**, 118–121.

Brown, G.W., Andrews, B., Harris, T., Alder, Z. & Bridge, L. (1986). Social support, self-esteem and depression. *Psychological Medicine*, **16**, 813–831.

Brown, G.W. & Harris, T. (1978). *Social Origins of Depression*. London: Tavistock.

Brown, G.W., Lemyre, L. & Bifulco, A. (1992). Social factors and recovery from anxiety and depressive disorders: a test of specificity. *British Journal of Psychiatry*, **161**, 44–54.

Burns, D.D. (1989). *The Feeling Good Handbook*. New York: Plume Books.

Burns, D.D. & Nolen-Hoeksema, S.N. (1992). Therapeutic empathy and recovery from depression in cognitive behavioral therapy: a structural equation model. *Journal of Consulting and Clinical Psychology*, **60**, 441–449.

Burns, D.D. & Spangler, D.L. (2000). Does psychotherapy homework lead to improvements in depression in cognitive behavioural psychotherapy or does improvement lead to increased homework compliance? *Journal of Consulting and Clinical Psychology*, **68**, 46–56.

Butler, G. (1999). Clinical formulation. In A.S. Bellack & M. Hersen (Eds), *Comprehensive Clinical Psychology* (vol. 6). Elsevier.

Crook, T., Raskin, A. & Eliot., J. (1981). Parent–child relationships and adult depression. *Child Development*, **52**, 950–957.

Dalgleish, T., Spinks, H., Yiend, J. & Kuyken, W. (2001). Autobiographical memory style in seasonal affective disorder and its relationship to future symptom remission. *Journal of Abnormal Psychology*, **110**, 335–340.

De Jong, R., Trieber, R. & Henrich, G. (1986). Effectiveness of two psychological treatments for inpatients with severe and chronic depressions. *Cognitive Therapy and Research*, **10**, 645–653.

Dickson, A. (1982). *A Woman in Your Own Right: Assertiveness and You*. London: Quartet Books.

Edwards, D.J. (1990). Cognitive therapy and the restructuring of early memories through guided imagery. *Journal of Cognitive Psychotherapy*, **4**, 33–50.

Elkin, I., Shea, M.T., Watkins, J.T., Imber, S.D., Sotsky, S.M., Collins, J.F., Glass, D.R., Pilkonis, P.A., Leber, W.R., Docherty, J.P., Fiester, S.J. & Parloff, M.B. (1989). National Institute of Mental Health Treatment of Depression Collaborative Research Programme: general effectiveness of treatments. *Archives of General Psychiatry*, **46**, 971–982.

Evans, M.D., Hollon, S.D., DeRubeis, R.J., Piasecki, J.M., Grove, W.M., Garvey, M.J. & Tuason, V.B. (1992). Differential relapse following cognitive therapy and pharmacotherapy for depression. *Archives of General Psychiatry*, **49**, 802–808.

Fava, G.A. (1999). Well-being therapy: conceptual and technical issues. *Psychotherapy and Psychosomatics*, **68**, 171–179.

Fava, G.A., Grandi, S., Zielezny, M., Canestrari, R. & Morphy, M.A. (1994). Cognitive behavioural treatment of residual symptoms in primary major depressive disorder. *American Journal of Psychiatry*, **151**, 1295–1299.

Fava, G., Grandi, S., Zielezny, M., Rafanelli, C. & Canestrari, R. (1996). Four-year outcome for cognitive behavioural treatment of residual symptoms in major depression. *American Journal of Psychiatry*, **153**, 945–947.

Fava, G.A., Rafanelli, C., Cazzaro, M., Conti, S. & Grandi, S. (1998a). Well-being therapy. A novel psychotherapeutic approach for residual symptoms of affective disorders. *Psychological Medicine*, **28**, 475–480.

Fava, G.A., Rafanelli, C., Grandi, S., Conti, S. & Belluardo, P. (1998b). Prevention of recurrent depression with cognitive behavioral therapy. *Archives of General Psychiatry*, **55**, 816–820.

Fava, G.A., Savron, G., Grandi, S. & Rafanelli, C. (1997). Cognitive behavioural management of drug-resistant major depressive disorder. *Journal of Clinical Psychiatry*, **58**, 278–282.

Fennell, M.J.V. (1989). Depression. In K. Hawton, P.M. Salkovskis, J. Kirk & D.M. Clark (Eds), *Cognitive Behaviour Therapy for Psychiatric Problems: A Practical Guide*. Oxford, UK: Oxford University Press.

Fennell, M.J.V. (1999). *Overcoming Low Self-Esteem: A Self-Help Guide using Cognitive Behavioural Techniques*. London: Robinson Publishing.

Fennell, M.J.V. & Teasdale, J.D. (1982). Cognitive therapy with chronic, drug-refractory depressed outpatients: a note of caution. *Cognitive Therapy and Research*, **6**, 455–460.

Garland, A. (1996). A case of generalised anxiety disorder. In I.M. Blackburn & V. Twaddle (Eds), *Cognitive Therapy in Action: A Practitioner's Casebook*. London: Souvenir Press.

Garland, A., Harrington, J., House, R. & Scott, J. (2000). A pilot study of the relationship between problem solving skills and outcome in major depressive disorder. *British Journal of Medical Psychology*, **73**, 303–309.

Garland, A. & Scott, J. (2000). Using homework in therapy for depression. *Journal of Clinical Psychology*. In session: *Psychotherapy in Practice*, **58** (5), 489–498.

Gold, P.W., Goodwin, F.K. & Chrousos, G.P. (1988). Clinical and biochemical manifestations of depression: relation to the neurobiology of stress. *New England Journal of Medicine*, **319**, 413–420.

Gonzales, L.R., Lewinsohn, P.M. & Clarke, G.N. (1985). Longitudinal follow-up of unipolar depressives: an investigation of predictors of relapse. *Journal of Consulting and Clinical Psychology*, **53**, 461–469.

Gotlib, I.H. & Hammen, C.L. (1992). *Psychological Aspects of Depression: Toward a Cognitive-Interpersonal Integration*. Chichester, UK: John Wiley & Sons.

Greenberger, D. & Padesky, C.A. (1995). *Mind over Mood: A Cognitive Therapy Treatment Manual for Clients*. New York: Guilford Press.

Greenhouse, J.B., Kupfer, D.J., Frank, E., Jarrett, D.B. & Rejman, K.A. (1987). Analysis of time to stabilisation in the treatment of depression: biological and clinical correlates. *Journal of Affective Disorders*, **13**, 259–266.

Guscott, R. & Grof, P. (1991). The clinical meaning of refractory depression: a review for the clinician. *American Journal of Psychiatry*, **148**, 695–704.

Hamilton, K.E. & Dobson, K.S. (2002). Cognitive therapy of depression: pretreatment patient predictors of outcome. *Clinical Psychology Review*, **22**, 875–894.

Hamilton, M. (1960). A rating scale for Depression. *Journal of Neurology, Neurosurgery and Psychiatry*, **23**, 56–62.

Harpin, R.E., Liberman, R.P., Marks, I., Stern, R. & Bohannon, W.E. (1982). Cognitive-behaviour therapy for chronically depressed patients: a controlled pilot study. *Journal of Nervous and Mental Disease*, **170**, 295–301.

Hellerstein, D.J., Kocsis, J.H., Chapman, D., Stewart, J.W. & Harrison, W. (2000). Double-blind comparison of sertraline, imipramine, and placebo in the treatment of dysthymia: effects on personality. *American Journal of Psychiatry*, **157**, 1436–1444.

Hollon, S., Shelton, R. & Davies, D. (1993). Cognitive therapy for depression: conceptual issues and clinical efficacy. *Journal of Consulting and Clinical Psychology*, **61**, 270–275.

Hooley, J.M. & Teasdale, J.D. (1989). Predictors of relapse in uni-polar depressives: expressed emotion, marital distress and perceived criticism. *Journal of Abnormal Psychology*, **98**, 229–237.

Ilardi, S.S., Craighead, W.E. & Evans, D.D. (1997). Modelling relapse in unipolar depression: the effects of dysfunctional cognitions and personality disorders. *Journal of Consulting and Clinical Psychology*, **65**, 381–391.

Imber, S.D., Pilkonis, P.A., Sotsky, S.M., Elkin. I., Watkins, J.T., Collins, J.F., Shea, M.T., Leber, W.R. & Glass, D.R. (1990). Mode-specific effects among three treatments for depression. *Journal of Consulting and Clinical Psychology*, **358**, 352–359.

Jacobson, N.S., Dobson, K., Fruzzetti, A.E., Schmaling, K.B. & Salusky, S. (1991). Marital therapy as a treatment for depression. *Journal of Consulting and Clinical Psychology*, **52**, 180–189.

Jacobson, N.S. & Gurman, A.S. (Eds) (1986). *Clinical Handbook of Marital Therapy*. New York: Guilford Press.

Jarrett, R.B., Kraft, D., Doyle, J., Foster, B.M., Eaves, G. & Silver, P.C. (2001). Preventing recurrent depression using cognitive therapy with and without a continuation phase: a randomized clinical trial. *Archives of General Psychiatry*, **58**, 381–388.

Johnson, J.G., Young-Sook, H., Douglas, C.J., Johannet, C.M. & Russell, T. (1998). Attributions for positive life events predict recovery from depression among psychiatric patients: an investigation of the Needles and Abramson model of recovery from depression. *Journal of Consulting and Clinical Psychology*, **66**, 369–376.

Judd, L.L., Akiskal, H.S., Maser, J.D., Zeller, P.J., Endicott, J., Coryell, W., Paulus, M.P., Kunovac, J.L., Leon, A.C., Mueller, T.I., Rice, J.A. & Keller, M.B. (1998). A prospective 12-year study of subsyndromal and syndromal depressive symptoms in unipolar major depressive disorders. *Archives of General Psychiatry*, **55**, 694–700.

Kazantzis, N., Deane, F.P. & Ronan, K.R. (2000). Homework assignments in cognitive and behavioural therapy: a meta-analysis. *Clinical Psychology, Science and Practice*, **2**, 189–202.

Keller, M.B., Gelenberg, A.J., Hirschfeld, R.M.A., Rush, A.J., Thase, M.E., Kocsis, J.H., Markowitz, J.C., Fawcett, J.A., Koran, L.M., Klein, D.N., Russell, J.M., Kornstein, S.G., McCullough, J.P., Davis, S.M. & Harrison, W.M. (1998). The treatment of chronic depression: Part 2. A double blind, randomized trial of sertraline and imipramine. *Journal of Clinical Psychiatry*, **59**, 598–607.

Keller, M.B., Klein, D.N., Hirschfeld, R.M.A., Kocsis, J.H., McCullough, J.P., Miller, I., First, M.B., Holzer, C.P. III, Keitner, G.I., Marin, D.B. & Shea, T. (1995). Results of the DSM-IV Mood Disorders Field Trial. *American Journal of Psychiatry*, **152**, 843–849.

Keller, M.B., Klerman, G.L., Lavori, P.W., Coryell, W., Endicott, J. & Taylor, J. (1984). Long-term outcome of episodes of major depression: clinical and public health significance. *Journal of the American Medical Association*, **252**, 788–792.

Keller, M.B., Lavori, P.W., Endicott, J., Coryell, W. & Klerman, G.L. (1983). Double depression: a two-year follow-up. *American Journal of Psychiatry*, **140**, 689–694.

Keller, M.B., Lavori, P.W., Rice, J., Coryell, W. & Hirschfeld, R.M.A. (1986). The persistent risk of chronicity in recurrent episodes of nonbipolar major depressive disorder: a prospective follow-up. *American Journal of Psychiatry*, **143**, 24–28.

Keller, M.B., McCullough, J.P., Klein, D.N., Arnow, B., Dunner, D.L., Gelenberg, A.J., Markowitz, J.C., Nemeroff, C.B., Russell, J.M., Thase, M.E., Trivedi, M.H. & Zajecka, J. (2000). A comparison of nefazodone, the cognitive behavioral analysis system of psychotherapy, and their combination for the treatment of chronic depression. *New England Journal of Medicine*, **342**, 1462–1470.

Keller, M.B. & Shapiro, R.W. (1982). 'Double depression': superimposition of acute depressive episodes on chronic depressive disorders. *American Journal of Psychiatry*, **139**, 438–442.

Kiloh, L.G., Andrews, G., & Neilson, M. (1988). The long-term outcome of depressive illness. *British Journal of Psychiatry*, **153**, 752–757.

Klerman, G.L., Weissman, M.M., Rounsaville, B.J. & Chevron, E.S. (1984). *Interpersonal Psychotherapy of Depression*. New York: Basic Books.

Kornstein, S.G., Schatzberg, A.F., Thase, M.E., Yonkers, K.A., McCullough, J.P., Keitner, G.I., Gelenberg, A.J., Ryan, C.E., Hess, A.L., Harrison, W., Davis, S.M. & Keller, M.B. (2000). Gender differences in chronic major and double depression. *Journal of Affective Disorders*, **60**, 1–11.

Kuehner, C. & Weber, I. (1999). Responses to depression in unipolar depressed patients: an investigation of Nolen Hoeksema's response styles theory. *Psychological Medicine*, **29**, 1323–1333.

Kupfer, D.J., Frank, E. & Perel, J.M. (1989). The advantage of early treatment intervention in recurrent depression. *Archives of General Psychiatry*, **46**, 771–775.

Kuyken, W. & Brewin, C.R. (1996). Autobiographical memory functioning in depression and reports of early abuse. *Journal of Abnormal Psychology*, **104**, 585–591.

Kuyken, W., Kurzer, N., DeRubeis, R.J., Beck, A.T. & Brown, G.K. (2001). Response to cognitive therapy in depression: the role of maladaptive beliefs and personality disorders. *Journal of Consulting and Clinical Psychology*, **69**, 560–566.

Lavori, P.W., Keller, M.B. & Klerman, G.L. (1984). Relapse in affective disorders: a reanalysis of the literature using life table methods. *Journal of Psychiatric Research*, **18**, 13–25.

Lee, A.S. & Murray, R.M. (1988). The long-term outcome of Maudsley depressives. *British Journal of Psychiatry*, **153**, 741–751.

Lewinsohn, P.M. (1974). A behavioural approach to depression. In R.J. Friedman & M.M. Katz (Eds), *The Psychology of Depression: Contemporary Theory and Research*. New York: John Wiley & Sons.

MacLeod, A.K. & Moore, R. (2000). Positive thinking revisited: positive cognitions, well-being and mental health. *Clinical Psychology and Psychotherapy*, **7**, 1–10.

McCullough, J.P. (1996). The importance of diagnosing comorbid personality disorders with patients who are chronically depressed. *Depressive Disorders: Index and Reviews*, **1**, 16–17.

McCullough, J.P. (2000). *Treatment for Chronic Depression: Cognitive Behavioral Analysis System of Psychotherapy*. New York: Guilford Press.

McCullough, J.P., Kasnetz, M.D., Braith, J.A., Carr, K.F., Cones, J.H., Fielo, J. & Martelli, M.F. (1988). A longitudinal study of an untreated sample of predominantly late onset characterological dysthymia. *Journal of Nervous and Mental Disease*, **176**, 658–667.

McCullough, J.P., Klein, D.N., Keller, M.B., Holzer, C.E., Davis, S.M., Kornstein, S.G., Howland, R.H., Thase, M.E. & Harrison, W.M. (2000). Comparison of DSM-III-R chronic major depression and major depression superimposed on dysthymia (double depression): validity of the distinction. *Journal of Abnormal Psychology*, **109**, 419–427.

Mercier, M.A., Stewart, J.W. & Quitkin, F.M. (1992). A pilot sequential study of cognitive therapy and pharmacotherapy of atypical depression. *Journal of Clinical Psychiatry*, **53**, 166–170.

Miller, I.W., Bishop, S.B., Norman, W.H. & Keitner, G.I. (1985). Cognitive/behavioural therapy and pharmacotherapy with chronic, drug-refractory depressed inpatients: a note of optimism. *Behavioural Psychotherapy*, **13**, 320–327.

Moore, R.G. (1996). It's the thought that counts: the role of intentions and meta-awareness in cognitive therapy. *Journal of Cognitive Psychotherapy: An International Quarterly*, **10**, 255–269.

Moore, R.G. & Blackburn, I.M. (1997). Cognitive therapy in the treatment of non-responders to antidepressant medication: a controlled pilot study. *Behavioural and Cognitive Psychotherapy*, **25**, 251–259.

Moore, R.G., Hayhurst, H. & Teasdale, J.D. (1996). *Measure of awareness and coping in autobiographical memory: instructions for administering and coding*. Unpublished manuscript. Department of Psychiatry, University of Cambridge.

Moore, R.G., Watts, F.N. & Williams, J.M.G. (1987). The specificity of personal memories in depression. *British Journal of Clinical Psychology*, **27**, 275–276.

Mynors Wallis, L.M., Gath, D.H., Lloyd Thomas, A.R. & Tomlinson, D. (1995). Randomised controlled trial comparing problem solving treatment with amitriptyline and placebo for major depression in primary care. *British Medical Journal*, **310**, 441–445

Nazroo, J., Edwards, A. & Brown, G.W. (1997). Gender differences in the onset of depression following a shared life event: a study of couples. *Psychological Medicine*, **27**, 9–19.

Nolen-Hoeksema, S.N. (1991). Responses to depression and their effects on duration of depressive episodes. *Journal of Abnormal Psychology*, **100**, 569–582.

O'Reardon, J.P. & Amsterdam, J.D. (2001). Overview of treatment-resistant depression and its management. In J.D. Amsterdam, M. Hornig & A.A. Nierenberg (Eds), *Treatment-Resistant Mood Disorders*. Cambridge, UK: Cambridge University Press.

Padesky, C.A. (1990). Schema as self-prejudice. *International Cognitive Therapy Newsletter*, **6**, 6–7.

Padesky, C.A. (1994). Schema change processes in cognitive therapy. *Clinical Psychology and Psychotherapy*, **1**, 267–278.

Padesky, C.A. (1996). Developing cognitive therapist competency: teaching and supervision models. In P.M. Salkovskis (Ed.), *Frontiers of Cognitive Therapy*. London: Guilford Press.

Padesky, C.A. & Mooney, K.A. (1990). Clinical tip: presenting the cognitive model to clients. *International Cognitive Therapy Newsletter* (special issue), **6**, 13–14.

Paykel, E.S. (1994). Epidemiology of refractory depression. In W.A. Nolen, J. Zohar, S.P. Roose & J.D. Amsterdam (Eds), *Refractory Depression: Current Strategies and Future Directions*. Chichester, UK: John Wiley & Sons.

Paykel, E.S., Ramana, R., Cooper, Z., Hayhurst, H., Kerr, J. & Barocka, A. (1995). Residual symptoms after partial remission: an important outcome in depression. *Psychological Medicine*, **25**, 1171–1180.

Paykel, E. S., Scott, J., Teasdale, J. D., Johnson, A. L., Garland, A., Moore, R., Jenaway, A., Cornwall, P. L., Hayhurst, H., Abbott, R. & Pope, M. (1999). Prevention of relapse in residual depression by cognitive therapy: a controlled trial. *Archives of General Psychiatry*, **56**, 829–835.

Persons, J.B. (1989). *Cognitive Therapy in Practice: A Case Formulation Approach*. New York: Norton.

Persons, J., Burns, D. & Perloff, J.M. (1985). Mechanisms of action of cognitive therapy: the relative contributions of technical and interpersonal interventions. *Cognitive Therapy and Research*, **17**, 123–137.

Peterson, C., Semmel, A., von Baeyer, C., Abramson, L. Y., Metalsky, G.I. & Seligman, M.E.P. (1982). The Attributional Style Questionnaire. *Cognitive Therapy and Research*, **6**, 287–300.

Post, R.M. (1992). The transduction of psychosocial stress into the neurobiology of recurrent affective disorder. *American Journal of Psychiatry*, **149**, 999–1010.

Quitkin, F.M. (1985). The importance of dosage in prescribed antidepressants. *British Journal of Psychiatry*, **147**, 593–597.

Rogers, C. (1951). *Client-Centred Therapy: Its Current Practice, Implications and Theory*. Boston: Houghton Mifflin.

Rush, A.J., Beck, A.T., Kovacs, M. & Hollon, S. (1977). Comparative efficacy of cognitive therapy and pharmacotherapy in the treatment of depressed outpatients. *Cognitive Therapy and Research*, **1**, 17–37.

Safran, J.D. & Segal, Z.V. (1990). *Interpersonal Process in Cognitive Therapy*. New York: Basic Books.

Scott, J. (1988). Chronic depression. *British Journal of Psychiatry*, **153**, 287–297.

Scott, J. (1992). Chronic depression: can cognitive therapy succeed when other treatments fail? *Behavioural Psychotherapy*, **20**, 25–36.

Scott, J. (1994). Predictors of non-response to antidepressants. In W.A. Nolen, J. Zohar, S.P. Roose & J.D. Amsterdam (Eds), *Refractory Depression: Current Strategies and Future Directions*. Chichester, UK: John Wiley & Sons.

Scott, J. (1998). Where there's a will. . . Cognitive therapy for people with chronic depressive disorders. In N. Tarrier, A. Wells & G. Haddock (Eds), *Treating Complex Cases: The Cognitive Behavioural Therapy Approach*. Chichester, UK: John Wiley & Sons.

Scott, J., Barker, W.A. & Eccleston, D. (1988). The Newcastle Chronic Depression Study: patient characteristics and factors associated with chronicity. *British Journal of Psychiatry*, **152**, 28–33.

Scott, J., Teasdale, J.D., Paykel, E.S., Johnson, A.L., Abbott, R., Hayhurst, H., Moore, R. & Garland, A. (2000). Effects of cognitive therapy on psychological symptoms and social functioning in residual depression. *British Journal of Psychiatry*, **177**, 440–446.

Segal, Z.V., Williams, J.M.G. & Teasdale, J.D. (2002). *Mindfulness-Based Cognitive Therapy for Depression: A New Approach to Preventing Relapse*. New York: Guilford Press.

Shaw, B.F., Elkin, I., Yamaguchi, J., Olmstead, M., Vallis, T.M., Dobson, K.S., Lowery, A., Sotsky, S.M., Watkins, J.T. & Imber, S.D. (1999). Therapist competence ratings in relation to clinical outcome in cognitive therapy of depression. *Journal of Consulting and Clinical Psychology*, **67**, 837–846.

Shea, M.T., Elkin, I., Imber, S.D., Sotsky, F.M., Watkins, J.T., Collins, J.F., Pilkonis, P.A., Beckham, E., Glass, D.R., Dolan, R.T. & Parloff, M.B. (1992). Course of depressive symptoms over follow-up: findings from the NIMH Treatment of Depression Collaborative Research Program. *Archives of General Psychiatry*, **49**, 782–787.

Shea, M.T., Pilkonis, P.A., Beckham, E., Collins, J.F., Elkin, I., Sotsky, S.M. & Docherty, J.P. (1990). Personality disorders and treatment outcome in the NIMH Treatment of Depression Collaborative Research Program. *American Journal of Psychiatry*, **147**, 711–718.

Sotsky, S.M., Glass, D.R., Shea, M.T., Pilkonis, P.A., Collins, J.F., Elkin, I., Watkins, J.T., Imber, S.D., Leber, W.R., Moyer, J. & Oliveri, M.E. (1991). Patient predictors of response to psychotherapy and pharmacotherapy: findings in the NIMH Treatment of Depression Collaborative Research Program. *American Journal of Psychiatry*, **148**, 997–1008.

Spitzer, R.L., Williams, J.B.W., Gibbon, M. & First, M.B. (1992). The Structured Clinical Interview for DSM-IIIR (SCID): I. History, rationale and description. *Archives of General Psychiatry*, **49**, 624–629.

Stravynski, A., Shahar, A. & Verreault, R. (1991). A pilot study of the cognitive treatment of dysthymic disorder. *Behavioural Psychotherapy*, **19**, 369–372.

Teasdale, J.D. & Barnard, P.J. (1993). *Affect, Cognition and Change: Remodelling Depressive Thought*. Hove, UK: Lawrence Erlbaum Associates.

Teasdale, J.D., Moore, R.G., Hayhurst, H., Pope, M., Williams, S. & Segal, Z. (2002). Meta-cognitive awareness and prevention of relapse in depression: empirical evidence. *Journal of Consulting and Clinical Psychology*, **70**, 275–287.

Teasdale, J.D., Scott, J., Moore, R.G., Hayhurst, H., Pope, M. & Paykel, E.S. (2001). How does cognitive therapy prevent relapse in residual depression? Evidence from a controlled trial. *Journal of Consulting and Clinical Psychology*, **69**, 347–357.

Teasdale, J.D., Segal, Z.V., Williams, J.M.G., Ridgeway, V.A., Soulsby, J.M. & Lau, M.A. (2000). Prevention of relapse/recurrence in major depression by mindfulness-based cognitive therapy. *Journal of Consulting and Clinical Psychology*, **68**, 615–623.

Thase, M.E. (1994). The roles of psychosocial factors and psychotherapy in refractory depression: missing pieces in the puzzle of treatment resistance? In W.A. Nolen, J. Zohar, S.P. Roose & J.D. Amsterdam (Eds), *Refractory Depression: Current Strategies and Future Directions*. Chichester, UK: John Wiley & Sons.

Thase, M.E. & Rush, A.J. (1995). Treatment-resistant depression. In F.E. Bloom & D.J. Kupfer (Eds), *Psychopharmacology: The Fourth Generation of Progress*. New York: Raven Press.

Thase, M.E., Rush, A.J., Howland, R.H., Kornstein, S.G., Kocsis, J.H., Gelenberg, A.J., Schatzberg, A.F., Koran, L.M., Keller, M.B., Russell, J.M., Hirschfeld, R.M.A., LaVange, L.M., Klein, D.N., Fawcett, J. & Harrison, W. (2002). Double-blind switch study of imipramine or sertraline treatment of antidepressant-resistant chronic depression. *Archives of General Psychiatry*, **59**, 233–239.

Thornicroft, G. & Sartorius, N. (1993). The course and outcome of depression in different cultures: 10 year follow-up of WHO collaborative study on assessment of depressive disorders. *Psychological Medicine*, **23**, 1023–1032.

Watkins, E. & Teasdale, J.D. (2001). Rumination and overgeneral memory in depression: effects of self-focus and analytic thinking. *Journal of Abnormal Psychology*, **110**, 353–357.

Watkins, E., Teasdale, J.D. & Williams, R.M. (2000). Decentring and distraction reduce overgeneral autobiographical memory in depression. *Psychological Medicine*, **30**, 911–920.

Wegner, D.M., Schneider, D.J., Carter, S. III & White, T. (1987). Paradoxical effects of thought suppression. *Journal of Personality and Social Psychology*, **53**, 5–13.

Weissman, A.N. & Beck, A.T. (1978). *Development and validation of the Dysfunctional Attitude Scale*. Paper presented at the 12th Annual Meeting of the Association for the Advancement of Behavior Therapy, Chicago, IL.

Wells, A. (2000). *Emotional Disorders and Metacognition: Innovative Cognitive Therapy*. Chichester, UK: John Wiley & Sons.

Wells, K.B., Stewart, A., Hays, R.D., Burnam, M.A., Rogers, W., Daniels, M., Berry, S., Greenfield, S. & Ware, J. (1989). The functioning and well-being of depressed patients: results from the Medical Outcomes Study. *Journal of the American Medical Association*, **262**, 914–919.

Williams, J.M.G., Teasdale, J.D., Segal, Z.V. & Soulsby, J. (2000). Mindfulness-based cognitive therapy reduces overgeneral autobiographical memory in formerly depressed patients. *Journal of Abnormal Psychology*, **109**, 150–155.

Williams, J.M.G., Watts, F.N., MacLeod, C. & Mathews, A. (1997). *Cognitive Psychology and Emotional Disorders*. Chichester, UK: John Wiley & Sons.

Winokur, G., Coryell, W., Keller, M., Endicott, J. & Akiskal, H. (1993). A prospective follow-up of patients with bipolar and primary unipolar affective disorder. *Archives of General Psychiatry*, **50**, 457–465.

Wright, J.H., Thase, M.E., Beck, A.T. & Ludgate, J.W. (1993). *Cognitive Therapy with In-patients: Developing a Cognitive Milieu*. New York: Guilford Press.

Young, J.E. (1990). *Cognitive Therapy for Personality Disorders: A Schema-Focused Approach*. Sarasota, FL: Professional Resource Exchange.

INDEX

Index by Sylvia Potter

The Wiley Series in

CLINICAL PSYCHOLOGY

Titles published under the series editorship of:

J. Mark G. Williams   *School of Psychology, University of Wales, Bangor, UK*